THE GOLDEN AGE
OF PINEHURST

The Story of the Rebirth of No. 2

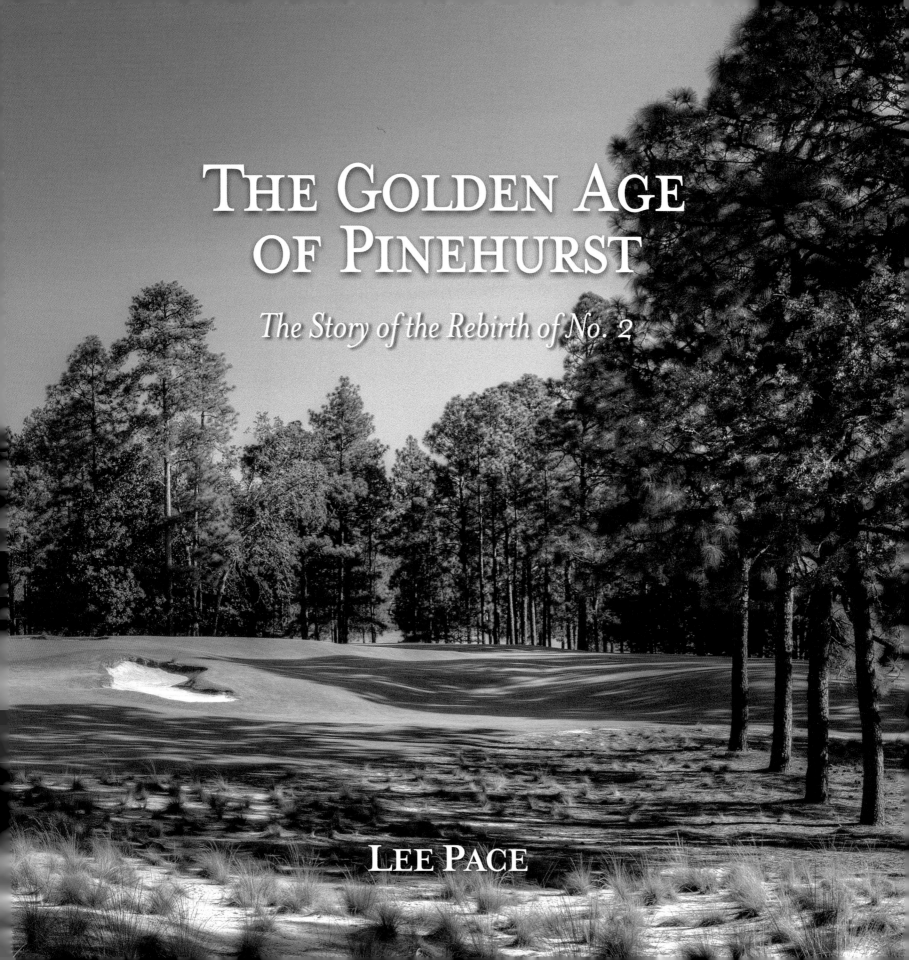

THE GOLDEN AGE
OF PINEHURST

The Story of the Rebirth of No. 2

LEE PACE

Published by Pinehurst LLC
P.O. Box 4000
Pinehurst, NC 28374

Distributed by
The University of North Carolina Press
116 South Boundary Street
Chapel Hill, North Carolina 27514
http://www.uncpress.unc.edu
In Association with the Tufts Archives

ISBN   978-1-4696-0790-0 (cloth)
ISBN   978-1-4696-0791-7 (e-book)

Printed in Canada by Friesens Corporation

Book Design and Production by Sue Pace

Front end sheet shows the sixth green of No. 2,
photo by Larry Lambrecht; back end sheet shows
the new "Thistle Dhu" putting green beside the
Pinehurst clubhouse, photo by John Gessner.

TO THE DEDMAN FAMILY,
STEWARDS OF PINEHURST
FOR MORE THAN A
QUARTER OF A CENTURY.

Wire grass, hardpan sand, rough-hewn bunker edges and random pine cones and needles define the restored look of Pinehurst No. 2 on the eighteenth (L), first hole (above) and tenth holes (overleaf) in 2012.

CONTENTS

CHIP SHOTS

The Pinehurst clubhouse as seen from the south side during an early 1900s match featuring (L-R) Willie Anderson, Bernard Nicholls, Donald Ross and Alex Ross; a similar view (overleaf) at dusk more than a hundred years later.

There is something in the air of Pinehurst that makes it insidiously attractive;

all who breathe it want more of it. Here, golf is the sport of sports; experts are counted by the dozens and enthusiasts of all kinds by hundreds. Every weekday on the links may be seen by many parties of players of both sexes and all ages, oblivious to everything but the fascination and charm of this most healthful and invigorating of all sports. Golf is popular everywhere, but particularly so at Pinehurst, where climactic conditions are ideal for the game and where players have the advantage of a course that is unquestionably the finest in the south, and which compares favorably with, if it does not surpass, any other in the United States.

H.C. FOWNES 1901

I've always felt...

... it's not what championships you won, it's where you won them. I have won in various cities, but winning in Pinehurst meant more to me. It was something totally different.

BILLY JOE PATTON

Two of the biggest winners in Pinehurst over a century were Billy Joe Patton and Ben Hogan. Patton (opposite) spent plenty of time tromping through the pine forests, as he did on this recovery shot during the 1962 U.S. Amateur, but he scrambled well enough to win three North and South Amateurs and one Southern Amateur on No. 2. Hogan, shown here hitting from a bunker on eleven in 1940, won three North and South Open titles. And the first was a biggie. He was winless in eight years on the pro tour, but his victory at Pinehurst in March 1940 set off a powder keg that led to the Hall of Fame.

Moments in Time

ayne Stewart's final stroke of the 1999 U.S. Open falls into the cup as caddie Mike Hicks raises his arms and Phil Mickelson walks in for a congratulatory hug and handshake. "Perfect—a perfect way to win," Stewart said. "I think everyone in the field will attest to how great No. 2 is, to what a special place Pinehurst is. To win here means a lot to me."

Other winners at Pinehurst (overleaf) have included (counter-clockwise from top left): Hale Irwin (1977), Tom Watson (1978-79), Curtis Strange (1975-76 in the North and South Amateur), Johnny Miller (1974), Raymond Floyd (1976), Paul Azinger (1992), Craig Stadler (1991) and Jack Nicklaus (1959 as an amateur and 1975 as a pro).

"Pinehurst was the most elite spot in the world as far as I was concerned. I have great memories of visiting Pinehurst in the old days. For a kid from Latrobe to visit the golf capital of the world was a special treat."

ARNOLD PALMER

Preface

IN CELEBRATION
of IMPERFECTION

ell, why not? Why *not* ask Ben Hogan if he would receive a visiting writer for the express purpose of talking about Pinehurst? The idea crystallized one day in December 1990 in the Tufts Archives while reading a *Pinehurst Outlook* account of Hogan's first professional tournament victory, his watershed triumph in the 1940 North and South Open.

"Mister Hogan received your letter, and he said he'd be happy to meet with you if you'd like to come to our office," his secretary said several days later, speaking by phone from the Hogan Company's Fort Worth headquarters.

Texas. Okay, who else in Texas might have an interesting story or perspective to tell about Pinehurst, about Donald Ross and their places at the head table of American golf history? Ben Crenshaw perhaps? He almost won that funky PGA Tour event back in 1973, when the traveling circus of the pro golf tour came to Pinehurst for two weeks and 144 holes, and

his passion and feel for the game's rich traditions were unmatched among contemporary tour pros.

"Call him," advised the old sage golf writer, Pinehurst's own Dick Taylor. "He loves the place. Bet he'd be happy to talk with you."

And so I set off to Fort Worth and Austin a couple of weeks later to talk golf and Pinehurst with Hogan and Crenshaw, beginning an odyssey that over the next five months included visits with Sam Snead, Jack Nicklaus, Arnold Palmer, Harvie Ward, Billy Joe Patton, Pete Dye, Bill Campbell, Curtis Strange and others.

The result was *Pinehurst Stories*, which came off the presses in October 1991, exactly one week before the Tour Championship on No. 2, with the eighteen stories augmented by contributions from golf writing heavyweights Taylor, Charles Price and Herbert Warren Wind. I was merely the pipsqueak with the tape recorder who organized it all.

More than two decades later, it's sad to leaf through that book and see so many central characters no longer around. Taylor, Price and Wind are gone. I still treasure a letter from Wind written in his distinctive cursive style saying that Dick Tufts of the founding family would "have softly allowed that he found the book interesting and sound." Hogan and Snead, who combined to win six North and South Opens over a decade in the 1940s, have passed. Patton and Ward, the two North Carolina boys who eschewed the idea of the pro tour and cavorted their way to two U.S. Amateur titles (Ward) and four North and South Amateurs (three for Patton, one for Ward) are now scrambling for pars in the wild blue yonder.

That book and the sequel to it published in 1999 were built around individuals—champion golfers and their good times in Pinehurst.

The next installment in this series of coffee-table books commissioned by Pinehurst LLC followed in 2004. The Spirit of Pinehurst was less about individuals and more about the singular character of the village and club and a gave a salute to Pinehurst's successful quest to bring major championship golf back following the demise of the North and South Open and the departure of the Ryder Cup—both in 1951.

The 1999 U.S. Open—likely the biggest sporting event ever held in the state of North Carolina—and Payne Stewart's memorable final stroke were a big part of that book. Photographer Rob Brown captured the final putt just as it rolled into the hole in a panoramic image used in that book (and repeated in a similar gatefold in this one as well), and the accompanying chapter traced the remark-able run of providence that led to Stewart's victory—his personal evolution and maturation, his return to equipment that felt comfortable and performed well, the pleasant vibes he got from the Pinehurst community dating back two decades, and an intricate game plan for attacking—and surviving—No. 2's greens.

Now it's time for another book. And a new central character—the No. 2 golf course itself.

The Golden Age of Pinehurst is the story of No. 2, its genesis, its creators, its advocates, its evolution. Within that process follows the story of Pinehurst itself, how an entrepreneurial family from Massachusetts and a golf architect from Scotland found themselves in the "jack pines of Carolina," as Donald Ross once said, and turned it into a bastion for the rapturous pursuit of the ancient sport of golf.

Pinehurst and "The Deuce," as the course was known through the mid-1900s, have never enjoyed the sexiness of a neighboring ocean, mountain range, river or waterfall. They've never benefited from being next door to a metropolitan beehive. The appeal has always been golf, pure golf.

"I could be happy playing this golf course and St. Andrews for the rest of my life," said Price, a national golf columnist, Pinehurst resident and regular participant in the North and South Senior Amateur up through his death in 1994. "Why would you need to play anywhere else?"

During my breakfast interview with Crenshaw in 1990, he suggested I call Bill Coore, his partner in the golf design firm they had founded in 1985. I had never heard of Coore at the time, but in a lengthy phone conversation he proved as articulate, nuanced and perceptive about the design elements of Pinehurst No. 2 as anyone I had encountered at the time or would since, for one reason because he knew the course intimately from having played often as a junior golfer in the 1960s. Coore and I had intermittent phone conversations over the years, another of them in 2005 after Coore & Crenshaw had assembled a portfolio of outstanding work borne of old-world golf tenets. Strategy and the ground game were more important than eye candy and herculean risks.

"Ben and I both hope the age of subtlety will continue to grow and expand," Coore said. "Subtlety and detail—Ben would call them 'brushstrokes'—hopefully will return. But they have not been in vogue through the eighties and much of the nineties. For so long, it was a question of how much paint can you splash on the canvas and how bright can the colors be?"

No. 2 fell prey over the two decades since *Pinehurst Stories* was published to a pair of factors that robbed it of the character Price, Coore and many others remembered so well. One, the market of golf—consumers, designers, superintendents, owners, promoters—moved in lockstep to a level of prettiness never known before. And two, the equipment revolution that rendered laughable Ross's idea of a driver and long-iron as a suitable test on a par-four forced No. 2's guardians, both in-house and those running the U.S. Open, to counterpunch with vast thickets of Bermuda rough.

Coore saw No. 2 for the first time in many years during an early evening stroll while in Pinehurst in 2006. "It was the most uninteresting golf course," he says. "It was nothing like I remembered playing as a kid."

Little did Coore know that three years later he and Crenshaw would be approached by Pinehurst officials to turn back the clock on No. 2, to strip out all of the grass beyond the fairways and return the course to its revered form of 1935 through the late-1960s. Coore and Crenshaw graciously permitted me carte blanche access to their plans, actions, thoughts, opinions and processes while they worked diligently from February 2010 through March 2011 and beyond to restore the hardpan sand, wire grass and the rumpled and disheveled look of the course away from the playing corridors.

"Mother Nature invented golf," Coore said one day. "But look around everywhere in this country, and you'll see every artificial contrivance imaginable."

The design story as seen through the eyes of Coore & Crenshaw is a fascinating and important one—important because it applies not only to Pinehurst but across a national golf inventory that has been over-built, over-greened, over-watered and over-fertilized. Former U.S. Open champion Geoff Ogilvy noted in an opinion piece in *Golf Digest* the week of the Players Championship in early May 2012 that he'd love to see the TPC Sawgrass look like it did when it first opened in 1980.

"The look," Ogilvy said, "was so cool. The fairways were beautifully maintained, but outside those playing areas there was an unkempt, Pine Valley-type feel to the place. I'd like to see the course allowed to be a little more 'wild.' It's a bit too neat. It would be nicer to look at if it wasn't so nice to look at, if you know what I mean."

That's exactly what Coore & Crenshaw said repeatedly on their walks around No. 2. The course looked too neat, too manicured, too organized, "too *perfect,*" as Coore said more than once.

In that context, No. 2 deserved a book of its own. It's a story of one course and, by extension, of hundreds of courses across the country.

The Golden Age of Pinehurst.

You mean then? Or now?

That's the beauty if it—it's open to interpretation.

Lee Pace
May 2012

The 9th Hole of No. 2 Course   Pinehurst, N. C.

Donald Ross follows the flight of his tee shot on the par-three ninth hole on Pinehurst No. 2 in this 1940s postcard.

Introduction

"An old Scottish saying goes that the best golf course is the course that fits the land you've got. What Donald Ross had to work with may well be the most naturally endowed stretch of golfing landscape in all of America.

It had gently rolling hills that could leave a course totally without blind shots and undulating stretches of ground that would make for the sort of tumbling fairways you find on seaside links in Britain. It had its share of dogwoods and azaleas.

But the course Ross had in mind wouldn't be the kind people would come to and smell the flowers.

Being a Scot, Ross interpreted the word "rough" to mean "broken ground." In other words, it was never tended in any other way. The "fairway" meant the same to him as the word does to a ship's pilot, a navigable channel through rocks, sand banks and other obstructions that is the safest way for a vessel to leave or enter a harbor—to leave the tee and enter the green. Consequently, he didn't create rough to border a fairway. He "dredged" a channel—a fairway—through the rough and left it as he found it.

What he found in the sandhills of Pinehurst was rolling sand spotted with wild "wire grass" indigenous to the region. After a rainstorm or a windstorm, pine cones and straw grass were naturally strewn about. Since the whole Chinese army wouldn't be enough manpower to pick it up, he simply left it there. Why not?

It was utterly natural.

Thus, overgrown fairway grass to be used or even called "rough" was loathsome to him. As a result, he left wide sweeps of turf cut no higher than the fairways to the left, right and even behind the greens, thereby permitting an errant shot to roll well away from the putting surfaces. The result was that No. 2 became one of the premier tests of chipping and pitching in the whole of golf, something no course prepared by the USGA for its championships has ever been. A ninety-foot chip or pitch is a much more sophisticated shot than a ninety-foot putt, which is more of a hockey shot than anything in golf."

CHARLES PRICE, GOLF Magazine, 1979

The august No. 2 course at Pinehurst is essentially vacant on this morning in February 2010, save for the odd squirrel or bird and the occasional interloping of a maintenance worker. Quietly in one of the far corners, three men make their way from hole to hole, scribbling notes, positioning colored flags, pointing, waving, stepping off yardages, occasionally using the modern vestiges of the GPS and the cellular telephone to measure distances and communicate with one another from three hundred yards apart.

They speak in measured tones, reverential at times, whispered at others, yet excited in some instances. This is serious work indeed: A significant tweaking of the Donald Ross *tour de force* that, by June of 2014, will have become the only course in the Milky Way to have hosted the U.S Open, U.S. Women's Open, U.S. Amateur, U.S. Women's Amateur, U.S. Senior Open, PGA Championship and the Ryder Cup.

"This is just an incredible place," Bill Coore says. "It was the foundation of my introduction to golf architecture."

"To be asked to contribute our ideas here is a high, high honor," adds the man walking alongside, none other than two-time Masters champion Ben Crenshaw. "We think the world of Pinehurst. Beyond the golf, the feeling of the place, it means so much to American golf. From the turn of the century, it has always been a leader, and it always will. It's been a mecca."

This golf design team, along with one of its key lieutenants, Toby Cobb, is making its first official visit to No. 2 as it embarks on an ambitious project to reconfigure the course's fairways back to the corridors and textures of the mid-1930s to the late-1960s, an era known by unofficial consensus as the golden age of No. 2. The period was marked on the front end by Ross's 1935 arrival at his final (and current) routing and conversion of the greens

Donald Ross (above) arrived at his final configuration for No. 2 in 1935, and more than seventy-five years later, Ben Crenshaw and Bill Coore (L-R opposite) came to restore that Old World ambience.

from a sand-clay mixture to Bermuda grass; it was denoted at the back end by a transition to a new owner that believed in the green-is-good mantra of modern golf course maintenance. Coore and Crenshaw were summoned for the project by Pinehurst officials (and with the blessing and encouragement of the United States Golf Association) because of their deep *curriculum vitae* of courses like Sand Hills in Nebraska and Chechessee Creek in the South Carolina Low Country designed with a classic, minimalist flair, and their deep reverence for the history and traditions of the game.

"It is not our intent to radically change this golf course," says Coore, who grew up in Davidson County, just southwest of High Point, N.C., and played No. 2 frequently in his youth and college days at Wake Forest. "This golf course has stood the test of time for decades. It is without question a masterpiece. It's like a work of art that has gathered some dust, is a bit covered by some things that have happened through time. We're trying to uncover it. We're in no way trying to pretend that I or Ben are Donald Ross or know exactly what he would say today or know exactly what he would do."

There are no major structural changes planned—perhaps a tee elevated for better view of the landing area and several new ones to add a few dozen yards, some bunker lips extended for improved visibility, two new pin positions on constricted greens. Essentially the task to be executed over the year or two—"It's hard to put a time frame on this job," Coore says—is to remove acres of existing maintained Bermuda rough and return them to a natural state more indigenous to Pinehurst and the Sandhills—hardpan sand, wispy wire grass and random pine straw. Coore and Crenshaw will use the center line sprinkler system, intact since 1933, and a variety of tools ranging from Tufts Archives photos to aerial images from the Department of

Before and After: A golfer tees off on the par-four second hole in the 1950s, aiming to a fairway lined with hardpan and wire grass . . .

THE GOLDEN AGE OF PINEHURST

. . . and Retief Goosen launches his tee shot on the first hole in the 2005 U.S. Open to a rough-lined, "bowling alley shaped" fairway.

THE BEGINNING GOLFER

Gee! but I'm glad to get back to Pinehurst

PINEHURST
NORTH CAROLINA

Free from climatic extremes, and wholesome in every respect

No consumptives received at Pinehurst

The Centre of Winter Out-of-Door Life in the Middle South

T o the timid man who has mowed a large field with a dull club for the first time, golf is an overgrown game of hide-and-seek which is played in a reformed cow pasture with clubs and a vocabulary. A golf course consists of eighteen four and half inch holes of the best quality, carefully concealed about a 180-acre field. The object of the game is to put an undersized ball into each of the holes in succession without breaking a blood vessel. Kicking the ball or attacking it with a knife is forbidden. One must do the trick solely by striking it with the club, counting each stroke doggedly and in a rich, redolent undertone.

The clubs which are used in herding balls over the course are many in number. There is the driver, which is used for driving the small rubber tee into the ground; the lofter, which raises small chunks of sod over trees, bunkers and other obstructions; the cleek, for weed-clipping; the niblick, for throwing sand at an adversary; the mashie, for pounding the ball into the earth; and the midiron, for punishing it until its maker would not recognize its battered shell. Other useful clubs are the brassie, the putter, the excavator, the whacker, the digger, the smasher, the chopper and the caddie driver. The latter is a common club, not turned up at the end, and is to be used to keep the caddie awake. A caddie is a parody on a small boy, who carries clubs and helps lose the ball. Expert golfers can drive both a ball and a caddie over the course at the same time without help.

The Pinehurst Outlook 1905

the Interior as their roadmaps.

"Think of it as uncovering the strategic principles," Crenshaw says. "We'll have a little less water here and there, fewer chemicals. We're not changing the skeleton of the course. We are changing the outline of the holes."

"The *picture* will remain the same," Coore adds. "It's the *frame* that needs some work."

The inverted saucer putting greens and intricate array of swales and knobs surrounding them provide much of No. 2's character. That element will not change.

"I can count on one hand the places in the world where two shots on and around the green mean more to a player than on Pinehurst No. 2," Crenshaw says. "These are works of art. How to play to them and how to recover when you miss? Invariably you have a shot you have to conjure up in your mind and you say, 'How am I going to play this one?' Those are the aspects that make Pinehurst what it is. The greens and their surrounds will always defend themselves, they're that spectacular. They are to be left alone. Everybody has always known players' hands are full when they approach the greens here."

This still-life painting by Bill Williams embraces the traditions of long-ago Pinehurst.

"We are not changing contours, not changing greens," Coore says. "If anything, we're trying to bring the latitude back, the strategy back, so there is actually a little more room to play. They had *room* to play in the 1951 Ryder Cup. Today there is little room to play."

"To have choices, you must have a little width through which to play," Crenshaw adds. "The strategy is the fascination with Pinehurst No. 2. Some of that has been lost."

There is also too much uniformity. Coore stands on the eleventh tee, a par-four with a gentle left-to-right swing, and points to the right side of the hole and the crisp delineation of the layers: first a pine forest, then sand cart path, next to it a sandy expanse with wire grass, then a strip of lush Bermuda rough, and, finally, the rich emerald fairway.

"It's all a little too perfect," Coore says. "We want it to look a little more random and natural. Straight lines are *not* what we want."

It so happens that as the restoration of Pinehurst No. 2 is commencing, the covers of the popular national golf magazines are plastered with photos of the newest of the four courses at Bandon Dunes on the Pacific Coast. Coore & Crenshaw designed one of these courses, Bandon Trails, and the quartet of layouts has been saluted for its old world appeal of sand, wind, taut surfaces and a lack of contrived features and appearance.

"You look at all the golf magazines today, the courses they are featuring have this very natural, evolved look to them," Coore says. "None of them portray the sense of the perfectly manicured look. Those are not the ones coming to the forefront. Bandon Dunes is in every magazine you pick up. Well, Pinehurst has been *that* since its inception. It was the leader in the beginning of very natural golf courses. It was one of the most natural looking golf courses in the entire country."

The early decades of Pinehurst golf courses featured fairways covered in coarse Bermuda grass and tees and greens made of a sand-

Equally as important but generally less discussed is the geometry of the course, which opened as eighteen holes in 1907 and was completed in its final configuration in 1935. Ross designed wide fairways to provide the skilled golfer with aiming latitude with the driver. Then he positioned bunkers and angled greens to offer even more choices—aggressive plays and safe plays, high rewards and hellish risks.

But the combination of lush maintenance standards mandated by the demanding club and resort golfer as well as the starkly pinched fairway dimensions of the 2005 U.S. Open set-up (average under twenty-five yards across) resulted in a course with constricted landing areas, lush thickets of Bermuda rough and minimum instances of the old-time sandy perimeters.

The fourth hole in the 1940s reflects the personality of No. 2 beyond the fairways. "Whenever you missed the fairway," legendary amateur Harvie Ward said, "you played out of wire grass and sand."

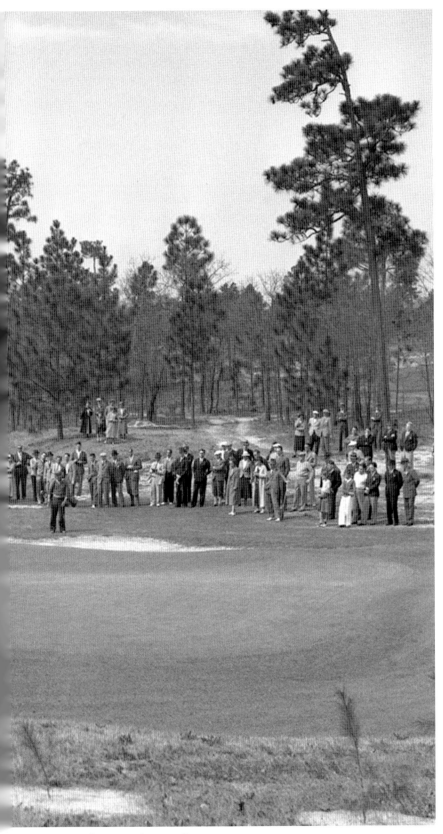

clay mixture. Ross and course superintendent Frank Maples developed techniques to plant and cultivate different grasses throughout the seasons and on different components of the course, and by 1928 Ross was experimenting with grass tees. That led to planting Italian rye (or "winter rye") on the fairways, and in 1933 they installed a sprinkler system on No. 2 to water the new rye grass. There was no thick Bermuda rough because there wasn't irrigation enough to throw water that far from the fairway centerline. The dominant grass in the roughs was native wire grass. The banks of bunkers were left in a semi-wild state.

"Whenever you missed the fairway, you played out of wire grass and sand," said Harvie Ward, the 1948 North and South Amateur winner who lived the last years of his life in Pinehurst before his death in 2004. "If you were lucky, you could hit the ball again. The course played fast. If you hit it off-line, the ball would roll and roll."

"I loved the way the ball went straight from the fairway into the wire grass and pine trees," adds Arnold Palmer, a contemporary of Ward's from their collegiate days in the 1940s.

As they walk around the course today, Coore and Crenshaw speak of the renovated course having more of a "laid quality" to it—that Ross found a great piece of ground and simply *laid* the golf course down on it. Crenshaw likes the term "poverty grasses" and believes the outlying areas of the holes should look more like Ross's native Scotland, where the irrigation fell from the sky and chemicals were reserved for the local apothecary. They want a broader color palette than the verdant fairways and white sand that dominate today. Straight lines and stark definition are out. They acknowledge the subjectivity of the enterprise.

"It's all judgment calls," Coore says. "Donald Ross is not alive, he's not standing here, he can't tell us what to do. All we can do is use our understanding of this golf course and our understanding through research of what it was like. We will take that perspective and try to come a little closer to what it once was.

"It is a daunting task," he says, his eyes directed down a fairway more than a century old. "It's an honor, but it's a nervous honor." 🌿

A gallery surrounds the second green of No. 2 during early 20th century North and South Open play.

Today nearly everyone plays...

...a coarse and vulgar pitch which punches a hole in the green. With the exception of the Old Course at St. Andrews and a few similar courses, there is rarely any necessity to play any other kind of shot. Golfers are losing the joy of playing the variety of approach shots that were so necessary in the old days.

ALISTER MACKENZIE

FUN TIME IN THE THIRTIES

By Dan Jenkins, *Sports Illustrated* 1963

Boy, those Thirties. Fun Time. The years when Sam Snead had hair, right there on his head, parted on the left; when Ben Hogan was a runt with a wild hook and a snap-brim hat; when Jimmy Demaret had pink shoes and violet pants; when Ky Laffoon anointed the greens with tobacco juice; and when Ruby Keeler and Dick Powell, in their sailor suits, couldn't do the Big Apple much better than Joan and Paul Runyan or Emma and Harry Cooper. It was Fun Time, all right, Fun Time on the pro golf tour—because if you couldn't laugh about it you might as well go back to mowing fairways and raking cottonseed-hull greens.

The game still belonged to the amateurs in the early Thirties, you see, to aristocratic young men with hyphenated names and blonde sisters. A professional was anyone who had caddied after he was fourteen, who could wrap leather grips and who took his meals in the kitchen. The exact date is not recorded when people first realized a pro could make a nine-iron back up better than an amateur, but it happened somewhere in the Thirties. At about the same time Walter Hagen finally convinced everyone you could let a pro in the front door and he wouldn't steal the crystal. These two circumstances began to combine, introducing America to the age of the alligator shoe.

To say it was more of an adventure in the Thirties would be like saying Cary Middlecoff's dental patients had to hold their mouths open a long time. Right away there was one primary challenge, to try to put chuck-burgers down your neck from Flagstaff to West Palm. If you shot over 74 in the first round you could forget it—fifteenth was the last pay spot and, of the thirty to forty regulars who were out there beating you, Ben Hogan was about the least known. But whether you won or lost, leaving town was always the same. You loaded into somebody's Graham-Paige or Essex and drove until you threw a connecting rod. Air travel? That was for Noah Beery Jr. up there in the sleet without any de-icers while Jean Rogers wept softly in the radio tower.

The tour began in Los Angeles. Everyone piled into the Hollywood Plaza for $1 a day, went directly downstairs to Clara Bow's It Cafe and began contemplating the happy fact that L.A. offered one of the biggest purses on the tour. And, next to the U.S. Open, it pulled the most spectators—so many one year, in fact, that in the congested excitement of a certain round Dick Metz had to park two miles away from the course and buy a ticket to get in. This would not have been so embarrassing for the sponsors if Metz hadn't been leading the tournament at the time.

From L.A. you went to Agua Caliente or Sacramento, maybe, or you scooped wedges around the Rose Bowl in the Pasadena Open. Wherever you were, you stuffed the bag with oranges from the citrus trees in the rough. It kept the food budget down. At the San Francisco Match Play you spewed challenges at anyone in the locker room you figured you could beat, and tried to get the pairings arranged accordingly. One tournament, the thirty-six hole Crosby at Rancho Santa Fe, was a little special, because a lot of Hollywood stars like Richard Arlen, Clark Gable and Randolph Scott were sure to be there, and, say, those lugs were just swell, to use one of Margaret Lindsay's more dramatic lines.

After the giddy times out on the Coast, fan belts permitting, the tour wended lazily through the Southwest, the South, the East and the Midwest until, quite sensibly, it ended as football season began. It embraced a variety of tournaments, many of which sounded as if they ought to be on the billiard circuit, namely, the Miami-Biltmore Four-Ball, the Goodall Round Robin, the Westchester 108-Hole Open, the Dapper Dan and the Vancouver Jubilee. It swung through San Antonio, oldest of the winter events (1922), for the Texas Open at Brackenridge Park, which was the place where sun-goggled Jug McSpaden once stunned himself by shooting a practice-round 59 at Ben Hogan, Byron Nelson and Paul Runyan. It was also there that Wild Bill Mehlhorn climbed a live oak beside the eighteenth green on the last day and loudly heckled Bobby Cruickshank, wishing for a three-putt so Wild Bill himself could win. Cruickshank survived, and Mehlhorn had to go on making most of his expenses at the bridge tables.

The tour moved on to New Orleans, where Lloyd Mangrum arrived one year so busted on Mardi Gras eve that he joyfully slept in the city jail. He remembers how the only bad part was going without cigarettes for two days. It hit Pinehurst for the North and South Open. There, busted or not, you had to wear a tux and your wife had to wear a formal gown if you wanted to eat dinner. There was Palm Beach, where Paul Runyan's partner in the Seminole pro-am one winter drove 310 yards on the first hole, hit his approach within eighteen inches of the cup but then—just as Runyan began to think the tournament was in the bag—putted eighteen feet past the hole! The partner's name was Gene Tunney.

In Florida the pros got their first inkling that they might be some kind of semi-celebrities. It was all because of the Miami-Biltmore Four-Ball, a partnership tournament sponsored by a hotel that figured sports-page stories with the word Biltmore in them might give rewarding ideas to tourists. The Miami-Biltmore also may have invented appearance money, for it always paid the Open and PGA champions $1,000 each to show up, as if they had anywhere else to go. The whole field got a bottle of White Horse Scotch and a tin of Lucky Strikes for each birdie. And every day both players and wives were hoisted by autogyros over to Miami Beach for a swim. When the tour moved through Greensboro there were no fish, but there was a weird species called "Sammy's Lambies," a name the pros gave the girls who traipsed after Snead. Arnie's Army was not golf's first militant unit. Georgia was quail-and-wild-turkey country, and part of the deal at the Thomasville Open was playing your round quickly so you could get out and hunt, slowly, no limit, to stock up as much free food as possible.

Suddenly, one fine spring there came what was to develop into about the most pleasant week of the year for everybody invited. It was a brand-new experience, the Masters, and while it did not have any turkeys it had a course that looked as opulent as a La Salle with chrome horns, it had outdoor barbecues, ham cooked in wine, biscuits bigger than head covers, corn whiskey in pitchers, Bobby Jones for a host and so many southern colonels sitting under crawling wisteria that you were tempted to look up who won the Civil War.

That was the way of the pro tour. There were no more than twenty to twenty-five tournaments a year. But if a man could reach most of them, if he knew how to fit the club heads that were made in Scotland onto the shafts that were made in Tennessee and if he could survive the nightly games of pitch, bridge and seven-card low, he could pocket maybe $6,000 and rank a whopping fifth on the money list.

(Reprinted by permission of the author)

Ben Hogan follows tee shot during North and South Open competition.

Hole of No. 1 Course. Pinehurst, N. C.

The Golden Age

To understand where Coore & Crenshaw are headed with their 2010-11 restoration of Pinehurst No. 2, it's incumbent to understand where the golf course has been. It lies today in Pinehurst through a fascinating series of coincidences, circumstances and twists of fate that have evolved over more than a century.

In truth, there is no good reason for Pinehurst to exist. There is no good reason that a patch of land known by locals in the late-1800s as the "pine barrens" should one day evolve into such a magnificent center for the care, nurturing and passionate pursuit of the ancient sport of golf. There is no seaside port, no river landing and no urban enclave of commerce and population nearby. There is no cooling mountain to have beckoned the lowlanders in the summer.

Yet Pinehurst came into being—the butterfly flapping its wings, if you will—on a chance meeting on a train in the late-19th century between James Walker Tufts of Boston and Colonel Walker Taylor of Wilmington.

Tufts made his fortune in patenting, manufacturing

Billy Joe Patton plays out of greenside bunker on the 17th during his run of three North and South Amateur championships from 1954-63.

and sales of apparatuses and syrups found on every Main Street in America in the late 1800s—the apothecary shop (today's drugstore or pharmacy). He concocted syrups for root beer and ginger ale and built the grand and ornate fountains used to dispense them. As he neared the age of sixty, Tufts turned his business operations over to subordinates. He was active in philanthropic work and sought on behalf of the Invalid Aid Society of Boston to locate a wintertime health resort for those suffering from consumption; he envisioned a location not as far from New England as Florida, a two-day train journey at the time.

Taylor was a sharp businessman himself and had opened an insurance agency in Wilmington in 1866 following the Civil War. He traveled extensively throughout the Eastern Seaboard, and having a gregarious personality, was wont to strike up conversations with perfect strangers. One day in 1895, pure happenstance landed Taylor and Tufts on the same train. They struck up a conversation, and Tufts explained his vision to Taylor.

Taylor, legend has it, suggested that the train station

The opening of The Carolina Hotel in 1900 illustrates the "oasis in the desert" phrase that depicted Pinehurst's early existence. The land was sandy, arid and dotted with scrub pines and oaks. In time, though, the landscape matured into a winsome haven for travelers from across the Eastern Seaboard and beyond.

The CAROLINA
PINEHURST
1895

80

the Carolina

Pinehurst
NORTH CAROLINA

Pinehurst
NORTH CAROLINA

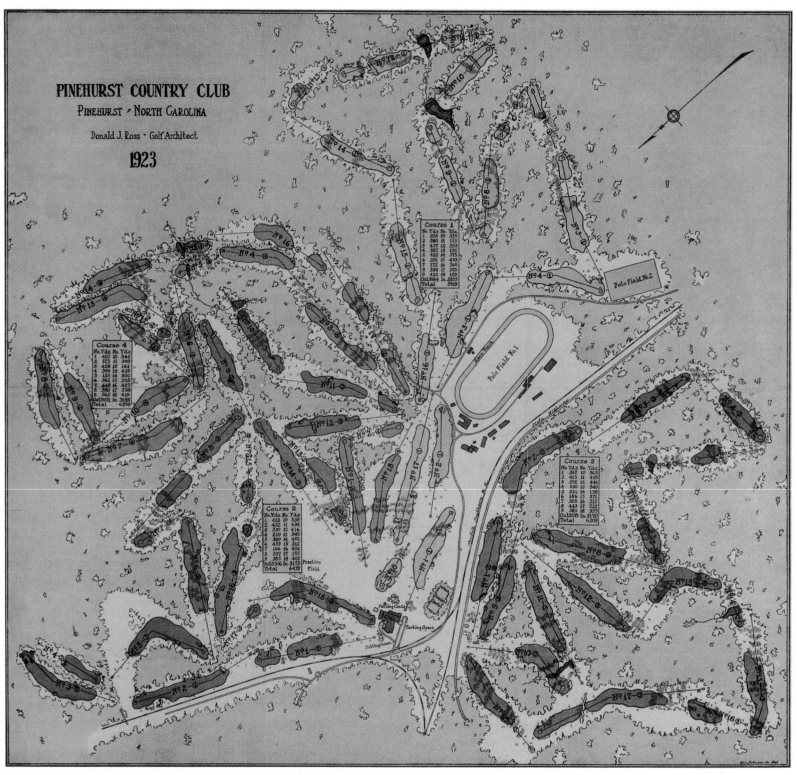

This 1923 map of Pinehurst's four courses includes No. 2 lower left, No. 3 lower right and courses 1 and 4 spread through the center. The current third and sixth holes of No. 2 are shown in the lower left corner when they played as holes three and four.

THE GOLDEN AGE OF PINEHURST

in Southern Pines might be a good starting point for Tufts' search for a site for his new resort. It was right on two of the nation's major north-south transportation arteries—the railroad and U.S. Hwy. 1. There was cheap land available, and it was halfway between Boston and Florida.

"It's an old family story," says Walker Taylor III, who was still active in the family insurance business in Wilmington in 2011. "I have no way of proving its authenticity. But my grandfather always said he directed Mr. Tufts to the Sandhills. True or false, he *did* get the Tufts' insurance business. He even opened an office in Pinehurst to service Mr. Tufts. He liked to tell the story of telling Mr. Tufts how much money he could save on his insurance bill by installing sprinklers in The Carolina."

So Tufts got off the train in Southern Pines, began exploring the area and eventually located and purchased in June 1895 from the Page family of Aberdeen some five thousand acres of cut-over, burnt-over, rooted-over timberland for the minuscule sum of one dollar an acre. Some thought Tufts was off his rocker.

"There is an old chap up in Boston who I fear has more money than good common sense, and has a wild scheme in the back of his head that he can make a resort up here in these barren sand wastes," wrote Walter Hines Page, the noted journalist from Moore County whose family owned and sold the land.

Undaunted, Tufts envisioned a New England-style village with broad, winding streets and walkways nestled in thick foliage and shrubbery and colorful flowers, and he wasted little time in visiting the top landscape architecture firm in the nation to plan his new village. By late June he called on the Brookline offices of Olmsted, Olmsted and Elliott, the celebrated concern whose resume included Central Park in New York and the Biltmore Estate in Asheville. He first spoke with John Charles Olmsted, nephew of the firm's founder, and returned in early July to meet with the esteemed Frederick Law Olmsted himself. Tufts paid the firm $300 for the land plan that he would immediately begin implementing.

Tufts constructed a trolley line from his new resort to the train station in Southern Pines, a water-and-sewer system and electrical grid and laid out the streets. He built a livery stable and an ice plant and cleared a sixty-acre peach orchard. Pinehurst's first build-ing, The Holly Inn, opened in December 1895, and the new resort was off and running. The infant resort answered to several names in the early days—from "Tuftown" and "Tuftstown" in honor of its founder to the names Tufts used in letters back home, "Sunalia" and "Pinalia." He eventually held a contest and the winning entry was "Pinehurst"—as in "pines on sandy, rising ground."

Tufts' grand scheme to help consumptives was derailed in short order by the realization in the late-1890s that the affliction was actually the highly contagious disease of tuberculosis. So he quickly adapted to make Pinehurst a leisure resort with activities such as horseback riding, dancing, recitals, carriage rides, cards and a croquet-like game called roque. There was no golf. But his vision for the resort further evolved in 1897 when it came to his attention that guests were hitting small, rubber balls with wooden sticks around the dairy fields and, in the process, aggravating the cows. Also affecting Tufts' plans was the fact that the peach business, very profitable in orchards around Southern Pines, took a hit with an infestation of the pest known as San Jose scale; the trees in the new orchard were killed, so the land was cleared for a golf course.

Tufts built nine holes as a lark in 1898, enlisting the help of Dr. D. LeRoy Culver, a Southern Pines physician who was an avid golfer, had played in England and Scotland and understood the gist of what a course should look like.

"A nine-hole golf course has been laid out after the famous St. Andrews, near Edinburgh, Scotland," *The Pinehurst Outlook* reported in February 1898. "Mr. Tufts is giving his personal attention to the construction and we may expect as fine a links as there are in the country. The spot selected is an ideal one, situated upon the hill south of the Village Commons. The grounds cover sixty acres of thoroughly cleared land, well fenced in, and covered with a thick growth of rye, which will be kept short by a flock of more than a hundred sheep."

But Tufts wasn't sold on the game's prospects and inquired of the manager of The Holly Inn, Allen Treadway, if he thought nine more holes would be a good idea.

"Save your money," answered Treadway, who later would be elected as a Massachusetts congressional representative. "Golf is a fad and will never last."

Tufts' instincts and better advice from others in his circle con-

Early North and South Open competitions were waged on a course that featured putting greens made of clay and sand. After golfers putted out, caddies would drag an apparatus resembling a mop across the green to smooth out footprints and ball marks. The greens were converted to Bermuda grass beginning in 1935.

vinced him otherwise, and soon he embarked on the expansion of the golf course to a full eighteen holes. Reaching back to his Massachusetts roots, Tufts hired a young Scottish golf professional working in Stockbridge, Mass., for the job. John Dunn Tucker came to Pinehurst and by the fall of 1899 unveiled the new eighteen-hole course.

English golf pro Harry Vardon visited Pinehurst in March 1900 as part of a tour that would culminate with winning the U.S. Open, and his appearance and favorable comments on the golf course excited the locals. "His visit was Pinehurst's first taste of big-time golf, the flavor was good and the resort wanted more," Tufts' grandson, Richard,

noted years later.

The Pinehurst story evolves with a twist of fate turning on a coin flip five time zones away in Scotland and a coincidental club connection in Tufts' home of Boston.

Donald J. Ross was born in 1872 in the village of Dornoch, on the northeast coast of Scotland, and learned as a boy to play golf, tend the greens and make clubs at Dornoch Golf Club (it was christened *Royal Dornoch* in 1906). His first club was a left-handed mashie he found abandoned in the whins bordering the course, and soon he graduated to a modest right-handed set fitted for him by club secretary John

THE GOLDEN AGE OF PINEHURST

In St. Andrews, Ross learned greenkeeping from Morris and also spent time making and repairing clubs in the shop of David Forgan. Though there was not at the time a formal occupation of golf course architect, no doubt Ross and others spending time in St. Andrews at the time like Alister MacKenzie, A.W. Tillinghast and C.B. Macdonald soaked up Morris's tastes and views on the proper design and construction of golf courses; Morris had a hand to one degree or another in designing Prestwick, Muirfield, Carnoustie, Dornoch and the Old, New and Jubilee Courses at St. Andrews.

"Old Tom Morris is the most remote point to which we can carry back our genealogical inquiries into the golfing style," said noted British golfer and writer Horace Hutchinson. "[Thus] we may virtually accept him as the common golfing ancestor who has stamped the features of this style most distinctly on his descendants."

Ross returned to Dornoch and in November 1894 was hired by Sutherland to work full time as the club's head professional, clubmaker and greenkeeper. In that capacity he made the acquaintance of an astronomy professor from Harvard University, Robert Willson, who was visiting Dornoch to play in the Dornoch Invitational. Willson took a liking to Ross—for one reason because Ross made a referral to a Dornoch tailor who treated Willson well—and suggested that Ross should come to America, where knowledgeable golf pros were in demand to service the burgeoning sport.

Sutherland had also thought of testing the waters of the fledgling American golf industry, and he and Ross considered the prospects. They agreed that one of them should remain at Dornoch to run the club, and the other was free to head to America. A flip of a coin would determine who would leave and who would stay home. Ross won the flip.

"My mother and Mr. Sutherland's daughter were great pals," says Donald F. Grant, a lifelong Dornoch resident and club member. "They lived side-by-side growing up. I heard the story often. I have no reason to doubt its truth."

Ross in 1899 sailed to Boston—despite the strong protestations from his mother—and upon arrival contacted Willson, who fed the hungry traveler a sandwich and a glass of milk and made arrangements to take him to Oakley Country Club in nearby Watertown and discuss the club's need for a professional and greenkeeper. Ross

Sutherland. His father, Murdoch, was a carpenter and fancied a career for young Donald as a tradesman, but Donald's affection for golf led the youngster to split his time as a carpenter's apprentice and a caddie. The fourteen year-old no doubt was quite thrilled in 1886 when Old Tom Morris, the four-time winner of The Open Championship, visited to begin redesigning the club's original links into a new layout. Sutherland convinced Murdoch and Lillian Ross to allow their son to travel as a teenager to St. Andrews and a year later to Carnoustie, where the ancient links and the tutelage of wise old heads in the golf world made indelible impressions on young Donald.

was hired by the club and immediately set out to remodel the club's eleven-hole layout. He staked out a new course, arranged for labor and began working toward a projected opening in the fall of 1900.

The Scotsman learned as November rolled into December that the winter weather of New England was significantly harsher from that of his homeland, despite the fact that Boston lies at forty-two degrees north latitude and Dornoch is at fifty-seven degrees—Scotland benefiting from the warmth of Atlantic Ocean current system known as the Gulf Stream. New England gets more snow and bitter temperatures, and playing the game and building new holes was severely limited from November through the spring.

And who should be a member at Oakley? James Tufts, who was looking for someone fluent in golf who could spearhead the Pinehurst operation.

Tufts asked Ross if he would be interested in traveling to Pinehurst to work in the Boston off-season. Ross agreed and began his new assignment at Pinehurst in December 1900. He was busy at first making clubs, managing the caddies, giving lessons and organizing competitions. He also tried his hand at designing and building new golf holes—and it just so happened that this ground 120 miles from the coast would consist of a similar soil structure Ross knew so well from his home along the Scottish coast.

Millions of years ago, the Atlantic Ocean covered what is now dry land along the East Coast. During the Miocene Epoch (circa twenty million years ago), the ocean receded and left a strip of what is now ancient coastline and beach deposits. The Sandhills are part of that band some thirty miles across and eighty miles long. One reason Tufts liked the land as he first found it was that its sandy composition drained quickly and was thought to have health-giving benefits.

Pinehurst was perhaps not oceanside itself. But its location was a kissing cousin to the seashore. The word "links" can be traced to the Old English word for lean, *hlinc*, meaning "lean terrain formed by receding seas." The ground was perfect for golf and Ross's tastes. It provided, in essence, an "inland links" terrain. British golf architect Donald Steel noted in his book *Classic Golf Links* that this ideal ground for golf "links the sea with the more fertile plains that may be only a couple of hundred yards distance. It is land with no agricultural value. The only vegetation it supports are the fine wire grasses

that, on top of a sandy base, make an ideal playing surface, especially for iron play."

The course at Oakley was built on high ground overlooking Cambridge and was rife with heavy clay, gravel and boulders. At Pinehurst, the earth was gently rolling and sandy. Rain water flowed through the sandy soil at Dornoch; it did so as well in Pinehurst, allowing for a golf designer's dream environment.

"He was particularly attracted to the soil conditions here, as they reminded him of the old links land at home," Richard Tufts said years later. "Even our native wire grass seemed to remind him of the whins he knew in Scotland."

The original Pinehurst course in 1901 had hazards described by *The Pinehurst Outlook* as ranging "all the way from the deadly 'whisker' (wire grass) bunkers and traps, the equally deadly mounded pits and other unique devices and the 'rough' bordering the course and laying in wait for topped drives in front of the tees.

"Combined with this is the unusual natural variety which has made the old Scottish courses famous: long level stretches and undulating fair greens, hidden holes, up and down grade approaches, two ponds and other varied features; the hazards, even when artificial, to all intents and purposes are natural ones for they are so constructed as to be a part of the landscape."

Soon Ross's attention was focused on rebuilding the resort's single golf course and adding to the inventory. He remodeled and expanded the original nine-hole design; he unveiled the stout No. 2 course as a full eighteen-hole layout in 1907; and he introduced in 1910 the No. 3 course, one that would prove popular over time with women and seniors with its shorter holes and small greens. Pinehurst No. 4 was unveiled in 1919.

The Tufts family and Ross proved to be shrewd promoters and businessmen. They created under the "North and South" banner an array of amateur competitions to draw guests and golfers to Pinehurst and instituted a professional event that attracted the top players of the day—the Walter Hagens, Jim Barneses and Macdonald Smiths. A New York advertising agency created the popular "Golf Lad" character that adorned ads, brochures, posters and calendars. As World War I ended in 1919, the United States economy expanded and golf rode its coattails into the "Golden Age of Golf Course Design."

Bobby Jones follows his tee shot during an exhibition at Pinehurst as course architect Donald Ross watches from the background (top left).

The Tufts were getting more business at their resort than they could handle during the winter "high season"—more than 100,000 rounds a year were being played in the mid-1920s—and joined investors to create one new private club and one new resort operation in nearby Southern Pines. Ross designed the courses at Mid Pines (1921) and Pine Needles (1928), and both courses remain in business today essentially as he designed them. He also built twenty-seven holes at Southern Pines Country Club during this period; eighteen of those holes remain in operation today. By 1910 Ross was focusing on golf course architecture and would become the most prolific golf architect of the first half of the 20th century, with nearly four hundred courses to his credit.

"Donald Ross was such a dignified man, a man from the United Kingdom, a place of royalty," says lifelong Pinehurst resident Marty McKenzie. "He brought a sense of decorum and class with him. Pinehurst marketed itself to the major metropolitan areas of the United States, and business executives came here to play this sport called golf. Ross taught them to play golf, and they said, 'Gosh, we've got to have one of these golf courses.' Pinehurst and Donald Ross were the Johnny Appleseed of golf."

So add up this flow of providence: The cue from Walker Taylor for James Tufts to get off in Southern Pines; the guests pinging the cows' backsides; Tufts' gut telling him not to listen to Allen Treadway; Donald Ross meeting a man from Boston and Ross winning the coin flip to come to America; the thread of Tufts being a member at Oakley Country Club and Ross being the

new professional there; and Ross finding a curious expanse of sandy ground inland in North Carolina that piqued his interest in designing golf courses.

The result is what you have today. Ben Crenshaw is taking in the ambience early one morning in the spring of 2010 and marvels at the scope of the story.

"You're struck standing here with the idea that this was Donald Ross's pet project for many years, and it was his portrayal of how he felt golf should be played on the best terrain he could find in North America," Crenshaw says. "Bill's ideas on architecture and mine as well incubated right here. I can't tell you how many places we've been where these principles are in the back of our heads every step of the way."

***

The lists of the finest golf courses in America as evaluated by the ratings panels of *Golf Digest* and *GOLF* magazine are dominated at the highest rungs by courses built through the late-1930s, an era known in design circles as the "Golden Age of Golf Course Design." Seventeen of *Golf Digest's* top twenty in 2010 and eighteen of *GOLF's* were built prior to 1937. Two exceptions to both lists are Coore & Crenshaw's Sand Hills (1995) and Tom Doak's Pacific Dunes (2001)—each a course that looks like it could have been conceived and constructed by your great, great grandfather.

Funny, that. Would an automobile designed and built in 1933 be ranked among the top one hundred cars on the road today? Would

	Yards	Par	Bogey	Strokes	Self	Op'nt		
1	430	5	5	10				
2	425	4	5	3				
3	367	4	5	12				
4	325	4	4	7				
5	427	5	5	5				
6	145	3	3	16				
7	537	5	6	1				
8	220	3	4	14				
9	140	3	3	18				
Out	3016	36	40					
10	332	4	4	9				
11	418	4	5	6				
12	390	4	5	11				
13	335	4	4	13				
14	432	5	5	2				
15	212	3	4	15				
16	387	4	5	4				
17	165	3	3	17				
18	402	4	5	8				
In	3016	35	40	IN				
Out	3073	36	40	OUT				
Total	6089	71	80	GROSS				
				H'D'P				
Date				NET				

PINEHURST COUNTRY CLUB
Course No. 2

SELF — Attested by Opponent

LENGTH OF THIS CARD IS STYMIE MEASURE

No. 2 played only 6,089 yards prior to 1923, when Donald Ross began a process over a dozen years of adding the current third through sixth holes.

anyone in his right mind still use a Royal typewriter with its click-clacking keys and return bell? Would anyone take daily delivery of their ice in a wooden box by the front door?

Indeed not, but golf courses built nearly a century hence glow with the same charm and fascination as cottages built by tongue-and-grove. Ben Crenshaw turns his attention from the fifth hole of No. 2 one morning in the summer of 2010 and nods toward the elegant home sitting fifty yards away.

"The classic lines, the detail on old homes like that are something to behold," Crenshaw says. "They last for generations. That beautiful old architecture adds so much character to our surroundings. The artisans who built that house are basically gone. It's the same with these golf courses. They should be preserved, for one reason for future architects and people who build golf courses to study. The way they were built, the attention to detail is amazing. The new stuff? It's not my thing."

The architects of the early 20th century worked with crude and limited implements, thus restricting their ability to move mountains of earth. So their focus was on strategy and on making mental dexterity as much a part of the game as physical skills. Donald Ross, A.W. Tillinghast, Alister MacKenzie, Charles Blair Macdonald, Seth Raynor, William Flynn, George Crump, Hugh Wilson and Perry Maxwell were the leaders of this neophyte profession.

Ross's Pinehurst No. 2 opened as eighteen holes in 1907, and Macdonald's National Golf Links followed in 1910. Gems such as Augusta National, Pebble Beach, Cypress Point, Winged Foot, Baltusrol, Riviera, Oakmont, Merion, Pine Valley, Bethpage Black, Pasatiempo, the Cascades Course at the Homestead and Old White at the Greenbrier were conceived and built before World War II. The number of golf courses in America had increased from under 750 in 1916 to 5,691 by 1930, and there were 2.25 million Americans playing the game.

"Early layouts were transformed from mundane and geometrically-edged mediocrities to grand-scaled, artistic and strategically designed masterpieces," Geoff Shackelford wrote in *The Golden Age of Golf Design,* a handsome volume that pays tribute to all the excellent design and construction work from 1910 to 1937. Following that period, however, Shackelford believes that the evolution of beautiful

venues and stroke-play competition as preferred tastes among golfers and architects changed the direction of course design.

"The primary inspiration back then was still the Scottish way of playing shots close to the ground," Shackelford wrote. "And, match play, which allowed architects more freedom to create daring holes where high scores might be racked up from time to time, had not been overtaken by stroke play as the primary method of competition. Also, luck was considered an interesting facet of the game during the Golden Age, whereas in today's game architects and superintendents are asked to do everything in their power to eliminate luck, which certainly limits the more creative design concepts."

Pinehurst No. 2 first opened as nine holes in 1901 at a length of 1,275 yards, and Ross stretched it to 2,750 two years later. *Golf,* an official bulletin of the USGA, said in 1903 that those nine holes "are intended for beginners. It is easier than the eighteen holes and more level," and a 1905 edition of *The Pinehurst Outlook* noted that No. 2 "will prove most attractive for many who do not desire as strenuous a game as the championship course provides."

That, naturally, would change when Ross expanded the course into what would become the premier course at Pinehurst. The new layout opened for the 1907 season, and the *Outlook* reported in the fall of 1908 that Walter Travis spent several weeks at Pinehurst the previous winter and "was greatly pleased with the new eighteen hole course, which was then being used in unperfected form … expressing the belief that the completed result would be a course absolutely unique in this country, a model from which other courses would be constructed."

Travis, a native of Australia then living in the States, was a three-time winner of the U.S. Amateur and the first non-British winner of the British Amateur. He was also an author (*Practical Golf* was published in 1901 and was considered an authoritative reference book) and in 1908 began publishing *The American Golfer* magazine. So his opinions carried plenty of weight in early American golf circles.

"I know of no course, north or south, which provides a more thorough test or better golf, and none which gives such diversity," Travis said. "You are exceptionally fortunate in length, there is no monotony—every hole is different—not an unfair hazard on the course, and, no hill climbing. Best of all, each

Narrow fairways bordered by long grass make bad golfers.

ALISTER MacKENZIE

Fairway width was one of No. 2's early calling cards. On the fifth hole, for example, a golfer could take a safe line out to the right; a more aggressive angle to the left shortened the hole but brought bunkers and a more severe fairway sideslope into play.

hole has a special shot of its own…and, mark my word, certain holes will be quoted from one end of the country to the other.

"When you get upon a tee you have to think how you are going to play that particular hole, for there is always the alternative; a hard shot followed by an easy, or an easy followed by a hard. If you elect to accept the risk involved and make the hard shot—the really difficult one—the second shot is comparatively simple; but if you are a little weak kneed and decide to make the easier shot first, you will assuredly be up against something extremely difficult on your second.

"There are always, as there should be, openings to the greens, permitting a player to make a low shot, with run, against the wind, if he elects to do so, and not a high shot compulsory."

The *Outlook* in 1909 hailed Pinehurst as being "the last word" in golf and observed that the resort has "been responsible for more players taking up the game and following it permanently than any half a dozen combined clubs in the country." By 1909 more than two thousand players were assembling at Pinehurst each year. "The great majority are lovers of the game who find in it beautiful recreation, who follow it just as the sportsman does his bird dog, the yachtsman the sea, the equestrian the horse, and so on down the line," the *Outlook* noted. Within two years, another course was opened and, with five-minute starting times, the three courses were swarming with golfers during any moment of the day.

Donald Ross set off on a major retooling of No. 2 in the early 1930s, the result unveiled in time for the arrival of the PGA Championship, held in November 1936 and won by Denny Shute.

The first and second holes of No. 2 and the eleventh through eighteenth remain in the same locations with the same numbers in 2011 as they did when the course first opened in 1907. Ross added and deleted holes on two occasions over the next three decades.

The original course turned at a right angle after the first two holes, with holes three and four being short holes and the fourth green positioned in the spot of the current seventh green. Then the current eighth, ninth and tenth holes were played in 1907 as the fifth, sixth and seventh, the last having been about one hundred yards shorter in its original form. After playing the original seventh, golfers ventured to the south and played three holes on land now occupied by the fourth and thirteenth holes of course No. 4; the water hazard around which those holes wrap was much smaller but was in play on the original ninth and tenth holes of No. 2. The ninth hole was a par-three of 140 yards—"This is the most unique and attractive hole on the course," the *Outlook* opined—and the tenth was 321 yards uphill with a water hazard fifty yards in front of the tee. From there the course reconnected with the current eleventh.

In 1923, Ross added the current third and sixth holes, which were played as the third and fourth at the time. The original third and fourth holes were converted into one hole, which is today's dogleg right seventh, and fell in order as the new fifth hole. The current eighth, ninth and tenth then were played as six, seven and eight. The three holes that skirted off onto the current No. 4 course were altered to two holes, nine and ten. Then the course resumed as always at the eleventh.

Five years later, Pinehurst opened a nine-hole course for employees, with much of that land occupied today by course No. 7. In 1935, Ross took the first and ninth holes of that course and added them to No. 2 as the fourth and fifth holes. He discarded the short holes where course No. 4 is today and had arrived at the final configuration. His last major hole alteration involved stretching what would now be the tenth hole by moving the green nearly a hundred yards farther toward eleven tee.

There was one other significant difference to the course from the one golfers know from recent times: The fifth hole was originally played as a par-five and the eighth hole as a par-four, five stretching 467 yards and eight measuring one yard shorter at 466. The eighth hole was the No. 1 handicap hole. The course measured 6,879 yards with a par of 72.

(The pars on five and eight were flopped fifteen years later, with eight being lengthened to 488 yards as a three-shot hole; five was shortened as a par-four and played at 440 yards for the 1951 Ryder Cup. Pinehurst resident and former U.S. Amateur champion Dick Chapman noted in the Ryder Cup program that the switching of pars led to a subtle subconscious change on the part of golfers.

("The fifth used to be a fairly easy par-five, where many fours were made," Chapman wrote. "On the other hand, the eighth was an extremely difficult par-four, where only the longest could hope to get up in two. As a result, very few fours were made. Strange, now that the par has been changed, fours are much less frequent on the fifth and more abundant on the eighth.")

The period of the 1920s through the mid-1930s was also marked by significant introduction and evolution of new agronomic practices and grass textures on land that Pinehurst owner Leonard Tufts termed "wretchedly poor." Years later during an after-dinner talk, Tufts looked back on the early challenge of growing grass and said the old story was that crows flying over Moore County "had to carry their own rations." Locals liked to say that during a rain storm, if you listened very closely when a drop of water hit the ground, you could hear a sizzle—it had struck Hell.

Ross, Tufts and greenkeeper Frank Maples had experimented for years with ways to grow a suitable stand of turf on the fairways and to replace the sand-and-clay greens with grass. Ross and Maples tried applications of nitrate of soda, barnyard manure, cotton-seed meal and fish scrap among other fertilizers in trying to get grass to grow and survive. Tufts remembered wryly in later years that some early guests asked them *not* to try to grow grass in the fairways because "the few clumps we did have interfered with the lie."

Years later other guests wondered why Pinehurst hung onto the sand greens when they had seen good grass greens in the Northeast (where courses were open only during the warm-weather months) and in Florida (which benefited from year-around warm temperatures). But Pinehurst was a wintertime resort. While the weather was mild enough for golf most of the year, it wasn't warm enough in the fall and winter to support healthy and closely cropped grass for a putting green.

"The play is so heavy here in the cold weather that the growth of the grass isn't sufficient to take up the wear during that time," Tufts said. "I feel sure that ninety percent of our guests would say that our good sand greens are much preferable to any grass green that can be grown north of Florida."

Ross began experimenting with grass tees in 1928. Several sample tees survived through the golf season and were applauded by guests, so every tee on courses Nos. 1, 2 and 3 was converted to grass during the off-season of 1929.

"The experiment with grass tees last year showed that most people preferred them, so as soon as the hotels closed in the spring all the clay tees on courses 1, 2 and 3 were remodeled and planted for grass tees, and now there is a good turf ready for play," Tufts wrote in his early season letter to guests in October 1929. "We learn a little every year about growing grass in this reluctant sand. The fairways show it, too. The turf is like satin."

Italian rye grass (or "winter rye") had been used successfully on golf courses over a base of Bermuda, but Ross knew it had to be watered carefully to survive. Five miles of irrigation pipes were installed on No. 2 in 1933, allowing Ross and Maples to overseed with rye and water it properly.

"With the help of this sprinkler system, we have been able to plant on the fairways of this course winter grass, such as that used around the greens and tees recently," Tufts wrote in his November 1933 letter

Among the lady golfers who enjoyed their annual visits to Pinehurst were Babe Zaharias and Patty Berg (far left) and Peggy Kirk Bell (far right), the latter of whom would later settle in the Sandhills and own the golf course and resort at Pine Needles.

THE GOLDEN AGE OF PINEHURST

to guests. "This assures us of a good green turf on this course throughout the season."

By 1934, Ross had experimented enough in the soil nursery maintained at Pinehurst that he believed he could grow grass on putting surfaces. He built three experimental grass greens on No. 2 for the 1934 season.

"You will find the first three holes of No. 2 course completely remodeled, with grass and sand greens for each hole," Tufts wrote in November 1934. "We are hoping this innovation will prove both practical and popular."

It did indeed. The nation's top professionals and amateurs lauded them during the North and South competitions that year, and Ross rebuilt all the greens on No. 2 for the 1935 season.

"No. 2 has always been a pet of mine," Ross said. "In building these fine new greens, I have been able to carry out many of the changes which I have long visualized but only now have been able to put into practice."

The revamped layout with its new holes, configuration and greens was christened in the competitive golf world with the staging of the 1936 PGA Championship. The event marked the first time the PGA had been held at a southern resort; in its twenty years of competition, the PGA had been held mostly at eastern clubs with an occasional trip to the Midwest or West Coast. Ross and Maples laid thousands of pounds of rye grass seed over the fairways of No. 2 to ensure a green and lush turf in the late autumn months, and Tufts agreed to delay the season opening to members and guests until after the mid-November competition.

"I'm happy that the PGA picked Pinehurst," defending champion Johnny Revolta said before the competition began. "For win, lose or draw at Pinehurst, there's just something about the place that makes you feel grand because you've played there.

"I don't see how a course could be any harder, but at the same time it's the most pleasant course I've ever seen. You have to play No. 2 with your head as much as your hands."

Perennial Pinehurst visitor Tommy Armour agreed.

"The man who doesn't feel emotionally stirred when he golfs at Pinehurst beneath those clear blue skies and with the pine fragrance in his nostrils, is one who should be ruled out of golf for life," Armour wrote in the championship program. "He is not qualified to enjoy golf or to contribute to its environment."

The PGA Championship was a match play event at the time, with Denny Shute edging Jimmy Thomson 3-and-2 in the thirty-six hole championship match. Shute held a 2-up lead through the fifteenth hole of the afternoon round, then laced a three-wood second shot to within five feet on the par-five sixteenth. Thomson was bunkered in two and conceded the eagle and the match to Shute, who collected a check for $1,000 following the second of his three career major championships.

And so for the next thirty-five years, through the sale of Pinehurst by the Tufts family to Diamondhead on the final day of 1970, No. 2 existed in its very own "golden age." Visit with any golfer of note through that period and they'll speak warmly of the Pinehurst experience and the magnificence of plying their skills on "The Deuce," as the course was often called. The amateurs knew the course from their participation in the North and South Amateur, and the pros from the tour's annual stop in March for the North and South Open.

"No. 2 presented challenges quite fair and consistent with the old game, the British game, and of course it was not unnecessarily penal," says William C. Campbell, who won four North and South Amateurs from 1950-67. "You had certain strategic choices to make. I played well over a hundred competitive rounds there and on each hole there are elements that make the player think. And it's not putting you out of business with one bad swing. You're not going to your hip pocket for another ball."

Ben Hogan was a struggling journeyman when the PGA Tour moved from Florida to Pinehurst in March 1940. Hogan had gone eight years without a victory and was on the verge of packing his dreams away for the sanctity of a club pro job back home in Fort

The front end of the decade of the Fifties included Jimmy Demaret putting from fringe as partner Ben Hogan watches (right) in the 1951 Ryder Cup; and 19-year-old Jack Nicklaus winning the 1959 North and South Amateur.

Worth. But a first-round 66 staked Hogan to a comfortable lead that he never surrendered, and he eventually won the North and South by three shots over Sam Snead. He followed that with victories in Greensboro and Asheville; emboldened by the confidence of victory, Hogan went on to a Hall of Fame career.

"The whole golf course was a most pleasant and testing golf course. It's a real test of golf," Hogan said in 1991. "The North and South Open was a major then. At least I thought it was. Pinehurst was a golf mecca. They had a very nice hotel, accommodations for everybody. It was great. It had a super reputation. Everybody wanted to go to Pinehurst."

Pete Dye was stationed at Fort Bragg during World War II and had the good fortune of having a superior officer who loved golf. Dye got out of doing KP duty by driving his boss across the back roads of Cumberland and Moore counties to Pinehurst, where Dye got to play No. 2 "more than the law should allow." He became a frequent competitor in the North and South Amateur, and his wife, Alice, played in the Women's North and South. The friendship and support they received from Richard Tufts were cornerstones in the embryonic golf design business the Dyes started in the 1960s.

Pete remembers a seat mate on an airplane once who had just played No. 2 and was delighted with the fact he played the round with one golf ball.

"Of course, he shot 105, but he was so happy with himself that he never lost a ball," Dye says.

"You take a golf course like No. 2. The first hole you've got a nice little change of elevation downhill. The next hole, a little down. The fourth hole, a *magnificent* natural elevation change. Down on five, then back up. Nice roll on eight. Nine and ten, *wonderful* changes of elevation. Eleven, nothing. Twelve, nothing. Thirteen, you get a

break. Sixteen, seventeen and eighteen—*wonderful* natural elevation. With all due respect to Donald Ross, I never in my life ever had a piece of inland ground like Pinehurst or remotely like Pinehurst. Pinehurst must have thirty or forty feet of change. It's just the right change of pace for a golf course. And the drainage. Hell, that sand is *perfect* for a golf course. Early in my career, I tried to do some of those hollows and dips around a green, but they won't drain in clay like they do in sand. Ray Charles could have built a course in Pinehurst.

"My wife loves No. 2. She can play it. You can dribble it on one, dribble on two, dribble on four, dribble on five, dribble on six, dribble on seven, dribble on eight, half-ass on nine. It's that way all the way around."

Harvie Ward learned to play No. 2 in the postwar 1940s, winning the 1948 North and South Amateur and finishing second a year

PINEHURST

A Winter Resort
in North Carolina
for Health Seekers and Golfers

Donald Ross presents the winner's keepsake and check to Paul Runyan following the 1935 North and South Open. The Open was considered one of golf's major championships at the time; it was discontinued in 1951.

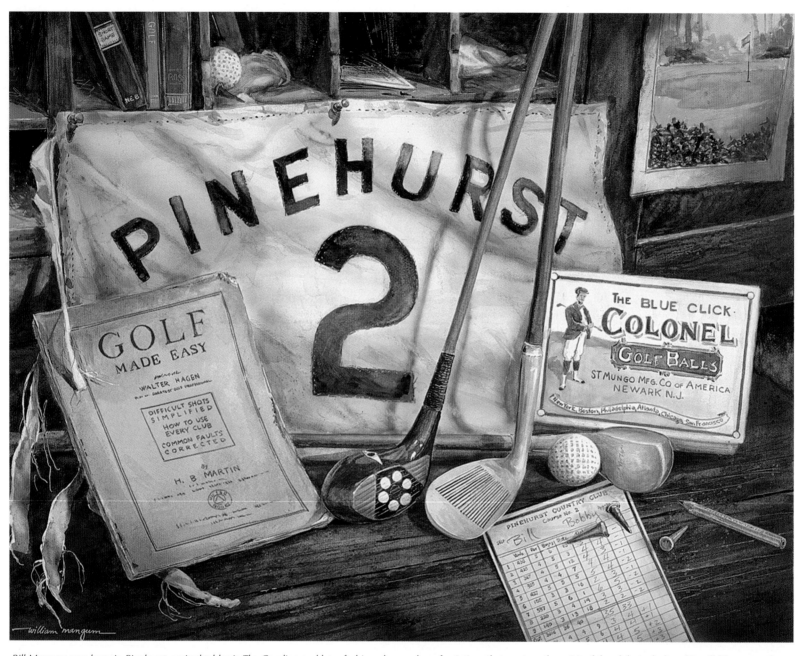

Bill Mangum was born in Pinehurst, waited tables in The Carolina and later fashioned a number of paintings that capture the spirit of the club, including this still-life watercolor.

later. In beating Frank Stranahan in the thirty-six hole championship match, he one-putted eighteen greens.

"You had to play a lot of bounce-up shots on No. 2," Ward said. "You couldn't play into the greens. It was more like Scottish golf—you had to bounce it in there. I grew up on sand greens in Tarboro. You used to have to hit the chip-and-run or putt from off the green. There and playing at Pinehurst helped when I won the British Amateur. They were amazed over there how good I was hitting the pitch-and-run versus the flop wedge, where you hit it in the air and stop it by the hole. I adapted to golf over there very easily."

Sam Snead won four North and South Opens and loved the short par-four third hole, one he called "one of the nicest little holes."

"It had chocolate drops down the left side," Snead said. "On the right side was sandy waste area. The fairway got narrower as you went. Then you had that bunch grass. If you got up against that, you'd have to pitch it sideways. There were more fives than threes made there. If you wanted to hit a big club, you go ahead, but brother you miss it to the left and you're up against one of those mounds—you're done for. It's a pitch-out, you see. And the same way in that waste bunker on the other side. Actually it was bare sand with that bunch grass. Had to play a two or three or four-iron off the tee, and they had four good pin placements. If the pin was on the left and you fooled around going for that flag, brother, you were going to get into trouble."

Billy Joe Patton of Morganton was one the game's consummate "career amateurs" in the mid-20th century, selling lumber during the week and pursuing his golf career on the weekends. He won three North and South Amateur titles and one Southern Amateur and advanced to the semifinals of the 1962 U.S. Amateur at Pinehurst.

"If I listed the five best golf courses I ever played, No. 2 would never leave my hand," Patton said. "I don't know if I ever thought any course was any better. I think Donald Ross just took what he had. It was a desert of sand and scrub oak and pine, and the fellow just built a golf course on it. He didn't build it around a lake because there wasn't a lake there."

Jack Nicklaus won the 1959 North and South Amateur as a nineteen-year-old, beating Gene Andrews, 1-up in the thirty-six hole final.

"The golf course was hard and fast," Nicklaus remembered in 1991. "The ball would hit the fairway and run right into the trees if you didn't hit it straight. There wasn't any rough, as it relates to grass. It was very thin around the greens. You couldn't use your wedge because you couldn't get your club under the ball. So you hit a lot of bump-and-run shots. There weren't really many good scores back then. I didn't feel I played all that badly, but I wasn't near par when I won.

"I've always thought Pinehurst to be one of my favorite designed golf courses in the United States. And the reason I say that is there's not any water on the golf course—well, there is on sixteen, but it's not in play—and there's not a tree in play on the golf course. It's a tree-lined golf course but the trees aren't a strategic part of the golf course."

Charles Smith of Gastonia won the North and South Amateur in 1960 and in recent times looked back in wonder over the difficulty of the course.

"This was back in the day of the balata ball and wooden clubhead," he said in 2006. "Beside Nicklaus and my brother, Dave, there really weren't any long hitters like you see today. That golf course was long and hard. I never hit anything less than a three or four-iron on the second hole. Today those kids hit nine-irons. Dave used to say the only thing they had to do to get No. 2 ready for the U.S. Open or the Amateur was to hang the USGA flag outside the clubhouse."

Vinny Giles was one of a number of Virginia golfers who routinely played competitive events at Pinehurst in the 1960s and '70s. Giles won the 1972 U.S. Amateur and 1975 British Amateur and later launched a career in sports management.

"Pinehurst was always natural, it was firm and fast and it was a little scruffy," Giles says. "You hit a funny shot and you're in a place you weren't used to. I can remember all down the right side of eleven, there was not a thing but sand and pine straw and whatever the heck you found—native grasses, weeds, whatever. You just tried to keep it between the green lines.

"I always said that architecturally, it might have been my favorite course ever. Every hole fit. The course had great ebb and flow to it. Nothing was out of place. There were holes you could attack, others that were back-breakers."

Toney Penna said in a 1983 *Golf Digest* story that if he could only play one course for the rest of life, it would be No. 2. "It's a course built by God, and Donald Ross knew how to take advantage of nature," Penna said.

Author Charles Price liked to talk of the *style* of No. 2 when holding court at the Pine Crest Inn bar.

"Think of the ten best-dressed men in America," Price once posited in a discussion about No. 2. "You don't notice what they're wearing. They're not in *Esquire* magazine. But they could step out of a photograph at the turn of the century and look presentable today. That's what Donald Ross did with No. 2. All these other golf courses built today are fashionable for the time. But they don't have an ounce of style.

"*Style* is what survives."

***

OFF FOR *Pinehurst*

Pinehurst generated plenty of
business from New York City
in the early days; the Golf
Lad makes his getaway from
Grand Central Terminal in
this iconic advertisement.

One of the beehives of activity in Pinehurst in 2011 is the Ryder Cup Lounge, a bar and dining area located in the front-right portion of the first floor of The Carolina Hotel. Guests enjoy a repast and beverage after their day on the golf course; all around them hang photos and assorted memorabilia from the 1951 Ryder Cup Matches at Pinehurst. There are images of Sam Snead hitting out of the wire grass, Ben Hogan following the flight of a drive, and several hundred spectators rimming the practice green for the closing ceremonies.

It's hard to comprehend amidst the frenetic competition of the modern Ryder Cup Matches, but in 1951 the Ryder Cup was a quaint, collegial gathering for serious players and golf wonks only. The American team won handily over the team of Brits and Irish at the inaugural matches in 1927 at Worcester (Mass.) Country Club and prevailed in six of the first eight meetings. Media coverage was limited, and so casual were the competitive juices at Pinehurst that the PGA scheduled a day off from golf on Saturday because of a football game in Chapel Hill between North Carolina and Tennessee (players from both teams were invited, but only three of nine Americans made the trip), and the No. 1 and 3 courses were busy with golfers on Sunday as the singles matches were being contested on No. 2.

"Richard Tufts agreed to stage the Ryder Cup as a gesture of support for the PGA of America, for which the match was then a financial burden," says Frank Hannigan, former executive director of the USGA.

Among spectators that week was the noted British journalist Henry Longhurst. He filed one report for *The Sunday Times* of London and later expanded on the trip to Pinehurst and the 1951 matches in an anthology of essays entitled, *Round in Sixty-Eight*. Longhurst played No. 2 before the competition and gave his British readers some insight into what was at the time a brutal challenge for average players.

"For minor fry, at 7,007 yards on the card and playing more like 9,000, it was murder—brassies, brassies all the way, as the poet might have said," Longhurst wrote. "It was not long before my partner and I agreed upon it as an admirable battlefield for the Sneads and Mangrums of this world but no fit stamping ground for aging investment brokers and golf correspondents. Still, we established one record which, unless some radical change comes over American golf, is likely to stand for years. We did it in two hours and twenty-five minutes."

The press information hand-out provided by the PGA included a hole-by-hole description of the No. 2 course. Consider the clubs commonly used for approach shots into the greens: three or four-iron to No. 1; three-wood to one-iron on No. 2; three-wood to one-iron on No. 6; five to seven-iron on No. 9; two to three-iron on No. 11; three to five-iron on No. 12; three to five iron on No. 14; three-wood to two-iron on No. 15; two to four-iron on No. 17; three to five iron on No. 18.

Richard Tufts noted that the course played even longer than its actual yardage of 7,007.

"This is due to the way its seven thousand-odd yards are distributed among the eighteen holes, there being three rather short par-five holes and no really long par-threes," Tufts said. "This places the extra yardage in the par-fours and calls for more use of the longer irons than is usual on two-shot holes. Since three of the par-five holes can be reached in two, a test for fairway woods is provided."

Dai Rees of the team from Great Britain and Ireland drew comparisons between the look and feel of No. 2 and his homeland layouts.

"This course is more like those we have at home than any other American course," Rees said. "It hasn't the subtlety of British courses and its fairways are broader. But in many respects, it is similar to those we are accustomed."

As competitions go, the matches were unremarkable. The United States team barely broke stride or a sweat in winning nine matches, losing two and halving one. Foursome matches were played in cold and wind and rain on Friday, Nov. 2, with the Americans jumping to a 3-1 lead. Then the ninth biennial competition wrapped up with singles on Sunday, the Americans winning six, losing one and halving one.

The other significant one-off event at Pinehurst during No. 2's mid 20th century glory days was the 1962 U.S. Amateur Championship.

The National Amateur through the 1940s and '50s had been held at some of the finest venues in the nation: Winged Foot, Baltusrol, Oak Hill, The Country Club, The Olympic Club and, in 1961, it made its first venture to Pebble Beach. Yet at no point had the championship been waged on what was by consensus viewed as a Top 10 course in the nation and one run by a gentleman who was certainly one of amateur golf's staunchest supporters.

By September 1960, Billy Joe Patton had had enough. It was time to get the Amateur onto the symphonic green settings, cushy beds of pine straw and acres of hardpan sand of Pinehurst No. 2.

"I just felt the players wanted to go to Pinehurst," Patton said. "I'd played in enough Amateurs, I knew enough people, it was like a fraternity. I knew everyone wanted to play Pinehurst."

The reason for the apparent oversight was quite simple. Richard Tufts, grandson of Pinehurst founder James Tufts and president of Pinehurst Inc. since 1935, was also a key volunteer, officer and championship official with the United States Golf Association. He had worked on every committee and sat in every officer's chair, culminating with his two years as president in 1956-57. At a time when resorts and chambers of commerce nationwide were quick to use golf tournaments as hooks for publicity and guest traffic, Tufts bent over backward in the opposite direction. Thus he never invited the USGA to Pinehurst for any of its championships. The U.S. Open was never really an option for No. 2, as the championship was played every June and the resort at Pinehurst closed in the summer until the advent and widespread use of air conditioning in the 1960s. But the Amateur was held in mid-to-late September, closer to the resort's customary early fall opening.

"Mr. Tufts was very reluctant to exploit his position with the USGA," remembers Bill Campbell. "He was the quintessential USGA president. For all of his ability, he was a very modest man, and also a purist. He did not want to take advantage in the sense of a conflict of interest."

The midwest region of the United States was affected by a drought in the summer of 1960 as the USGA prepared to take the Amateur to St. Louis Country Club, and when the field arrived for play that September, it found the greens thin and splotchy.

"The players wanted to get the best courses for the Amateur championship, and obviously Pinehurst No. 2 was one of the great ones," Campbell says. "It seemed odd that of all the golf courses the USGA conducted the Amateur and its other championships on, none had been at Pinehurst."

So Patton drew up a petition at St. Louis in 1960 requesting that the UGSA, instead of waiting for an invitation from a potential venue, actually approach Tufts and Pinehurst and ask that they agree to host the Amateur. The players readily signed. The gesture took Tufts off the hook for any real or perceived conflict of interest issues and allowed the USGA to set the Amateur for Pinehurst No. 2 on Sept. 17-22, 1962.

"It was an easy sale for Billy Joe to get the rest of us to sign up," Campbell says. "Everyone was happy to do it. It allowed Mr. Tufts to relent without feeling guilty."

"It was a difficult thing for Pinehurst," Patton added. "They had to open the hotel early, get the golf course ready early. It was quite an undertaking. We were delighted when he agreed."

Donald Ross had been dead for twelve years in 1960 when the Amateur was scheduled for Pinehurst two years hence, so Tufts personally took on the job of renovating several holes to strengthen them in the face of improved golf equipment and longer ball flights. He carefully studied the lengths of tee shots and the high-traffic landing areas during the 1961 and '62 North and South Amateurs and made changes during the summer leading up to the U.S. Amateur. By studying tee shots on the second and fourteenth fairways, Tufts found that the modern player was driving the ball beyond the established obstacles. Target areas were narrowed at the 250-yard range. New tees at four and eighteen stretched the course from 7,007 yards to 7,051. New bunkers in the right corner of the dogleg on the seventh hole and to the left of the fourteenth fairway were added.

The Amateur would be without its defending champion, Jack Nicklaus, who had just turned professional, but there were plenty of outstanding players left in the amateur ranks to give the event proper electricity. North Carolina native Harvie Ward was thirty-seven years old and traveled from his new home in San Francisco to vie for the title he'd won in 1955 and '56. Among other favorites were Deane Beman, former champion of the U.S. and British Amateurs; Charlie Coe, a two-time Amateur winner and second-place finisher to Gary Player in the 1961 Masters; Homero Blancas, the runner-up in the most recent NCAA Championship; Campbell, the three-time winner of the North and South Amateur; and, of course, Patton, the native North Carolinian who had won two North and Souths and challenged for the 1954 Masters title.

"Quick-witted and hopelessly gregarious, Patton is perhaps the most popular amateur in American golf today, and nothing would please his colleagues more than to see him win at Pinehurst," Herbert Warren Wind wrote in a *New Yorker* piece previewing the event.

It turned out that none of those favorites would make it to Saturday's final following six rounds of match play, though Blancas and Beman staged one of the week's most memorable matches—a twenty-four hole, see-saw affair that saw Blancas win with a 20-foot birdie putt on the par-three sixth hole, the sixth hole of a playoff. Patton lost to eventual champion Labron Harris Jr. in the semifinals.

"That one hurt," Patton remembered years later. "*What* it was, *where* it was, made it very disappointing. The Amateur, the national Amateur, on one of my favorite golf courses … if you were going to have an examination of your golf game, it suited me fine to have it there. Back then we weren't smart, we didn't know you could win on and on. But then I was about forty, and I kinda felt it was my last chance."

The championship match featured Labron Harris Jr., a twenty year-old graduate student at Oklahoma State University, and Downing Gray, a twenty-four year-old insurance man from Pensacola, Fla. Gray was in control through eighteen holes, taking a five-up lead in shooting a medal score of 70. But his troubles began on the fourth hole in the afternoon, when he drove wildly into the woods to the right, lost the hole and then lost four more in succession. The match was all-square through eight. Harris, who would go on to a career on the pro golf tour, took a 2-up lead through sixteen and held on for the win, dropping a four-footer for par on the eighteenth green to secure the victory.

That 1962 U.S. Amateur would be the last competition of any national scope at Pinehurst for more than a decade. By the time the pro golf tour returned in 1973 in the form of the World Open, the golf course had morphed from its rugged eccentricity to a more serene palette of green. Old-timers like Bill Campbell hung tightly to their mid-20th century Pinehurst utopia.

"Pinehurst was such a salutary experience," Campbell said years later. "Pinehurst is more than good golf courses. It is a state of mind and a feeling for the game, its aesthetics, courtesies and emotions."

Pete Dye wondered in the spring of 1991 what Donald Ross might do if he knew the Tour Championship, the season-ending climactic event on the PGA Tour, was going to be held that fall and that the course they would play was essentially the same one that Ross finished routing in 1935. In an expansive conversation for the book *Pinehurst Stories,* Dye told of the extensive lengthening and comprehensive greens rebuilding job he did at Crooked Stick in Indiana prior to the 1991 PGA Championship.

"Now I've been wondering what Mister Ross would do if today he woke up and knew that the pros were coming," Dye says. "When he built it in 1930, or whenever he finished, he had to envision it, I would assume, as the players played at that day and that given time.

"I wonder about all this talk about the 'subtleties' of Mister Ross. I don't think when he built this thing in the early '30s that he felt the golf course was *subtle* at all. I think he thought he built a golf course that was *severe* and challenged the hell out of the great professionals at that time. I know he was very upset he couldn't build a golf course for Bobby Jones at Augusta.

"If he woke up and saw Brandie Burton, that young girl, stand on the first tee of the Women's Amateur and knock a drive down there and hit a wedge to the first green, I wonder if he wouldn't take the first tee, pick it up and put it in the parking lot. I wonder if he was alive today, and he could see the great players play and how they play, if he thought a *challenge* was a drive and a long iron to a par-four, if he wouldn't do like I did at Crooked Stick and modify the whole damn thing, to try to give these guys the same challenge that their peers had fifty years ago. I always wonder what he would do."

There's no way of knowing, of course, Ross having died in April 1948. But many would make a study of considering that very question for decades to come. ❧

***

MUSIC TO GOLF BY

M usic and golf are strange bedfellows unless it's Barry White's *Love Theme* harkening back to ABC's old U.S. Open telecasts or Dave Loggins' lilting instrumental used by CBS for its Masters telecast theme. But in Pinehurst, the soothing strains of the Coe Memorial Carillon emanating from the Village Chapel bathe the town and Pinehurst No. 2 in a sensory delight that complement the crisp pine scent, the deep blue sky and the contrasts of the emerald fairways and sepia sandy roughs.

"You hear the bells, and you know you're in Pinehurst," says Ben Crenshaw, who visited the resort frequently over eighteen months from 2010-11 to help supervise the restoration of No. 2. "It's yet another little connection to the past, another little statement that this is no ordinary place in golf."

John Shannon, director of music at the Village Chapel since 1982, remembers considering the collision of concentration and ecclesiastical knell when the 1999 U.S. Open was approaching. He suggested the chimes be silenced during competition.

"I didn't think the finest golfers in the world should be putting for half a million dollars and all of a sudden the quiet is interrupted," Shannon says.

Chaplain Ed Galloway thought differently.

"The carillon is part of Pinehurst," he said. "They'll just have to accept it."

Indeed they did, only a programming error led to Christmas music being woven into the queue of music emanating over the proceedings that week in June. Shannon was on a European trip at the time, and no one else knew how to reprogram the apparatus.

"The announcers on national TV remarked what a charming village this is—'They even celebrate Christmas in summertime,'" Shannon says with a smile.

Payne Stewart had a one-shot lead as he addressed his tee shot on the eighteenth hole in the final round of the 1999 Open, with Tiger Woods up ahead on the green. Woods was grinding over a potential birdie putt; Stewart needed a par to cling to his lead over Phil Mickelson. The chimes from the chapel rang out.

"Was that an omen?" Stewart wondered later. "Was that a sign? Maybe it was. When I heard the church bells, I relaxed more."

Fifteen minutes later, he drained a fifteen-foot par putt to win the championship.

Bill Campbell vividly remembers hunkering down over a four-foot putt on the seventeenth green of No. 2 in the 1950 North and South Amateur. He needed to make the putt to remain even with Wynsol Spencer in the championship match.

The bells from the chapel interrupted his concentration. It was six o'clock. Unsettled, Campbell backed away. A few in the gallery chuckled a little. Then Campbell settled back over his ball. He drained the putt and then won the match a few minutes later on the thirty-seventh hole; the victory was the first of four North and South titles he would win in eighteen years.

Jack Nicklaus II closed out Tom McKnight on the seventeenth hole in winning the 1985 North and South Amateur just as the 6 p.m. bells were ringing. Lifelong Pinehurst resident Marty McKenzie puts the celebratory scene of Jack Sr. and son among the top in his considerable memory bank of significant Pinehurst episodes.

The intra-denominational Village Chapel has been a cornerstone of the Pinehurst experience for nearly a century. Miss Mary Bruce donated $5,000 in 1923 to launch a fund-raising campaign for the building, and the Tufts family contributed land at the base of the Village Green. The distinguished church architect Hobart Upjohn of New York designed the structure in the Georgian style popular at the time—wielding symmetry and order with red brick and a white New England spire to create a structure that nestled seamlessly into the landscape. The cornerstone was laid on April 13, 1924, and the first service was held the following March.

The original carillon gave out in the 1980s, and the music today is the gift of Marybelle Coe, who contributed funds in 1987 in memory of her late husband, Vincent. The apparatus is composed of fifty strips of bronze metal that are struck by

The Village Chapel sits serenely amidst the pines at the base of the Village Green in Pinehurst. The Coe Memorial Carillon serenades townsfolk and golfers with music selections on the half hour throughout the day.

mallets; the sound runs through a set of four speakers positioned in the steeple. The carillon rings the hour from 8 a.m. to 10 p.m. and plays a pealing at two minutes after the hour at 9 a.m., noon, 3 and 6 p.m. It plays two hymns each half hour, the selections coming from a library of about a hundred—hymns of praise, prayer, celebration, holiday and patriotism.

Around Easter you might be walking the second fairway of No. 2 and be serenaded with *Christ the Lord Has Risen Today*.

On the Fourth of July you might be debating a four-iron or a five and hear *God Bless America*.

As Christmas approaches you might be blowing warm breath on your hands while *O Holy Night* courses through the chilly air.

And at any point during the year a traditional hymn like *Holy Holy Holy* might punctuate your address of a nasty bunker shot.

"At Pinehurst, it's impossible not to get caught up in the great history," says David Fay, former executive director of the United States Golf Association. "It's everywhere. It's where you look, it's in the air, it's in the turf, it's in the images on the walls, it's in the church bells. You can almost feel the ghosts coming out."

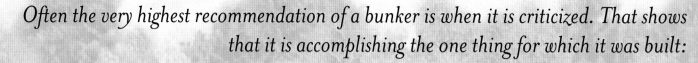

Often the very highest recommendation of a bunker is when it is criticized. That shows that it is accomplishing the one thing for which it was built:

A golfer aiming at the flag on the par-three ninth hole had better take enough club, else a sandy demise awaits.

It is making players think. DONALD ROSS

HEART AND SOUL

Richard Tufts as a young man not long after his graduation from Harvard in 1918 and subsequent service in World War I.

He was known, simply, as "Mister Richard." Richard Tufts was an excellent golfer and well-versed in agronomy, golf design, carpentry, finance, the rules of golf, tournament administration and club management. He was soft-spoken, reserved, quite intelligent and a stickler for details.

Tufts, the grandson of Pinehurst founder James Tufts, spent half a century in various administrative roles for the resort, club and village—from his graduation from Harvard University in 1918 and service in the Navy in World War I until the Tufts family sold Pinehurst to the Diamondhead Corporation in December 1970.

He was also a giant in international golf administrative circles, particularly in the 1950s with his ascension to the presidency of the United States Golf Association. Tufts served as secretary of the USGA in 1950-51 and vice president in 1952-55 before beginning a very active and successful two-year term as president in 1956. There were few parts of the game that his expertise and good sense did not touch:

* Tufts was an authority on the rules of golf and he played a central part in a 1951 summit conference at which the USGA and R&A agreed to uniformity, which he summarized in a book, *The Principles Behind the Rules of Golf*. His two great principles: Play the course as you find it and play your own ball and do not touch it until you lift it from the hole.

* In concert with USGA Executive Director Joe Dey, Tufts formulated the standard USGA set-up for championships—tight fairways, graduated rough both off fairways and surrounding fast, firm greens. This move came in the 1950s in reaction to a series of wildly disparate U.S. Open set-ups contrived by host clubs.

* He was the primary creator of the modern USGA handicapping system, which broke away from the old method in which only the most recent scores were considered, to one that uses an average of many rounds.

Today it's the ten best of the last twenty.

* He made the radical decision to convert the USGA Green Section into a national array of agronomists who visit courses to diagnose turf problems and prescribe cures. Before 1953, the USGA Green Section was only a modest support of research projects. More than any other single factor, the USGA visiting service has changed the look and feel of American golf.

* He was the creator of the USGA junior and senior championships. Tufts was not excited about the USGA branching out beyond its basic Open and Amateurs, but other groups were running what were regarded as national events for juniors and seniors. He figured if they were inevitable, they might as well be done right.

Tufts was a traditionalist and slow to adapt to modern tastes; it took repeated requests from members and guests for Pinehurst to slowly begin building a fleet of motorized golf carts in the late 1950s and early 1960s. He disliked gambling and grumbled often about the large Calcutta pools that were a part of the Masters week in Augusta. He also abhorred slow play and artificial measuring devices. Tufts rued the discontinuation of thirty-six hole Saturdays in concluding championship events, believing the double round was an excellent test of physical and mental endurance.

One of Tufts' lasting legacies of the game was his commitment to the spirit of amateur golf. "The Amateur Creed," which he authored, is an excellent reminder to golfers of all abilities of the true meaning of the game.

"An amateur is one who competes in a sport for the joy of playing, for the companionship it affords, for health-giving exercise, and for relaxation from more serious matters," Tufts wrote. "As a part of this light-hearted approach to the game,

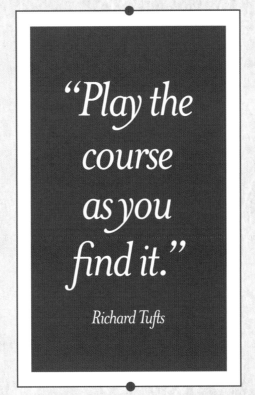

"Play the course as you find it."

Richard Tufts

he accepts cheerfully all adverse breaks, is considerate of his opponent, plays the game fairly and squarely in accordance with its rules, maintains self-control, and strives to do his best, not in order to win, but rather as a test of his own skill and ability. These are his only interests, and, in them, material considerations have no part. The returns which amateur sport will bring to those who play it in this spirit are greater than those any money can possibly buy."

The "Creed" was his most lucid and direct assault on creeping commercialism in golf, but over the decades Tufts spoke and wrote with force and passion in trying to keep the amateur spirit intact.

In 1960 he told the annual meeting of the Southern Golf Association at Myrtle Beach that the game is getting "soft." He said the game was getting too expensive, that excessive demands were being put on green superintendents and that use of motorized carts by those who do not need them was "almost degenerate."

"The game's standards are being lowered and subtly, bit by bit, golf is losing its character," Tufts said. "Those unable to meet the challenge of the game seem to find a vicarious pleasure in destroying it."

In 1963 as captain of the United States Walker Cup team, Tufts told his players that their two goals were to retain the cup in the competition against Great Britain and Ireland and to cement friendly relations with "our friends" from across the water.

"Failure in the first undertaking is acceptable if we succeed in the second," Tufts told his players. "But the trip will be a complete loss if we win the match but lose the good will of our friends. We can stand criticism of ourselves as golfers but not as sportsmen and gentlemen."

Golf Course, Dornoch

Scottish Invasion

Tom Watson had won three British Opens and become a national hero in Scotland by July 1981when he visited the Scottish Highlands burgh of Dornoch with Sandy Tatum, a long-time family friend and the just-retired president of the USGA. They played on a blustery Saturday afternoon in front of a gallery of several hundred spectators, then repaired to the bar on the second floor of the clubhouse. As he visited with the locals, Watson told head professional Willie Skinner to keep their clubs at hand, and he whispered to one of the caddies, a young man named Dennis Bethune, "Don't go anywhere."

After downing a pint and hobnobbing with the locals, Watson and Tatum slipped back onto the golf course early in the evening (the summer gloaming in Dornoch lingers past eleven o'clock), this time with no swarm of onlookers.

"They had a gallery of two—a man walking his dog," says Skinner.

They ventured out amid the wind and rain and played the difficult par-three second hole, with the green perched on the kind of plateau that the course's co-designer, the devout Old Tom Morris, was fond of because it kept the golfer looking toward heaven. They walked down the path thirty yards toward the third tee, through the thick bushes of yellow whins, then turned the corner where the vegetation gives way and a panorama of the Dornoch Firth opens up. They continued along, carefully aiming their tee shots to steer clear of the oval pot bunkers and tack left or right, depending on the direction and force of the gales.

Donald Ross was the golf pro and green superintendent at Dornoch during the era of the postcard at left (1895) before staking his claim to fame in America.

"We were walking down the third fairway, and Watson stopped," Tatum remembers. "He said, 'Tatum, I want to say something. This is the most fun I've had playing golf in my whole life.'"

They continued to the fifth tee, tucked alongside a ridge that runs the length of the course. Below them in one direction was the fifth fairway, below them to the right were the eleventh and twelfth holes and the beach.

"We were standing right at the very back of the tee," says Bethune, in 2011 the captain of Royal Dornoch. "The wind and rain and squalls were blowing and Watson said, 'This is what golf's all about.'"

Watson and Tatum spent the night next door to the club in the Royal Dornoch Hotel and on Sunday morning went back out to play again. Watson surveyed the townsfolk gathered around the first tee, like the day before an ample gallery of several hundred. "I thought all of you

3

The best golfing grasses vary in color.

They may be red, brown, blue, dark green, light green, yellow, and at times even white and gray. A golf course that is consisted entirely of one shade of green would be merely ugly. There is great charm and beauty in the varying shades of color on a golf course.

ALISTER MacKENZIE

The fifth and sixth holes at Dornoch (fifth green to the left, sixth to the right) sit beneath a gorse-covered hillside in the Scottish Highlands.

people would be in church this morning," he said.

"We can't," one of them replied, then nodded to a man standing a few yards away. "The minister's right there."

The sport of golf is quite the religious experience in Dornoch, the Scottish hamlet with profound physical and emotional alliances with Pinehurst and the Sandhills. Both are small and remote (though Dornoch more so than Pinehurst). Golf is the mother's milk of daily life at both addresses. Both have world-renowned courses—Royal Dornoch and Pinehurst No. 2, and it's perhaps no coincidence that in 2011 they were ranked No. 15 (Pinehurst) and No. 16 (Dornoch) in *GOLF* magazine's Top 100 World Courses. There is no noise pollution or visual obscenity in either.

And, of course, there is the considerable thread of one Donald James Ross.

Ross was born, raised and introduced to the sport and the business of golf in Dornoch, furthering his education under Old Tom Morris at St. Andrews. He immigrated to the United States at the age of twenty-seven, first settling in Boston but soon connecting with James Walker Tufts and his fledging resort in the North Carolina Sandhills. Pinehurst's sandy soil reminded him of Dornoch, and the region's signature wire grass was reminiscent of the ever-present Scottish whins. The design values Ross first absorbed at Dornoch followed him throughout nearly four hundred North American course creations.

"You can see the characteristics of Dornoch in Pinehurst No. 2," says Tom Weiskopf, winner of some two dozen professional events and architect of more than fifty courses. "The perched greens are certainly a similarity, though some of the greens at Dornoch are more of a flat grade. This is a look everyone is doing now. What would you call it? Retro? Retro 20th century? It's out of respect to the great architects like Donald Ross and Alister MacKenzie that everyone today is trying to capture that classic look."

Americans limiting their Scottish golf excursions to the trophy courses of the British Open rota—St. Andrews, Turnberry, Troon, Muirfield and the like—are missing the experience of their lives if they let Dornoch's remote location, some two hundred miles north of the capital city of Edinburgh, spook them from the effort. The A9 highway snakes its way northward, through villages like Killiecrankie

Dornoch pro Willie Skinner (center) and caddies Dennis Bethune (left) and Jim Seatter (right) prepare to set off with Tom Watson and Sandy Tatum in 1981. Skinner was retired in 2012 while Bethune was club president and Seatter served as finance committee chairman.

and Kingussie, beneath the barren mountain peaks and alongside the salmon and mussel-rich River Tay. There are no billboards, just an occasional square sign with the outline of a cow, signaling motorists to watch for wayward farm animals. Sheep chew their cud in a pasture to the left; acres of blazing yellow rapeseed scream from the right. Castles and cathedrals and whisky distilleries dot the landscape.

Pinehurst owner Richard Tufts made the drive in the 1950s—and this was before the construction of two bridges trimmed the journey considerably. So profound was the effect of the Scottish golf experience and the umbilical cord that nourished Pinehurst in the early days that he named his 1962 history of the resort, *The Scottish Invasion*. Tufts dedicated the book to "that most important person, the amateur golfer," and included a page on "The Pinehurst Ideal." That was his grandfather's vision of establishing a "small friendly community where those in need of it could find health-giving relaxation." The fulfillment of that vision was, over time, entrusted to the game of golf. "Golf came to America as a great amateur sport, rich with tradition and enjoying the best possible standards of ethics and good sportsmanship in its play," Tufts wrote.

Tufts also talked architect Pete Dye and journalist Herbert Warren Wind into the trip north to Dornoch. Wind wrote about the experience in *The New Yorker* in 1964, prompting many more Americans to make the pilgrimage. Ben Crenshaw has been to Dornoch and said he "very nearly didn't come back." David Fay, the USGA executive director for two decades, made the journey and played fifty-four holes in one day. Craig Stadler came north and told the locals, "Don't change a thing."

Two more Americans who have made the drive up A9—and, in fact, *did* stay—are Don Greenberg and Chris Surmonte. Greenberg came to Dornoch from California in 1985 on vacation, joined the club and now splits his time between Dornoch and Tampa. Surmonte grew up in New Jersey, loved golf and, while traveling to various British links courses in 1997, was told he could probably get a job caddying at Dornoch. He was smitten and has been there ever since.

Greenberg cites the par-four fifteenth hole, a short one of just over three hundred yards with a green sitting cliffside above the beach, as a hole that reflects the aesthetics and challenges of links golf and the kind of holes Ross built in the United States.

"This course was Donald Ross's introduction to golf," he says. "I have played a number of Ross courses in America, and you very much see Dornoch in them. When I was caddying here, I would walk people to the mound on fifteen, drop a ball a hundred yards from the green, look around and tell them, 'This is what Donald Ross and Dornoch are all about.'

"You can make anything from a two to a seven without hardly doing anything wrong. You can run it up, lob it up—it all depends on the wind and the pin position. You can knock it fifteen feet from the hole and still walk away with double bogey, not even hitting a poor putt. When the breeze picks up, it definitely affects balls on the greens, and fifteen is one of the more exposed greens."

"Dornoch has that perfect blend of charm and challenge," adds Surmonte, who now runs Luigi's, likely Dornoch's best restaurant. "All golfers love it—from the pros down to twenty-five handicaps. You can go to Carnoustie, where you have your hat handed to you, or you can play holiday golf, where it's charming. But if you want charm and challenge and eighteen perfect holes, Dornoch is it. You come all the way up here and you're rewarded—the views, the village, the golf. Dornoch has it all."

The best vantage point for the Dornoch experience is the Royal Golf Hotel, where the front door is about fifty paces from the first tee. The lounge has nearly a thousand bag tags from golf courses around the world pinned to eaves above the bartender's area—and one from Pinehurst is front and center. There's a room off the lobby devoted to drying your clubs and clothes quickly after a squall, and the laundry slip in each room has a price for cleaning your kilt. If you're lucky enough to get a room on the southeast corner of the hotel, you'll wake to a view of the rumpled ground, the golden whins, the odd rabbit scooting across the fairway, the symphony of puffy clouds and sunlight over the Dornoch Firth in the distance.

One such morning in May 2011, I rose to this visual array, tucked into some coffee, cereal and a few slices of meaty British bacon and was off to the first tee, where I found Roddy Roderick resplendent in his kilt as he sent golfers about their merry way.

"Aye, it's pretty mooch as God left it," he said.

What more reason do you need, then, for an adventure into the Scottish Highlands?

***

Of course, some people *left* Dornoch, and that's what is on the minds of two long-time Dornoch residents as they sip coffee one morning in the lounge area of the Royal Dornoch clubhouse. Dennis Bethune, the caddie to Tom Watson three decades earlier, has completed a career in health-care administration and now spends considerable time on the golf course and in his role as captain of the club. Alongside is Donald F. Grant, another lifelong Dornoch resident and club member, and spread on the table before them is a poster heralding the village's production of young golf talent in the early 1900s.

Headlined "Dornoch to the U.S.A.," the poster features photos of eight golfers—most pictured wearing ties on the course, some with tweed caps, one with a pipe in his mouth—and short descriptions of their accomplishments in the New World.

There is Bob MacDonald, who was a founding member of the PGA of America and instructor to Gene Sarazen, Horton Smith and Babe Zaharias, and his younger brothers Bill and Jack. There is Bob Grant, who helped light the golf fire in Chicago and later was a respected club pro in Indiana. There is Don Sutherland, a longtime club pro in Vancouver and winner of the 1934 B.C. Open. There is Alex Murray, who died two years into his American adventure, and whose son was later secretary at Royal Dornoch.

And, of course, also pictured on the poster are Donald Ross and brother Alex, the former the foremost golf architect in the United States during the first half of the 1900s and the latter the 1907 U.S. Open champion.

"All these boys went out and were successful," Grant says. "They head off to America with their clubs and a hold-all, and with very little money. No one here had any money."

"Imagine, Donald, what they had to do to *get there*," Bethune says. "There was no railway station in Dornoch at the time. A horse to Inverness, a train to Glasgow, a boat to Liverpool, then another boat to New York."

"We're very proud of them," Grant says. "They should be remembered."

Grant's family-run grocery store and butcher shop, John Grant & Sons, sits at the corner of Castle and Bridge Streets in the village of Dornoch, and just a few yards to the west on St. Gilbert Street is a row of gray sandstone homes. One of them, No. 3, has an oval blue plaque posted beside the front door marking the birthplace of *Donald Ross, Golf Architect*.

"Ross sent money home to his mother," Grant says. "That money allowed her to expand upstairs. American golf money, that is. Local boy makes good. Quite a story how a little village like this can have such an influence on the States."

Farming, fishing, coal mining and the construction of ships and locomotives were staples of the Scottish economy in the late-1800s, but the remote Highlands region was poorer and more sparsely popu-lated, in part because of the potato famine and an outbreak of cholera in the 1800s, but mostly because of the ravages of The Clearances — the century-long forced exodus of natives off their land in favor of the more profitable enterprise of raising sheep and cattle. English aristocrats paid dearly for wool and beef, making the inland acres of the north more valuable with animals grazing than with humans planting. Many families shoved off to America and Canada and would often send younger members to establish a beachhead before the rest of the clan joined them. Dornoch in the late 1800s was an outpost described by one observer as an "old fashioned, outlying, outlandish grey net to which no stranger ever thinks of going."

Tom Tew is a Dornoch beekeeper by vocation and a golfer and historian by avocation, serving as archivist for the golf club and as a board member for the Historylinks Museum in the village.

"Donald Ross was the right man at the right time," Tew says. "Ten years more or ten years less … it might have been quite different. He went over at the right time. And he had the guts to do it! Imagine taking that boat ride to the other side of the world. What a decision that was! I don't think we have any idea the hardship these people had.

"Sometimes I'll sit down and think and concentrate on what it would have been like on those ships, all the sorts of people escaping. Hundreds of people, all with their little stories. There he was, with another hurdle to get over. 'Have I made the right decision?' He came from a pretty hick spot here, let's be crude about it. This was a poor, desolate little town.

"*But* … this is a town of survivors. And he was certainly one of the better ones."

Golf is woven into the soul and fabric of Scottish life—in the Highlands and elsewhere. The game is part of the curriculum in grade school. Matrons and geezers play. It's inexpensive because land was cheap when the old courses were built and the golf consumer doesn't demand perfect playing conditions. Most every course exists as an end in itself—not as a means to sell real estate or hoity-toity club memberships.

Grant Shannon, a retiree to Dornoch, marvels at the grip golf has on the national psyche. Shannon was on a flight departing Edinburgh Airport one day in 2011 when he looked out his window and saw Turnhouse Golf Club, which sits just to the east of the airport and has

DORNOCH TO THE U.S.A.

the early 20th Century a number of Scottish golfers emigrated to the United States of America professionals at the many clubs that were appearing there. Among these were several from Dornoch:

DONALD ROSS

Born in St Gilbert Street, Dornoch in 1874, Donald Ross emigrated to the United States in 1899. His first job was professional at Oakley Club, Boston. He was later appointed manager at Pinehurst Country Club, North Carolina. He became a legendary architect of many great courses including Pinehurst No.2, Braeburn, Oakland Hills, Interlachan, Inverness (Toledo, hio) and Seminole. In total he was architect for proximately 500 courses.

BOB MACDONALD

Born at Evelix, Dornoch. Emigrated to the United States in 1910. Bob was professional at a number of Chicago clubs including Evanston and Edgewater and was the first winner of the Texas Open in 1922. He was a founder member of the U.S.P.G.A. and later became it's president. He coached legendary U.S. golfers Gene Sarazen, Horton Smith and Babe Zaharias. His book, "Golf", published in 1927, was a classic of it's time.

ALEX ROSS

in St Gilbert Street, Dornoch, brother to d. Alex emigrated to the United States of a in 1900. He played out of Brae-Burn y Club, West Newton, Massachusets, previously played out of Pinehurst and lmington, Del. He won the U.S. Open t Philadelphia and had 4 more top 10 that Open. He also won the North en 5 times and the Massachusetts es (in succession).

BILL MACDONALD

Born at Evelix, Dornoch, brother to Bob and Jack. Emigrated to the United States in 1912. He became professional at Door County, Sturgeon Bay, Wisconsin then later at Springfield, Illinois and Illini Country Club, Illinois. Bill managed city tournaments for many years.

BOB GRANT

och. Bob was a golf professional f which his final 21 were spent at ry Club, Indiana. He was a highly er of the U.S.P.G.A. and served officer in the Indiana section. He rumental in the early growth of

JACK MACDONALD

Born at Evelix, Dornoch, brother to Bob and Bill. Emigrated to the United States in 1919. He was professional at Lynx Club, Milwaukee and then later, professional at 4Gs Driving Range in Chicago and Stop and Sock 'Em Range in Springfield, Illinois.

ALEX MURRAY

Born in Dornoch in 1891. Emigrated to the United States in 1925. Alex became the first professional at Granville Golf Club, Ohio. Sadly, he died after only 2 years in the United States, aged just 36. His wife Grace stayed on to manage the clubhouse and sons Dick and Ken played and caddied at the club. Later, Ken (also in picture) became Secretary at Royal Dornoch Golf Club, retiring in 1987.

DON

Born in Little Emigrated to Va where he became & Country Clu Don at the clu Life Members complete Dorn successes was w

been there for more than a century (James Braid tweaked the original layout in the 1920s). He told his seatmate about his father, a scratch handicap, being on that very golf course with three of his closest golf buddies on Sept. 3, 1939, the day Britain delivered an ultimatum to Adolf Hitler: "Cease hostilities by 11 a.m., or we go to war." Hitler did not respond to the threat, issued about the time the elder Shannon and his group teed off. At 11:15 a.m., Neville Chamberlain, Britain's prime minister, went on the radio and announced the nation was at war with Germany. Every able-bodied male in Britain from eighteen to forty-one was called into service.

"The siren went off at the RAF station nearby, and they realized it meant, 'War,'" Shannon says. "They were on the ninth hole. My father always said to me, 'We had a decision to make—would we go on or would we go in?' He said they decided to play nine more holes. They made the right decision. Two of his friends died in the war and they never again played as a foursome."

Noted American amateur golf champion William C. Campbell has deep Scottish roots. His ancestors came to the United States from the Highlands during the "Clearances," arriving in Philadelphia and then migrating in a southwest direction roughly on the path followed today by Interstate 81. His paternal grandfather was one of ten children, and all were college educated.

A bag tag from Pinehurst hangs amidst hundreds above the bar of the Royal Dornoch Hotel (R).

"The Scots brought with them religion, and more importantly, they brought an *attitude* with them," Campbell says. "They were in favor of education and they were honest people. Years ago when a house was sold, the buyer would say, 'Where's the key?' Well, there were no locks on the doors. Grocers would take deliveries overnight on their doorstep. No one would think of taking the milk.

"Life wasn't always easy for the Scots. They had a lot of fight in them. They had to. They had to fight for everything."

Englishman Alistair Cooke moved to the States as a young man and was a midlife convert to golf. He pursued the game passionately while forging a career as a noted journalist and television personality.

"Golf was just what the Scottish character had been seeking for centuries," Cooke observed. "The main tenants of the Scottish faith are that life is grim and uncomfortable and that human vanity cannot prevail. Humiliations are the essence of the game. The golfer's credo is that man should expect very little here below and strive to gain it. Golfers are the only worldwide secret society that revels in the mutual display of human frailty."

Man has enjoyed games of sticks and balls throughout history, and Europeans in the Middle Ages even played from one village to the next by striking an object, finding it and hitting it again toward a predetermined target. "Kolf" as it was known in the Netherlands and "Goff" as Englishmen termed it were early ancestors to the modern game of golf. The towns of St. Andrews, Leith and Aberdeen on Scotland's east coast were among the early hotbeds of "gowf" in the mid-1700s. The first printed reference to golf in Dornoch came in 1616, and fourteen years later, Sir Robert Gordon wrote of his journey to the Highlands:

"About this toun along the sea coast, are the fairest and lairgest links of green fieldes of any pairt of Scotland. Fitt for archery, golfing, ryding, and all other exercises, they doe surpass the fields of Montrose or St. Andrews."

Bethune tells Grant he recently watched a film about the War for American Independence and the role the Scots played in the events from 1775-82.

"I thought, Donald, 'Here in Dornoch, we were *playing golf* then,'" Bethune says. "Thousands were getting killed on the battlefield, but someone here was worrying about getting down in two from the fringe."

"We're going to celebrate four hundred years of golf here in 2016," Grant says.

"Four hundred years that we can *prove*," Bethune adds. "It's documented that golf was here in 1616. We think it was played here before

"CALLING GOLFERS HOME..."

Getting a Texas boy to play a bagpipe and wear a kilt is not necessarily an easy undertaking. But Ian Staten has an umbilical cord to Scotland—his mother is a native of Edinburgh. Staten began playing the pipes in 1998 at age eight and was a member of a world championship bagpipe team at St. Thomas Episcopal School in Houston in 2004. His family moved to Laurinburg in 2005 and Staten found a gig at Pinehurst playing for special events and regularly at dusk on weekends during spring and fall. He begins his march at the traffic circle and moves along Carolina Vista to the front of The Carolina Hotel, playing traditional marches and "calling golfers back to the hotel after a day on the golf course."

then, but we can't prove it."

Another lad who left Dornoch for the States was Thomas Currie, the golf pro who replaced Ross upon his departure in 1899. Currie left for the States in 1922 and landed at Inverness Club in Toledo, Ohio; the club was named for the Scottish Highland town and had just christened a Ross-designed course in 1918. Currie's daughter, Mamie, wrote back home to a friend in Dornoch years later, and the spell the village cast on her resonates through her words:

"Frequently I daydream about Dornoch," she wrote. "Do the blue-bells still grow in profusion in the hollow down by the bathing-shed? Are the breezes across the links filled with the intoxicating sweetness of broom and whin in blossom? Do the skylarks sing their hearts out away high out of sight? To complete my daydream I can still see the rain-clouds and the falling showers making beautiful rainbows in the rain."

Grant Sword grew up in Aberdeen on the northeast coast of Scotland, entered the hotel and golf development business and today is a partner in the Royal Dornoch Hotel and a developer of Castle Stuart Golf Links, a 2009 course just outside Inverness (an hour's drive from Dornoch) that was heralded upon its opening with landing the Scottish Open Championship for 2011-13. He easily clicks off facts vouching for golf's hold on Scotland in general—5.6 million people in the country and 587 golf courses—and its concentration beyond that in the "Highlands and Islands" region in the north.

"Up here we have the highest concentration of golf courses for the population of any place in the world," Sword says. "We have ten percent of Scotland's population and we have two hundred of those 587 golf courses. Most of the courses were built in the late-19th century. Land and labor were so inexpensive—both were in plentiful supply. Many who built golf courses were farmers who had the land. So we have this legacy which is absolutely wonderful. The game is so inexpensive here. That you can play for twelve pounds is truly amazing. It's a great pastime—it's healthy, it's safe and kids love it."

Those you might not suspect as being competent golfers sprouted from every crevice of the village. Newspaper magnate Lord Rothermere owned the Burghfield House Hotel in Dornoch in the first part of the 20th century. His gardener was Walter Ross, who was a scratch handicap but didn't look the part to guests at the hotel with his over-

alls and soil-crusted hands. Rothermere would often engage guests in conversation and casually mention he didn't think the guest could beat his gardener in a match.

"I'll bet you a hundred pounds you can't beat him," Rothermere would venture.

More times than not, the guest took the bait and lost a pocket of cash on the Dornoch golf course, with Rothermere earning a commission from his gardener on the bet.

In Dornoch Donald Ross played with the baker T.E. Grant, who had the misfortune of having lost the thumb on his left hand to a power machine accident during his tenure as a baker's apprentice. Grant had to turn his left hand fully over the top of the club, promoting a tendency to draw the ball. Grant would make two waggles and then step back eight inches with his right foot—for more power and a more hard-running draw along the firm Dornoch fairways.

The village has fewer than 2,500 permanent residents but that number swells during the summer as golfers come to play the two courses at Royal Dornoch (there are the Championship Course and the Struie Course, the latter playing just under 6,200 yards as an amalgam of the club's original Ladies Course and newer holes designed by Donald Steel). Visitors also stroll the beaches and nature park and explore such attractions as a 13th-century cathedral.

"Everything in the town depends on golf and the beach," Donald Grant says. "If you can walk, you play golf. You *have* to."

"Kids grow up playing golf," Bethune adds. "Everyone plays golf. The junior golf program is very strong. They play for virtually nothing."

Willie Skinner was the club professional from 1973-98 and was succeeded by his son, Andrew. He still plays golf and afterward enjoys the fellowship in the lounge that overlooks the first tee and eighteenth green.

"Dornoch was such a small village," Willie says. "There was nothing to do—there were no computers, no television. Youngsters played golf. They came by it naturally. Their parents played as well."

The club is committed to making the game as affordable as possible for the majority of people and to ensure that it keeps its place within the community; thus the membership fee in 2011 was £410 (about $660 in the States).

John Sutherland (opposite) was Donald Ross's mentor at the club; Ross (back row, second from left above) poses with family members on a return trip to Dornoch in the early 1900s. The antique box of Dunlop golf balls are among the artifacts on display at a replica clubmaking shop at the Dornoch History Museum.

DUNLOP
The best Golf Balls
in the world.

DUNLOP
GOLF · BALLS

"And so the postman, the grocer, the schoolteacher—everybody plays golf up here," Shannon says. "Kids are started young. It's never been looked upon as a socially elite game as it was in England."

The village emanates from the ancient Dornoch Cathedral, which was first constructed in the 13th century and later rebuilt and expanded following a fire and general neglect. The organ has operated since 1893, and the gargoyles around the eaves have warded off evil spirits for centuries. There is a castle across the street that was once the bishop's residence and serves today as a hotel, and the Market Square commercial district bustles with residents and visitors buying lamb cutlets and haggis at the butcher's counter and mahogany sideboards at the antiques shop. The village glows in a patina of weathered gray and brown sandstone and slate roofs.

There's no glitz or neon. There are no chain stores and certainly not a Big Mac.

"Dornoch is in its own little world," says Sword. "It has a warmth all its own. Stand outside at midnight and look up and you'll see stars like you've never seen them. There's no light pollution. The sky looks fantastic."

"Anywhere you go, if you say you're from Dornoch, the response is, 'Oh, it's so lovely,'" says Neil Hampton, club general manager.

"'Quaint' is another word you hear often," says course manager Eoin Riddell.

Donald Grant nods knowingly when talking about the magic of the little town.

"Strangers say they sleep very well here," he says.

***

Exit the clubhouse door, walk past the first tee, skirt the putting green and stop beside the elongated sign reading "Royal Dornoch Golf Club." The brisk and salty wind funnels up from the Dornoch Firth and the beach below. Inhale, close your eyes, let your imagination run more than a century back in time …

Perhaps you can see a young man hunched over on the grass nearby, tools splayed around him, sculpting and scraping the ground.

"I would go out in overalls and get down on my hands and knees and care for the turf and the bunkers and the greens," Donald Ross remembered years later. "And how I used to hate it. But, as it turned out, that was the best training I could have had for what turned out to be my future."

Conjuring your powers of fantasy, picture a small shed off to the side, no more than twelve by fifteen feet, equipped with vises, tools, sandpaper, pots of varnish and shellac, and a stock of steel golf club heads with *D.J. Ross, Dornoch* stamped on the back. There are blocks of persimmon wood and barrels filled with hickory shafts. A young man with carpentry skills honed from a boyhood apprenticeship and a recent year at St. Andrews labors away at assembling the components into golf clubs for the Dornoch membership. Donald Ross, a Dornoch native trained under Old Tom Morris at St. Andrews, was the ideal occupant of the little workshop.

"Donald had brought with him something of the golfing prestige historically associated with St. Andrews, Prestwick and Musselburgh, these southern schools of golf," one local historian observed.

"He knew how to select the proper piece of hickory to give you the kind of shaft you wanted and how to shape the shaft to give the kind of 'whip' which best suited your swing," Richard Tufts, grandson of Pinehurst founder James Tufts, commented years later.

Listen closely, those festive notes wafting from the village center a quarter of a mile to the west are from a teenaged Donald Ross and the local brass band playing at the summer Dornoch Highland Games; those melancholy strains following moments later are the boy and his parents singing with their fellow Free Church parishioners the haunting Scottish psalms that would remain locked in Ross's soul for

The green of the par-three sixth hole at Dornoch is guarded by a bunker on the right and steep slopes to the front and right sides.

life. After a mid-1930s showing of the movie *The Little Minister,* a tale set in 1840s rural Scotland, Ross said: "When I was a young man, I used to think of Scotch village life as very narrow and hard. Life was limited to work and the church. The faces of the elders in *The Little Minister* brought back the elders I used to know at Dornoch. The older I get the more I can feel myself turning back to their way of thinking. At least they never compromised their honesty."

Turn toward the golf course and there you'll see Ross, his friends and club members playing across the links, through the thick, thorny whins and over and around the knobs and bumps. The firm ground and ever-present winds combined with the confining attire of the day and the stiff wooden shafts forced Scottish golfers into playing low running shots with strong grips and short backswings. Clubs were longer and heavier than today, and golfers generally drew their right foot back three or four inches to encourage a wind-cheating, right-to-left ball flight. They carried at most a half dozen clubs.

"When golf was *golf,* the player had to make a number of shots with the same clubs, half shots, three-quarter shots and so forth," Ross said many years later, prompting one to wonder what he'd say about the modern exercise of dialing in a sixty-degree wedge with a three-quarters swing from fifty-five yards to a puffy green. "I doubt that there are half a dozen players today who can bring off fractional shots with any degree of confidence."

These are the spawning grounds of Donald Ross, the young man who left Scotland some eleven decades ago and had a profound effect on golf in America and, certainly, in Pinehurst.

"I don't believe the world of golf has ever seen a course architect that was his equal," Tufts said in 1978. "He was a gentleman with the very highest standards, he knew the game of golf very well, loved it and served it to the best of his ability. His career was as a professional, but he was a true amateur at heart. We badly need his spirit in golf today."

Ross was born in 1872, the eldest of six children of stonemason Murdoch Ross and his wife, Lillian. His early days consisted of school, church, choir and golf, the latter activity mostly as a caddie on the local course. Donald's formal schooling ended at age fourteen, and he graduated into an apprenticeship with Peter Murray, a Dornoch carpenter whose projects around the village and club included

building eighteen wooden tee boxes to hold the sand used to fashion rudimentary "tees" before wooden ones came in vogue in the early 1900s. The youngster's interest in golf was apparently stoked in 1886 when four-time Open champion Tom Morris visited to upgrade the club's crude nine-hole layout into a more formal display of tees, fairways and greens. Morris returned again in 1892, and local speculation and some educated guesses hold that at this point club secretary John Sutherland introduced Ross to Morris and suggested Ross as an ideal candidate for an apprenticeship at St. Andrews.

Ross spent a year in St. Andrews, where the insights and education he received from Old Tom and clubmaker David Forgan were pivotal in his development in the golf business. Ross may have helped Morris prepare for or even build a course along the dunes, just to the east of the existing course, that came to be known as the New Course, which opened in 1895 and likely would have been in some planning or early construction stage in 1893. He certainly learned of course maintenance, clubmaking and teaching the game to the locals, and there is no telling whose acquaintance he made along the way: Charles Blair Macdonald kept a locker in Tom's shop; Harry Colt spent boyhood summers at St. Andrews; and Alister MacKenzie and A.W. Tillinghast both learned the game and the art of golf design from Morris.

Author Kevin Cook wrote in *Tommy's Honor,* his splendid account of Morris's life and that of his son, that Morris's "influence on Ross would still make him a crucial figure in the game's evolution." Later, when Ross went to America, Cook wrote, his head was "full of pictures of Tom's links: elevated greens; grassy hollows and hungry bunkers; subtle deceptions that rewarded local knowledge ..."

Morris's mentorship of the young man from Dornoch extended beyond the shop and course. He invited Ross to attend his kirk, and there on Saturday nights Ross could contribute a penny and enjoy entertainment and a good dinner. His salary was seven and six pence (about $1.50 worth of mid-1940s American currency).

Old Tom was against gambling in golf and advised Donald to never bet on the golf course beyond a small wager. "Why make a horse race out of a game like golf?" Morris posited. Donald took Tom's words to heart and for the rest of his life rarely played for stakes beyond a quarter Nassau. Ross said that Calcutta pools "don't belong

A SIDELINE FOR MR. ROSS

The Holly Inn opened in 1895 as Pinehurst's first lodging house and was followed five years later by the opulent Carolina Hotel. Within a decade, Pinehurst had three golf courses and the village and resort were drawing visitors *en masse* from October through April to experience this curious game made popular by the talents of visiting experts like Walter Travis.

While the Pinehurst Inc. operation owned by the Tufts family would forever be the driving force in the Sandhills golf explosion, there was ample opportunity for savvy entrepreneurs to grasp onto a coattail.

A case in point: Emma Bliss and the Pine Crest Inn.

Mrs. Bliss and husband John had managed the Ocean Forest Hotel at Myrtle Beach and moved to Pinehurst in 1903 to operate the Lexington Hotel, which was essentially a boarding house for Carolina Hotel employees and sat on the site where the Manor Inn sits today. Ten years later, she believed there was demand for more hotel rooms and purchased a lot across the street from the Lexington. Ground was broken on Feb. 13, 1913 for the Pine Crest Inn, and the inn opened nine months later.

"It comes as a delightful addition to the list of hotels; its comfort is suggested by the charm of the exterior—radiant with fresh air, sunshine, good charm and hominess," *The Pinehurst Outlook* reported.

While the community welcomed the new enterprise, there was one concern: The inn was snug with the baseball field that sat between it and The Holly Inn. Fortunately, there were no reported instances of baseballs hitting the side of the Pine Crest.

Donald Ross and close friend Jim MacNab bought the inn from Mrs. Bliss in 1921 and ran it for twenty-five years, until leasing it to the Arthur Roberts Hotel Co. of Minneapolis in 1946. So for a quarter of a century, Ross was actually in competition with Pinehurst Inc. in the hotel business while working for the Tufts family in managing its golf operations.

In a 1939 letter to a prospective buyer of the inn, Ross noted the "attractive and cheerful lobby" and the outdoor porch that is "much enjoyed on pleasant days." He said he had put all of his profits back into the inn and was proud that each room had a telephone. Ross listed more than $100,000 cash he had invested in the property—from the original purchase price of $52,500 and improvements that included a sprinkler system that cost more than $10,000. He was willing to sell it for $65,000—with half cash up front.

"I have had an opportunity to sell the inn but refused to do so because I wasn't favorably impressed with the party who wanted it," Ross wrote. "The only reason I have for wishing to sell it is that my connection with Pinehurst Inc. makes it impossible for me to give it my personal attention."

The inn was run by the Roberts group for four years. Then in 1950, Carl Moser, retired as manager of the Carolina Inn in Chapel Hill, leased it and purchased it two years later. He operated it until 1961, when he sold it to Bob and Betty Barrett of Erie, Pa.

Barrett was a newspaperman who had visited Pinehurst regularly over the years—"At the beginning for two days, then for a week, then for two weeks," he said. He also bought the cottage across Dogwood Drive for his family to inhabit, saying he didn't want to raise sons Bobby and Peter in a hotel.

"I didn't know a thing about running a hotel, but I learned the key is to treat visitors warmly," Barrett said. He also joked often of running a "third-class hotel with first-class guests."

Donald Ross's portrait hangs above the fireplace in the lobby of the Pine Crest Inn, which will turn 100 years old in November 2013.

Following his wife's death in early 1975, Barrett wrestled with the idea of selling the inn and moving to Hilton Head. He actually found a buyer and initiated the transaction, but the buyer defaulted and within a couple of months the inn was back in Barrett's hands.

"The luckiest day in my life," says Peter, who prepared for a career running the inn with a degree from Chapel Hill and one in hotel-restaurant administration from Florida International.

The inn has remained in the family ever since, Bob passing away in 2005 and Peter, Bobby and his wife Andy Hofmann running it with help from a loyal staff. "Mr. B's

Old South Bar" has become an institution in Sandhills night life as traveling golfers and locals converge to enjoy the piano music and practice their chipping into the wooden frame target conceived years ago by Bob Barrett and Lionel Callaway, a pro on the staff at Pinehurst Country Club. In 2003 *GOLF* Magazine listed the Pine Crest as one of the "50 Coolest Places in Golf."

"I have a lot of great memories not only of playing golf at Pinehurst, but staying at a neat old place like the Pine Crest Inn," says Curtis Strange, a two-time North and South Amateur champion in the mid-1970s. "From the moment you get into town, you know this is a serious golf environment."

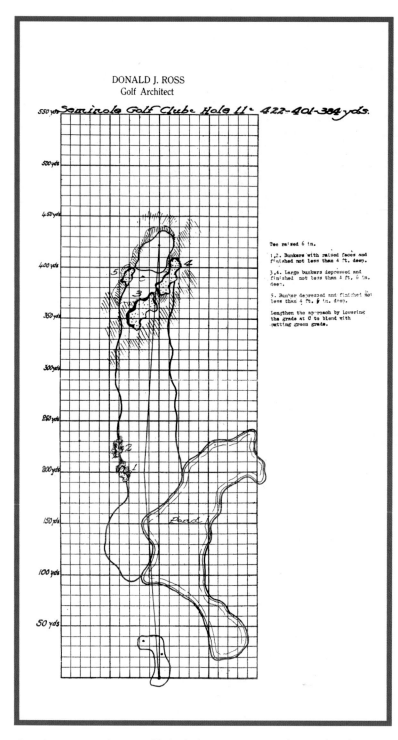

DONALD J. ROSS
Golf Architect

550 yds *Seminole Golf Club: Hole 11: 422-401-384 yds.*

500 yds

450 yds

400 yds

350 yds

300 yds

250 yds

200 yds

150 yds   *Pond*

100 yds

50 yds

Tee raised 6 in.

1,2. Bunkers with raised faces and finished not less than 4 ft. deep.

3,4. Large bunkers depressed and finished not less than 4 ft, 6 in. deep.

5. Bunker depressed and finished not less than 4 ft. 6 in. deep.

Lengthen the approach by lowering the grade at C to blend with putting green grade.

Ross drew intricate diagrams of holes for his construction workers, such as this one from Seminole Golf Club in Florida. There are no such illustrations for Pinehurst No. 2 as the course was built by Ross and superintendent Frank Maples by hand with Ross on-site every step of the way.

in such a fine, clean game."

Once at Pinehurst, a young man who didn't know Ross asked him for a game and a $25 Nassau.

"Let's just play for the fun of the game," Ross countered.

The young man insisted, so Ross relented, played the visitor and beat him soundly.

"I built the course," Ross told his opponent. "Let this be a lesson to you: Don't play for high stakes with a stranger."

After his year at St. Andrews, Ross moved thirty miles up the east coast of Scotland to Carnoustie, where he spent the 1894 golf season working under pro Archie Simpson, a close friend of Old Tom's who had assisted with the Dornoch design project several years earlier. When Donald returned to Dornoch in November, he was ready: John Sutherland hired him full-time as head professional, clubmaker and caddie master.

"I also became the greenkeeper, although we didn't dignify the task by any such title," Ross said.

Ross's good name and reputation helped him early in his days in his Dornoch post. He needed money to purchase materials and supplies to build clubs over that first winter, but his pockets were empty. He appealed to a banker named Urquhart, who loaned him one hundred pounds forthwith. The banker told Ross that his reputation and character were the best collateral he could have, and Donald repaid the loan within the year.

That reputation endured many years after Ross left for America. Buck Whittemore, a former Harvard baseball and football star, was on a hunting trip in the Highlands in 1936 and lacked cash. He visited the Dornoch bank, presented a letter of credit and requested fifty dollars.

The cashier called the manager, and the manager called the president.

"I don't doubt that this paper is quite good," the president said, "but we can't be too careful about these things. I'll have to ask for references from a local citizen."

Whittemore said he didn't know a soul.

"But I know a man who used to live here. His name is Donald Ross."

The president shook his hand, patted him on the back and offered him a hundred dollars.

Ross was very busy for four months of the year, making clubs, giving lessons, managing the caddies and supervising a maintenance team of two workers. He could make a golden half-sovereign from wealthy visitors from the south giving lessons.

Ross in the summer of 1898 met a Harvard astronomy professor named Robert Willson, who was an avid golfer and frequently played abroad. Willson told Ross that an ambitious young man well versed in the business of golf could find a profitable and fulfilling niche in an American landscape increasingly inclined toward leisure and recreational pursuits.

"Americans in those days did not have much time for play—it was all work," Ross said. "In Scotland every man, woman and child had some interest outside his work. I knew that America some day would find time to play.

"I began to think about it. That was three times what I was making in Dornoch."

Ross discussed the idea with Sutherland, his mentor and an important man in the town and club. Sutherland was a golfer and sportsman and became Club Secretary in 1883; he was the Burgh Collector and later Town Clerk and also a coal merchant. He found time as well to write a Sunday golf article in the *London Daily News* in the early 1900s and contribute monthly pieces to *Golf Illustrated*. Sutherland was a crack golfer; he and Dornoch golfer Tommy Grant competed in a tournament at Muirfield and stunned the field by beating Open champion Harold Hilton and former Amateur champion John Ball. The losers decided to visit Dornoch to see what type of course had spawned such excellent competitors, and their praise of the course gave fellow golfers reason to investigate.

"A few visitors began to come, and we took great care of them," Sutherland said. "We saw visions of prosperity for a dying little place with only the Law Courts, held once a week, to maintain life. We had a history and some of us thought it was worth fighting for. We were a cathedral city, a royal burgh with a charter granted by Charles I."

Sutherland confided to Ross that he had considered going to America as well. They decided to flip a coin—with the winner going to the States and the loser remaining to tend to the Dornoch course and club. Ross won. His future was then in America, while Suther-

land remained and served as Club Secretary until 1941. It is Sutherland's portrait that hangs in the clubhouse at Royal Dornoch.

"Having played Ross courses in the States, you can see he's taken some inspiration from his formative years here," says Hamish MacRae, a lifelong Dornoch resident and former captain at Royal Dornoch. "But he was just somebody from Dornoch who disappeared and made good for himself. We just accepted him for what he was, a Dornoch man, end of story, not a great designer of golf courses. John Sutherland really brought golf to Dornoch; he was a lot more proactive in bringing tourism to the area. His history is very important to this place as well."

Ross's parents were against the thought of their son leaving Scotland, but Ross won his mother over by promising to send home as much salary as he could to help expand their two-room home on St. Gilbert Street. According to a story by Bob Harlow in a 1945 *Pinehurst Outlook*, Ross's mother did not speak to Sutherland for months because she believed Sutherland unduly influenced her son to leave home. And according to another by club historian John MacLeod, Lillian had to keep a close eye on the money Donald sent home, lest it be traded by her husband for beverage: "Rather snide local comment says it would have been better if so much of the money had not gone over the bar at the Eagle, the pub round the corner. However, having seen them all, this is the best of the conversions of old Dornoch property, in my opinion."

Ross sought out Professor Willson upon his arrival in Boston in April 1899, was introduced at Oakley Country Club and hired on as the golf pro. New England winters were not conducive to an outdoor sport like golf, so Ross was amenable in his second December in Boston to an offer from Oakley member James Tufts to move south for the offseason and run the golf operation at Tufts' new resort in North Carolina.

"My friends laughed at me," Ross said in 1930. "They said it was folly to try to make a winter golf colony down in the jack pines and sand of Carolina."

But in Pinehurst Ross discovered land forms that harkened to his homeland, to wit, pure sand. He set about retooling Pinehurst's modest golf offering and expanding it. Golf's popularity was spreading like wildfire in the early 1900s, and Pinehurst was at the epicenter.

Ross (left) poses in March 1914 with two U.S. Open champions: Francis Ouimet (second from left, the 1913 winner), and Alex Ross (second from right, the 1907 victor). Jack Jolly (right) rounds out the foursome.

daily." He spent at times as many as twenty-five days a month traveling, and one estimate pegged three thousand men working on the construction and maintenance of his courses in the mid-1920s. Ross's likeness sold rooms at Pinehurst and golf clubs as well, and Ross advertised his services: "Donald J. Ross makes a specialty of laying out golf courses on modern lines, and of re-arranging existing ones. He is justly regarded as being preeminent in his line," read one advertisement.

Two of Ross's brothers were key lieutenants. Alex Ross followed Donald to Pinehurst in 1900 and forged an impressive competitive resume—1907 U.S. Open champion and six-time North and South Open winner. Alex spent much of his time teaching beginners the nuances of grip, stance and stroke and was hired in 1916 as the first full-time professional at the Detroit Golf Club, where Donald would design thirty-six holes. Aeneas Ross was a construction supervisor from 1922-30 until he returned to Dornoch; some speculate he was an economic casualty of the Depression, perhaps laid off by his own brother when course construction work dried up.

"Pinehurst was absolutely the pioneer in American golf," Ross said. "While golf had been played in a few places before Pinehurst was established, it was right here on these sandhills that the first great national movement in golf was started. Men came here, took a few golf lessons, bought a few clubs and went away determined to organize clubs."

And when these new clubs were formed, Ross was invariably hired to design their courses.

"His ability to choreograph Mother Nature into a beautiful and playable golf course convinced wealthy and influential lovers of the game to hire him for their clubs and private estates," said Ross historian Pete Jones.

At a time in the early 1900s when purses for professional tournaments were just a thousand dollars, Ross was clearing thirty grand designing golf courses. An *Outlook* story in 1919 noted Ross "is a busy man these days and, like Thomas Edison, sleeps only four hours

Ross formed Donald Ross Associates in 1916 and hired a pair of key engineers—Walter B. Hatch of Amherst, Mass., and J.B. McGovern of Wynnewood, Pa. Ross worked from Rhode Island in the summer and Pinehurst in winter. Walter Irving Johnston was a civil engineer who joined the firm in 1920 and worked from his office in Pinehurst.

Ross's first task upon undertaking a design project was to walk the site, selecting a handful of the best hole locations and trying to work them into the final routing. He and his associates used sketch cards for each hole, the left side of the card having a grid for the outline of the hole and the top-right quarter showing a separate cross-section to draw the undulations and elevation changes. Separate grids for greens provided space for Ross to sketch the outline, bunker placement,

THE GOLDEN AGE OF PINEHURST

ridges, furrows and swales in more detail.

Ross did not grant many interviews or regularly commit his thoughts to paper. He compiled a manuscript prior to World War I, but it was never published. Eventually golf architect David Gordon found the manuscript among the effects of his father William, also a golf architect, and brought it to the attention of Paul Fullmer, executive director of the American Society of Golf Course Architects. The ASGCA teamed with Ross's family, *Golf Digest's* Ron Whitten and Sleeping Bear Press to publish the edited manuscript under the title, *Golf Has Never Failed Me.* The book was published in 1996 and more than any source provides some insight into Ross's design philosophy.

He spoke of undulations around putting surfaces: "Ideal golfing terrain, such as Ballybunion, consists of knolls and dips that reach right onto the greens to test stance, swing and shot placement," Ross noted, adding that the most desirable elements of British courses were "an approach which takes the ball over little knolls, undulations and hillocks instead of absolutely flat and smooth country."

He noted that punchbowl greens are not "genuine testers of skill, as their sloping sides draw balls toward the center and offer equal advantage to both good and poorly played shots." The inverted-saucer greens and saddle shapes with a ridge through the middle were designed to allow good drainage.

Ross wanted short holes to be difficult and thought every course should have a hole five hundred yards or longer.

He advised limiting the number of water hazards to three, two being better. "The repeated loss of balls by those to whom the hazard is difficult is apt to create dissatisfaction."

He said he liked blind shots "as they add spice to game. But of course do not overdo it—one or two on a course are okay." He liked to build one or two drive-and-pitch length par-fours. "Both the drive and approach should be difficult," he advised.

He didn't like long walks from one green to the next tee—"long walks cause much dissatisfaction."

Ross recalled that many of his "best golfing friends complained bitterly" about what they felt were radical use of bunkers in the construction of Pinehurst No. 2; Ross was told the course would get minimal interest and play from members and guests.

"At the time, our No. 1 course was rather easy and quite free from bunkers, and was not comparable in difficulty or as a test of golf," Ross said. But he added that once No. 2 opened, the early critics were quickly converted. "Those men who were so skeptical are now No. 2's strongest admirers."

Ross believed there is no such thing as a misplaced bunker. "Regardless of where a bunker may be, it is the business of the player to avoid it," he said.

He spoke of the manufactured look of some courses and their features.

"If you use a line and square to build a bunker, the result is sure to have an artificial-ness akin to hideous. It's just as easy to break up all the lines and avoid such a regrettable result," and observed that "man cannot do in a few days what nature took years to accomplish."

Ross loved the pocks and pimples on courses at Dornoch, St. Andrews and Prestwick, calling them "tantalizing little hummocks" and "charming variation" in lies one gets playing around and on top of them. The mounds Ross built in America, particularly in the Northeast where the ground was inundated with rocks and boulders, were often the result of seeking cost savings in construction; it could take $2,000 in men and machines to cart rocks away. Many of his "chocolate drop" features were merely boulders covered with piles of dirt and finished with loam and seed.

Ross was a perfectionist and expected those around him to be as well. A man's word was his bond. Once he scolded his Pinehurst clubmakers for letting the edge of a wood-working tool go blunt; standing before them, he used his considerable carpentry skills to provide a sharpening demonstration. Another time he popped an uppity caddie on the noggin with a five-iron, saying that would be the only "strike" of the day when the caddies were threatening a walk-out over wages. Yet Ross possessed a soft side as well. He loved flowers and gardening—a passion he inherited from his mother—and his daughter, Lillian Ross Pippitt, remembered that he "always brought to the dinner table a choice rose, freshly clipped from his carefully tended rose garden."

"I remember seeing Donald Ross as a child of six or eight years old," says Wilmington's Hugh MacRae II, whose ancestors worked with Ross in building courses in Wilmington and Linville. "He was a fine-looking man with a tweed cap and tweed suit and knickers and

Three bunkers guard the small green on the par-three tenth hole at Royal Dornoch. After playing in a northward direction for eight holes, the course turns and heads back toward the village with the Dornoch Firth to the left.

long stockings. He had a mustache. He was very pleasant and kindly. His Scottish brogue was very thick and difficult for a child to understand. He was very impressive."

"He was very quiet, a bit stern, dignified," Tommie Currie, a club employee, remembered in an interview in the Pinehurst *Gazette*. "All you had to do was just what you were supposed to do, and you never had any problem with him. There was not a nicer person you'd ever meet. If you were wrong, he'd let you know, and you'd better shape up, and you knew it."

Currie once fielded a complaint that a foursome was playing very slowly and asked the golfers to let the group behind play through.

"No one plays through me," snapped one of the offending golfers.

Currie reported to Ross, who got in a buggy and drove out to confront the slow players. The man refused Ross's request to step aside.

"Sir, we don't need any player on our course like you," Ross told him. "You can leave right now."

The man knew Richard Tufts and immediately appealed to the owner. Tufts sided with Ross, saying that Ross was the club manager and his authority was unquestioned.

Richard Moss in his book, *Eden in the Pines*, told of Ross going to Florida to build a course in the mid-1920s and writing back to Tufts that he didn't like what he saw. Ross noted that the hotels were full of land speculators and that "many of the best people" were leaving the more prominent hotels to relocate away from "the undesirable element" brought by the real estate boom. Ross told Tufts the opportunity was there for Pinehurst and other mid-South resorts to capitalize on those leaving the Florida market.

Ross's stern nature led to moments of tension with his bosses. One year Leonard Tufts wrote to son Richard about problems in the putting greens and potential causes and solutions. He referenced a meeting with Ross and course superintendent Frank Maples.

"I am sorry but as you noticed yesterday, Donald gets mad every time I discuss this subject and Frank, who is glad to work with me, has to do as Donald says," Tufts wrote.

To Ross, the principles of life were the same as those in golf: tell the truth, take things as they come, assume total responsibility. There was no better metaphor for life than playing eighteen holes and posting a score, as Ross noted over the years in various comments:

"If you want to know a man, take him out on the golf course."

"I believe wholeheartedly in golf. I consider it a game of honor. It does more to bring out the finer points in a man's character than any other sport."

"A country which gets golf-minded need not worry about the honor, the integrity and the honesty of its people."

"Every golfer is on his honor. As long as we keep golf a game of honor, we're on the right road."

Ross's early ties in American golf were with the affluent—at a Boston country club and a southern resort—but his modest Scottish roots allowed him to stay anchored in the idea that anyone could and should have access to quality golf. He visited Asheville in the mid-1920s to survey the site for a new municipal course east of town, and *The Asheville Citizen* noted the occasion with a large headline: "Municipally Owned Golf Courses Needed Here Says Donald Ross On Arrival."

"It is the consensus of opinion of almost all that a municipal course will go a long way toward drawing winter and summer tourists," the story said, then quoted Ross that a new course would "prove one of the chief assets in advertising for visitors."

Asheville Municipal Golf Course opened a year later and was dedicated on May 21, 1927. Ross followed his work in Asheville with a municipal course in Wilmington; those eighteen holes were completed in 1929. In 1930 he was in New England looking at a site for a potential municipal course and told a local newspaperman that he saw a "brilliant future for the pay-as-you-enter golf courses of America, a tremendous big, new industry.

"I am positive that a city cannot expend its money for a better, more worthy cause than a municipal course such as this," Ross said. "From a business standpoint, it is money well-spent. It means an enormous increase in real estate values in that section. And like every

The seventh tee is the highest point at Dornoch, affording golfers a view for miles in every direction.

other municipal course in country, this one will support itself."

The Donald Ross Society, founded in 1987 by a group of Ross devotees, serves as a clearinghouse for plans of Ross courses through the Tufts Archives in Pinehurst. It regularly awards scholarship funds to young, aspiring architects as well as grants toward the restoration of Ross courses, like the $7,000 it contributed in 1998 for work on Wilmington Municipal. The course suffered from the lack of a proper maintenance budget and was beaten up from heavy traffic. The money went toward retaining the services of Ron Prichard's design firm, which proposed a bunker restoration plan. The city then contributed $100,000 toward the reconstruction work.

"I think there's real value in complete restoration, allowing for some changes mandated by technology," says Prichard, a Philadelphia-based architect who has supervised several Ross overhaul projects. "You can't have the contours today with the speed we maintain greens, for example. But if you restore it carefully, you suddenly have a masterpiece hanging in a museum. You have a fabulous piece of artwork people can visit and actually play."

***

Roly Bluck can't be sure of the year in the mid-to-late 1970s when he and his wife Pat first visited Dornoch from their home far south in England, but he remembers playing golf in the morning, fishing in the afternoon and having the blissful feeling of finding a personal Shangri-la.

"We walked from the second green to the third tee, and all of a sudden this vista just opened up," Bluck says. "I just stood there in a trance. I was shocked by the sheer beauty of it all. I fell in love with it instantly. We returned every summer after that. Two weeks became three. Three became four. Four became five."

The Blucks were on the ninth fairway in 1985 when Roly floated the idea of a Dornoch retirement to his wife, who promptly shot it down given the distance from children and grandchildren in England. Three years later on the very same hole, Pat out of nowhere said she'd now consider a move to Dornoch if the family supported the decision. The Blucks in 1990 found a home literally steps from the third tee, expanded it to accommodate house guests and have been there ever since.

"I've played most of the championship courses in Britain and the States—Pine Valley, Cypress Point, Baltusrol—and to me there's only one No. 1, and that's Royal Dornoch," Bluck says. "That's not just because we live here, but because of the complexity of the course. The course is shaped like an inverted 'S,' and the winds change from hole to hole, day to day. It never plays the same. On the twelfth hole, for example, from the medal tee you can drive into the wind, your second shot is across the wind and your third can be down wind. That kind of thing sets it apart."

The course that exists today was ranked sixteenth in the world by *GOLF* in its 2011 rankings; it would certainly be good enough to host The Open Championship, but its remote location and lack of infrastructure limit Dornoch to the occasional tidbit of an event like the 1985 British Amateur.

"Forget Cypress Point and the others," *Golf Digest* columnist Peter Dobereiner once said. "Dornoch is easily the finest course in the world—the absolute No. 1."

Written documentation verifies golf was played in Dornoch as early as 1616, but the first formal club was the Sutherland Golfing Society (named for the county in which Dornoch is located). The club was formed in 1877 and used a nine-hole course on the eastern edge of the village as its competitive venue; the original layout consisted of nine holes set in the ground with no formal putting surfaces or bunkers and the next tee set several club lengths from the cup.

Like many old courses that span generations, the layout is a porridge of ideas from different individuals. John Sutherland took over as club secretary in 1883 at the age of nineteen and, three years later, invited Old Tom Morris up from St. Andrews to restructure the layout into a more formal presentation.

"We raised a few pounds among ourselves" to hire Morris, Sutherland said.

"There canna be better for gowf," Tom told the Dornoch citizens and members.

Whether Morris fashioned nine or eighteen holes at this point has been debated. Some believe he completed nine holes in 1886 and finished a new nine in 1892; others assert that the entire routing was finished in 1886 and Morris tweaked the layout upon his return six years later. In either event, the 1892 course measured 5,285 yards and proved sufficient until the advent of the rubber golf ball in the early 1900s. Sutherland and five-time Open champion J.H. Taylor, a regular visitor to Dornoch, lengthened the course by some eight hundred yards to accommodate the livelier ball in 1904. Ross himself designed the first and second holes as they sit today in 1921 on a visit from the States, but the work wasn't actually done until 1927-28 because of cost and land access issues.

Several holes on the south side of the course were lost during World War II when the Royal Air Force commandeered the ground for an airstrip. Then at the end of the war, four new holes were built at the north end of the course—through some combination of ideas from 1920 Open champion George Duncan, who was paid £25 for a one-day visit, and greenkeeper Robbie Grant. No significant changes have been made in more than half a century, with the exception of a few holes lengthened with new blue tees. The course today plays at a maximum of 6,697 yards with a par 70.

"It was all here whenever Tom Morris and John Sutherland built it," Chris Surmonte says. "The flow and rhythm of the holes are unmatched. There are the coolest landforms—with the ridge and the raised beach and the curvature of the beach. The course goes out and then back, but the holes don't really run perfectly parallel like so many links courses. You are constantly changing directions."

The distinctive plateau and inverted-saucer green profiles have been part of the Dornoch flavor from the beginning. In 1907, a golfer named Anthony Spalding visited and wrote, "The plateau greens are difficult to understand because of the undulations which are not always so real as they look, or look so real as they are."

"Surely no one can forget the feeling of joy after placing his second shot on the plateau greens on the fourth or eighth at Dornoch, my old home course, one of the best and most enjoyable courses in the world," Ross wrote in *Golf Has Never Failed Me*.

KINDRED GOLFING SPIRITS

Former USGA Executive Director David Fay has called St. Andrews, Pinehurst and Pebble Beach "the three-legged stool of golf." Fay was a champion for Pinehurst's quest to land a U.S. Open in the early 1990s, relishing is the fact that Pinehurst, like the Old Course and Pebble Beach, is accessible to the man on the street.

"You knew going in to this week that the ambiance and flavor of the area were going to be a home run," Fay said at the 2005 U.S. Open. "You knew it. The United States may not have a St. Andrews, but Pinehurst is the closest thing to St. Andrews we have in terms of the feel for the history of the game, the passion of the game. The whole place just exudes golf."

Pinehurst's roots in Scotland trace to the mid-1700s, when Scottish Highlanders traveled south from Pennsylvania on the "Great Wagon Road" and northeast from Wilmington along the Cape Fear River and settled in what would become Moore County. They named villages in the area Aberdeen and Carthage; they buried McCaskills, Mathesons and McDonalds in a cemetery to the west of Carthage. The county to the south was named Scotland County. The ground, which Leonard Tufts of the Pinehurst founding family would later term "wretchedly poor," was hardly friendly to farming, so the Scots focused on harvesting naval stores from the pine trees.

But the sandy loam was ideal for golf, as Dornoch native Donald Ross discovered when he first came to Pinehurst in December 1900.

Today the fabric of both Pinehurst and St. Andrews are woven around golf, though St. Andrews adds the considerable influence of some seven thousand students at the University of St. Andrews.

Pinehurst has over eleven decades of golf history; St. Andrews over six centuries.

Moore County has sand and wire grass; the Kingdom of Fife is rich in sand, whins and heather. The dogwoods are white and pink in Pinehurst; the gorse is yellow, the heather purple in Scotland.

In Pinehurst you have the Pine Crest Inn, in St. Andrews the Dunvegan as consummate nineteenth-hole watering spots. Here you have Old Sport & Gallery; there you have Auchterlonies Golf Shop. Fletcher Gaines and Hardrock Robinson paved the caddies' path in Pinehurst; Tip Anderson was among the most colorful of the St. Andrews caddie fraternity.

Pinehurst salutes Donald Ross with two statues—one in the center of the Village and one by the eighteenth green of No. 2. St. Andrews remembers Young Tom Morris with a bas-relief sculpture on his gravestone and a display of Old Tom's workbench in a shop bearing his name.

There is one golf course that stands above all in each town—No. 2 in Pinehurst and the Old Course in St. Andrews. But there are seven more courses at Pinehurst proper, six more under the St. Andrews Links Trust umbrella—not to mention excellent venues nearby such as Pine Needles and Crail.

"Golf was born in Scotland, but it lives in Pinehurst," said Laurie Auchterlonie, the Scottish clubmaker who visited Pinehurst most every winter beginning in 1973 in his role as "international curator" of the World Golf Hall of Fame.

His father, Willie Auchterlonie, won the 1893 British Open and two years later established a club-making business in St. Andrews with two brothers; the business remains today at the corner of North Street and Golf Place, just a block from the first tee of the Old Course. Laurie donated the family's extensive collection of antique clubs to the World Golf Hall of Fame upon its opening in 1973.

"America has done so much for the game of golf that I thought it would be great to donate the collection to the Hall of Fame," Auchterlonie said. "I wanted to have a good home for the clubs and keep the collection in its entirety. Pinehurst was the natural choice."

Auchterlonie died in 1987, and the Hall of Fame has since moved to St. Augustine, Fla., but a kindred spirit remains in the Village in the person of Tom Stewart, a former PGA club professional who moved to Pinehurst in 1996 and opened Old Sport & Gallery, an enclave of books, artwork and collectibles. Stewart spent time in the early 1970s at St.

The work of noted British golf artist Richard Chorley—such as this depiction of the first and last holes of the Old Course—is on display at Old Sport & Gallery in Pinehurst. "Old golfers never die," says proprietor Tom Stewart (pictured). "They just eventually move to Pinehurst."

Andrews, initiating his extensive golf library when he discovered a librarian throwing old books away to make room for new ones.

"If it's true that old golfers never die, they just eventually move to Pinehurst," says Stewart, "then I'm just following in the best traditions of the game. The only other place I could do what I do and get the fulfillment I do here would be at St. Andrews."

Herbert Warren Wind had visited Pinehurst frequently and was quite familiar with Ross's work in Wind's native New England by the time in 1964 he first visited Dornoch. He noted the similarities between Dornoch and Ross's American designs in an essay in *The New Yorker.*

"The Dornoch golfer learns how to improvise the delicate little lob-and-run shots," Wind wrote. "In America, Donald Ross rarely found the kind of terrain that would permit him to reproduce the touchy subtleties of Dornoch's green areas, but their lasting influence on him is visible in the hilltop 'crown' greens he built wherever he worked."

The Dornoch Firth is the true architect of the course, the water and wind and sand getting assists from the rabbits and burrowing animals in shaping the land forms. The firth is visible on every hole except the eighth, and seven miles of beach stretch above and below the town. Your concentration is challenged on the ninth, tenth and sixteenth tees from the crash of surf below the tee box. On clear days, you can see Dunrobin Castle, a dozen miles to the northeast.

"Unrivaled stretches of fine seaside turf, hillocks, banks, promontories, hollows and humps," wrote Donald Grant in his booklet, *Personal Memories of Royal Dornoch Golf Club, 1900-1925.* "Everything in terms of terrain for modern golf had been provided by the age-long forces of nature."

"No other links has quite the ageless aura Dornoch does," Pete Dye observed in his book, *Bury Me in a Pot Bunker.* "When you play it, you get the feeling you could be living just as easily in the eighteen hundreds, or even the seventeen hundreds."

The weather is a part of the story as it is on any seaside links, but the rain-bearing clouds that move from Ireland to the west coast of Scotland are often halted or slowed by the mountains in the Scottish interior. Thus the east of Scotland gets less rain than the west.

"The east coast gets twenty-two to twenty-four inches of rain a year," Grant Sword says. "The west coast near Glasgow gets seventy or more. The mountains block a lot of the bad weather. Not all of it, but some of it."

The ground is firm; everyone walks and everyone plays no matter the weather.

"It's only *water,*" Bluck once said to an American who blanched at the idea of playing in the rain. "What are you going to do? Melt?"

"There is something about the excitement of playing the most northerly championship course in the world," says Grant Shannon. "So it's unique for that. We are two degrees below the Arctic Circle, yet we play our golf all year round. And flying into America, we went over just to the east of the Hudson Bay. And it's *frozen.* And Dornoch is on the same latitude as that. Our daughter used to complain about the winters here. Then she spent two winters in Chicago. She'll never grumble again."

Adding to the Dornoch elixir is the frequent blanket of sea fog or "haar" that engulfs the course. Don Greenberg and head pro Andrew Skinner once played six rounds of golf in one day, starting at three in the morning and finishing at seven at night. A year later, they did a repeat performance, this time going seven rounds and raising money for junior golf. At times they had to play through the "haar" and used the sound and feel of the ball to estimate where it landed.

"The haar enveloped us like cotton and you couldn't see ten yards in front of you," Greenberg says. "You had to rely on feel. 'Ah, that's a good one, it's on the middle of the clubface.' I probably hit it more consistently during that stretch because I was thinking of process more than the result."

The Dornoch course sets off in a north-northeast direction for eight holes, then turns and tacks back toward the south along the beach for eight holes. Seventeen cuts back north and eighteen reverses south. Greens bounded by stark slopes like the second play the devil on recovery shots, and canted fairways are forever reflecting balls toward treacherous bunkers. The traps seem to inhale shots because there is no rough to absorb the bounce of the ball.

The challenges as you dig into a round at Dornoch are varied. Seven requires a muscular approach into the prevailing north wind to reach home in regulation; ten demands a surgeon's touch to loft a short iron with the wind and stop it on a small green just beyond three bunkers. Greens such as two and seven have subtle spines running from the front into the putting surface that can deflect shots left or right. The whole course is fescue grass, the greens rolling about ten on the Stimpmeter on an average day, perhaps a little quicker for competitions. Learning the nuances takes some time for Americans— hitting short shots off firm turf requires touch rarely developed on soft, verdant layouts. The best advice Skinner can give to Americans suitably frightened of the steep sod-wall bunkers is, simply, "Stay out of them." Beyond that, you need a sand wedge with plenty of bounce.

"Open the face and take a full swing," he says. "The sand is soft, it'll stop the club from coming through. You have to swing right through the sand. In Pinehurst, the sand has a firmer base. You can clip it out easier."

In 2011 Gary Dingwall was in his ninth year on the Dornoch professional staff. He grew up in Wishaw, a small town midway between Glasgow and Edinburgh. He says he's come so far north for one reason: the golf course.

"It's the best I've seen," he says. "I thought Turnberry was the best until I came here. It blew me away the first time I played. It changes every day. The wind changes, the playing conditions change. It's fair but difficult. For the higher handicap, it's hard to lose a ball until you hit into the gorse bushes. For the scratch golfer, you have to position yourself off the tee to have the proper angle to the green. But that's not easy because of the way the wind might be blowing. Every day is a new challenge.

"People come in and say, 'Thank you,'" Dingwall says. "I say, 'What for?' They say, 'For letting us play this magnificent golf course.'"

"It's in my top five, and I've played a lot of golf courses," says Dick Mayberry of Chicago, who's been coming to Dornoch for twelve years and has been a member for eight.

Eoin Riddell has been working on the course since the age of sixteen, joined the staff full-time in 1986 and has been in charge of course maintenance (his title is course manager) since 2005. Asked if

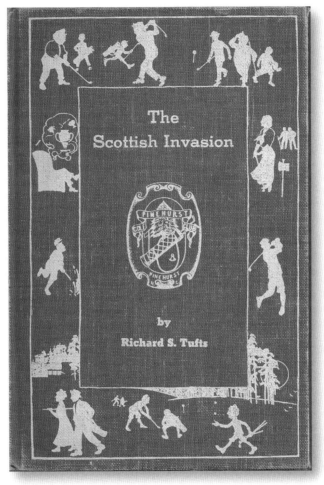

Richard Tufts wrote "The Scottish Invasion" in 1962 to tell the story of golf's development at Pinehurst: "The world is indebted to Scotland for giving us the game of golf, and America's debt to the Scots was further increased by the arrival of many Scottish professionals."

he sees the course as something of a national treasure, he says, "I don't know about that, but I just see it as *mine*. If someone takes a divot, I want them to fill it out. If I see something happening that shouldn't, it annoys me. The golf course is for me to look after and I try not to break it. It's like one of my children."

It was not until around 2000 that the club installed disks in the fairways to mark two hundred yards and one hundred fifty from the green. There are no other yardage markers on the golf course.

"I was against *any* yardage markers," Riddell says, "but at the time, I didn't have a say in the matter. This is a links course. Sometimes you have to land the ball a hundred yards short and let it roll on. Sometimes you hit a three-wood one-fifty into the wind. The yardage doesn't matter. All I want is a sign on the tee—'par-four, four hundred yards.' That's it. Go for it."

The ebb and flow of the holes, the history of the village, the Ross connection—they all add up to making Dornoch a special experience.

Certainly for visitors …

"When you play a course like Royal Dornoch in Scotland or Royal County Down in Ireland—magical, classic links courses—between the setting and the people, it becomes a spiritual experience," American actor Michael Douglas told *GOLF* Magazine in October 2011.

And natives as well …

"Modesty forbids me saying more than Dornoch is the most beautifully situated links in the world," Donald Ross said, "and that no American golfer should omit to go there, where he will find the best golf, a royal welcome and no rabble."

PINEHURST DESIGNERS' INCUBATOR

The American Society of Golf Course Architects was founded at The Holly Inn in Pinehurst in December 1947, with thirteen architects approved for charter membership: William Bell, Jack Daray, William Diddel, William Gordon, Robert Bruce Harris, Robert Trent Jones, William Langford, Robert Lawrence, Perry Maxwell, J.B. McGovern, Donald Ross, Stanley Thompson and Robert White.

Harris was elected president, Thompson vice president and Jones secretary-treasurer. Ross was named honorary president, and throughout its history, the trade association for golf's design community has paid frequent homage to the man considered the dean of early golf designers in the United States.

The red plaid jackets worn by members at their annual meetings were designed in the Ross Tartan and adopted in 1973.

The Donald Ross Award was created in 1976 and is presented annually to a person who has made a significant contribution to the game of golf and has spotlighted the contributions of the architect.

"I consider my Donald Ross Award to be my Heisman, my Oscar, my Pulitzer, my Grammy," said *Golf Digest* architecture editor Ron Whitten upon receiving his award in 1996.

The group took its 1980 annual meeting to Dornoch, Ross's home in Scotland, and for its fiftieth meeting in 1996, it returned to Pinehurst. One highlight of that gathering was a discussion headed by Pete Dye and Jack Nicklaus on why No. 2 was such a special place in golf.

Nicklaus spoke of growing up playing Scioto Country Club, a Ross-designed golf course in Columbus, Ohio.

"I always felt comfortable playing No. 2 because I was familiar with the look and feel of a Donald Ross course," Nicklaus said. "It looks very natural, like it's always been there, and can be played by every level of golfer. The greens will accept high shots if the course is wet and it's been raining, but you can also bounce the ball into the greens if it's dry and firm."

Nicklaus observed that trees along the fairways of No. 2 "didn't come into play," whereupon he was interrupted by the crusty Dye. "Maybe not for you, big guy, but they do for the rest of us," Dye said to a round of laughter.

Dye then told of frequent visits to No. 2 in the early 1940s from Fort Bragg and taking money from a colonel "who thought he knew how to play golf." Dye said he was often asked why he frequently built a par-five, par-three and par-four as his finishing holes, and he pointed to No. 2's closing configuration.

"If it was good enough for Mister Ross, it was good enough for me," Dye said.

Indeed, five of Dye's most acclaimed golf courses conclude in a 5-3-4 pattern—the Ocean Course at Kiawah, the Stadium Course at PGA West, the Players Course at TPC Sawgrass, Whistling Straits and Oak Tree.

Tom Marzolf, a design associate on the staff of Fazio Golf Course Designers, was ASGCA president in 2006 and took the annual meeting to Pinehurst. Marzolf was the lead designer on the new No. 4 course that opened in 1999 and arranged a hickory tournament on that course. His connection to Pinehurst extends to attending golf camp at Pinehurst in 1973, and Fazio's firm has done work of some sort on every course at Pinehurst except No. 7.

"No. 2 has always been my favorite golf course," Marzolf says. "From forty yards in, you can get a Ph.D. in golf course design by studying those greens and surrounds. It is a special place."

The formative meeting of the ASGCA in 1947 included an address from Pinehurst's Richard Tufts, who spoke about research the USGA was conducting on an ongoing basis into the issue of the length of ball flight.

"We feel that a golf course is designed for a certain type of shot to the green, and that as you increase the length of the tee shot, you throw the golf course all out of scale," Tufts said. "Therefore, it spoils the pleasure of the play to have this continual increase in the flight of the ball. We feel that the question involves not only the ball but also the equipment of the game; that possibly the shaft has something to do with the increased length of the ball."

Tufts said that research by the USGA and ball manufacturers since 1942 had shown little increase in the properties of the golf

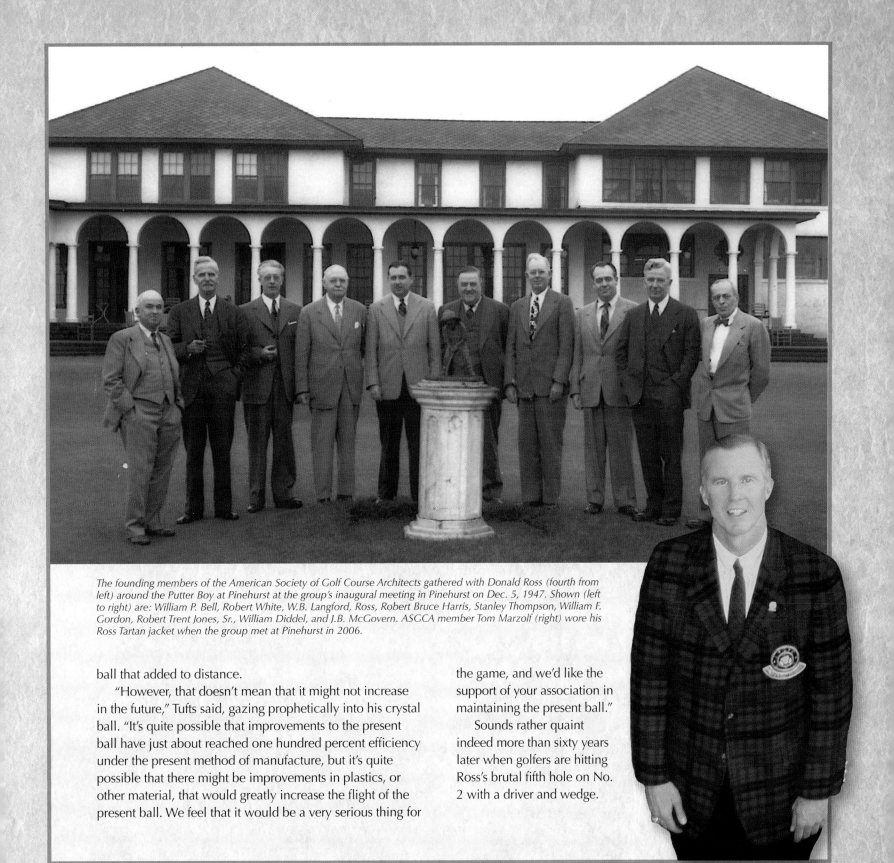

The founding members of the American Society of Golf Course Architects gathered with Donald Ross (fourth from left) around the Putter Boy at Pinehurst at the group's inaugural meeting in Pinehurst on Dec. 5, 1947. Shown (left to right) are: William P. Bell, Robert White, W.B. Langford, Ross, Robert Bruce Harris, Stanley Thompson, William F. Gordon, Robert Trent Jones, Sr., William Diddel, and J.B. McGovern. ASGCA member Tom Marzolf (right) wore his Ross Tartan jacket when the group met at Pinehurst in 2006.

ball that added to distance.

"However, that doesn't mean that it might not increase in the future," Tufts said, gazing prophetically into his crystal ball. "It's quite possible that improvements to the present ball have just about reached one hundred percent efficiency under the present method of manufacture, but it's quite possible that there might be improvements in plastics, or other material, that would greatly increase the flight of the present ball. We feel that it would be a very serious thing for the game, and we'd like the support of your association in maintaining the present ball."

Sounds rather quaint indeed more than sixty years later when golfers are hitting Ross's brutal fifth hole on No. 2 with a driver and wedge.

Architect Bill Coore referred often to this photo of a golfer playing from a bunker on the tenth hole in the mid-1900s in communicating with his construction staff the goal of the 2010-11 restoration.

If I had my way . . .

. . . *there would be a troupe of cavalry horses running through every trap and bunker on the course before a tournament started, where only a niblick could get the ball out and then but only a few yards. I have seen a number of traps and bunkers that afforded better lies and easier strokes than the fairway. This, of course, is ridiculous.*

C.B. MACDONALD

LAD TURNS A HUNDRED

For more than a century the little boy with the floppy hat on his head and golf club in his hands has represented Pinehurst in newspaper ads, on shirts and caps and in the hands of championship golfers. The Golf Lad and his offspring, the Putter Boy, are among the most famous inanimate objects in golf.

"The Lad truly represents what Pinehurst is all about—youthful enthusiasm and walking No. 2," says Stephen Cryan, director of retail operations at Pinehurst from 1995-2012. "He's been a part of our history since the early 1900s."

The Lad has been the focal point of U.S. Open logos in 1999, 2005 and leading into 2014, and a series of posters also used on the faces of tickets for the 2005 Open featured him in a variety of settings around the resort. And his offspring, the Putter Boy, is the official resort logo, appearing in various vestiges in fabric, leather, bronze and even in the resort kitchens in chocolate and butter.

"The Lad is the life, the Putter Boy the foundation and the rock," Cryan says. "The Lad is always moving, going places, while the Putter Boy, as a statue, is right there today where he's always been—just outside the clubhouse by the putting green."

Frank Presbrey, Pinehurst's first advertising counselor, created a young boy that appeared in the resort's early 1900s advertising and calendars who was called "The Golf Lad," "The Golf Boy," or "The Golf Calendar Lad." Later he was replaced on the calendars sent annually to hotel guests by photos of architect and club professional Donald Ross play-

2005
UNITED STATES OPEN

Pinehurst no. 2
NORTH CAROLINA
JUNE 16 - 19, 2005

ing the Pinehurst golf courses. He is believed to have made his debut in a 1906 ad that appeared in newspapers in the Northeast.

In 1912, sculptress Lucy Richards used the Lad as the model for her bronze statuette in sundial form. Since Richards wasn't a golfer, Ross demonstrated the proper grip and stance for her—but the image, contrary to lore, is not of Ross, who was a grown man at the time. The shaft of the club created the shadow that would be used on the sundial to tell time, and in order to get the proper angle, the length of the club had to be inordinately long.

The statue was known as "The Sundial Boy" until the 1970s, when "The Putter Boy" name caught on. For many years the statue sat on a concrete base between the two large putting greens beside the clubhouse. It was moved in 1978 to the PGA/World Golf Hall of Fame but returned to Pinehurst around 1990 and now is displayed prominently once again outside the south side of the clubhouse. The Putter Boy is the most cherished award a golfer can win at Pinehurst; a bronze statuette goes to the winner of all North and South competitions.

The Lad was the focal point of the logos created for the 1999 and 2005 U.S. Opens. The mark for the former event was patterned from the "Off for Pinehurst" ad from the early 1900s that showed the Lad carrying his golf clubs through New York's Grand Central Terminal. The logo for the 2005 championship was modeled from the Lad swinging a club in a 1906 ad titled, "Back to Pinehurst," and the image of Payne Stewart making the winning putt in

PINEHURST.
1895

The Golf Lad was the centerpiece a poster heralding the 2005 U.S. Open (opposite) and was used in a variety of scenes on that year's tickets. Meanwhile, the original Putter Boy statuette has attracted the attention of juniors and pros over a century.

USGA
2005 U.S. Open Championship
Pinehurst No. 2

Sunday, June 19, 2005
GROUNDS

Conducted by the United States Golf Association

1999 and moments later cradling the Open trophy in his arms generated themes for two of the eight posters created by artist Eric Johnson prior to the 2005 Open.

The Lad embracing the trophy image was the foundation for the next generation of Open marks; it's the centerpiece for the 2014 Men's Open.

"There's a little of the Lad in all of us," Cryan says. "In the posters we created, he's doing everything you want to be doing at Pinehurst—from walking into The Carolina, hanging out on the porch, taking a nap, making the putt on

eighteen, holding a trophy, playing golf and carrying your clubs in the afternoon. It's all there. The beauty is, he can be anybody."

To celebrate the Putter Boy's centennial birthday, Pinehurst public relations officials dispatched him on a worldwide tour in 2012. Putter Boy statuettes were sent to various locations domestically and abroad—New Orleans, San Francisco, Paris, Madrid, New Zealand among them. His hosts took photographs and posted them on Facebook in the "Where Is Putter Boy Tour?"

Greening of Pinehurst

Ben Crenshaw is bundled in layers and a stocking cap as he rides around Pinehurst No. 2 on a chilly, windy first day of December 2010. He parks his golf cart on the side of the eighth green, inspects the bunker that's been reconfigured to the side of the putting surface, then walks to the green and stops in the middle, about eight yards from the front edge.

"It's a repeatable theme when you play a Donald Ross course—if you hit the ball right here," he says, pointing to the area front-center of the putting surface, "you can play all day. No matter what the course is, no matter where it is. Front and center is the ticket on a Donald Ross golf course."

The thirteenth green (opposite) in an early 1900s postcard and (above) in all its emerald glory at the turn of the 21st century.

He motions to the extremities of the green and notes in particular the danger to the rear of the putting plateau.

"You go this way, that way, long, you ask for trouble," he says. "If you come right to the front and the center, you're fine. You can play. You're safe."

Crenshaw should know—his 64 on this very golf course nearly four decades earlier remains one of the best rounds he's ever played and one of the finest rounds crafted over more than a century of No. 2's existence. It came in taxing weather in the sixth round of the 1973 World Open and catapulted Crenshaw from deep in the field to a contender's role in the one-off, eight-round event conceived by Pinehurst's new owners to fill the void left by the 1952 disbanding of the North and South Open. It was only Crenshaw's second event as a PGA Tour professional, and he finished second by three shots to Miller Barber, who took home the first prize of $100,000—an outlandish sum for the day.

"It was a cold day, much like today," Ben says. "The wind was really blowing. It was one of those days I hit the ball on the green just far enough. I had good range with my irons. I played front-and-center. I made just about every putt I had. It sticks out in my mind as one of the best rounds I've ever played. I leapfrogged so many people that day. I was way back and everyone's shooting big numbers in that wind. It was a very special round, that's for sure."

The ironies are deep that a golfer in the thick of the drama that week in 1973 should now be a leading character in the 2010-11 restoration story. That World Open serves as a prism into the changing of the guard taking place at Pinehurst in the early 1970s— the greening of Pinehurst and the transition from the staid Tufts family to the chic Diamondhead operation.

Marty McKenzie and Peter DeYoung were both in their early twenties at the time—McKenzie, a native of Pinehurst, as a bellhop at The Carolina, and DeYoung, from Rochester, N.Y., on the tournament administration staff at the country club.

"Pinehurst was always a 'dress-for-dinner' kind of place," McKenzie says. "As soon as Diamondhead came in, out went the jackets and neckties for dinner and it became open-neck shirts and gold chains and the volume was turned up in every corner of the resort. They were all from California and thought we were all Podunk, dumbass, redneck southerners."

"At the time there were maybe five hundred residents of Pinehurst," says DeYoung. "Then the place started exploding. If you were one of the newcomers, you thought it was all very exciting. If you were the old guard, your jaw dropped. Condos were literally growing overnight. One day it would be woods and fairways and that's it. And the next day there are condos on both sides."

Pinehurst—the village, the resort and the country club—had been owned and managed in a state of "benevolent dictatorship" by the Tufts family since the beginning in 1895. As the 1960s evolved, the third generation now in control was aging. There was new competition in golf travel from Florida, Hilton Head and a burgeoning resort area within easy driving distance, Myrtle Beach. Pinehurst Inc. was controlled by brothers Richard, James and Albert Tufts and a fourth stockholder, Isham Sledge, the company's long-time secretary-treasurer. It would take a considerable infusion of cash to upgrade the careworn resort, and the specter of inheritance taxes loomed over the family as well. As the nation's economy soured in the late 1960s, James, Albert and Sledge voted to sell the resort; Richard bitterly opposed the idea.

Into the breach stepped Malcom McLean, a native of nearby Maxton in Robeson County who had made his fortune in the trucking and shipping businesses. McLean in 1969 formed Diamondhead Corporation, and within two years the company was involved in residential-resort developments in Mississippi, Alabama and Oklahoma. Diamondhead bought Pinehurst for $9.2 million dollars, the deal closing on Dec. 31, 1970. James Tufts later said the price was a fair one if you considered the profit the company was making at the time, but it was a steal if you considered the value of the land. McLean installed Bill Maurer as president and Maurer, in turn, hired Eddie Susalla as director of golf.

Where the Tufts were conservative, reserved and cautious, Diamondhead brought a fire-ready-aim mentality to the peaceful village and resort. Where the Tufts preferred understated décor with whicker and wing-backed chairs in the hotel lobby, Diamondhead remodeled the hotel with the greens and golds and shag carpets of the era. Where the 1960s era of Pinehurst was described as "dusty" and "old folks eating cornflakes," the new owners zeroed in on youth and family, spending over $11 million on recreational amenities outside of golf. Where the Tufts were slow to react to the new market of golfers spawned by the appeal of President Dwight Eisenhower and Arnold Palmer in the 1950s and '60s, Diamondhead was aggressive in its sales and marketing approach—TV sets and even "Putter Boy" statuettes were premiums for real-estate purchases at the time. The Tufts planned for slow and steady growth; Richard, Albert and James remembered the pain of the 1930s and abhorred debt. Diamondhead had built 556 condominiums in four years, hopelessly cluttering the aesthetics of the No. 3 and 5 golf courses. (A Diamondhead official later admitted to the *News & Observer* of Raleigh that the company had "swallowed too much" and "overbuilt a little.")

The idea for the World Open was hatched at the Masters Tournament in 1971, when Maurer looked at the largesse of the annual assembly at Augusta National Golf Club, at the talented golfers, the energetic galleries, the fawning media and weekend television commercials for the club via CBS Television—and the event was not yet forty years old.

"I was thinking to myself that it is unfortunate a tournament as great as the Masters is not in its fiftieth year at Pinehurst," Maurer recalled later. "But the people who had Pinehurst before us apparently didn't think that way."

Indeed, Richard Tufts decided in early 1952 that he'd had enough of professional golf at Pinehurst. Professional golf to Tufts' taste was too much like a carnival, and he was stung by what he perceived as a slap in the face by the 1951 U.S. Ryder Cup team. After whipping

Ben Crenshaw at Pinehurst in 1973; the recent University of Texas graduate was playing in his second tournament as a professional and finished second in the World Open, the highlight a 64 in the sixth round of the 144-hole event. "It sticks out in my mind as one of the best rounds I've ever played," Crenshaw says.

the team from Great Britain and Ireland in the Ryder Cup in early November, only five members of the nine-man contingent remained in Pinehurst for the North and South Open the following week. The pros squawked about the North and South's relative low purse; Tufts countered that some of that prize money went to players in the form of free room and board in The Carolina. Tufts discontinued the North and South Open and replaced it with the North and South Senior Amateur.

Now Maurer, a former club professional, wanted to come full circle. It was time Pinehurst had another professional event.

"We're always talking about Pinehurst being the golf capital of the world, so you could have the 'World Championship' at Pinehurst," Maurer ventured.

It took some schmoozing with PGA Tour officials, but eventually Maurer sold Joe Dey, commissioner of the Tournament Players

Division of the PGA of America, on the idea of a "World Open" at Pinehurst—eight rounds over two weeks for the astronomical purse of half a million dollars and $100,000 to the winner. The dates were blocked for November 1973.

"If we do a first-class job, we'll earn a place somewhere down the road," Maurer said. "It could take ten years."

Fraser Smith was eight years old when his family moved to Pinehurst in 1946, and he spent his adolescent and teen years in Pinehurst before going off to the University of North Carolina and a northeastern newspaper career. He returned to Pinehurst early in the fall of 1973 to look under the hood of the new ownership operation, and his findings were published in a lengthy essay in *Sports Illustrated* the month before the World Open. The Tufts family, Smith observed, thought that professional events like the one Maurer was planning "over-shadowed their town and made the game secondary

TRUCKING ALONG WITH McLEAN

Malcom McLean grew up on a farm near Maxton, N.C., graduated from high school and went directly into business for himself, purchasing a used pick-up truck for $120 with savings from his gas-pumping job. He and two of his six siblings—sister Clara and brother Jim—then opened McLean Trucking Company, expanding their fleet and hauling crops from farm to market and empty tobacco barrels from market back to farm.

Some three decades later, McLean would return home to North Carolina and buy Pinehurst. He was the "bridge owner" in the 1970s between the past and present of Pinehurst.

Frustrated in 1937 by having to wait days at a New Jersey dock to unload his cargo of cotton onto a ship bound for Istanbul, McLean groused "there must be a better way" than loading a ship with cargo piece by piece. The idea fermented for two decades until McLean acted on his instincts in 1956—designing cargo containers that could be easily separated from the truck bed and then neatly stacked on a ship designed to haul hundreds of containers at a time. He bought a fleet of old tankers, converted them to cargo ships and was off on his next venture, one that would revolutionize the shipping industry.

Maxton native Malcom McLean on deck at a New York shipping harbor in the 1970s.

The eventual sale of Sea-Land Service Inc. to R.J. Reynolds in 1969 made the McLeans multimillionaires—the sale price was $531 million.

One of Malcom's sidelines in the late 1960s was the resort and residential development concern that he named the Diamondhead Corp. and that had projects under way in Mississippi, Alabama and Georgia. He was one of a number of potential suitors for the resort when the Tufts family looked to sell in 1970, and he eventually bought the resort on Dec. 31, 1970, for the price of $9.2 million.

The decade was a difficult one taken as a whole as Diamondhead attempted to transition from the conservative, highbrow stewardship of the Tufts family into a new era marked by golf becoming a game for the masses. Two of Diamondhead's early executives were well versed in golf, President Bill Maurer and Director of Golf Eddie Susalla, but the executive and management staff as a whole lacked the golf pedigree commensurate with the "St. Andrews of American Golf." At a planning meeting for the World Golf Hall of Fame that would open in September 1974, one executive mentioned a new inductee and said, "We're pleased to announce the first woman to the hall, Francis Ouimet."

McLean in later years regretted that the demands of running Sea-Land for his new bosses at RJR limited his hands-on influence in Pinehurst. As Diamondhead was losing the resort to the banks holding the company's loans in the early 1980s, McLean changed the name Diamondhead to the "Purcell Corporation"—Purcell being McLean's middle name.

"Malcom had a lot of old friends in Pinehurst who constantly berated him about the way Diamondhead was developing Pinehurst," says Marty McKenzie, who worked for both the Tufts family and Diamondhead in various capacities as a young man. "He changed the company name to try and rid himself of what he perceived to be a major black mark on what was otherwise a wonderful business career."

McLean died in 2001 at the age of eighty-seven, but the McLean connection extended for many years, however, as Clara McLean rented a suite of eight rooms in the East Wing of The Carolina from 1976, when she turned sixty-five, until 2008, when she bought a house in the Village of Pinehurst. She paid in-season rates for the rooms that were converted into a luxurious apartment. She died in 2010.

to the tournament."

"One served golf, they thought, not with the traveling circus of the tournament and its superstars but by their absence," Smith wrote. "The old Pinehurst approach was not an attempt to bring true altruism into resort management. It was the result of traditions that dictated certain rules: you made your money first and then you came to Pinehurst where gracious living was the primary occupation. Hard driving for bucks would have been seen as crass and disruptive, particularly if the owners of the town had done it.

"The Tufts family, owners of Pinehurst for three generations, represented that era in American and golf history in which the professional was thought of as a hustler with no credentials for entering the front door of a clubhouse. Beyond this—and, more important—professionals and their tournaments got in the way of Pinehurst's reason for being, the care and pampering of its guests. The Tufts family considered guests in their hotels as house guests. And they had more to offer than golf. Their Pinehurst stood for congeniality, exclusivity and immunity from all but the most benign forms of commercialism and politics. It was a tolerable system for a company town with benevolent owners who thought their reign would endure forever."

Maurer was stung out of the gate in his World Open venture when some high-profile members of the pro tour were cool to the idea. The incumbent U.S. Open champion (Johnny Miller), the British Open champion (Tom Weiskopf), the PGA Championship winner (Jack Nicklaus), the best player from Britain (Tony Jacklin) and one of the top gallery draws (Lee Trevino) all had reasons to be somewhere else that November when the World Open came to Pinehurst. Trevino said he couldn't "go anywhere for two weeks," Weiskopf planned to go elk hunting, and Nicklaus said he needed the window of time for rest and relaxation at home.

Maurer said he was "disheartened and bitter" that such prominent players chose not to support the tournament.

"I thought the players would gravitate toward the tournament," Maurer said. "I thought it would be good for pro golf, that it would mean even bigger and better tournaments. I've made a mistake in judgment. I can't understand it. This is their business. Is this good for the Tour?"

Pinehurst needed a second golf course for the event and hired

Robert Trent Jones to oversee a renovation of the No. 4 course. That, too, proved to be a controversial turn of events as Jones extended the course in length by more than seven hundred yards to a total of 6,903 and increased the par from 70 to 72. But Jones had neither the time nor budget to rebuild all of the greens to accept the longer approach shots now required (four new greens were constructed). His son, Rees, would return in 1983 to rebuild the greens, and the entire course was razed in 1999 in favor of a new Tom Fazio creation.

DeYoung traveled to Pinehurst in the 1960s with his parents, who were non-resident members of the club. DeYoung is of the same vintage as Bill Coore; both beam when remembering trips to Pinehurst where, for a pittance, they could play two or three rounds on summer days on No. 2.

"I came with a buddy in the summer of '65, stayed in an RV park down the road and played unlimited golf on No. 2 for ten dollars a day," DeYoung says.

"The thing I always remember my dad saying about No. 2 is that guys with fifteen to twenty-five handicaps would come down here and play their best rounds, because there are no holes where they'll make doubles or lose their ball," DeYoung says. "It's not like going to Sawgrass and having a couple of Xs on your card. Everyone can finish this one."

Several years later, DeYoung had just graduated from college and came to Pinehurst in the summer to help his parents finish the house they were building in the Village. He and his father spent a number of days the summer of 1970 helping the construction workers in the mornings and playing golf on No. 2 in the afternoons. As soon as the house was finished, DeYoung planned to go to Atlanta and find a job.

"Clyde Mangum was the club manager at the time and he told me they were looking to fill an opening on the golf staff," DeYoung says. "At first, it didn't sound like much.

"Then he said, 'You can play No. 2 for free every day after work.' I was on the payroll by the end of the week."

DeYoung never made it to Atlanta. He spent four years as an administrator on the Pinehurst tournament staff before moving on to a career with the Western Golf Association and then as an independent golf tournament promoter and administrator. He lives again in

Pinehurst, where for nearly twenty years he has run the Winternational Series of golf competitions for juniors. Sitting in the 91st Hole bar in the Pinehurst clubhouse one winter morning in 2011, DeYoung can nod toward a window on the south wall and see where his desk was located all those years ago.

"It never seemed to bother anyone in the sixties that the golf course was not particularly pretty," DeYoung says. "That would change. The new guys had different ideas."

Eddie Susalla was born in Michigan in 1923, turned pro at the age of sixteen, served in the Army in World War II and after the war settled into the golf business in California's Coachella Valley, the desert patch two hours east of Los Angeles that in the postwar days was morphing into a playground for Hollywood's rich and famous. Some credit a man named Merle Williams with popularizing the motorized golf cart in the early 1950s, but Susalla in other circles is considered the "father of the golf cart." Susalla, an assistant pro at Thunderbird Country Club in Rancho Mirage, got the idea from seeing a handicapped man in Long Beach wheeling down the sidewalk in a gas-powered mini-car called an Autoette. Susalla commissioned the manufacture of carts that seated two golfers and had "wings" on the side to hold golf bags; they were an instant hit among Thunderbird members.

Susalla was an inventor and innovator in many other areas as well. In 1956 he was one of the founding partners of Indian Wells Country Club (Desi Arnaz at the height of his *I Love Lucy* fame was another partner) and later a co-founder of La Costa Resort & Spa in nearby Carlsbad. He had the idea for what would become the Bob Hope Desert Classic and the Tournament of Champions on the pro golf tour. Susalla ran with big names in all of sports—from Arnold Palmer to Dodgers pitcher Don Drysdale; and with the big names in entertainment—Perry Como, Lawrence Welk, Frankie Avalon and the like. Marty McKenzie remembers helping Phil Rodgers unload his car at The Carolina bell stand at the 1972 Liggett & Myers tournament held at the Country Club of North Carolina and Rodgers asking, "Where's Eddie Susalla?" Years later, McKenzie and his wife Susan were visiting the Hope Classic and standing behind the eighteenth green when Palmer came through, spotted Susalla and gave him, McKenzie says, "one of those special smiles Arnold always had

This late 1980s watercolor from the late Vivien Weller captures the soothing spirit of the Village of Pinehurst—no matter the era.

Diamondhead executive Bill Maurer presides at World Golf Hall of Fame induction ceremonies in 1974. At left in yellow jacket is TV-radio commentator John Derr; on the other side of Maurer are (L-R) inductees Arnold Palmer, Jack Nicklaus, Gary Player and Gene Sarazen.

for people he loves."

So you have a man who came to Pinehurst from the California desert where all of the visual appeal was manufactured and the history book spanned all of two decades; who thought the golf cart was the finest invention since the gutta-percha replaced the feathery; and who came from a place where kinetic nightlife was as important as a day on the golf course. He brought with him associates with slick-back hair and lots of vowels in their names, guys like Sal and Bruno and Carmen and one nicknamed "Mad Dog." One long-time club member groused that with the new Diamondhead staff and the influx of "99ers"—golfers paying less than a hundred bucks for a weekend package—that "it was impossible to keep Vitalis and combs in the locker room." In hiring Susalla, Maurer incorrectly bet that Susalla's

skills and savvy in the California desert would translate to the North Carolina Sandhills.

"From where they came from, it's all about beauty," McKenzie says. "Eddie thought the sand and wire grass was ugly. That's why they changed it—not to improve the golf course but to make it look prettier. It just was never a good fit. Pinehurst was never California—thank God. They didn't understand that."

Joe Inman is a North Carolina born and bred golfer who, like Bill Coore, grew into adulthood in the 1950s and '60s with fond memories of long summer days playing golf in Pinehurst. The Greensboro native graduated to the PGA Tour and lamented the early 1980s malaise that had gripped the golf course and resort. The PGA Tour event that had been coming to Pinehurst since that 1973 World Open was on the brink of death because of poor dates and lack of sponsorship dollars. The resort itself was near bankruptcy, the result of Diamondhead's ill-fated stewardship.

"It makes me sad. To me, it's a tragedy," Inman said the week of the final Hall of Fame Classic in September 1982. "So many people here today don't know the *real* Pinehurst. They don't remember what it was like in the '50s and '60s, when there weren't any condominiums, when you could come out here with your caddie and not hear a sound, no golf carts, no nothing. It was the most beautiful place in the world … To a golfer who grew up in the Carolinas, that's what Pinehurst was. That's not what it is now."

DeYoung acknowledges that it's easy to blame Susalla for "ruining No. 2" by planting so much grass on a course that had developed its character over decades with its rough-hewn look.

"But you know what?" DeYoung muses. "Eddie was trying to make a buck for the people that hired him, and he probably wasn't too far wrong in what he did. Not for the purists, but for the everyday northerner, you know they want green grass. That's all they cared about. We were in business against Hilton Head and Myrtle Beach and people like that. We had to get northerners to stop here and play golf."

So fond was the new management of green and lush that all the fertilizer and water around the greens spawned a thicket of grass that made balls difficult at times to locate. DeYoung remembers the playoff in the 1975 World Open when it took several minutes to find a ball in rough around a greenside bunker on the sixteenth hole.

"The only way they found it was by Jack Nicklaus accidentally kicking it," DeYoung says. "That's how deep the rough was. I mean, you can't even fathom that right now."

DeYoung worked under tournament director Hubie Smith in

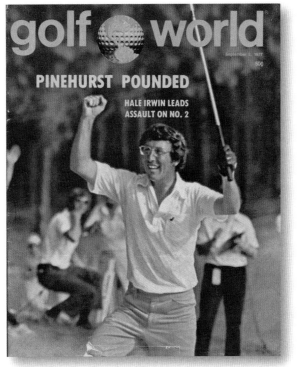

Hale Irwin celebrates on the cover of "Golf World" magazine following his victory in the 1977 Colgate Hall of Fame Classic at Pinehurst.

the inaugural World Open and remembers the sense of being overwhelmed. The tournament ran Thursday through Sunday, took two days off and continued Wednesday through Saturday. Temperatures were in the thirties during parts of two rounds the first week, with players wearing stocking caps and Gary Player making a run to the department store for long underwear.

"We had 240 players, two golf courses, four starting tees—people going to the wrong tee, cold weather—and we knew we were going to lose money going into it," DeYoung says today. "No television. It was unbelievable. We had the largest purse in the history of golf and we couldn't get Nicklaus, Trevino, Weiskopf or TV."

One attraction the World Open did have, however, was Ben Crenshaw. The twenty-one year-old had won two NCAA titles and shared a third at the University of Texas, finished first in Tour Qualifying School at The Dunes Club in Myrtle Beach and just won his first tournament as an official member of the Tour—the San Antonio Texas Open.

"The best cure for whatever ails the game was obvious to the loyal hundreds who followed the World Open," Dan Jenkins wrote in *Sports Illustrated*. "Ben Crenshaw had blondish, mod hair covering his ears, a campus-hero smile, the warmth and excitement of a young Arnold Palmer, the classic swing that is seen so rarely. He has it all. As Miller Barber said, 'He's the best that's come along since Nicklaus. He's gonna be the new gunner. I knew when I beat him that I'd done beat somebody.'"

Gibby Gilbert and Tom Watson, in his second year on Tour, posted course record 62s, Gilbert's coming in the first round and Watson's in the fifth. Then Crenshaw moved into contention with his 64 in round six, notching nine birdies and two bogeys. He vaulted from eighteen back to a tie for second as Watson careened to a 76 in the

THE ART OF HITTING IT SHORTER

Neckties, plus-fours and hickory-shafted clubs accent this Sandhills "throwback" golf competition held at Mid Pines Golf Club.

The hard and dense wood from hickory and persimmon trees has been shaved and whittled into bows, flutes, spoons, billiard cues, tool handles, drumsticks, skis and walking sticks over many centuries.

Golfers up through the 1920s knew hickory for the shafts in their clubs and persimmon for the heads of their driving clubs, but those materials gave way to technology as steel, titanium, graphite and other lighter and more malleable materials came to the fore. When the Taylor Made Company developed metal driver heads in the early 1980s, the company broached each corner of the Periodic Table of Elements by naming the clubs "Pittsburgh Persimmon."

Today a cadre of golf traditionalists cling to the old ways by playing pre-1935 clubs and trekking around vintage golf courses wearing plus-fours, argyle socks, tweed tams, button-down shirts and neckties. There are national championships for hickory golf played in Australia, Canada, England, France, Germany, Scotland, Sweden, Finland and the United States.

The genesis of the modern hickory golf movement traces to thirty-five acres of ancient farmland outside White Sulphur Springs, W.Va. A group of Scottish, English and American gentlemen in 1884 laid out nine golf holes on land owned by a Bostonian named Russell Montague, who had purchased land close to the area's renowned "healing springs." The course was later abandoned but was restored in 1994, and Oakhurst Golf Links—resplendent with its sand tees and 2,250 yards of fairways groomed by two dozen sheep—was the venue for the inaugural U.S. National Hickory Championship in 1998.

One of the participants was Jay Harris, at the time a dentist from High Point and, since 2004, the occupant of a home along the seventh hole of Pinehurst No. 2.

"Slowly but surely the interest in hickory golf has grown," Harris says. "Some of the people at that very first tournament have become very good friends. My day has come and gone as far as tournament golf. Playing hickories, I am not unhappy with bogeys. Before, if I made three bogeys in a row, I was really hot. Par for me in hickory golf is high 70s, so I have room for some bogeys."

As a teen and young adult, Harris played in the North and South Amateur at Pinehurst against the likes of Billy Joe Patton. Then he spent his working life fixing stuff, specifically his patients' molars, incisors, gums and other contents of the mouth. Now his hands are occupied with vises, sanders, saws, epoxy and solvents as he restores and repairs antique clubs.

"Working with my hands and fixing something has been a natural transition," he says.

The Hickory Nut is the retirement sideline Harris launched several years ago in his workshop to repair vintage clubs and supply rental sets to hickory tournament competitors nationwide.

"Most of us are older, we're tired of trying the next five hundred dollar driver," Harris says. "What you find out is, if you have good hickories, you can play anywhere from 5,300 yards to 6,100 with no problem. A lot of golf courses that were gems in their day, the young long hitters thumb their noses at today. Hickory golf brings the old, classic course back into play."

Donald Ross and other golf designers from the early 1900s would be smiling from their wooden boxes. Pinehurst courses Nos. 1 and 3, Mid Pines, Pine Needles and Southern Pines Golf Club are popular among the hickory gang in Moore County; there's an active group at Sedgefield in Greensboro, and in late May 2011 the Carolinas Hickory Golf Association conducted a one-day tournament at Hope Valley in Durham; the 2010 U.S. Hickory Open was held at Mimosa Hills in Morganton, and the 2011 competition was waged at French Lick, Ind.; all the above have that delightful patina of Ross's handiwork.

The challenge, the venues, the tradition, the camaraderie—many elements unite the avid hickory golfer.

"The game's too easy with modern clubs," says Randy Jensen of Omaha, Neb., a multiple winner of the U.S. National Hickory Championship. "You can hit the ball all over the clubface and still hit good shots. Playing with hickory is more of a challenge. It's more fun."

Rob Pilewski was head golf professional at Mid Pines in 2004 when he learned of the U.S. National Hickory Championship at Oakhurst and attended with the thought of drumming up some new business for the 1921 Ross layout that plays a perfect length for hickory golf from the member tees—6,114 yards. That led to Mid Pines hosting its own hickory tournament that fall, and the event was in its eighth year in November 2011. Pilewski is now head pro at Pinehurst No. 6 and has his own set of hickory clubs and participates periodically in hickory competitions.

"They're the neatest folks," he says of hickory devotees. "They're all traditionalists, they love the history of the sport and they enjoy each other's company."

The wooden shafts, tiny sweet spots and unforgiving club faces also encourage golfers to sharpen their games.

"You know that sting you feel in the winter if you hit the ball thin?" Pilewski asks. "That's what you get every time when you miss-hit a hickory. It forces you to slow your tempo down and focus on good contact. You have to learn different shots, too. You can't sail the ball in high with all the lofted wedges we have today. You've got to learn the run-up shot."

Hickory clubs are available from a variety of sources—from antique club dealers to Ebay to guys like Harris who attend hickory tournaments at various locales. It's easy to buy modern clubs via the mail as clubs are made to exacting specifications by machines. The quest for good hickory clubs is a sport in itself, as is tweaking them to an individual's feel and taste, such as breaking a soda bottle and using the sharp glass to whittle a shaft a few millimeters thinner for a bit more of a whippy feel.

"There's an art to finding good clubs," says Kelly Miller, proprietor of Pine Needles Golf Club in Southern Pines. "A lot of guys love the thrill of the hunt. They shop and trade and experiment until they get their set right."

The hickory golf movement is here to stay. Its connoisseurs are passionate. They march to a different beat and aren't looking for a better game through science. After all, as Miller muses, "Who wants to hit it shorter?"

wind and Gilbert ballooned to an 82.

"Crenshaw crashed onto the scene in the sixth round, shooting a seven-under 64 in a high, vicious wind on the architectural monument known as Pinehurst No. 2, and it was said that this round under those conditions was probably the best ever on a course that has felt the cleats of the game's finest players for fifty years," Jenkins wrote.

Crenshaw and Barber were tied for the tournament lead through thirteen holes in the final round, but Barber birdied fourteen and eighteen and Crenshaw bogeyed sixteen after a wild hook to provide the final chapter.

Thirty-seven years and two Masters titles later, Crenshaw can't help but look to the left of sixteen whenever he's touring the course with Bill Coore.

"I was trying to hit it five hundred yards and it went seventy yards left," he says with a smile. "Miller Barber and I have talked about that day a lot over the years. But boy, what an education that week was. I had never seen Pinehurst No. 2 before that tournament. The old guys, the writers like Charlie Price and Dick Taylor, told me about it. They said you've got to see it to believe it. And they were right about that."

Richard Tufts discontinued the North and South Open in 1952 to focus on competitions for senior amateurs. The golfers came in all shapes, sizes and wardrobes for the Men's North and South Senior Amateur in 1962 (above) and the Women's event in 1963 (opposite).

***

The greening of Pinehurst commenced with Eddie Susalla and Diamondhead in the 1970s. It continued with Pinehurst's storybook quest to land a U.S. Open, with modern maintenance practices and the USGA's effort to defend par amidst equipment revolutions at the turn of the 21st century. The evolution is the result of marketing, water, fertilizer, titanium club heads and urethane-covered golf balls.

"It is interesting how from the early nineties when Pinehurst No. 2 started hosting big events again, you can almost trace how it became greener and greener and prettier and prettier," says Southern Pines' Ran Morrissett, who runs the *GolfClubAtlas* website and is a partner in a Nova Scotia golf course. "And it is such a slippery slope when you host big events."

And the biggest event in the equation is, of course, the U.S. Open.

Pinehurst had been the site of one of golf's premier tournaments in the first half of the 20th century. The North and South Open ran from 1901-51 with Walter Hagen, Jock Hutchison, Macdonald Smith, Bobby Cruickshank, Horton Smith, Paul Runyan, Henry Picard, Ben Hogan, Sam Snead and Byron Nelson among its winners. It was the only tournament in the early days of the professional golf tour that wasn't a "championship" of anything but was nonetheless one of the most important and prestigious events of the year. The U.S. Open, British Open, PGA Championship, Western Open and British PGA Match Play were among other tournaments loosely considered of "major" status. And in a day when turning professional was not automatic for a quality player—after all, pros weren't even allowed in the clubhouse in many places—you can easily throw the U.S. and British Amateurs into the majors pot.

"The North and South had an immediate atmosphere of class and elegance," Dan Jenkins wrote in *Golf Digest* in 1990. "Dress for dinner, veranda stuff. In fact, the North and South was the Masters before there *was* a Masters (1934) and for many years before the Masters finally out-southerned the North and South."

Pinehurst owner Richard Tufts eventually sniffed at the churlish attitudes of many pros and their incessantly outstretched hands, and the club and tour officials jockeyed back and forth over the level of the North and South purse. The tour wanted more prize money while Tufts believed the room and board offered players at The Carolina should count in the equation. Tufts reached his limit in early 1952 and terminated the event, scheduling in its place a tournament for senior amateurs (which still runs today). For two decades, Pinehurst made no effort and had no interest in staging a professional golf event.

That changed when Diamondhead Corporation and its brash president, Bill Maurer, conceived the World Open in 1973 and later in the decade when its director of golf, Lou Miller, began courting USGA officials on the idea of an Open at Pinehurst. The prospects for an Open were slim, though, because one key USGA insider who knew No. 2 intimately from the 1950s was adamantly opposed to the idea.

P.J. Boatwright was a native South Carolinian and lived in the Village for four years in the 1950s while running the Carolinas Golf Association before moving to New York to the join the USGA staff under then-executive director Joe Dey. Boatwright later became executive director and then was executive director of rules and competitions. Those who heard him reminisce about his days in the Sandhills were struck by the contrasts of his reverence for the old ambience and his disdain for the new ownership.

"P.J. said, 'They've ruined it. They've just ruined it,'" recalled Grant Spaeth, USGA president in 1990-91. "He said the course had become such a contrast to way it was in the old days. He just didn't think it could ever be right for an Open."

"It was clear to me, P.J.'s most enjoyable time during his working life was when he was executive secretary of the Carolinas," says David Fay, the USGA's executive director from 1989-2010. "Things would get a little quiet in the afternoons and he'd play golf with Pete Tufts. He described the way it was, with fairways and sandy soil, pine straw, pine cones and wire grass. P.J. talked so lovingly about what No. 2 had been years ago. That picture he painted of No. 2 has always remained in my mind."

Boatwright's opinions marinated in Fay's memory bank as Fay rose up the USGA administrative ranks, taking over the executive director's post in 1989. Despite Boatwright's recalcitrant views (and Boatwright would no longer have a voice following his 1991 death at the hand of cancer), others in the USGA hierarchy joined Fay in thinking that an Open at Pinehurst had possibilities. Spaeth and Fay drove through Pinehurst on the way to Augusta and the Masters Tournament one year in the late-1980s, played No. 2 and thought the layout itself would provide an outstanding Open venue. Of course, there were the issues of the quality of the putting surfaces and the village infrastructure—could you find enough ticket buyers, sponsors, hotel rooms, restaurants and parking spots?

"We agreed: 'Can't we take a second look? How can we *not* go the extra mile to see if it will work here?'" Spaeth said.

Fay believed a U.S. Open at Pinehurst could be "Tracy-and-Hepburnesque, a match made in heaven."

"Early on in this process I thought Pinehurst No. 2 was one of great courses in the world," Fay says. "It's the United States' answer to St. Andrews. Opens are usually played in and around large metropolitan areas, but there are a couple of exceptions. It might be that arguably two of the most outstanding sites for the Open are played quite far away from these metropolitan areas—Shinnecock and Pebble Beach. You look at the pattern of the British Open, which is actually played *away* from metropolitan areas. My feeling was, if you can have an Open at Pebble Beach, if you can have an Open at Shinnecock Hills, you can have an Open at Pinehurst."

Fay reveled in the tradition and mystique of the golf course, the resort and the village. An avid baseball fan, Fay believed a visit to Pinehurst was like a trip to Wrigley Field or Fenway Park.

"How many times today do you hear some hot young star in any sport hear the name of a Hall of Fame player in his sport and say, 'Who was *he?*'" Fay muses. "When you get to Pinehurst, that changes. It's impossible not to get caught up in the great history. It's everywhere. It's where you look, it's in the air, it's in the turf, it's in the images on the walls, it's in the church bells. You can almost feel the ghosts coming out."

P.J. Boatwright in his signature button-down shirt, necktie and floppy hat. He lived for four years in Pinehurst in the mid-1950s.

Any significant competition in golf has two core components—inside the ropes and outside the ropes. Pinehurst and the vision of a U.S. Open had significant hurdles to leap on both counts.

Boatwright's concerns were founded primarily on the putting surfaces. The USGA's template for Open venues featured firm, lightning-quick greens. Given that the championship was conducted in mid-June, southern venues were essentially off the table given that

their greens were either Bermuda, which can get only so quick in the summertime, or Penncross bent, which required substantial application of water to keep them healthy in the hot weather.

Pinehurst and its No. 2 course were conceived as wintertime playgrounds and operated from September through May through the 1960s. A base of Bermuda grass overseeded with rye during the winter worked fine for many decades, providing the course with firm greens that needed little additional watering.

That changed in the 1970s. Diamondhead had owned Pinehurst for eighteen months in August 1972 and was moving the resort more toward a year-around operation with the installation of air conditioning throughout the resort. The Bermuda-and-rye structure was fine for the eight months the course was once open; it didn't do as well over twelve months, especially since it required two transition periods in the fall and spring. The consensus at the time was that Penncross bent provided a smoother year-around putting surface. Smoother, yes. Firmer, no, particularly since the bent grass of that era was not very heat tolerant in the summer and required careful watering.

Pinehurst officials had already changed the greens on courses 1, 3, 4 and 5 to bent and followed suit on No. 2 in August 1972. They considered rebuilding the greens' foundations to allow for better drainage of the additional water the bent would require, but with the PGA Club Professional Championship scheduled for October, there wasn't time. The maintenance staff merely killed the Bermuda and seeded bent that August.

The result was a course with pliant greens during July through September—exactly the time period that PGA Tour events were con-

The PGA Tour returned to Pinehurst for the 1991 and '92 Tour
Championships. Craig Stadler and Paul Azinger (insets) won the
events over competitors like Fred Couples and Davis Love III,
captured above leaving the eighteenth green.

The Pinehurst Golf Lad was depicted with his golf bag slung over his shoulder for this poster commemorating the 1999 U.S. Open at Pinehurst.

ducted on No. 2 from 1974-82. Granted, two of the lowest scores ever shot on No. 2 came during the month of November in cool conditions (the 62s by Gibby Gilbert and Tom Watson in the 1973 World Open), but the course was regularly poached in the 1970s by aggressive players able to fire at the flag, knowing their shots would check up quickly on the soft greens.

"Any ball that landed on the putting surface stayed right there," says Hale Irwin, who shot a 62 in 1977 and won the Colgate Hall of Fame Classic with a 264 total (fifteen and sixteen shots below the totals posted by Payne Stewart and Michael Campbell, respectively, in winning U.S. Opens more than two decades later). "It essentially took away the fear of missing a green and having those funny little chip shots. I don't remember having any of those shots that week."

"The bent was like a sponge in that summer heat," adds Miller, the resort's director of golf from 1976-80.

Miller led the move in 1979 to return the greens to the Bermuda surfaces and hopefully restore the firmness that was always part of Ross's original design philosophy. But that wasn't a panacea. Resort guests complained about the bumpiness of the greens during the transition seasons, and nearly all southern resort courses were moving toward the smoother bent greens. Yet another conversion in 1987 from Bermuda to bent was haunted by imperfections in the original sod that left inconsistencies in the texture of the bent grass, and the root system of the sod never took hold as expected.

By the early 1990s, Pinehurst had successfully hosted two season-ending Tour Championships on the PGA Tour (1991 and '92), and Fay and USGA officers and staff had overcome their "outside-the-ropes" concerns about staging their marquee event in a remote village. Resort President Pat Corso and his staff argued that Pinehurst was not, in fact, "in the middle of nowhere," but was actually in "the middle of everywhere"—pointing to the vibrant Piedmont Crescent region of North Carolina that ran from Charlotte to Raleigh and had more than six million citizens in its midst within a two-hour drive of Pinehurst.

The USGA announced in June 1993 that it was awarding the Open to Pinehurst for 1999, the caveat being that USGA agronomists would work with Pinehurst staff in determining the best new strain of bent for another greens conversion. They decided on Penn G-2, a

grass developed at Penn State University that promised a hearty blade with a deep root structure. It could be close-cropped for fast putting speeds but would need only modest amounts of water, even in the hottest summer months. The greens were rebuilt in 1996 and held up well for the 1999 Open, won by Payne Stewart with a 1-under-par score of 279.

The 1999 event was a success on every level—ticket sales, corporate sponsorship, logistics, course playability and overall atmosphere. Within a year, the USGA had awarded Pinehurst the 2005 Open.

The 2005 championship proved a perfect complement to the 1999 event given the contrasting menus of conditions from the first to the second. The week of the 1999 event was unseasonably cool. A heavy shower hit the afternoon before the tournament opened, and more rain fell Thursday morning. The final round on Sunday was played in near-British conditions—fog, mist, intermittent showers. The 2005 Open week was hot and sunny with temperatures in the 90s, and not one shot all week was affected by rain.

"If it doesn't rain, you can't stop the ball on the greens," said Vijay Singh before the 2005 championship began. "I've been hitting wedges and it's not spinning back. It's taking one big hop and stopping. The rough is a lot harder than it was the last time I played here. You can get the best of lies, and you can move it 150 yards, max."

The scores were remarkably consistent from the 1999 Open to 2005.

The average score was 74.55 in 1999. The winner finished at one-under and his was the only 72-hole total under-par. Twenty-eight players shot rounds under-par through four rounds. The cut was at seven-over.

The average score six years later was 74.16. The winner was even-par. Twenty-eight players bested par. The cut was at eight-over.

Keeping the scores low in 2005 was not without a price, however. Pinehurst officials and the USGA had solved the vexing issue of getting firm greens in June and preserving one element of No. 2's personality. It lost another essential characteristic, though, with all the grass everywhere else.

***

A ritual throughout 2010 when either Bill Coore or Ben Crenshaw comes to Pinehurst is dinner at Raffaele's, an Italian restaurant in Southern Pines that has been a favorite of Pinehurst executive Don Padgett II since moving to town in 2004. Owned and operated for three decades with hands-on care and attention by Raffaele Grionda, the restaurant offers excellent pasta, pizza and Parmesan in a comfortable environment.

"I could eat here three or four times a week, everything's good," Padgett says. "My dad used to get the veal Marsala with mushrooms. Raffaele's in here every night, making sure people are well fed and looked after properly. My wife and I come on Fridays a lot, eat pizza and hang out. It's a comfort zone for us. It's like *Cheers*."

Usually on the first day Bill or Ben have spent on the golf course, Padgett reserves a table, invites the architect(s) and design associate Toby Cobb as well as several key Pinehurst staff members to dinner. Padgett sits at the head of the table, engineering the deployment of large platters of brochette, chicken wings and oysters around the table before the main courses are served. Everyone's stuffed by the time the last strand of spaghetti or crumb of pizza is consumed. Padgett is quick to pay the bill and make sure everyone's on their way at a reasonable hour.

"Some people hire Ben and Bill and think they've got them all night drinking wine and telling stories," Padgett says. "I think it's the proper thing to do to feed them a good meal and talk about the project. But we're gone by eight o'clock."

For nearly a quarter of a century, a member of the Padgett family has held a key executive role at Pinehurst. Don Padgett Sr. was director of golf from 1987 until his retirement in 2002, and Padgett II has been president and chief operating officer since 2004.

Padgett II actually was approached in 1987 about the job his father eventually took.

He had been at Firestone Golf & Country Club in Akron, Ohio, since 1980, first as director of golf and then adding the responsibility of general manager. One of the first tasks for Pat Corso upon taking the job as new president and CEO at Pinehurst in 1987 was to hire a director of golf. Corso and Padgett were fellow Indiana natives, and Corso knew Padgett had played the PGA Tour for three years in the mid-1970s—his highlight being a 66 in the third round of the 1977 U.S. Open—and was well-connected in golf competitive and admin-

istrative circles. That was the kind of man Corso needed as he sought to restore Pinehurst to its proper place in golf circles.

"Pat, it sounds like you want my *dad*," Padgett said of his father, a former president of the PGA of America and long-time Indiana club pro. "He'd be perfect for the job."

So Corso phoned Padgett Sr., at the moment just beginning a new job at one of the Phoenix area's top new golf clubs. The position appealed to Padgett, sixty-two, who was told by Corso that he had one job responsibility: "Restore Pinehurst to its proper place in the game of golf and bring championship play back to Pinehurst."

Over the next decade and a half, Padgett Sr. helped shepherd Pinehurst to landing and/or successfully staging two U.S. Opens, two PGA Tour Championships, a Senior Open, a U.S. Amateur and a U.S. Women's Amateur.

"We needed a lot of things with that hire, but most of all, we needed a mentor," Corso says. "We needed a mentor for a very young staff. And I needed a mentor. Believe me, that's exactly what we got."

Through the 1990s, Padgett II settled into the successful management of one of ClubCorp's top properties and one of its most visible through Firestone's annual hosting of the PGA Tour's World Golf Championship on the Robert Trent Jones-designed South Course. When architect Tom Fazio completed his new design at Firestone in 2002 on ground previously occupied by the West Course, Padgett believed his career had reached a plateau.

"I had been at Firestone for twenty-five years, and by then there was not one single thing conceptually that I wanted to do there," Padgett says. "I was nearly fifty-five. The next ten years looked to be pretty boring. It was a good time to leave."

Padgett knew that ClubCorp owner Robert Dedman Jr. and Rich Beckert, the company's executive vice president for the resorts division, were looking in the spring of 2004 for a replacement for Corso, who left Pinehurst to launch a consulting firm. At first Padgett thought their search universe was limited to hotel executives, so Padgett didn't give the position much thought. Then he learned a potential candidate was the general manager at a prestigious Eastern country club that was a regular host for the U.S. Open.

"I told Rich that if the new guy didn't have to be a pure hotel guy,

I'd be interested," Padgett says.

Padgett was a comfortable fit for the Dallas home office and for Pinehurst on a variety of levels—from his familiarity with the village and resort through visits to his parents and the fact both Pinehurst and Firestone were top-rung ClubCorp properties. Several weeks later, Padgett met with Dedman and Beckert in Dallas.

"Both assumed I was so comfortable at Firestone I'd never want to leave," Padgett says. "They both asked, 'Are you *sure* you want this job?' I told them I was."

Padgett was hired in May 2004 and assumed his new position in July. The machine working toward the 2005 U.S. Open was in smooth operation at that point—both inside and outside the ropes—so Padgett's job the first year was essentially to get out of the way and let everyone do the jobs they had handled so well in 1999. But when the event came and left, Padgett continued doing what his father had done so well—observing, strolling, asking questions, quietly processing inputs from a variety of angles and taking action if and when necessary.

"It took a while for my dad to figure Pinehurst out," Padgett says one night at Raffaele's over a steaming bowl of spaghetti. "It did for me as well. He used to say he didn't care much for history because he was always looking forward. But the more time you spend here, the more you understand how important that history is in everything we do. You have to be here a while before you truly appreciate that."

Given that resort guests playing No. 2 want to see the course set

Don Padgett Sr. as a club professional in Indiana early in his career (above); in Pinehurst posing with The Putter Boy shortly before his retirement in 2002 (L).

up as closely as possible to Open conditions (minus, perhaps, the lightning quick green speeds) and that the U.S. Amateur was coming in 2008, Padgett saw no reason to change the fairway mowing patterns or otherwise tinker with the course set-up. But one by one, dominos were falling as the first decade of the 21st century passed.

A CENTURY OF THREADS

Ben Hogan wore a woven collared shirt and a necktie the week he won the 1940 North and South Open at Pinehurst.

Johnny Miller sported plaid polyester slacks, a white belt and a wide-collared shirt when he won the World Open in 1974.

And Payne Stewart collected the 1999 U.S. Open on No. 2 wearing his ubiquitous plus-fours and a rain jacket *sans* the sleeves—he cut them off with a pair of scissors that morning.

"It's fascinating to me to look at all the photos on the hallways at Pinehurst and the clothes they were wearing," says Chris Knott, founder of the Raleigh-based Peter Millar apparel manufacturer. "You wonder how they could swing the club in those restrictive clothes.

"Today what's neat is to walk onto the first tee on a cold day and see a guy in a polyester, tight-fitting mock next to his body, a merino or cashmere sweater over that and then a sleeveless piece of outerwear that's built to repel water. You can stay warm and dry on a thirty-five degree day but still be stylish. That's the best of the old world and today's high-tech."

When Danny Lee won the 2008 U.S. Amateur at Pinehurst, he sported the look popularized by all the twenty-somethings on the pro golf tour like Camilo Villegas and Anthony Kim—the "Full Cleveland" look with big buckles, white belts, white shoes, form-fitting garments and bright colors. That was all the rage in the 1970s and has returned today, accented by the second coming of polyester.

The prevalent trend *du jour* is the return of polyester in the form of "performance fabrics"—names like Climalite, Dri-FIT and CoolMax filling the shelves and hangers of golf shops hither and yon.

"It's such a world market now," says Knott, who founded Peter Millar in 2001 and has seen the company thrive over a decade in selling cashmere sweaters and brightly colored golf, leisure and business attire. "What's acceptable now is amazing. If you told me five years ago you could go to super high-end clubs and their best members would be wearing all-polyester shirts, I've had said no way. But it's happening everywhere, and it's great."

Adds Stephen Cryan, director of retail operations at Pinehurst: "Today you might ask a guy if he has any polyester shirts. He'd say no, but he probably does. This isn't your father's polyester."

Cryan points toward a stack of polyester shirts with the Pinehurst Putter Boy and the Nike swoosh.

"Dry-FIT is a hundred percent polyester," he says. "The reason a majority of people like this fabric is its easy care. You throw it in the washer, put it on a hanger or dry it a few minutes and you're good to go. It doesn't need much ironing—if any ironing."

Yet there will always be a place for the golden age elegance of natural fibers like cashmere and wool. Chris Dalrymple, proprietor of the Gentlemen's Corner in the Village of Pinehurst, points to a framed black-and-white photo of Jack Nicklaus and Arnold Palmer hanging on his store wall, both of them in cashmere sweaters on a dark day at the British Open.

"I think golf was meant to be played in a cashmere sweater," Dalrymple says. "It feels so good. I've heard stories about when cashmere was so cheap, guys would buy an extra one at the British Open, cut the arms out and wear it on their legs, under their pants, to keep warm.

Early golfers in Great Britain and then in the States wore knickers, heavy tweed jackets, starched collars and neckties—no wonder their swings were compact and powered with the wrists and hands. By the 1920s, jackets were less common, and many golfers favored cardigan sweaters over their white shirts and neckties or bow ties. Golf attire took a more casual direction following World War II; players were tired of cutting their neckties off after they knotted up with perspiration, and the game was being played not just on the windswept links of Scotland but amid the palm trees of South Florida. The knit tennis shirt popularized by Rene Lacoste featuring a tiny crocodile on the chest found its way onto the course in the 1950s, and lighter-weight slacks of varying colors replaced the drab flannel slacks worn by an earlier generation.

Golf attire in the 1930s featured neckties, heavy sweaters and plus-four trousers; Danny Lee was cool and lithe in the 2008 U.S. Amateur in his trim, athletic threads.

Fashion designers apparently ingested their share of LSD and other hallucinogenics during the 1970s, and their bad taste certainly infected the golf world. The crescendo of tacky threads reached its nadir with the 1980 movie *Caddyshack*, as actors Ted Knight and Rodney Dangerfield strutted the fairways of Bushwood Country Club attired in neon duds with patterns banging one another with sledgehammers. At least someone like Gary Player had the good taste to find a signature style and stick with it—black on black.

The 1980s evolved with new superstar Greg Norman dashing down the fairways in his signature "Shark" line of clothes with bold prints and wide-brimmed straw hats. Polyester and Pickering were hauled off to Goodwill, and cotton found its bull market along with metal drivers. Fred Couples set the standard as the 1990s evolved with his

khaki trousers and oversized Ashworth shirts. Payne Stewart inked a deal with the NFL and for a period in the early 1990s wore plus-fours and his Kangol-style cap in the colors of pro football teams. The idea of a refrigerator company like Amana paying players to display its logo on hats expanded as corporate sponsors found advertising space on every chest, sleeve, cap and visor.

Today you can find styles all over the map—straight-laced with tan pants and white shirts or Euro-chic with carnival colors, vented trousers and mock-turtle collars. The looks are trim and athletic and reflect the time golfers spend today in the fitness trailer. Modern golf is a game of grip-and-rip, bomb-and-gouge. No way Danny Lee could have cut the corner and driven the green of the par-four seventh at Pinehurst No. 2 wearing a tie and long-sleeve shirt.

Padgett was struck the week of the 2005 Open by how much the buzz about the golf course seemed to have quieted from six years earlier.

"The difference between '99 and '05 was amazing," Padgett says. "So much of what you read in '99 was how great the golf course was. Tom Watson came out of the press room the first day and I said, 'Tom, how'd you do today?' He said, 'I shot 75, but man, the golf course was just great.' When these guys shoot 75, they are *hot*. They're not going to tell you how great the course was, that it was their fault for not taking advantage of their opportunities. That stuck in my mind.

"But in '05, you did not hear that."

It was irksome to watch as No. 2 slipped in the annual rankings of America's 100 Greatest Golf Courses as compiled by *Golf Digest* and to read salty remarks directed toward No. 2 in certain enclaves of thoughtful architecture discussion.

No. 2 was listed by *Golf Digest* as ninth greatest from 1995 through 2001, but when the 2005-06 list was published in May 2005, just a month prior to

A team of mowers coifs the fifth fairway at daybreak during the 2005 U.S. Open; there will be no rough to mow when the Open returns in 2014.

the 2005 Open, the course slipped to No. 14. It fell to No. 19 in 2007 and No. 32 in 2009. Though Padgett and fellow Pinehurst officials knew the rankings could be capricious, political and subject to the whims of individual raters, it was nonetheless unwanted publicity for the course to fall from the Top 10.

Pinehurst's John Dempsey, a member of the rating panel of *GOLF* Magazine, was asked in the spring of 2009 for his perspective on No. 2's slide.

"I think part of what has happened with No. 2 is a reflection of tastes today," Dempsey said. "Take a baseball game, for example. I go to a lot of baseball games. Used to be between innings, everything was quiet, except for maybe the old lady playing the organ. Now some

hot babe is on top of the dugout giving away T-shirts. Every second is accounted for. Our need for sensory activation is acute. Go to any sporting event today and everything is loud and boisterous and in-your-face. No. 2 is not that way. It never has been and never will be. And it shouldn't. But there are certainly a lot of golf courses today with more bells and whistles than No. 2. That has an effect in the minds of some panelists, I'm sure."

The course had long been a favorite of golf architect Tom Doak, garnering ten stars from Doak in his 1996 book, *The Confidential Guide to Golf Courses*. Doak wrote that No. 2 was Donald Ross's masterpiece "and a certifiable work of genius." He lauded the green complexes and said: "It amazes me that a style so brilliant has never been copied or emulated by another designer, and one of these days I'm going to try and imitate Pinehurst No. 2 myself, just to see if it can be done." The photograph used in Doak's book to illustrate the passage was of the ninth hole and showed a foreground of pine straw and wire grass and a thin strip of grass through the middle for walking from tee to green. Within a decade, that very same view showed nothing but lush Bermuda grass between tee and green.

A couple of years after the 2005 Open, Doak was traveling the East Coast with an intern at his golf architecture firm, Renaissance Golf Design, and visited Pinehurst. He was disappointed in the look of No. 2 and said so on the message board of *GolfClubAtlas.com*. Among the comments he made was that No. 2 looked "like an aged relative with dementia. It was sad." Pinehurst marketing director Tom Pashley printed out the entire thread of the conversation and passed it along to Padgett and others on the management team.

"I first saw No. 2 in the early 1970s," Doak elaborates in 2011. "I was ten or twelve and was visiting with my parents. I've seen it at

PRELUDE IN PINEHURST

As the name Hank Haney rose up *The New York Times* best-seller list in the spring of 2012 for his book *The Big Miss*, some still around Pinehurst thought back thirty years ago to when Haney spent his days on the practice tee at Pinehurst Resort & Country Club, teaching swing plane to guests and members and running the resort's golf schools.

"Hank walked into one of the first staff meetings and said, 'I'm going to be the best teacher you've ever had here,'" remembers Rich Wainwright, an assistant pro at the time now on the Pinehurst executive staff. "He had plenty of confidence. And he was good. He could back it up."

Haney was twenty-five years old and working his way up the ladder on the John Jacobs Golf Schools staff when he came to Pinehurst for a school in 1980. He made the acquaintance of Pinehurst Director of Golf Mike Sanders, who soon offered him a job as the resort's lead instructor.

"It was my first opportunity to do things my own way," Haney says. "What an opportunity for a young kid."

Haney was in his office late on the September Friday afternoon of the 1982 Hall of Fame Classic when Ken Crow, another young member of the golf staff, said there was a struggling golfer out on the range. The player had missed the cut and was totally lost with his golf swing; he was desperate for some help.

Haney walked outside and was surprised to find Mark O'Meara, the 1979 U.S. Amateur champion. Haney watched O'Meara hit balls, took him inside for a talk and outlined a program to fix O'Meara's swing. Something inside told O'Meara that Haney knew what he was talking about. Within two years, O'Meara won almost half a million dollars and was No. 2 on the tour money list. He won the Masters and British Open in 1998 with Haney in the gallery.

"This is where it all started," Haney said at the 2005 U.S. Open at Pinehurst. "I owe a lot to this place. The three years I spent in Pinehurst were probably the most instrumental of my career."

Haney moved to Texas in 1984 and later opened the Hank Haney Golf Ranch outside Dallas. His stature in the golf instruction business grew, and in 2004 Tiger Woods asked if Haney would become his coach.

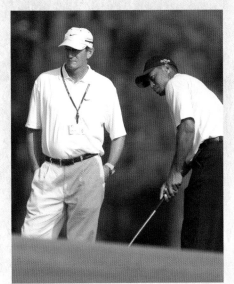

Hank Haney and Tiger Woods on practice green at Pinehurst for 2005 U.S. Open.

The six years Haney spent working with Woods were the subject of *The Big Miss*, ghosted by noted golf writer Jaime Diaz, a long-time *Golf Digest/Golf World* staffer who lives outside Southern Pines. The book was lauded by some for the fascinating glimpse it offers into Woods' world and the tensions and pressures of performing at the top echelon of the golf universe. It's been panned by others for violating some unwritten code of silence that the inner workings of athletes' lives should remain private—not that Jim Bouton and Jerry Kramer didn't begin the genre four decades ago with *Ball Four* and *Instant Replay*.

Haney had a front-row seat for six years to one of golf's finest talents. He simply wanted to preserve for posterity the experience.

"When you're in a position to observe greatness like I was for six years, you're asked about it every day," Haney says. "I wanted to share it. These are Tiger's memories. They are my memories, too. I wanted to talk about it, I wanted to write about it. I'm not the first coach or manager who's ever written a book. I wanted to write about what makes Tiger so great, how he is as a person and what contributes to him being such an incredible golfer."

various times over forty years. It's always been one of my favorite golf courses. What made it cool was a bunch of little stuff, little ridges, touches of wire grass here and there. The strategy of the fairways stood out. There used to be places on the golf course where the fairway would widen out behind a bunker and you'd try to get way over in the left corner of the fairway to get at a pin on the right side of the green.

"On my last trip, it seemed like all of that had gone away. They were narrowing it up for major championships and getting the grass to grow nice and thick. All the texture and angles were gone. That's what made the golf course—all the subtleties. I said that if I were to rate it again, I'd give it a seven or eight—but not a ten."

One of the final straws in Padgett's thinking was a round on No. 2 with Lanny Wadkins on Father's Day, 2008. Wadkins was a long-time devotee of Pinehurst, harkening to his days as a junior golfer in Richmond when Willow Oaks Country Club pro George Bird would chauffeur a group of boys to the Donald Ross Junior Championship in December. His memory bank grew during his days at Wake Forest and playing in the North and South Amateur in the 1960s. Wadkins's perspective on the course was so deep that he was invited by the PGA Tour to attend a press day in the summer of 1991 to promote the PGA Tour Championship, scheduled for No. 2 that October.

"I could hang around Harbour Town and Augusta National and Seminole and Pinehurst for as many days as possible and play all day long and never get bored," Wadkins said. "There's something about those courses that invigorates you and makes you want to get out there and play."

Wadkins's son Travis had just completed his second year on the Wake Forest golf team in June 2008, and Wadkins was in the area and set up a game with Travis. Wadkins and Padgett knew one another from their days on the PGA Tour in the early 1970s, so Wadkins asked Padgett to join them.

"Padge, I can't comprehend what's been done to this golf course," Wadkins said, looking at all the uniformity of the grass surfaces.

"When did all this take place?"

Padgett shakes his head remembering Wadkins's comments.

"I said, 'Wow,' and I started to get the conviction that this had gotten out of hand," he says.

Still, Padgett's growing suspicion that it was time to roll back the clock on No. 2 would have gone for naught if those in charge of the U.S. Open had not blessed the idea as well. After all, the biggest push toward the narrow fairways and thick rough had come from the USGA itself at the turn of the 20th century. Tom Meeks, the USGA official in charge of course set-up at the time, asked Pinehurst to install some four hundred new sprinkler heads in the roughs to ensure a sharp poke in the eye to anyone straying from the narrow fairways.

"If you ask, 'What happened to the golf course?' the answer would be, the golf ball," Padgett says. "The '99 Open was the last one before the new Pro V1 and Pro VX balls came out. After that, everyone was hitting the ball twenty or thirty yards longer. Tom Meeks was doing what he thought needed to be done—grow the rough to fight the longer ball."

The 1999 Open was the last before solid-core, multi-layer golf balls and oversize titanium-faced drivers were used by nearly the entire field. Most of the driver head sizes in 1999 were 260cc; six years later, most players carried drivers with heads at least 400cc. Seventy-three percent of the drivers were titanium in 1999; all were in 2005. Eighty-five percent of the players used wound balls in 1999; hardly any did in 2005. John Daly led the field in driving distance in 1999 at 286.3 yards; six years later, three quarters of the players who made the cut matched that number. The field's driving average in 2005 was 292 yards—*thirty-two yards* more on average than 1999.

"It's not the club or the ball," Frank Thomas, an equipment expert and former USGA official, told *Golf World's* Bill Fields in 2005. "It's a combination of the two. The ball and club are working together to optimize launch conditions. There is a synergy, where one and one makes three."

Meeks retired following the 2005 Open and was replaced by Mike Davis, who would prove more open to letting a course's native personality shine through and not simply boilerplate an age-old set-up template. It turns out that fellow USGA officials David Fay (the executive director) and Jim Hyler (vice president at the time, later to become president) joined Davis in coming to the conclusion that there was something missing at Pinehurst as they were preparing for and conducting the 2008 U.S. Amateur on No. 2. Padgett and the USGA brass bandied ideas about, found they had similar views, and the concept came to a concrete plan of action during a meeting at the 2009 Open at Bethpage with resort owner Bob Dedman Jr., Padgett and several USGA officials. Everyone was on board at that time, and the next move was to approach Coore & Crenshaw.

"It took a while to have any conviction," Padgett says. "After a while, you start to get validation, validation, validation, then you realize, 'This is a pretty solid concept.' From there the project never lost any momentum."

That validation came from a number of sources, among them Fay, who had never forgotten what P.J. Boatwright used to say about Pinehurst No. 2.

"I thought it would be a bold stroke to attempt to take Pinehurst No. 2 back to the way it looked for all its glory days—*after* sand greens, that is, we don't want to go quite that far," Fay said in November 2010, just six weeks before announcing his retirement from the USGA. "It would be much the same as Oakmont showed its boldness by pulling out all those Christmas trees planted in the 1950s."

The architects realized in the planning stages that less rough *could* make for lower scores. But Fay, Hyler and Davis agreed that a sympathetic restoration project engineered by Coore & Crenshaw and a return to the true character of Ross's design trumped all issues of scores.

"Mike, it's possible you could get some rain and the golf course might not be as hard and fast as you'd like it," Coore said before he and Crenshaw would commit. "If that happened and nine- or ten-under won the Open, would it bother you? Would that be an issue?"

"No," Davis said. "As long as the golf course plays true to its character, plays the way it was intended to play, then the best player would have won that week."

That was an instrumental threshold to cross in getting Coore &

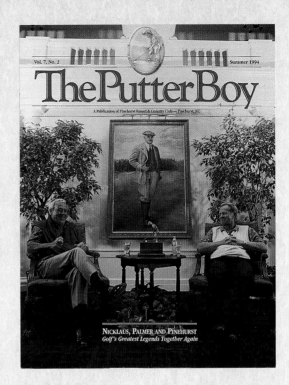

Arnie and Jack in Pinehurst

L ong-time rivals Arnold Palmer and Jack Nicklaus were jovial and relaxed in April 1994 when they visited Pinehurst to play No. 2 in a made-for-TV match as part of a modern incarnation of the old *Shell Wonderful World of Golf* series. Nicklaus shot 67 and Palmer 74 in the competition that was secondary to seeing two of golf's all-time greats on stage on No. 2. "Jack and I haven't always agreed over everything, but I think we've found one common ground here," Palmer said. "I agree with him that No. 2 has been one of the greatest golf courses I've ever had the opportunity to play. And I go back to when he was wearing three-quarters pants when I first came here. That would have been 1947."

Robert Dedman Sr. follows the flight of his tee shot during a pro-am in the early 1990s; below he and son Robert Jr. stand behind Payne Stewart during the trophy presentation ceremony following the 1999 Open. A statue of Dedman stands today alongside those of Donald Ross, Richard Tufts and Stewart beside the eighteenth green.

THE GOLDEN AGE OF PINEHURST

Crenshaw to sign on to the project. Padgett admits that had they turned the job down, he's not sure who the next choice would have been. Fay believed from the outset that they were the ideal team for the project.

"Coore and Crenshaw are great tailors," Fay says. "A suit by those guys is never 'off-the-rack.' It's original stuff, it fits perfectly, every stitch is in exactly the right place. Their courses are ones you enjoy and you look forward to playing."

Padgett knew Crenshaw from their days on the PGA Tour in the mid-1970s (both were in the field when No. 2 was host to the 1973 World Open), but he'd never met Coore until August 2009, when Coore was in Pinehurst working on Dormie Club. They discussed the concept over the fall of 2009, then reached a green light just as 2010 dawned. It was pure coincidence that the project evolved as the United States was in the early stages of digging out from the Great Recession of 2008-09 and, if a success, could provide the resort with a valuable buzz in a beleaguered golf industry.

"This was never about being a business decision," Padgett says. "It was about restoring No. 2 to the tradition and concepts of Donald Ross. Will we have business benefit from it? Yes. But never did anyone run a pro forma on the money we'd spend and the money we'd get back. There was never one conversation about that between me and the CFO or me and the owner—at all.

"I feel good about the fact if the golf course plays out the way I think it will, it will set Pinehurst up for the future. It will put No. 2 back to where it was. If I can be a small part of that, it's pretty gratifying."

***

Pinehurst Resort & Country Club was losing $1 million a year in the early 1980s under control of the syndicate of banks that had seized the property from its delinquent owner, the Diamondhead Corporation. Employees exhaled when the bank deemed their paychecks good. A butcher fell through a rotting floor in the kitchen at The Carolina. On rainy days, buckets were deployed in public areas of the careworn building to snag the raindrops.

A new suitor, a Texan named Robert Dedman Sr., saw an opportunity.

"Partner, I think this place is worth saving," Dedman told an associate with his Dallas-based company, Club Corporation of America, during his 1984 due diligence. "This is one of those places you can't duplicate—it's kind of like buying the St. Andrews of America."

A dozen years later, Dedman had already spent a sizeable chunk of the $100 million he would pour into Pinehurst over nearly two decades—remodeling the entire resort, building a new meeting facility, hiring Tom Fazio to design course No. 8 and being granted by the USGA the privilege of hosting the 1999 U.S. Open on the No. 2 course. He talked often about resurrecting a "fallen angel."

"Robert loved golf and took a lot of pride in owning No. 2," says Pat Corso, who directed the resort as president and chief executive officer from 1987 until early 2004. "The pride he had at the beginning remained at the end. He was passionate about his ownership of Pinehurst. Guys like Robert usually caution themselves not to get too emotional about their assets. But he was emotional about this place."

"Pinehurst was the love of his life," adds Beth Kocher, Pinehurst's executive vice president for more than two decades and one of Dedman's first staff postings at Pinehurst upon his purchase of the property in 1984. "From the day he first saw Pinehurst, he wanted it. He said we were just caretakers, we were just stewards passing through and had an obligation to maintain it."

Dedman was the quintessential rags-to-riches story—childhood in rural Arkansas, where his family of six existed in two bedrooms with no electricity or running water; high school in Dallas, where he and his brother moved to live with an aunt; voracious appetite developed at an early age to learn and work and guarantee a better life than his parents knew. He began his working life as a lawyer but quickly realized the path to true wealth came through creating a product and finding a receptive market. He did so by expanding access to a country club from the top one percent of the 1950s population to the top ten percent—parlaying the postwar economic boom and the growing popularity of golf spawned in part by President Dwight Eisenhower and later by Arnold Palmer. Club Corporation of America began with Brookhaven Country Club in Dallas in 1957 and by 1975 had grown to fifty clubs, including its most recent purchase of Inverrary Country Club in Lauderhill, Fla., the site of a PGA Tour event.

Robert Dedman Jr. (second from right) joins Mike Davis and Jim Hyler of the USGA (left) and architect Bill Coore (right) around the Putter Boy statue outside the Pinehurst clubhouse.

Dedman spent $15 million to buy Pinehurst in 1984, overcoming objections from some advisors that the resort business was a different animal altogether than running clubs. "Partner, this is just a country club with rooms," Dedman said. The company that evolved into ClubCorp International would eventually own and operate more than two hundred clubs and have assets of more than $1.6 billion at the turn of the 21st century.

The Dedman family spent many Thanksgivings at Pinehurst, and Senior's deep feelings for the resort were evident to all. "He loved the feeling you get standing on the first tee, he loved walking up the eighteenth fairway," Bob Dedman Jr. says. "He loved everything about the experience."

Dedman Sr. died in August 2002 and four years later his family sold its seventy percent interest in ClubCorp. The family did, however, keep the crown jewel, Pinehurst.

"There was an emotional component to keeping Pinehurst—I think we were dealing with both our heart and our head," Bob Jr. is saying one morning in September 2010. "Pinehurst is a magical experience. It confirms why you play the game of golf. Keeping Pinehurst gave us the opportunity to build on my father's legacy, to preserve and enhance a special place in the world of golf."

Bob worked as a teenager in the tennis and golf shops at Brookhaven, then earned a degree in economics from the University of Texas in 1979, a masters in business a year later and law degree from Southern Methodist in 1984. He spent three years in mergers and acquisitions with Salomon Brothers in New York, then returned to Dallas to join his father in 1987. Bob became ClubCorp president and COO in 1989 and CEO in 1998.

Since the 2006 sale of the rest of ClubCorp's assets to KSL Capital Partners, Dedman Jr. has divided his time on his family (wife Rachael and two daughters) and the family's considerable charitable endeavors (from Boys and Girls Clubs of America to the Dallas Museum of Art). His business interests are mostly restricted to running his family's trust under the auspices of DFI Management Ltd.. and overseeing Pinehurst through its ownership entity, appropriately named Putterboy Ltd. Dedman has funded a total overhaul of guest rooms in The Carolina Hotel, led the resort and club through dicey economic times and now is eagerly following the most ambitious initiative at Pinehurst in many years—the overhaul of No. 2. Nearly every trip to Pinehurst includes an early morning round on No. 2 with Chief Operating Officer Don Padgett.

"It's like walking on hallowed ground to me," Dedman says. "I think we really have connected to the past, with our restoration and with letting Mother Nature have her will once again. I think it makes it even more special. I'm overcome every time thinking of all the greatest players in the game having walked before you over the last century and those that will come over the next century. It's fun to be a part of that history."

Coore & Crenshaw are six months into their restoration process, and Dedman sees notable differences each time he plays the course.

"It's so much more visually appealing than before," he says. "Because of all the green, you never saw some of the mounds that are tucked off to the side—like on No. 1. They were covered in grass and in the shadows. Now they've reappeared. I love the wire grass creeping into the bunkers.

"The course had become too manicured. I think it's the right thing to do for golf, the right thing for Pinehurst, and we've got the perfect team in Ben and Bill. Long before our stewardship, Pinehurst was a leader in the game. This focus on a natural look rather than a fully manicured look is the right thing to do for golf. We're proud to hopefully lead that charge. Obviously, the USGA has been a strong proponent of that, and we certainly agree with them."

Pinehurst rebounded from its financial duress in the early 1980s to hosting a U.S. Open in the final year of the 20th century through the ownership of Dedman Sr. and astute leadership of a management team that included Don Padgett Sr. Dedman provided the resources and the commitment, and Padgett Sr., hired in 1987 as the resort's director of golf, opened doors into the corridors of influence and power in the world of golf. As a former president of the PGA of America, Padgett was on a first name basis with golf's *Who's Who*. The kindred spirits died within one year of each other from the late summer of 2002 to the spring of 2003.

"Don and I chose our dads pretty well," Bob says with a smile. "We both have great memories of sitting around and listening to our dads talk and tell stories, needle one another. It was a real treat to be around them. I think Don Sr. once said, 'The role of a leader is to

Among the many legacies of the Dedman family has been returning championship golf to Pinehurst; the grandstands were jam-packed in 2005 when Tiger Woods hit his approach to the eighteenth green.

preserve order amidst change and change amidst order.' That's pretty profound. Don Sr. had an incredible love for the game. But for him and his real passion for the game, I don't think Pinehurst would have made the progress we did in the time frames we did. It took someone with a steady hand on the tiller to navigate through the changes that needed to be made."

The Dedmans have shared a love of poetry and quotations (Bob has published two volumes of his favorite passages), but their essential personalities are quite at variance. While Dedman Sr. was totally at ease with a microphone and an audience, the somewhat bashful Dedman Jr. has had to practice his oratory skills and his comfort level in groups. While Senior was gifted in the art of finding and making the deal, Junior is skilled in executing the details the next day, the next week, the next month.

"No question about it," Dedman Sr. once said. "Bob is more organized, more detail oriented that I ever was."

It's fair to say the legacy of Dedman Sr. was his purchase of Pinehurst and the resort's subsequent rebirth. The legacy of Dedman Jr. will now be a similar renaissance of the prized No. 2 course.

"Bob Dedman took a big risk in this," Bill Coore says. "I hope in time the Dedman era will be as revered as the Tufts era was."

"The Dedmans are like the 'anti Wall Street," adds Mike Davis, the long-time USGA staffer promoted to executive director in 2011. "They're not worried about the next quarter. They're looking at the long term."

Indeed, Dedman is proud that his family's stewardship of Pinehurst is now more than a quarter of a century old. That longevity is starting to make a dent in the century-plus existence of the resort.

"You have to have an incredible appreciation for the traditions of this place," Bob says. "It is an incredible place to me and to many other people in the world. We have reverence for the past, while at the same time, we need to evolve. Pinehurst has seen a lot of glory in its 115 years, but I firmly believe its best years are ahead."

JUNES TO REMEMBER

For one week in June, they were the very best in the business, this Missourian named Payne Stewart and this New Zealander named Michael Campbell.

Each had paid his dues in professional golf by the time the 1999 and 2005 U.S. Opens came to Pinehurst No. 2. Stewart was forty-two with eleven PGA Tour wins, Campbell was thirty-six with six victories on the European Tour. Both were married and the father of two children.

Each had rebounded from earlier slumps, Stewart going nearly four years from 1995-98 without a win after an unfortunate change of equipment, and Campbell losing his exempt status on the European Tour in 1996 after a severe wrist injury sustained in the New Zealand Open in late 1995. He threw his clubs across a hotel room in 1998 and vowed to quit the game.

Each had been steeled by earlier setbacks in major championships, Stewart losing a four-shot lead in the U.S. Open one year before at The Olympic Club and Campbell sleeping on a third-round British Open lead at St. Andrews in 1995 before yielding on Sunday amid the pressure to eventual champion John Daly.

Each had ignition sparks earlier in their respective championship years, Stewart winning at Pebble Beach in February 1999 and Campbell missing five cuts in early 2005 before swing changes made under the tutelage of new full-time coach Jonathan Yarwood started nestling in. "We've redone everything," Campbell said. He also retained a new sports psychologist and joined the management stable of IMG's London office.

Each was in good rhythm and comfortable mindset on Thursday morning as curtains lifted on the Open. Stewart missed the cut in Memphis the week before, arrived in Pinehurst on Saturday and had mapped out his game plan for attacking the devilish greens by Sunday night. Campbell checked into Pine Needles on Sunday, played a practice round on No. 2 on Monday morning and spent five hours back at Pine Needles that afternoon working with Yarwood on adjustments to his putting stroke and lagging long putts with his eyes closed.

Each benefitted from a golf tip from a random source, Stewart's wife Tracey telling him after Saturday's third round he was moving his head on his putting stroke and Vijay Singh critiquing Campbell's bunker play during their Monday practice round. Singh told Campbell that he was cutting across the ball on his sand shots and spinning it too much. Singh showed Campbell how to flop the ball out high and let it roll out with less spin, and Campbell used the technique to hole out from a bunker on seventeen on Saturday and get up-and-down on eleven and fifteen for pars on Sunday.

Each played solid if unspectacular golf for three days, jockeying expertly into position and letting the field melt away with a cacophony of mistakes amid the heinous rough and blazing greens of Pinehurst No. 2. Stewart shot rounds of 68, 69 and 72 to earn a spot in the final pairing on Sunday, and Campbell carded rounds of 71, 69 and 71 to start the final round one group behind leader Retief Goosen.

Each heard the roars up ahead in the final round as Tiger Woods mounted a charge. In 1999, Woods missed five-footers for par on eleven and seventeen and then agonized as a potential tying putt on eighteen hung on the lip; he finished two strokes back. Just three years into his professional career, Woods would learn to make those five-footers in major championships. Six years later, the noise emanating from Woods' birdie on fifteen cutting the lead to one momentarily distracted Campbell back on fourteen, but the Kiwi collected himself and nailed his four-iron to five feet, made the putt and was never bothered again as Woods bogeyed sixteen and seventeen and finished second, two strokes back.

Each, of course, made a lot of putts. Stewart took 111 putts for seventy-two holes and twenty-four on the final day, most notably his downhill birdie bomb from twenty-five feet on sixteen and his fifteen-footer for par on eighteen. Campbell took just 113 putts for four rounds, fourth best in the field, including ten one-putts on Sunday.

Each birdied the seventeenth on Sunday, Stewart spearing a six-iron to four feet for a birdie and Campbell stroking a twenty-five footer into the hole, the kind of lag putt he'd

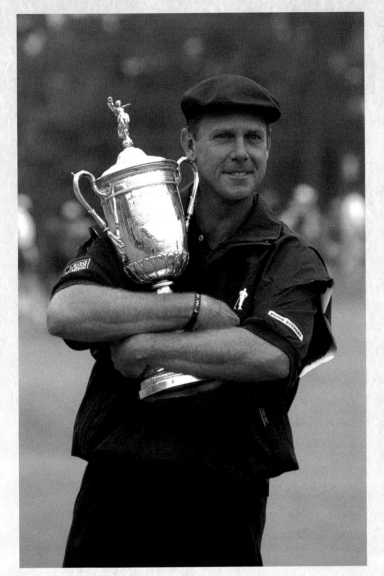

Payne Stewart (left) cradles and Michael Campbell kisses the U.S. Open trophy following championships in 1999 and 2005, respectively.

worked so hard to perfect on Monday afternoon at Pine Needles. Campbell hit his tee shot on seventeen, then ducked quickly into a port-a-john in the woods to the right. But he was there not for the usual reason; instead, he spent forty-five seconds doing a series of eye exercises mandated by a doctor months earlier.

Each partied long into the night after all the requisite autograph and interviewing duties of a new champion. Stewart drove ninety miles to the Hillsborough home of caddie Mike Hicks that night for a charity exhibition scheduled for Monday, and they joined Paul Azinger, Fred Couples and Hal Sutton at Hicks' home watching replays of the final round on TV until 4 a.m. Campbell returned to Pine Needles, where he joined a half dozen fellow Kiwis, their host Peggy Kirk Bell and her family and others for a party that lasted past 3 a.m. Campbell poured Dom Perignon champagne into the Open trophy, drank from it and passed it around to everyone.

And each, sadly, reached the pinnacle of his golf career

Stewart was back on his game in 1999 after several fallow years; here he's launching a tee shot on the par-four seventh hole.

on those third Sundays in June. Payne Stewart died on October 25, 1999, when the Learjet he was riding from Orlando to Dallas lost cabin pressure, killing two pilots and four passengers. Michael Campbell won the HSBC World Match Play Championship at Wentworth in September 2005, but soon his game went into a downward spiral. He's not made a cut in the Masters since and only one in the U.S. Open. In March 2012, he was ranked No. 783 in the World Golf Ranking.

***

Michael Campbell was still plugging away at his golf game in the spring of 2012. In 2011 he hired a new swing coach, Gary Edwin. He moved his wife and two sons from New Zealand to Switzerland so he could be closer to the European Tour and cut out a full day of travel to and from

New Zealand. He took heart watching forty-something friends Darren Clarke and Thomas Bjorn have good years in 2011 and believed a similar comeback was in the cards for him. He has a full-time physiotherapist to help monitor and treat the effects of a shoulder injury in 2010. Under the tab "Career Highlights" on his website are the words, "The Story So Far," implying there is more news to come.

"My play has always been streaky," Campbell told John Huggan of *Golf World* at the 2010 U.S. Open at Pebble Beach as he shot 78-83 to miss the cut. "Ever since I was a little kid, I've always done this. I'm used to it."

Eighteen months later, he sounded optimistic as a new season on the European Tour beckoned. His ten-year exemption in the U.S. Open by virtue of his 2005 victory will allow him to play at Pinehurst in 2014.

"I said to my family that we could relocate to Europe or I could do something else for a living," Campbell says. "They

Campbell used a tip from Vijay Singh on bunker play to get up-and-down for par on the fifteenth hole on Sunday.

were really encouraging and supportive and said, 'So let's give it another go.'"

Meanwhile, the spirit of Payne Stewart remains through the hallowed ground of No. 2 and the Village of Pinehurst—indeed, throughout the game of golf.

The statue beside the eighteenth green is a magnet to resort guests. Rarely an hour goes by from April through October without a golfer posing beside the bronze replica of the "Payne Pose." The maintenance staff has trouble keeping the grass healthy around the statue with all the traffic it gets and has had to solder the putter back on because visitors have leaned on it and broken it. On Sundays the hole on eighteen is cut as it was on June 20, 1999—twenty-five paces in, six from the right, and the flag features the silhouette of Stewart's victory form. Stewart's bust, final-round scorecard and assorted memorabilia are displayed in a case in "Heritage Hall" in the clubhouse.

Early in the week of the 1999 Open, Stewart was having dinner at the Pine Crest Inn and renewed acquaintances with owner Bob Barrett, whom he had met when staying at the inn in the summer of 1979. Stewart had just graduated from Southern Methodist University and was in the Sandhills area for a series of mini-tour events, and years later he recalled his visit at the Pine Crest as feeling like "a month at golf camp." Barrett introduced Stewart to his nine-year-old grandson, Patrick, who was not yet terribly interested in golf, having sloughed off lessons when all he cared about was "banging the ball as hard as I could and driving the golf cart." But Stewart signed a napkin and wrote, "Patrick, keep swinging, Payne Stewart." That week Patrick went to the golf course at daybreak, stayed all day and hounded autographs from players like Jack Nicklaus, Tiger Woods and Vijay Singh.

"I was so short, I couldn't see much of the action, but I could feel the energy," Barrett says. "I was more interested in autographs and celebrities than the golf. But that week I decided I wanted to play golf, to learn the game."

He did just that, taking lessons from Eric Alpenfels at Pinehurst and playing around the clock on summer days at the Country Club of North Carolina and Knollwood Fairways between Southern Pines and Pinehurst. In 2003 he tied for second in the Donald Ross Memorial Junior in his age bracket. For the 2005 Open, he got a job with the Associated Press as a "runner"—shuttling film from photographers on the course back to the lab in the media center. His badge gave him access to the interview room and the practice range, and he used it to full advantage.

"The Open in '05 was much more relevant for me," Barrett says. "I had been playing a lot for several years and understood what was going on. I remember sitting twenty feet from Tiger watching him hit balls—it was unlike anything I'd ever seen or heard, the sound of his club striking the ball."

Barrett in the spring of 2012 was a senior at the University of North Carolina and one of the top golfers on the Tar Heels' roster. He doesn't know what the future holds—perhaps a try on the professional tour—but he knows that golf is a part of his life forever.

"I would not be playing now if not for that '99 Open," he says. "I was there every day from 8 a.m. until they kicked me out at night. By 2005, I was a golf nut. That year it was so fun to see that I could hit my drives past where some of the short-knockers hit it. That pushed me to keep getting better and better."

One of the prime storylines of the week was the impending birth of Phil and Amy Mickelson's first child. Mickelson didn't decide until Tuesday night of Open week to come to Pinehurst, and he promised his wife he'd leave immediately to return home to Phoenix if she went into labor. Mickelson had a private plane waiting on Sunday as he teed off with Stewart in the final pairing and had calculated that it would take just over five hours from golf course to hospital. Amy felt contractions on Saturday night and asked for medication to slow the process and hopefully delay the baby's birth until after Sunday; she watched the final round on the sofa with her pelvis propped up on pillows to prevent the baby dropping any further.

"I was totally in tears," she said. "The worst thing that could happen was I have the baby Saturday night and he's leading the U.S. Open."

The beeper carried by caddie Jim MacKay never went off, so Mickelson made it through eighteen on Sunday, shooting a 70 that fell one shot behind Stewart. After Stewart made his fateful putt and hugged caddie Mike Hicks, he approached Mickelson, put his hands on either side of Mickelson's face and said, "You're going to be a father, and there's nothing greater in the world."

Mickelson was back home on Monday when Amanda Brynn Mickelson was born. She was the four-year-old with big blonde curls and cream dress whom Mickelson lifted for a hug outside the scorer's hut at Augusta in 2004, just moments after collecting that elusive first major championship in the Masters Tournament.

"Even though I was disappointed about the Open, the excitement and memory I have of seeing my child born, and taking care of her, will far surpass any letdown I felt," Mickelson said. "I've thought about the final round a couple of times, but not nearly as much as I thought I would."

Shortly after congratulating Mickelson on his impending fatherhood, Stewart connected with Pinehurst owner Robert Dedman Sr. The trophy presentation was about to begin on the eighteenth green, and Stewart noted the navy blue and red attire he was wearing and said to Dedman, who had given considerable millions of dollars to Southern Methodist, "I wore my SMU colors today." Ironically, Stewart had been flying to Dallas to look at a potential site for a new SMU home golf course on Oct. 25, 1999, when he died.

Watching from home in Orlando that day was Aaron Stewart, Payne's nine-year-old son. Aaron was not an avid golfer, but he gravitated toward the game through his teens and became an excellent player. Aaron followed his father to SMU and played on the golf team, and in 2009 and 2010 he entered the North and South Amateur. With his father's regular caddie, Mike Hicks, on the bag, Stewart shot an 83 in qualifying that first year and failed to advance to match play. The next year, he improved to 73 and then lost to Lee Bedford of Cary in nineteen holes in the first round of match play.

The Payne Stewart Match Play at Pinehurst event was created when Bob Dedman Jr. suggested to SMU head golf coach Josh Gregory and associate coach Jason Enloe that a collegiate event at Pinehurst in Stewart's honor would be an

A solitary Aaron Stewart putts to the Sunday hole location on the eighteenth green of No. 2 and poses with his father's statue while in Pinehurst for the 2009 North and South Amateur.

excellent means to further Stewart's legacy. The inaugural event was scheduled for Oct. 7-8, 2012, with SMU hosting Wake Forest in a competition that would include golf alumni from each school and a thirty-six hole match between the college teams on Monday on No. 2.

"We see the event growing over time and becoming a great fund-raiser and opportunity to remember Payne and the impact he had on the game of golf," Enloe says. "He was one of the first really outgoing and colorful golfers of our generation. He was fun and full of life. It's important we keep those traditions alive and pay our respects to him."

PRACTICE MAKES PERFECT

T he ground is beaten, bludgeoned, sliced and diced. Divots morph into craters. Blades of grass pray for their lives, only to be thwacked with a six-iron at daybreak. Water and sun and fertilizer only go so far. This is Pinehurst, and the math doesn't work—high demand by golfers and limited acreage for hitting balls.

It's got to be well into the millions of balls hit a year on the Pinehurst practice range dubbed "Maniac Hill" during the old North and South Open days.

Figure one hundred and fifty thousand rounds a year out of five courses at the main clubhouse, and each golfer hits thirty balls. That would be 4.5 million. That doesn't count people practicing or in golf schools.

Chad Campbell, Pinehurst's director of golf, has run some numbers. The maintenance building, tucked amid a covey of trees below and to the left of the main hitting area, houses eight forty-four gallon barrels filled with balls.

"And the barrels are industrial strength," Campbell notes. "If they're not, the handles will break."

Each barrel holds eight cases of Titleist Pinnacle balls. A case comprises twenty-four dozen. Campbell works the numbers on his hand-held PDA.

"Eighteen thousand, four hundred and thirty-two golf balls at any given time," he says. "We have two pickers running all day during high season just to keep up. We have a specially made loading platform so that the guys don't have to lift the barrels of balls off the carts. The balls are pre-soaked, washed and the machine spits them out. They're ready to go back out."

Surely Donald Ross never dreamed his modest 1913 experiment would evolve into such a production. Pinehurst had three golf courses open by 1910 but no dedicated practice facility. Early lessons were conducted in the Scottish style of the teacher accompanying the student onto the golf course. But in the spring and summer of 1913, Ross allocated the ground covered by the first, second and 18th holes of course No. 1 exclusively for practice and built new holes further southward from the clubhouse.

The concept of practice was slow to evolve, as Richard Tufts, grandson of the resort founder, once observed: "I always thought it very strange that Walter Travis persisted in practicing chip shots, putting and even full shots when a vacant fairway was available. Why should he, of all golfers, need to waste time practicing?"

But consider the incubator that Pinehurst provided golfers—both pros and amateurs—in the early 20th century. The North and South Open was one of the premier competitions in pro golf at the time, and players the ilk of Tommy Armour, Walter Hagen, Horton Smith, Paul Runyan and Henry Picard relished having this ample laboratory to practice, share swing tips and ideas and experiment with the several dozen clubs allowed in their bags before the fourteen-club limit took effect. Armour said that Maniac Hill was to golf "what Kitty Hawk was to flying." The pros also had hundreds of pigeons fluttering about—club members or resort guests anxious to take lessons and improve their own ability.

"The lessons had to be good," historian and author Herb Graffis once noted. "If they didn't pay off for the amateur during the daily competitions at Pinehurst, there was a quick switch of teachers."

Ross's early course designs never accounted for practice grounds. But Graffis said Ross told him years later that after the success of the Pinehurst practice tee, he began incorporating practice ranges at all his courses beginning in 1914. Still, they were largely afterthoughts—practice tees were never considered destinations in and of themselves.

Tom Fazio entered the golf design and construction business under the tutelage of his uncle, tour pro George Fazio, in the early 1960s and remembers the landscape for golf practice:

"Every good player had a shag bag in the trunk of his car and his caddie would stand in the distance with the bag," Fazio says. "The caddie opened the bag up and caught the ball on one bounce. You only needed a very small area. Back in the day, only the good players practiced, and some of them didn't practice much. If they did practice, it was on the golf course. How many stories have you heard about Walter Hagen and Jimmy Demaret showing up on the first tee after partying all night? The pros back then went from the golf course to the bar.

"Today professional golf has evolved that there is so much money and so much good competition, a work ethic has taken over. Today they sign their scorecards and go to the fitness trailer or back to the practice tee."

The importance of the practice environment today is underlined by the fact that over the last decade, Pinehurst has resculpted the hitting area with target greens, lengthened the depth of the range by fifty yards, built a state-of-the-art teaching facility and eliminated the practice of distributing balls via tokens or bags in favor of leaving them free for the taking by members and resort guests at each hitting station. The club installed all-weather mats at the top the hitting area early in the 2000s that are used during the winter and to take wear and tear off the hitting turf at other times of the year.

"The all-weather stations give us thirty percent more life with the turf," says Bob Farren, Pinehurst's director of golf course and grounds management.

Still, it's quite a battle for Pinehurst staff to keep the turf up throughout the year. When the weather turns cool in October, golfers are still pounding the turf, but it's too chilly to generate new Bermuda. Then it turns cold in December and there's never enough time to develop a reasonable thatch of winter rye—which isn't even a good practice turf to begin with. After a miserable winter in 2010, March dawned with hardly a healthy blade of grass on the practice ground. So Pinehurst officials summoned Sandhill Turf Inc., and the company brought six truckloads of sod one day. Workers laid out some 55,000 square feet of Patriot Bermuda covering 1.5 acres by the end of the day.

"A football field gets beat up in the fall just like we do," Farren says. "But then they have until August to grow back. We have to be ready in the spring. The practice facility is the first impression for many people. It's important for guests to have a good experience when they hit balls."

Indeed, the resort has 18,432 reasons to have a nice stand of grass on Maniac Hill.

Tour pros brought their own shag bags to "Maniac Hill" in the early days of the North and South Open.

Country Club Porch Pin[ehurst] N. C.

PINEHURST N.C. FEB OP 191
U.S. POSTAGE ONE CENT

Bill and Ben

Nearly half a century later, Bill Coore can reach back into his memory bank and take hold of the sights, sounds and textures of his teenage Pinehurst experiences—the car ride down country roads from Davidson County with his pals or perhaps an adult golfing friend and mentor, the anticipation of arriving at this cathedral of golf, the quiet ambience and immersion in nature and sport. For Coore and his friends, there was nothing like a summer day in Pinehurst.

"We'd tee off at daybreak," Coore says. "It was five dollars. You got a little tag, a paper tag to put on your bag. We would start walking and playing. They had a marshal who would check to see that you'd paid your fees. We were so early there was nowhere to check in. I remember an elderly fellow. He would stop us and say 'Boys, when you get through you know you have to go back in and pay.' We'd say, 'Yes sir.' We would pay our five dollars and continue to play. Far more than a few times we'd play fifty-four holes in one day, carrying our bag, on the No. 2 course. That was my earliest memory. It's just an incredible place."

Coore was born in 1946 and grew up in the Davidson County countryside, just south of Thomasville and a few

The firm of Coore & Crenshaw was formed in late 1985 and over a quarter of a century had designed golf courses across the United States and as far away as China and Tasmania.

minutes north of Denton (the home also of noted sports journalist Furman Bisher). He loved all sports and played baseball and basketball in high school but sat out football because of poor eyesight—"I couldn't see the ball and couldn't wear glasses playing football," he says.

But he gravitated mostly to golf. His parents divorced when he was young, and Bill was an only child. Golf was a game he could play in the wide open spaces around his home and do so by himself.

"There were not many people around where I grew up," he says. "The kid next door was eight years older than me. You could have great fun playing golf all by yourself. I could hit balls in our backyard, around to the front, aim for the mailbox or a fence post."

The man next door befriended young Coore, hiring him as a caddie and taking him to play golf, often to Lexington Country Club. Donald Jarrett would become one of the early influences on Coore's understanding of golf and how it's played. One day in the late-1950s, they were playing the third hole at Lexington, a short par-three, slightly downhill, to a green bordered by a hillside to the left and a stream front, back and to the right. The fact that the green was tilted slightly away from the golfer made it more of a challenge to hit and hold. Coore, an early teen at the time, routinely took a lofted club, aimed for the pin and had decidedly mixed results. Jarrett's idea was to punch a seven-iron left of the green, let it bounce off the hillside and trickle onto the putting surface.

"I would complain about how the hole was messed up, that he was hitting trick shots on the green nine of ten times," Coore reflects with a smile. "I was playing the game way it was *supposed* to be played—from point A to point B.

"One day he said, 'William, you're a bright boy. I wonder how long it's going to take you to figure out how to play that shot. Keep playing it your way if you want.' That was the first time the light went on, that I realized maybe there was more than one way to play a golf hole. It was like, 'Hmmmm, okay, no one said you *had* to play on a straight line.' That was the beginning of my education in golf course architecture. I'll never forget that day as long as I live."

Jarrett on occasion drove Coore and some of his friends to Pinehurst, as did another older golfer who would influence Coore's perspective on the game and its venues. Stuart Kennedy was a Thomasville businessman and a Pinehurst Country Club member and a good player himself (Kennedy won the 1987 North Carolina Senior Amateur).

"It was a fascinating thing to watch Stuart play and come up with all these little shots around the green," Coore says. "He'd bumble them up from off the sides at different angles and trajectories, and I'd be standing there and say, 'I'm not sure that's how you're supposed to play that.' But he'd get it up and down and say, 'It works, doesn't it?' It was the beginning of my education to know that imagination is such

Owner & Architect in the 1940s (L-R): Richard Tufts and Donald Ross

an important part of golf and, particulary, *this* golf course."

Coore remembers lively discussions about No. 2 and its difficulty. Coore himself didn't think the course was that tough.

Kennedy's standard response: "So what did you shoot?"

"Well ..."

"So what did you shoot?"

"Well …"

"It's a little harder than you thought."

Over time, Coore has developed a deep appreciation for the point Kennedy was trying to make.

"No. 2 is not the most visually spectacular golf course in the world," he says. "But the subtleties that go into making it what it is are almost beyond comprehension. You can be here almost all your life and still have some little different shot, some little different place to be, and it holds your interest."

Coore attended Wake Forest on an academic scholarship to study classical languages and was a member of the Deacon golf team for two years but never a varsity competitor of any note.

"I was a participant on the team, I was not a player," he says. "It didn't take a very bright person to figure out that 75s and 76s and 77s didn't quite match up with the red numbers Jay Sigel and Leonard Thompson and Jack Lewis were throwing up."

Coore is quick to make light of his own golf abilities, noting that his penchant for hitting low running shots helped him develop a taste for a course like No. 2. He didn't care for forced carries and approaches to greens bordered by water as it was tough to carry the ball to the target and get it to stop. He learned to appreciate the beauties of the ground game.

"I could work my way around No. 2," he says. "I could tack my way around the course. I could run a four-wood up on a green. I had a chance against better players. I have a healthy respect for width on a golf course and the angles that width presents. I like the ground game because I never got the ball much in the air. The ground game isn't as important in our country today as it was when Donald Ross built No. 2. But you go to Great Britain or Australia, the ground game is all they know. It's a wonderful form of golf."

The Tufts family was generous with providing playing opportunities to area college teams, and the Deacon golfers would frequently make the hundred-mile drive southeast to Pinehurst, where Coore further soaked in the ambience he'd known as a youth. He and the Wake Forest golfers practiced and played daily at Old Town Club in Winston-Salem, another classic in golf design created by Perry Maxwell.

"Old Town was a wonderful place," Coore says. "It had the most pristine set of Perry Maxwell greens anywhere. I enjoyed looking at golf courses, trying to figure out why one was better than another, why one hole went here and another went there. But I never thought of it as a career. My plan was to go to grad school and then become a college professor."

Owner & Architect in 2011 (L-R): Bob Dedman Jr. and Bill Coore

Coore earned his degree in 1968 and spent two years in the Army, much of that time at Fort Bragg in Fayetteville, and once on leave to visit his mother in Davidson County, Coore drove to High Point to investigate a new course under construction. Oak Hollow was going to be a public golf course and was designed by an architect named Pete Dye, who was just coming into some acclaim for his innovative new design on Hilton Head Island, Harbour Town Golf Links.

"In 1971 every golf course had the Robert Trent Jones Senior look," says Coore. "They were the proverbial 7,000-yard-plus championship golf course—and 7,000 yards at that time was a long golf course. What Pete was doing was so different. I was enamored with it. I had no clue who Pete was, but I liked what I saw. Oak Hollow was like Harbour Town. It was based on finesse shots, shorter shots, precision and placement. I was fascinated."

Coore struck up a conversation with one of the course maintenance workers and eventually got Dye's home number in Florida. He had applied to Duke University's graduate program in classical languages, but the more he thought about working on a golf course in some capacity, the more he liked the idea. Coore called Dye repeatedly and left messages but never got a return call. As his Army stint neared its ending, he called more regularly.

"I hate to say it, but I made up a story," Coore says. "I got him on the phone one day and told him I was coming to Florida, maybe I could drop by and talk. He said, 'Well, all right, if you're in the area …' So I drove to Florida *specifically* to see Pete Dye. I got there and called him one Sunday afternoon. He was a big Miami Dolphins fan and there was a game on TV that afternoon. So we sat there and watched the football game and talked a little golf. In essence, he said I had about as much chance of becoming a golf course architect as I did getting struck by lightning.

"I told him I would start at the bottom, I would just like to learn. I was single, I didn't need much money, and I could go anywhere."

By this time Coore was set on becoming a golf course architect and had the conviction to follow the values instilled by his mother, Clara Coore. She worked two jobs while Bill was a boy and fought the mindset of the mid-1900s that worked against a divorced working mother.

"She was my hero," he says. "She didn't have anything when I was growing up. But what an inspiration. She was amazing. I'd come home with these hare brained ideas. 'I'm going to be an astronaut,' I'd say. Instead of, 'Well, that's a stupid idea,' she'd say, 'Okay, how do you become an astronaut? What do you have to know?' She was used to a man's world, to having people say, 'You can't do that.' She would not let me fall into that trap. She enabled me to become a golf course architect."

Dye eventually told Coore that he was close to embarking on a new project in Greensboro for a new development company, Landmark Land Co., a concern headed by a two former golf professionals, Ernie Vossler and Joe Walser. Dye said perhaps Coore could go to work on the construction crew on what was to become the Cardinal Golf Club. Coore's friend and mentor Stuart Kennedy "thought I'd lost my mind," Coore says, but nonetheless gave him work in his Thomasville factory until the Cardinal construction job commenced.

In Greensboro Coore learned to run a bulldozer and tractor and read engineers' drawings. He soaked up ideas from Dye and his wife and design partner, Alice. He was, in his own words, "a general flunky." The unfinished golf course was sold by Landmark, and Dye never completed it (a contractor recommended by architect George Cobb finished the course for the new owner), but Coore had made an impression on the Dyes. They asked him to move to the next job at John's Island, near the Dye's Florida home in Jupiter Beach, and Coore often served as house-sitter and dog-sitter for the Dyes' German shepherd, whiling weekend hours away pouring through Dye's library of golf books. Coore was, coincidentally, finding his bearings in golf design by reading many of the same classics from authors like Alister MacKenzie, Bernard Darwin and Horace Hutchinson that Ben Crenshaw had been reading in his dorm room at the University of Texas.

"Pete was a tremendous influence," Coore says. "He was so good to me, he and Alice both. He thought I was just nuts. I started to get a sense of how the all the pieces fell into place. Before, I knew what I liked, but I had no idea how to get from theory to reality. If nothing else, they were great just allowing me to eavesdrop on their conversa-

tions about golf architecture."

Coore worked for Dye for a decade and then moved to Texas in the early eighties to work for Pete's brother, Roy, on the design and maintenance of Waterwood National, just north of Houston. His memories of Pinehurst No. 2 were always part of most any design or maintenance decision he ever made; once in the late 1970s, in fact, Coore brought one of his bulldozer operators to Pinehurst specifically to see for himself what Coore meant when he referenced the personality of No. 2 and Donald Ross design. Coore inherited the superintendent's job at Waterwood and then learned of a distressed project farther south, near Corpus Christi. The owners of Rockport Country Club were in a bad way.

"They were really desperate," Coore says. "They said, 'Here's the thing, we can't spend a penny more. Make something out of this and start it now.' I didn't know any better, so I dove in."

***

And just what, exactly, is the two-time Masters champion doing in the men's locker room at Pinehurst? Why is he bent over at the waist between the stalls and lavatories, pointing to the squares of tile on the floor? Ben Crenshaw is doing what he always does—he's living and breathing the game of golf.

"With the right kind of marble, you can find some really neat golf holes. Look at these beautiful lines," Crenshaw enthuses. "You can find some really good stuff, and the reason is that man had absolutely nothing to do with it. There are some unbelievable looking holes."

He runs his finger along splotches of dark and lighter areas of the marble.

"Use your imagination," he says. "This is the fairway. This is a green. This is a bunker. You can find them. There are plenty here."

Resort guests come and go around him and wonder if Crenshaw is looking for loose change or has lost his marbles. He points to another potential hole.

"Look at that: That's a nice angled bunker … you have a nice green here … you're hitting over a lake here …"

He straightens up and laughs.

Three highlights of Ben Crenshaw's competitive career have included making a long putt on the tenth at Augusta in winning the 1984 Masters (above); celebrating with Phil Mickelson during the 1999 Ryder Cup at Brookline (above right); and weeping with joy after his final putt in the 1995 Masters (right).

Two Crenshaws at Pinehurst: chipping in the 1973 World Open and teeing off on the first hole in the 1999 U.S. Open.

"The product of an idle mind," he says.

Inspiration for golf holes can come from most anywhere, Crenshaw says. He tells of a construction associate at Coore & Crenshaw finding ideas for bunker designs in clouds. He remembers one of his favorite passages from the British writer Bernard Darwin.

"One day Darwin was sick and spent the whole day in bed," Crenshaw says. "He wrote the most unbelievable article called 'The Links of Eiderdown.' He was lying in bed and envisioned all these golf holes in the folds and curves of the bed spread. It was a lot of fun to read."

Indeed, the Darwin passage is interesting:

"In my warped mind's eye I continually saw golf holes designed on the 'land of counterpane' before me. It is not an uninteresting one, this links of eiderdown, and is laid out on what an ingratiating prospectus would call fine, undulating country. Moreover, by undulating himself in bed the patient can in a moment change the contour of his course."

Another morning Crenshaw is meeting design associate Toby Cobb at the Track Restaurant, a rectangular cement building that serves down-home cooking to the locals who like the reasonable prices and lack of pretension. The restaurant is located on a 111-acre site that houses the Pinehurst Harness Track, which has been a winter training venue for trotters and pacers for nearly a century, and the ground around the tracks has never been burnished with water, fertilizer and intense hand labor like all of the golf courses surrounding it.

Crenshaw exits his rental car with his ever-present cup of Starbucks coffee and surveys the earth around him.

"There's some fabulous ground right here," he says. "It looks like Britain. Over there they say, 'We can't use this ground to farm, so we can recreate on it. We can play golf on it.' These are what I call 'poverty grasses.' If you don't use water and chemicals, this is what it looks like. It's potluck if your ball runs into it. But you can find it and get your club on it and keep playing the game. Tournament golf has gotten to be 99.9 percent 'pound it out of heavy rough.' To me, it's very boring. I've gotten sick of it. There's got to be something different from that. Yet that's the mainstay of defenses put on courses. It's anything but interesting.

"I sense that other players feel that way also. And I think Mike Davis and the USGA recognize that. I think Mike has the idea that maybe, just maybe, you can have a U.S. Open that's just a little bit different …"

Crenshaw joins his partner and design soulmate Bill Coore in agreeing that golfers should find quality turf on tees, fairways and greens. Together they *disagree* with the idea that every other square inch on the property should be buffed, coiffed and manicured to perfection. It costs too much money, for one thing, and it's unnatural for another.

"You have to go to Dornoch and to the old country to understand the appeal this ground had for Mr. Ross," Crenshaw says, surveying the acreage around the track. "You set your feet on links turf for the first time and you say, 'My gosh, this is bone dry, this is different.' The only water on those golf courses is what falls from the sky. The ball takes off and you just say, Wow. The turf conditions there are very different. There are only a few spots where you can emulate Dornoch, and this is one of them."

Crenshaw makes his way inside, greets the proprietor and says he hopes they don't mind him importing his own coffee.

"Good morning, Toby," Ben says, slipping into a seat beside Cobb at a corner table. He peruses the menu, places his order and then reads a passage set in front of him written by Charles Price. The words are the very ones at the start of the introduction to this book, crafted by a man who competed on No. 2 in the North and South Open back in the 1940s and lived on two separate occasions in Pinehurst.

"That guy was amazing and so talented," Crenshaw says. "God, could he write. He was fun to talk to. He could talk about many different things. He had very sophisticated tastes in music and art. He knew world affairs."

Crenshaw was a fifteen-year-old growing up in Texas when his father gave him Price's 1962 book, *The World of Golf*, a treatise to the game's venues, champions, implements and traditions. The 308-page compendium of prose and pictures offered a fascinating panorama of six centuries of the game of golf. Ben adored the game and was quite good at it, but his universe then extended only as far as the out-of-bounds stakes at Austin Country Club and the local municipal course.

A match was lit.

"It's a great piece of work," says Crenshaw, who has now acquired more than eight hundred golf books. "I couldn't have cut my teeth on a better book. It has a little bit about everything. When I first read that book, I began to understand the rich history and colorful stars of the game of golf."

Soon after, Charlie Crenshaw suggested to Ben that he attempt to qualify for the 1968 U.S. Junior Amateur, scheduled for The Country Club in the Boston suburb of Brookline. Ben made the field, and the Crenshaw boys flew to Boston on Braniff Airlines. They attended a Red Sox game at Fenway Park, and Ben met in person some of the national golfers he'd read about in *Golf World*, top juniors like Eddie Pearce and Gary Koch. He lost in the quarterfinals but had a mesmerizing week—"The ground was so perfect, I was scared to take a divot," he says—and the experience ignited a magical circle that ended in 1999 when Crenshaw captained the U.S. Ryder Cup team to its memorable final-day rally at The Country Club. No wonder he subtitled his autobiography *To Brookline and Back*.

"I couldn't have been luckier to see Brookline early on, when I was so young," Crenshaw says. "It was rustic, it was New England, it seemed like the other side of the world from Austin, Texas. It was perfectly natural. It was so history laden. You had to ask yourself: 'Why? Who put this together? Who started this? Who nurtured it?' There was so much romance about it, and then I learned about it being one of the founding clubs of the USGA and the place where Francis Ouimet won the Open.

"Together, Charlie Price's book and my trip to Brookline set me off on a path I've enjoyed the rest of my life. They opened my eyes to a different world."

That world, of course, was at first built around competitive golf. He won two NCAA championships outright as a Texas Longhorn

A MASTERFUL STROKE

Don Padgett swore to himself when Coore & Crenshaw were hired that at no point would he act like a tourist and buttonhole Ben Crenshaw with questions about putting technique. He made it for a number of months before caving.

"Well, I promised myself I'd never do this with you, but now I'm going to …" Padgett said.

"What?" Crenshaw answered.

"Where is your grip pressure with your putter?" Padgett asked. "Every idiot in the world has asked you about putting, now I'm one of them."

Crenshaw laughed and answered that Harvey Penick taught him as a junior to assert the pressure with his thumbs on the top part of the putter, the flat face on Crenshaw's grip.

"Harvey said if the thumbs were in the right spot, the palms and everything else would be where they're supposed to be," Crenshaw said. "That's what I think about."

Crenshaw won two Masters and seventeen more PGA Tour events with his Wilson 8802 putter known as "Little Ben." Padgett played often with Crenshaw in the early 1970s and marvels at how his stroke hasn't changed in four decades.

"Ben's an old soul," Padgett says. "His golf swing is old school, his putting stroke is old school. You look at guys from his era, no one has the long, slow, flowing stroke he has."

Bill Coore says he's always thought one reason Crenshaw was so good on the greens was that he could read them better than anyone and see breaks that were not visible to others.

"I think part of it's his incredible eyesight," Coore says. "We'll be standing on a tee somewhere and he's pointing out a rock four hundred yards away. It's like he's seeing every single blade of grass in a fairway."

Crenshaw applies his smooth stroke to the greens on No. 2 during a media exhibition in April 2011.

from 1971-73, shared a third with Tom Kite and debuted on the PGA Tour in the fall of 1973 with a win in his first competition, the San Antonio Texas Open. His next event was a second-place finish in the 144-hole World Open at Pinehurst, with Crenshaw shooting scores like 64 by day and listening to host Peter Tufts of the Pinehurst founding family regale him with stories of the resort's history at night.

Crenshaw trailed Miller Barber in the final round by one stroke on the tee of the sixteenth hole, which then was a regulation par-five at 504 yards. He wanted a birdie in the worst way and hit the gas a bit too hard with his driver, pull-hooking the ball seventy yards left of the fairway in the woods at the base of the practice tee. He bogeyed the hole and finished three shots behind Barber.

"I was just trying to hit the ball five hundred yards," Crenshaw says.

Many years later, country-western singer Larry Gatlin was playing No. 2 with Pinehurst native Marty McKenzie. Gatlin and Crenshaw are pals from Austin and Barton Creek Country Club, and McKenzie told Gatlin about Crenshaw's errant shot on sixteen, whereupon Gatlin pulled out a cell phone, got Crenshaw on the line and proceeded to rag him about the shot.

"I rope-hooked it all the way to Aberdeen!" Crenshaw told Gatlin.

Riding a silky smooth putting stroke, a deft ability to read greens and a friendly Bulls-Eye putter named "Little Ben" (a Wilson 8802 he found in a municipal golf shop rack as a teenager), Crenshaw evolved into one golf's luminaries through the close of the 20th century. He won the 1984 and '95 Masters, seventeen other tour events and played on four Ryder Cup teams. The apex came at Brookline in '99 when he predicted his team's miraculous Sunday rally from four points down by concluding his Saturday night press briefing by winking, wagging his finger and saying, "I'm a big believer in fate."

The Americans rallied with a fury, clipping the European team, 14.5 points to 13.5, with a fiery charge that saw six straight Americans win their matches and fellow Texan Justin Leonard cap the victory with a forty-five foot putt against Jose Maria Olazabal. That glorious stroke set off an exuberant celebration by the Yanks on the seventeenth green that was deemed unsportsmanlike by the Europeans.

"The momentum of that final day carried us to different emo-tions," Crenshaw says. "The crowd played a big part. They sensed they were witnessing a comeback, something really special. We had the momentum the entire day and it continued on with Justin making that putt. That's what went over the top on seventeen. We simply couldn't contain ourselves. That's what we apologized for."

Since then, Crenshaw has settled into regular appearances on the PGA Champions Tour (he averaged just under twenty events and some $300,000 earnings a year in the three seasons from 2008-10) spending the rest of his time tending to his wife and three teenage daughters and the design business he and Coore started in 1985. He visited Pinehurst a half dozen times in 2010, spending three to four days on most visits and reveling in walking the fairways of No. 2 and interacting with resort staff, members and guests.

Most notable beyond his passion and feel for classic golf design is the fact that this very famous and revered man in golf is simply an in-ordinately nice man. Not only does he make eye contact with golfers spotting him on the periphery, his smile invites them to say hello and come and talk. He shows golfers photos of what No. 2 used to look like and tells them about the changes. Ben is too polite to correct one fellow who says his father met Crenshaw's father when they were both living in Ohio, knowing full well that Charlie Crenshaw never lived in Ohio a day in his life. He politely puts in his wallet a business card from a man with an audacious request for Crenshaw to send him an autographed photo.

Until the course closed in November 2010 for the heavy work, the designers and construction guys have to work carefully during the day while golfers are making their way around the course. That invariably leads to idle moments while golfers play their shots, and Ben and Toby Cobb frequently pass the time by making bets on how successful various golfers might be in executing their shots. A testament to Crenshaw's inherent good nature is that he always bets *for* the golfer.

"A dollar someone hits the green," Crenshaw says as they wait for a foursome to hit their tee shots on the long and difficult fifteenth.

"A dollar someone makes par," he says from beside the fifth green, waiting for a foursome of players to attempt to scramble for pars from the outskirts of the difficult green complex.

A golfer hits a good drive and Crenshaw says, "Great drive. Keep hitting 'em just like that."

This photo of Donald Ross playing on unkempt ground in Pinehurst "speaks volumes" to the philosophy Coore & Crenshaw brought to the restoration of No. 2.

Cobb remembers the design and construction process at Friar's Head in New York State several years earlier. Crenshaw, Cobb, the client and several other individuals were walking the course when Ben ventured off on the fifteenth hole to talk to a man charged with chiseling down a huge boulder in the middle of the fairway.

"Thirty minutes later, they're still talking," Cobb says. "The rest of us have moved on and we're two holes ahead. You can be the President of the United States or you can be a guy sitting on a piece of equipment, and Ben will talk to you."

"So many highly recognized people are different in public than in real life," Coore says. "Ben is not. He's the same person. He's got his values and priorities in the right place."

One high school golf coach would vouch for that when he spots Crenshaw standing outside the Starbucks in Aberdeen early one morning. Crenshaw is getting his caffeine fix and enjoying one of his rituals of the road. "For a traveling guy, Starbucks is a sense of familiarity, a little feeling of home," he says.

The coach is on his way to his team's competition that day in the North Carolina state high school championships at Pinehurst Country Club.

"I'll tell the kids I saw you," the man says. "I'm sure it's a good omen."

Crenshaw smiles. "Tell them to play well," he says. For Crenshaw, that's no idle throwaway line. He means it.

***

Bill Coore is sitting in the grill room at Pinehurst Country Club one afternoon in July 2010, looking at a photo of golf architect Donald Ross that hangs on the south wall of the expansive room. The image shows Ross in a follow-through position after striking a golf shot. There is a small water hazard behind him, so perhaps the setting is the sixteenth hole on No. 2 or even the abandoned tenth hole on No. 2 that ran over ground where the No. 4 course sits today. The ground around him is rugged—sand, wire grass, stray weeds—and the trees are spare and scraggy; one assumes Ross is playing from a spot between a tee and the fairway. Ross is not a young man in the photo (his mustache has turned gray), but the teeing area in the background has not been grassed, meaning the photo was likely taken sometime in the mid-1920s, before Ross's late 1920s experiments with rye grass led to a uniform planting on all tees.

The photo illustrates the idea that the quality of golf years ago was judged more on strategy than the cultivation of grass.

"That picture speaks volumes," Coore says. "Donald Ross didn't just go out there at random and pick that spot. It doesn't have anything to do with trees, it doesn't have anything to do with beautiful turf. He's hitting the ball out of sand and wire grass. To Ben and me, that means something."

Ben and me has been in business of designing new golf courses and restoring old ones for more than a quarter of a century now. The firm of Coore & Crenshaw was formed in December 1985 and had completed approximately two dozen golf courses by the end of 2010 and done so in landforms as diverse as the meadows and hillsides of Colorado, the low country of South Carolina and the coastal dunes of Tasmania. Ideally they work on no more than two courses at a time, melding Coore's background in golf course construction and maintenance and innate feel for routings with Crenshaw's perspective as a competitor at the highest levels, a tourist on many of the world's finest courses and a master of the delicate brush strokes around greens complexes.

After Coore completed his first solo design at Rockport Country Club in Corpus Christi in 1982, he stayed on as course superintendent and then took on a design job at another Corpus Christi club, Kings Crossing. By then Crenshaw was interested in learning golf course design and had served as a player consultant to designer Jay Moorish on the TPC at Las Colinas in Dallas.

A man named Charlie Bellaire was going to be project manager of a proposed course on the Gulf Coast in Corpus Christi. He knew Coore and liked his work at Rockport. He asked Coore why he didn't hitch his talents to the name of a well-known professional golfer. Coore answered in throwaway fashion that he'd never given it much thought, but if he did, "it might be someone like Ben Crenshaw." Bellaire took it upon himself in summer of 1984 to invite Crenshaw and Coore, who had never met one another, to a luncheon announcing that they were going to team up and design this new course.

"It was one of the most embarrassing moments I've ever been

though in my life," Coore says. "We're sitting in this room with all these people and Ben and I had barely shaken hands. We both had a blank stare on our faces."

That project never had a chance of proceeding, but Coore and Crenshaw used that afternoon to drive to Rockport and tour Coore's handiwork.

"I liked what I saw," Crenshaw says. "I liked how natural it looked. I was fascinated with architecture, always had been."

Thus began a friendship that evolved with frequent phone calls and Coore's visits to PGA Tour venues in Texas to watch Crenshaw play golf. Over dinner in the evenings they would discuss golf courses they liked and didn't like, golf books they'd read and people they'd met.

"Eventually I just blurted out that maybe we could think about a partnership," says Crenshaw. "Bill said he would need to really think on that. It was not that he was totally against the idea, but it took a while."

Crenshaw smiles.

"He had no idea what he was getting into."

Design associate Toby Cobb hears the story and notes the odd circumstance of pursuer and pursuee.

"That's the exact *opposite* of what normally happens," Cobb says. "Usually it's the budding architect going to the big-name player with the idea to join forces."

Coore actually cannot recall the circumstances of them deciding to form a partnership in the fall of 1985, some eighteen months after Crenshaw shot a final-round 68 to beat Tom Watson by two shots at Augusta.

"That's so strange, isn't it?" Coore marvels. "But that proves to me how natural the union was. It was not a memorable event, and you'd think it would have been very memorable. But it was just a natural occurrence."

Coore does remember an interview in late 1985 at Barton Creek

outside Austin when Ron Whitten of *Golf Digest* sat down with the two budding architects.

"His first question was, 'What's the name of your firm?'" Coore says. "Ben and I looked at each other. We'd never given it any thought, which goes to show how naïve we were about business. So here we were, we'd just become partners and we flunked the first question.

"But Ben didn't miss a beat. He answered, 'The name is Coore and Crenshaw.' That tells you a lot about Ben. I can confidently say I don't know of another highly accomplished touring professional that would have made that decision and put his own name second."

The early road was fraught with ditches, obstacles and bad luck. Coore chuckles ruefully when he says the firm had "the dubious distinction" of working on four jobs in the mid and late 1980s, none of which was ever completed. Deals faltered, the savings and loan crisis reared its ugly head, leveraged buy-outs impacted ownership groups. Meanwhile, the firm did some remodeling jobs and Coore worked independently designing a course in France—Golf du Médoc in the wine-centric city of Bordeaux.

"We had four years and nothing to show for it," Coore says. "Ron Whitten wrote another piece for *Golf Digest* and said we were the only guys he'd even seen who formed a partnership and immediately retired. That's what it looked like."

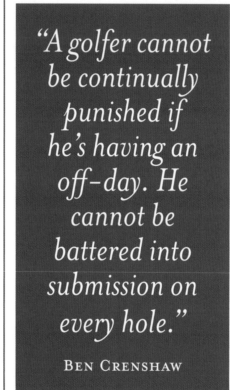

"A golfer cannot be continually punished if he's having an off-day. He cannot be battered into submission on every hole."

BEN CRENSHAW

"Gosh, I remember getting static at home," Crenshaw says. "Julie couldn't understand what we were doing, and rightly so. We had this partnership to design golf courses and we couldn't get one finished."

Finally, two jobs came along with staying power—Barton Creek in Austin and Kapalua on Hawaii. They both opened in the spring of 1991.

Crenshaw talked one morning at Barton Creek in December 1990 about the flavor and style of the course growing in to a spring opening—it had wide fairways, greens with open entrances and chipping areas around the greens to provide recovery options, all with direct connections to Coore & Crenshaw's fancy for understated features. Golf was riding the worldwide economic boom of the late 1980s and courses were sprouting up in every corner of the nation. The golf media universe was expanding and filling its pages with sexy photo spreads, the course ranking business was gaining momentum and the heroic hole—the "signature hole"—was an important marketing element of any project. Ben and Bill were not jumping on that bandwagon.

"I think this instance of all or nothing on so many golf courses is totally wrong," Crenshaw said that day. "First of all, golf was never meant to be a death or glory situation on every hole. It hasn't been that way for a hundred years. A golfer cannot be continually punished if he's having an off-day. He cannot be battered into submission on every hole.

"That's why St. Andrews is so great. You can make a lot of bogeys, but it's hard to make a double. At the same time, you have to play excellent golf to make a birdie. That's what Pinehurst is all about."

It was at Barton Creek that Bill and Ben made their first connection with Dick Youngscap, a building architect from Lincoln, Neb., who had recently made his first foray into golf development with the 1985 opening of Firethorn Golf Club. Pete Dye designed the course with a links-style flavor, and the project whetted the maverick Youngscap's vision of creating a unique golf experience somewhere amidst the 18,000 square miles of north-central Nebraska—the windy, sandy, grass-covered dunes known as the Sand Hills. Youngscap had identified some land near the town of Mullen (population five hundred), an hour from the nearest airport and approximately three hundred miles between Lincoln to the southeast and Denver to the southwest. He was attempting to entice investors to what would be a private club with a "Field of Dreams" vision: There is no market in central Nebraska for such a club, but if you build something special, the members will come.

Youngscap took Coore, Crenshaw and business manager Scotty Sayers on a helicopter inspection of the site.

"We were blown away by how natural the site was," Crenshaw says. "Bill and I said we'd do it for nothing. Scotty just about choked on that one."

They took the job, Crenshaw even putting personal money into the project as an investor.

Coore wandered the site frequently over two years in the early 1990s, often by himself and sometimes for four or five days at a stretch, looking for the best holes amidst the ridges and "blow-outs"—the natural bunkers created by eons of wind blasting against the land—while Youngscap was trying to raise funds for what Coore says "most considered a complete folly." Coore carried in his pocket a piece of company letterhead on which he drew tiny drawings of potential holes; there were more than a hundred sketches of potential holes by the time Youngscap acquired his financing and they were ready to break ground in the spring of 1993.

"It was so virgin, so pristine, so fabulous," Coore says. "We planned it for over a year. It was actually hard to pull the trigger on the final design because we had so many holes, so many options. It was tough to pick eighteen. It was so beautiful, we didn't want to mess it up."

Coore says he'll never forget seeing construction chief Dave Axland sitting on a backhoe on what would become the eighth hole, steeling his nerves to take the first bite from the ground.

"Dave sat there a good while," he says. "All of us knew we'd never get a shot like that again. The one thing everyone thought about was: 'Don't mess this up.'"

The result at Sand Hills Golf Club was roundly applauded upon its opening in 1995 by Youngscap, the 140 members who joined, the golf press and anyone who made the effort to get there. It cost only $1.2 million to build (the going rate at the time was from $5-10 million) and the architects disturbed only three thousand cubic yards of dirt, essentially, as fellow architect Tom Doak noted, "moving the dirt in spoonfuls" to create greens and tees. The course was pegged No. 8 in the United States in *GOLF* Magazine's 2011 list of the Top 100 Courses in the United States and No. 9 in *Golf Digest's* 100 Greatest Courses in the United States.

Hanging today in the clubhouse is Coore's original map of holes, the kaleidoscope of lines named "The Golf Constellation" because it looks like a map of the heavens.

"It was a hodgepodge," Coore says. "It looked like an explosion in a spaghetti factory."

TUFTS TOWN TIME CAPSULE

Located in a wing of the Given Memorial Library in the Village of Pinehurst resides a microcosm of life a century ago. Within the Tufts Archives is stored as a complete a record of the early years of Pinehurst as you could find—short of hearing the New England accent of James W. Tufts or the Scottish brogue of Donald Ross himself.

Letters that today might be sent via e-mail or broken into fragments of text messages were written in longhand or dictated, typed and duplicated with carbon paper. Thousands of them are stacked neatly in file folders on the Archives' shelves.

Images that today are compendiums of 0s and 1s and transmitted through thin air were captured on film in the 1920s and printed onto glossy paper. Cans of negatives rest in cold storage downstairs and the images have been digitally copied.

Golf courses that are planned today on sophisticated Cad systems were sketched by Ross in pencil on grid-lined paper with cursive notes in the margins. More than three hundred of his original field sketches from courses around the country are catalogued in the Archives.

"We have such a thorough history of an urban movement," says Audrey Moriarty, executive director of the Archives since 2002. "What happened here mirrored what was happening around the country. We have such an intricate and precise record of what happened. It's so clean and well document-

ed. We have every single letter that Pinehurst management wrote and mailed out and every one it received. It's a very, very complete history."

The Archives were created in 1975 at the behest of Richard Tufts, grandson of the founder, and are funded today by the Tufts Foundation, various fund-raising projects, sales of archival images and donations from supporters.

On display in glass cases are an array of photographs, documents, maps and artifacts dating to the beginning in Pinehurst. James Tufts' marble and silver 19th-century Arctic Soda Fountain Machine and items from the Tufts silverplate business are among the artifacts. Visitors can view the original landscape plan of the Village by Frederick Law Olmsted, and photos and plans of many of the original cottages are catalogued as well.

The Archives has more than eighty thousand negatives from the John Hemmer collection. Hemmer was the official photographer for Pinehurst from the late 1920s through the 1960s, and his images appeared in the pages of newspapers and magazines around the nation.

Moriarty and her staff have taken various initiatives in the last decade to enhance the historical experience of Pinehurst and the Archives, including construction of a replica sand green outside the building, publication of a Pinehurst Walking Tour Book and hosting monthly "Gathering at Given" events featuring speakers of local interest.

> "We have such a thorough history of an urban movement."
>
> AUDREY MORIARTY

Display cases, book shelves and computer storage drives in the Tufts Archives are filled with the history of Pinehurst—including the original crest of The Carolina Hotel, golf bag tags from the country club and a pack of vintage Pinehurst brand cigarettes.

Pointing the way: Ben Crenshaw makes a point on the design nuances on No. 2 while Bill Coore tells Mike Davis of the USGA (opposite) how he envisions tweaking a bunker.

locked into specific par or yardage for a course— "We just let it evolve," Coore says.

In the end, Coore says, the architect's job is to take a piece of land and build something that entices people to play golf.

"Mother Nature does that better than we can," he says. "All we're trying to do is imitate nature. The variables in nature are never-ending. That's what we're trying to do here. Donald Ross took what was naturally here and built a golf course around it. Over time, it got away from that natural look. We're trying to put Mother Nature back into Pinehurst No. 2."

No matter the verbiage, the results have garnered critical acclaim in any geographical venue. Representative of quality of job sites and developer missions that have come Coore & Crenshaw's way since their early success with Sand Hills is Chechessee Creek Club, a course nestled in a bucolic setting between Beaufort and Hilton Head on the South Carolina coast.

Jim Chaffin grew up in rural Halifax County, Va., and earned money as a boy in the 1950s caddying on a nine-hole course with greens made of clay and sand. After each hole, the caddie would drag the green with a piece of carpet, smoothing out the surface for the next group, just as the old caddies did in Pinehurst in the early 20th century. There he developed a deep and abiding love for the game, its traditions and the innate simplicity of enjoying sport in the great out-of-doors.

"Golf was a real gift to me," says Chaffin, who went on to play golf at the University of Virginia, then began his life in the residential and golf development industry working for Charles Fraser at Sea Pines Plantation.

"I really have gratitude for everybody who has protected the essence of the game and who has tried to keep it unpretentious and low-key and dedicated to civil behavior," Chaffin says. "And, frankly, I think fundamental to golf's appeal is the simple

The result also quieted the skeptics in the local community who could not for the life of them reconcile the concept of the emerald green golf courses they'd seen on television from California and Florida with the raw land in the Nebraska outback.

"Nobody could quite understand what we were trying to do at first," Crenshaw says. "The local people didn't know what we were about at all. They said, 'You're gonna build a golf course out here?' Their idea of golf was to build lakes and to plant trees. We showed them holes of historic golf courses in England, Scotland and Ireland, and they said, 'Well gosh, that looks a lot like our ground.'"

The Sand Hills job helped catapult Coore & Crenshaw's brand into a targeted niche that can't be easily categorized. Fifteen years later, Coore looks befuddled when pressed by a lunch companion in Pinehurst to apply a label to the firm's style of design. The word *minimalist* has been used. The term *least disturbance* has been thrown about. Coore shrugs and says that *site specific* might be accurate. He tells of a marketing executive at the Golf Club of Cuscowilla in Georgia asking him for the "signature hole" to put on a brochure cover. "I had no idea where to take him," Coore says. They are never fact that it's played outside. Those early guys with crooked shafts, they weren't worried about the quality of their lie or the Stimp-meter on the greens. They were just outside. They were outdoors in a little friendly competition. And I think that when you create a golf experience, you want people not simply to be challenged by the experience, but enriched by the environment in which they are playing."

Chaffin and partner Jim Light developed twenty-one golf courses and communities from the Pacific Northwest to Colorado to the South Carolina coast, two of them outside of Beaufort—Spring Island and Callawassie Island Club. In the mid-1990s they acquired 360 acres between the entrances to Spring Island and Callawassie, and Chaffin says the mix of open fields used for agriculture in earlier times, the tidal marshes and the canopy of three-hundred-year old live oaks was the ideal setting for an understated club and golf course built, simply, for the love of the game.

"We wanted a course that felt like a group of folks had come down from Chicago in the 1930s when land was cheap and bought some land and built their own golf course and a sweet, small, unpretentious clubhouse and then a group of cottages, one for each family," he says. "Old-fashioned golf—a golf course that is authentic to the land and takes whatever integrity there is in the ground and evolves from there. We wanted a walking course, no long hikes from one hole to the next. You know, there's nothing really wrong today with the game of golf. What's wrong with the game is what developers have done to sell real estate around golf courses. Land planners have not always given the best land to the golf course architect."

Chaffin/Light Associates had worked over two decades with Tom Fazio, Arnold Palmer and Ed Seay, Rees Jones—almost everyone who was anyone in the golf architecture business. They knew the vision and the land were perfect for Coore & Crenshaw. Chaffin wondered what would happen if you brought Donald Ross, A.W. Tillinghast, Seth Raynor and Alister MacKenzie back to life, what would their collaboration at Chechessee Creek have looked like?

"I'm not sure you can find two people who have protected the essence of the game any better than Ben and Bill," Chaffin says. "They are authentic and they have this incredible partnership and an innate feel for one another. We just knew anyone else would come in here and start pushing up a lot of dirt. And we knew that Ben and Bill would, one, be very respectful of what was here, and, two, move a minimum amount of dirt. I remember one of Bill's first visits here. He'd been out walking the land all day and said, 'I can really *feel* the golf course here.'"

Chaffin wanted a hands-on designer—or two hands-on designers, as the case may be. He remembers their energy walking the golf course on hot afternoons, the hours Coore spent floating greens himself on a small machine that looked like a riding lawnmower.

"Both of these guys are muddy-boots guys," he says. "Ben would come here about every third visit that Bill made and he'd have his boots with him. He didn't want me riding him around in a cart."

Most golf architects work from intricate topographical maps and

Crenshaw & Coore on site at Sand Hills in the early 1990s. The course opened in 1995 to rave reviews and has been ranked consistently among the top 10 of American golf courses ever since. At right, the green of the par-three seventh hole at Chechessee Creek along the South Carolina coast is fronted by gnarly bunkers and native grasses.

most likely an early on-site visit to draw a comprehensive set of routing plans, hole configurations and construction blueprints. When those plans are approved by the course developer, the architect is paid from fifty to seventy percent of his design fee and the developer then sends the plans out to bids from construction companies. The architect earns the rest of his fee by making periodic visits to inspect the ongoing construction process.

Coore & Crenshaw knew from the beginning they lacked the skills to provide those kinds of drawings upfront and that they wanted their designs to be more hands-on than the standard process allowed. They receive a ten percent retainer upfront and the rest of their fee is paid in incre-

ments as the project evolves. One of the tenets the company was founded on was, "Know what you know, know what you're good at, and be realistic enough to know what your limitations are."

"Our idea was not to establish a large firm with many associates who would be producing those plans," Coore says. "We knew this process would limit the number of jobs we could handle. But that was okay. We conceived the business to work on one job at a time, ideally two at a time. We hoped we would have choices. And in the beginning, most of our inquiries came through Ben's name recognition. If we were fortunate to be able to choose, our thought was to pick the ones that would be fun, that provided us an opportunity to do something special and memorable.

"All we could promise a prospective client was to take his money and, in many cases, his dreams, and deliver the very best result within our capabilities. Growing the business has never been our goal. It's

odd, I guess—most businesses *want* to grow. We just chose to not grow. Philosophically, we're at a comfort level exactly where we are."

Coore insists on walking a new site frequently—sometimes even a dozen times—before arriving at a final routing. The fourth hole at Bandon Trails in Oregon would never have utilized a dramatic sand dune if the course had been drawn from a map as the dune didn't show up on the map. Coore says if he'd worked from wetlands maps in routing Dormie Club, just northwest of Pinehurst, he'd have handed the drawings back to the developer and told him, "No dice. You can't build a golf course here."

Instead, Coore walked the course and routed it by feel up and down the ridges and hills.

"It just proved to me that if you lay the golf course out the way the land wants to go, in most cases the wetlands are going to be okay," Coore says. "The topos will tell you a lot of things, but they won't tell you the feel of the place. You have to go walk a site and experience it, walk it up and down, get a feel for the way the golf course will circulate. Sometimes a map will appear totally uninteresting, but you get to the site and find all kinds of interesting features that didn't show on the map."

In Pinehurst from the launch of the No. 2 restoration project in February 2010 through the summer of 2011, at least one of the partners visited every month, Coore giving Cobb the down-and-dirty mandates on where to strip and spray unwanted grass, plant new wire grass and rework the bunkers, and Crenshaw fine-tuning the process, providing ideas and the perspective of the elite player.

"I have learned from Ben that a subtle contour or the consideration of a wind angle will serve the purpose of good golf more than any heavy-handed creation could ever achieve," Coore says.

Pinehurst President and COO Don Padgett once asked Cobb who had the trump card if they disagreed.

"Toby kind of laughed," Padgett says. "He answered that it would depend on what feature they disagreed on. He said if it was around the greens, Ben would probably prevail. If it was on routing, angles, approaches, it would be Bill."

The image of Donald Ross stands sentinel in this statue of the architect of No. 2 standing today in the Village of Pinehurst.

Crenshaw can remember only a couple of conflicts in all their years together, and those were minor.

"Both were totally off the beaten path, like whether to use the left hand side of the eleventh green at Colorado Golf Club a couple years ago, and we had a little disagreement at Barton Creek early on about the shape of the thirteenth green," he says.

Sometimes one of the partners will pull out his cell phone walking a hole and call the other to discuss the nuances of the question at hand. More common is Cobb taking notes and passing directives back and forth between each partner's visits.

"There's a lot of give and take between them," Cobb says. "They don't argue over things. They're very cooperative, they have a great deal of respect and admiration for what each brings to the table. A lot of times they have different ideas, but it never leads to an argument. There are no egos in this company. Ben is amazing. Here's a two-time Masters champ, and the other night we were down at Chili's for dinner and he's mobbed. But he interrupts his dinner to take time for pictures. He's very engaging.

"Outside our little world, everyone knows Ben. I mean, he's won the Masters two times. Not many people can say that. But in the golf design and construction business, Bill Coore is more of the rock star."

***

Bill Coore spends a hundred percent of his working life on Coore & Crenshaw design projects, traveling from his home in Scottsdale, Ariz., to sites as varied as Long Island, Nebraska, Tasmania and China. Ben Crenshaw travels once or twice a month to job sites between competitive forays onto the PGA Champions Tour. He and Coore communicate daily by cell phone, but they are decidedly low-tech. Coore doesn't use e-mail, do text messaging or carry a laptop computer, and he jokes that his cell phone is so old he can't always find a replacement battery on the road. It wasn't until Crenshaw's wife bought him an iPhone in 2010 that he ventured into the digital revolution. The firm is run and administered from the Austin, Texas, offices of Scotty Sayers, an attorney who has managed Crenshaw's business interests for some four decades.

Meanwhile, out in the field is a cadre of design and construction associates who execute and supervise the firm's projects on a day-to-day basis. They all have homes and families elsewhere but work roughly a three-weeks-on, one-week-off schedule. The man assigned to Pinehurst is Toby Cobb, a father of three who lives in the west Texas town of Canyon. Cobb met C&C associate Dave Axland in Nebraska in 1999 and a year later was offered the chance to work for the firm in the construction at Friar's Head on eastern Long Island. Since 2007, his post has been in the Sandhills managing the firm's design job at Dormie Club, a private golf club northwest of the Village of Pinehurst. The timing was perfect for Cobb to maintain his rental house in the interior of the No. 3 and 5 courses at Pinehurst Country Club when the Dormie construction wound down in the fall of 2009 and the No. 2 project commenced early the following year.

"You can't help but fall in love with Pinehurst the minute you get here," Cobb says. "It's sort of like Mayberry. Everybody's friendly, everybody's helpful. I'm just glad Bill and Ben got this assignment—it means I can work here a while longer."

It's quite a contrast, though, to have spent two years working on the Dormie course—out in the hinterlands of Moore County with no one around and a blank canvas in front of you—versus nipping and tucking on a century-old layout regarded as one of the nation's finest with golfers playing it every day.

"We're kind of tippy-toeing around out here," Cobb says during the early stages of the project. "We're not bringing in a lot of big machinery and making noise. We're clipping here, clipping there, trying to stay out of golfers' way."

On the Friday before Easter 2010, Cobb is busy on his "mini-ex"—shorthand for the compact excavator he uses to shape ground on a job site—and has recently put the finishing touches on a new bunker to the right of the thirteenth fairway, about a hundred yards short of the green. He deftly works the controls on the machine, scraping the sandy ground here, dumping and filling there, smoothing it all out in the end. Cobb draws on Pinehurst's maintenance crew for help as needed, but mostly in the beginning he's a one-man band, executing the decisions his bosses have made on their last visit and using his own skills and judgment to fill in the blanks.

"I like to take my time," Cobb says. "I'm not like a big golf-course contractor, who if I work fast I make more money. I just like to do it well. The other day a guy driving a tractor behind me said, 'You're really good on that machine, but you sure are slow.' He's right. I'd rather be good than fast."

Once the heavy work is completed on the mini-ex, Cobb takes a shovel to tuck and trim the bunker edges. There's no single template for creating bunkers; the idea is to give them a rough edge and hap-

hazard appearance that might have evolved over decades. The early bunkers in Scotland were nothing but crevices dug by sheep seeking refuge from the elements blowing off the North Sea; it's instructive for modern designers to keep that mental snapshot in mind.

"Some of what we're doing is taking the perfection out," Cobb says. "Bill talks about bunker edges being so perfect that it looks like they're 'painted' on the fairway. We try to give them a little bit of an 'edgy' look.' Ben uses the term 'spic-and-span.' We don't want the bunkers to have a 'spic-and-span' look to them. In other words, clean is not the look we want."

Much of their work over the coming year in Pinehurst will be shaped by the images Cobb carries on his ever-present clipboard—a stack of black-and-white prints of No. 2 taken from an airplane nearly seventy years ago. The images were provided by Craig Disher, a resident of suburban Washington, D.C., who has developed a network and skill set to locate aerial photos of golf courses nationwide taken by government workers in the World War II era. Disher is coincidentally a Pinehurst homeowner and Pinehurst Country Club member, and upon hearing of the Coore & Crenshaw project, he located photos from 1943 and provided the architects a set of enlargements.

The photographs gave Coore & Crenshaw a visual record of bunker placement and, combined with the center-line irrigation heads, an additional reference to the fairway boundaries as they existed five years prior to Donald Ross's death.

"The center lines and the aerial photos—those will take a lot of the guesswork out," Coore says. "We can base what we're doing on fact, not supposition or opinion. We can be bold now."

"Look at this—Christmas Day, 1943," Cobb says, holding his clipboard out for inspection. "Some poor guy had to go fly. His mission apparently was to take photos of the shooting range and fields at Fort Bragg. But the camera just kept running, so everything he flew over got photographed. Lucky for us."

Cobb holds the clipboard closer and uses a pen to point out the tiny specks of golfers on the sun-drenched fairway.

"Golf on Christmas Day," he says. "Not a bad way to enjoy the holiday."

He rummages through the photos, each eight-by-twelve print showing two holes, and runs his pen along the perimeters of the trees, bunkers and fairways.

"The photos are very revealing—bunkers have moved, gotten bigger or smaller or gone away totally," he says. "The grass lines are different. Bill and Ben like to say that over time, this golf course has just kind of lost its way. It had no shape. With practically wall-to-wall grass, there was no movement."

He points to the fourteenth hole.

"Look how the grass line sweeps around from left to right and then around the green," he says. "Today it's all grass, there is no definition."

As Cobb talks standing under a canopy of a half dozen pines between the thirteenth and fourteenth fairways, a ball lands nearby, hops once and skids into the new bunker.

"That bunker's getting a lot of business," he says. "This is a short hole, and it had gotten so that there was no fear off the tee. Hopefully this will give players a little something to think about."

While Cobb provides the day-to-day presence for Coore & Crenshaw in Pinehurst, an assortment of company associates and freelance designers and shapers will move in and out throughout the year—some staying a week or two, others coming for a stretch of months. Long-time Coore & Crenshaw associates Dave Axland, Dan Proctor and Jimbo Wright will lend a hand, while freelancers Kyle Franz, George Waters and Brian Caesar are recruited from a pool of guys who have worked for architects like Coore & Crenshaw, Tom Doak, Gil Hanse and Kyle Phillips.

Spending the most time in Pinehurst beyond Cobb's permanent posting will be Franz, who came to Pinehurst in August 2010 and would remain for ten months. Franz, a twenty-nine year-old native of Oregon, decided at a young age he wanted to be in the golf design business and has worked for Coore & Crenshaw on a project basis over the last decade.

"No. 2 might be the most study-able golf course I've ever seen

other than the Old Course," Franz says, one month into his arrival in the Sandhills. "That makes perfect sense—Donald Ross grew up just a few hours away from St. Andrews. He learned the nuances around those greens. There is so much intelligent stuff at the Old Course and right here—where to miss shots, where not to miss shots. It's fun to be out there and take it all in. I'm just scratching the surface. If I ever get the chance to do my own course some day, I'd love to do one with eighteen greens as interesting as these. I'm a total golf design nerd, for lack of a better term—so I'm in heaven here."

Franz has spent time in Dornoch as well and draws parallels easily in the ancient links on the northeast coast of Scotland and Pinehurst No. 2. One of Franz's favorite holes at Dornoch is the par-four fourteenth. The "Foxy Hole"—each hole at Dornoch is nicknamed—runs 445 yards with a slight turn from left to right. There are no bunkers, and the green sits on a plateau.

"If you pick up the grassing pattern and green arrangement of that hole and put it on top of the second hole here, they're identical," Franz says. "Both greens have a bump front-right of the green that is a form of hazard, that kind of defines the hole. The swales on the Foxy Hole are like little hazards. They're in the same places as the bunkers on the second hole here. It all lines up exactly the same."

Another nuance to No. 2 that Franz likes is the small spine running into the green on the eighth hole that, he says, serves the same function as a tiny ridge on the front of the second green at Dornoch. The ridge begins just under a hundred yards from the green and runs toward the putting surface.

"Ross mentioned the eighth green site in a couple of places I've read," Franz says. "He was so in love with that little spine. He wanted you to be on one side of the fairway or the other, depending where the pin was that day. That green, if you miss it left, right or rear, you're in big trouble. The concept is the same on the second hole at Royal Dornoch. The whole front approach area is pretty calm, but there is one

"No. 2 might be the most study-able golf course I've ever seen other than the Old Course."

KYLE FRANZ

little feature, one little mound, on the front of the green. You have to land your ball to one side or the other, depending on where the pin is. And if you miss the green left, right or rear, it's a killer coming back."

As the months evolved and the workload ramped up after the closing of No. 2 in mid-November, Cobb and Franz reached out to other contacts in the golf design and construction business, offering work to a pair of West Coast residents, Waters and Caesar.

Waters came across the country from San Francisco, where he is an assistant superintendent at California Golf Club and enjoys a liberal allowance from his bosses to take time off if interesting golf course construction jobs come along. Waters met Franz in 2003 when both were working on Doak's Australian design, Barnbougle Dunes.

"I had been on Kyle ever since I heard he was coming to Pinehurst—'If you need any help …'" Waters says.

"George was the first person I called when we got in a bind," Franz says.

"What an education," Waters says. "You're getting to immerse yourself in one of the greatest golf courses in the world and spend time with two of the greatest architects of the modern era."

Waters had visited Pinehurst about five years earlier, around the time of the 2005 U.S. Open, and remembers being struck by the "monochrome look" of the course.

"It was a sea of green, huge corridors of stark green with a smattering of bunkers," he says. "No. 2 had become too homogenized. What we did was reveal what had been there originally. We brought the strategy back to life. It had been all grassed over. This has been a remarkable transformation for such a great golf course. I've never worked on one that was so well established but had such a major facelift."

Caesar, who lives in Bend, Ore., met Franz and Waters working on The Dukes Course at St. Andrews.

"No. 2 is simple, yet well thought-out," Caesar says. "It's very subtle. It's been exciting to help bring it back. I love the way we added some speed to the golf course. If you hit it crooked now, it's going to go further from the fairways. I hope they keep that part of it going after we leave—get it really firm and really fast."

Axland and Proctor are two of the longest tenured staff members on the Coore & Crenshaw shingle. Axland came to Pinehurst for three weeks in November 2010 and Proctor chipped in for a month after the New Year. They have worked on various Coore & Crenshaw courses over more than two decades and have collaborated outside the Coore & Crenshaw umbrella to design a course in Gothenburg, Neb., Wild Horse Golf Club. Coore traveled to Pinehurst in the early stages of his design career, once with Proctor and another time with a shaper, Jerry Clark, for the express purpose of communicating to them what a quality golf course should look like. Clark, for example, had built only roads before and Coore wanted him to see the flow of the ground on No. 2 and the gentle pitches and nooks around greens like the fourteenth.

"The inspiration for our greens comes from Pinehurst," Proctor said one January afternoon. "You can see it in our work.

"Bill always drills into us the 'fun factor,'" he says. "You could tell there were a lot of fun little shots around here, that it wouldn't beat you to death, that you could walk it and enjoy your round. You got a sense for how low to the ground the course was but still how much it all moved. It's subtle stuff, it's fascinating to study."

Proctor enjoyed seeing the course, in effect, evolve backward into its classic bearing of yesteryear.

"It's looking older by the day," he said another afternoon. "There are a lot of golf courses like this across this country—over watered and over fertilized. This will be a dramatic improvement. I love it."

The talent and dedication of the staff are never lost on the bosses. Coore, in fact, laments the state of the golf economy as 2011 evolves and the fact there is little new golf construction work available.

"Some of this business can be taught, the rest is innate talent," Coore says. "It's like Ben just can't believe that everyone can't make putts like he does. He says, 'Just roll the ball to the hole.' Ben Crenshaw has a gift. I think our guys have a gift to take the ground and create interesting looking features on a golf course.

"These guys are so talented. They study this stuff beyond belief. It's sad in that in today's golf industry, there is just not enough work for them. There are no jobs out there, certainly not much new. They've gone from having all kinds of opportunities five years ago to next to nothing now. But they love it and they're good at it. They are really, really good at it."

"IT'S A BEAUTIFUL DAY ..."

At the opposite end of the phone line, is flesh and blood. There is a real person—not a computer navigated by a series of keyboard punches.

"It's a beautiful day in Pinehurst."

Ring the main number at The Carolina Hotel and Pinehurst Resort and you find Gloria Spencer or one of her fellow phone operators.

"People say I make their day, pump them up a little bit," says Spencer, who began working the resort phone lines in 1985. "It makes me feel good to say it. Rain or snow, it doesn't matter, people call and say, 'I called just to hear you say that.' It's a personal touch that's important."

Spencer and a staff of five operators work the phones around the clock, presenting a subliminal message to callers that Pinehurst is a better place than any they might be calling from.

"Pinehurst to me means serenity, it's peace, it's the people," Gloria says. "When I first came to work here, I thought I was going on a picnic, it's such a place of beauty. Pinehurst is such a peaceful, calming place."

Another signature greeting of Pinehurst is the three hundred yards of Carolina Vista, the lane that runs from Hwy. 2 north to The Carolina Hotel. The stately white building sits grandly in the distance with its copper roof and signature cupola, framed by a canopy of seventy-eight hollies and pines and hundreds of flowers nestled along the street. Travelers often have driven from distant parts or ridden for ninety minutes from the airport in Raleigh and are

taken aback as they pass from the here-and-now into antique nirvana.

Jack Kennally has worked on the transportation staff at Pinehurst for a decade and has heard first-time visitors grouse about the long drive from Raleigh-Durham International.

"They ask, 'Why'd they build it so far from the airport?'" says Kennally, who then tells them Pinehurst was built *before* the airport. That gives them some perspective and puts them in the proper frame of mind when his shuttle turns off the round-about and winds its way up the Vista.

"They love the architecture of the houses along the lane," Kennally says. "They say, 'Oh, it's lovely.' They imagine what it looked like back in the thirties, that kind of thing. The big dome, the copper cupola, are very striking. The drive up the Vista sets a nice tone for the visit."

Carolina Hotel General Manager Scott Brewton drives out of his way each day coming to work—eschewing a more direct route into the employee parking lot in back of the hotel in favor of entering via Hwy. 2 and Carolina Vista and passing by the old world grandeur of Ailsa House, Beacon House, Heartpine House and Little House.

"You swing off the traffic circle and there's a gentle rise, and it's like the hotel comes out of the ground," Brewton says. "There are flowers on your left and right, people walking dogs or carrying tennis racquets. It's a nice visual to start every day."

May Wood, a golfer at Vanderbilt University

in 2002 and the winner that year of the Women's North and South Amateur, remembers her first drive along Carolina Vista.

"It was electrifying," she says. "I almost teared up the first time I saw it. It was the most beautiful place I'd ever been."

A smile and warm welcome at the bell stand continue the transition from the kinetic energy outside the bubble of Pinehurst.

"The first thing we want to do is say, 'You're at home, relax and come in,'" says Eddie Mitchell, a long-time bellman. "It's our job to make sure people decompress as soon as they get here. If we do it right, by the time you get to the front desk, you're ready to rest and relax."

The white rocking chairs around the porch wrapped to the south and west sides of The Carolina take relaxation to a higher notch. They're perfect early on a Sunday morning with coffee and a newspaper, late in the afternoon with a good novel or at midnight over cordials and fond memories of the day past.

The *beautiful day* theme carries from the hotel into the Village, where there are no right angles in the roads and no large signs on the shops and you half expect to see Beaver Cleaver or Barney Fife walking down the side-walk. James Tufts' New England roots dominate the architecture—the arched doorways, the Colonial Revival facades, the sharply pitched roofs and the gables, the cedar and redwood

trim, the white picket fences, the cabins built of juniper logs, the original heart-pine columns of the "Casino" building (now a real-estate agent's office). Pinehurst has no drive-up windows, but one bank has a "Walk-Up Garden." And then there are the colors, the two best being the forest green throughout the village and the sepia on the old photographs preserving the history— from the halls of The Carolina Hotel to the file books in the Tufts Archives.

"Each day you spend in Pinehurst, you escape the real world," says clothier Chris Dalrymple, who owns Gentleman's Corner. "You mark it off as a day you succeeded."

Scott Straight has visited Pinehurst frequently from his home in French Lick, Ind., sometimes as a guest of the gathering hosted each fall by Fluor Corporation and other times on a spring golf outing with friends and family. When he first came in the early 2000s, cellular service was spotty in the Sandhills.

"It's like going back in time, back to a much simpler time," Straight says. "I couldn't believe it when I first visited. Here I was in this little village, this golf resort, with no cell service, no e-mail, totally removed from the world."

He smiles, noting the evolution of technology.

"Unfortunately, somebody went and put a cell tower nearby," he says.

Still, Pinehurst is in a beautiful world of its own.

Playing a round of golf is not merely a question of getting around, like traveling over a race course or walking around the block. It's rather a question of taking nine or eighteen separate and distinct little journeys, each of which presents its own distinct pictures and its own distinct problems as part of the grand tour.

CHARLES BANKS

The pre-restoration seventeenth green (inset) was enveloped in smooth bunker dimensions and thick rough. Today the look is anything but.

PINEHURST COUNTRY CLUB TERRACE, PINEHURST, N.C.

Yearbook

Bill Coore is standing one morning in late April 2010 to the right of the second fairway of Pinehurst No. 2, some ten yards removed from the short grass and another ten from the thicket of pine trees that separate it from the forest bordering the length of the hole. He nods toward a general area of hardpan sand and wire grass and tells a story of watching U.S. Open qualifying in Pinehurst at some point in the 1960s and seeing Phil Rodgers facing a difficult shot from that general vicinity.

"I thought, 'Oh gosh, all he can do is advance it.' The lie looked like he was hitting off rock," Coore says. "But he picked that ball off the hardpan and knocked it on the green. I was stunned. The sound the club made hitting that sand was different from anything I had ever heard. It was so interesting

Mother Nature's handiwork adds texture to the right of the par-three sixth hole.

to me. I thought that if he had been three inches to the side, he might have been against a tuft of wire grass and had no shot at all. Instead, he had a little bit of an opening and had the skill to pull it off.

"I remember standing there and thinking, 'This is infinitely more interesting than if he'd been in grass three inches thick.' It's a vivid memory. We're going to try to bring a little of that back."

That's the goal of Coore, partner Ben Crenshaw and

their design and construction associates over the coming year—resurrect the aura, flavor and personality of the old Pinehurst No. 2. Coore is making his way around the course with design associate Toby Cobb upon returning to Pinehurst for the first time since late March. The water has been turned off, except for the center-line irrigation heads, and that combined with a dry spring is starting to give No. 2 a hint of the look to come—bright green tees, fairways and putting surfaces, a paler hue and even some tan and brown everywhere else.

"What I see is the attractiveness of a different palette of color," Coore says. "Before, you had just one shade of green everywhere. Now you have everything from all shades of green and brown to all the stuff in between. That, in and of itself, is an attractive picture."

Every few yards around the course, Coore sees something that ignites an opinion, a memory, a plan for the restoration job. Moving toward the green of the second hole, he motions to the hump at the front of the putting surface, the rise that casts balls left, right or even over the green, depending on where the shot lands on or around the hump. Crenshaw says the knob "defines the hole" and dictates every shot, and Coore elaborates on the roles that a design

6

element like that can have on the strategy of a hole.

"So many holes that are interesting have one dominant feature," he says. "It could be a big hump in the green like this or a large mound with scruffy stuff or a dip in the fairway. It's nothing that whacks you over the head. It can be very subtle. But it's the right touch at just the exact spot."

Coore stands on the front of the green and looks at the pocks in the ground surrounding it—the dips made possible by the excellent drainage quality of the sandy soil.

"What is so difficult is to *think* random," he says. "It goes against all human nature. You want to structure things, put them in an orderly fashion or what looks like a studious fashion. *They really studied that, they did that just right.* The best golf courses I've seen, you look and you say, 'How did they ever think of that?' You can't figure out how they thought of it. Most golf courses you can see them and say, 'Okay, you can follow the thought process. They did this and this and this, you follow the structure.' What you like to find are things that don't follow any logical thought pattern. That is certainly what Donald Ross created on this golf course."

Coore has marveled for some four decades at how No. 2 adds strokes to your scorecard in a drip, drip, drip fashion—not so much in a waterfall cascade but a quiet leakage that has a five-handicapper writing down 83 at the end of the day.

"The golf course lulls you into mistakes as opposed to bludgeoning you with them," he says. "In my opinion, a golf course is like a good book, there's an ebb and flow to it. The theme runs throughout the story, but it's presented, then fades away, then is presented again. If you're reading a drama and it continues to build constantly without a lessening of tension, the effect is lost. You build up and then soften, step back a ways, set the tone for the next stage of development. Mister Ross did that so well."

Among the themes of the restoration that are never far from Coore's mind are reintroducing the element of intrigue to shots that miss the fairway and the absolute need to void the course of the straight lines that dominate. Picking up on the story of Rodgers and his ability to cleanly pick a long-iron off a thin, firm lie, Coore bemoans the prevalence of thick rough and the sameness of the penalty it invokes—at Pinehurst and everywhere else in golf.

"One thing we will introduce is the threat of the unknown," he says. "The fairways will be bigger. You can miss them and can be perfect on a hard, sandy spot. Or you can be behind wire grass or in a cuppy spot in the sand. When you've got rough four inches high on both sides, you go find it and hack it. You know what you're going to do, you grab the wedge when you're two hundred yards from your ball."

Coore notes the vast expanses between the tree lines. That breadth was originally one of No. 2's charms; players had enough space to work the angles from tee to fairway, from fairway to green. Standing on the fifth tee, he looks at an aerial photo from 1943 and contrasts it with the narrow avenue he and Crenshaw found earlier in the year.

"When you study the aerial photographs from bygone days, the fairways *moved*," Coore says. "They were constantly moving as opposed to a bowling alley appearance that went in straight lines. What's happened in recent years with all the Bermuda from tree-line to tree-line is the fairways were mowed in very, very narrow corridors. These narrow corridors were very straight. That's exactly the opposite of what No. 2 was known for, which was width in the fairways but also movement in a serpentine fashion as they worked their way from tee to green. We'll see more of that old movement as we eradicate the Bermuda."

Coore had not been to Pinehurst in many years when he visited in 2006 to inspect a potential site at the behest of Bob Hansen, who just happened to live in the former Donald Ross home beside the third green of No. 2. Hansen and some business partners had in mind a club northwest of Pinehurst and he wanted Coore & Crenshaw to design the course—this would open in 2010 as Dormie Club—and Coore remembers walking out of Hansen's house, strolling a few holes of No. 2 and thinking, "What has happened here?"

"It was the most uninteresting golf course," Coore says. "It was nothing like I remembered playing as a kid."

Standing on the thirteenth tee two hours later, Coore looks down the fairway and to the green in the distance, perched on a hillock some 350 yards away. The hole bends slightly from left-to-right, and the visual directly in the distance as one stands on the tee is a slope of ground that runs from the left side of the fairway into the woods. On their very first day in Pinehurst two months earlier, Coore and Crenshaw had noted the greenness of that area—the grass enriched

Maintenance workers leave pine cones where they fall from the trees under the Coore & Crenshaw restoration regimen. Note the haphazard planting of wire grass and the jagged bunker edges around the twelfth green of No. 2.

PLAN OF Nº 2 GOLF COURSE
PINEHURST COUNTRY CLUB — PINEHURST — N·C·

VILLAGE
GREEN

This blueprint of No. 2 from May 1911 shows the first and second holes and eleven through eighteen in essentially the same locations as they are a century later. Among those plying their skills on "The Deuce" in the early days was amateur great Bobby Jones (above).

with a thick coat of winter rye grass—and cited it as an example of what would change over the coming year.

"Let it go distressed," Coore said in February.

"If you could see some brown off the tee, it would be kind of neat," Crenshaw concurred. "There needs to be more color out here, more hues."

Now, after two months of the irrigation having been turned off and the rye beginning to wane in the warmer spring weather, Coore sees some positive results, both in the color of the extremity of the hole and placement of the new bunker on the right side of the fairway.

"It's starting to get a little of that look of distressed turf," he says. "Eventually it'll have more of a sandy appearance. We'll see what happens more naturally with water restriction. We'll see what nature does with some of this stuff. There will be other areas that, by the end of June, nothing will have happened and we'll have to increase the stress. Chemicals are a bad word these days. Let's say we'll 'manipulate its demise.'

"But it's a start. There is a little sense of something here, a little color on the hill. We're starting to get a sense of this hole. We're miles from being finished, but it's quite a difference from when we stood here two months ago. This is getting close to the old pictures. I think the addition of the bunker might concern a couple of people who are long players."

A few minutes later, as Coore and Cobb are walking up the thirteenth fairway, Pinehurst President and Chief Operating Officer Don Padgett drives up in a golf cart. The spring golf season is hitting its high gear, and some golfers playing No. 2 have voiced a concern about the apparent lack of grooming attention to the course. He looks toward the putting surface and points to an area to the left—the very spot that Coore was just talking about.

"Help us tell people what those areas are supposed to look like," Padgett says. "They think we are not taking care of the golf course. Maybe you could sign a letter, maybe we could give them a 'white paper' of sorts before they play. People look at the brown grass and think we don't have the money to maintain the golf course. We have to educate the average guy and tell him what the course is going to look like and feel like."

Over the next half hour, as Coore and Padgett move along the course, they trade memories of their early days on this and other golf courses and how tastes in course maintenance have evolved over several decades.

"Seeing all of this makes me feel like a kid again," Padgett says. "The golf course I grew up on in Indiana had single-row irrigation and a lot of areas had that brown look. They didn't water every square inch of a golf course back then."

"I never played any course that looked any different," Coore agrees. "Everything was single-row irrigation. Then you had Augusta and Muirfield Village—'son of Augusta.'"

Coore remembers his tenure at Rockport Country Club in Corpus Christi, Texas, in the early 1980s (he designed the course and remained as course superintendent for two years) and one instance when PGA Tour officials came to town to mark the course for an upcoming Tour Qualifying School. The tour staff had just been to Muirfield Village, Jack Nicklaus's opulent club in his hometown of Columbus, Ohio, to mark the course for the Memorial Tournament on the PGA Tour.

"They talked about how they didn't use *one single spot* of white paint on eighteen holes at Muirfield," Coore says. "They did mark a few little spots at the end of cart paths. Nicklaus immediately had the maintenance guys come out and re-sod those spots so there would be no white paint *anywhere*. That struck me. I thought, 'That's just not right.' You're trying to make every square inch of a golf course *perfect*."

It was such a seminal moment to Coore that he can remember exactly where he was standing when Wade Cagle of the Tour staff related the incident.

"I was standing on the steps of the eighth tee," he says ruefully. "I thought, 'Oh my God, is this where we're going?'"

Indeed, that's exactly where course maintenance has gone over three decades—perfect green on every square inch, a brown patch the size of a dime anywhere enough to sound the alarm in the maintenance shed. Coore shakes his head while musing that the toughest week for any private club superintendent is the one in April immediately following the Masters. Members have watched all weekend on television as the game's finest players compete on a course coiffed and buffed with an unlimited budget for staff, equipment and materials.

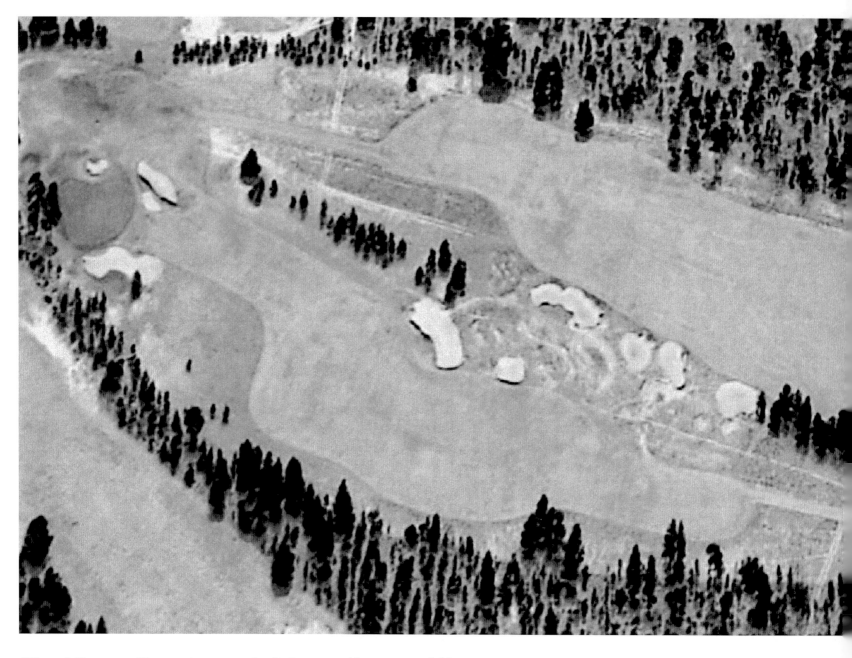

"To me," Coore says, "Augusta is an example of a fantastic golf course and a wonderful club. But to hold it up as the model for all golf courses is just not right."

Coore appreciates Padgett's worries about the perception from golfers, ultimately the people paying the bills. Padgett and the rest of Pinehurst management understand the restoration of No. 2 will be an evolving process—one that could take a couple of years or more. An important component is communicating the story to the resort and club's constituents.

"Think of this as a work in progress," Coore says. "It's hard to imitate Mother Nature and it's hard to reverse evolution. It took four decades to get to this point. It's not going to get back to that natural look overnight. I just hope people will be patient. What we're doing *sounds* easy—you just kill some grass. It's not that simple. I'm afraid people will look out here and say, 'What the hell are they doing?' By October, I think, you'll see a lot of areas that look about right."

The design team meets with Pinehurst and Tufts Archives staff to pore over hundreds of photos in their quest to find the proper Golden Age feel of No. 2. One important tool was a set of aerial photos from 1943, like this one (left) showing the thirteenth and fourteenth holes.

Padgett nods, gets back in his golf cart and is ready to drive back to the clubhouse and his office.

"I put my head on the pillow at night and go to sleep because I know we're doing the right thing," Padgett says.

***

Ben Crenshaw is in town for two days the second week of May after some time at home in Austin and before rejoining the PGA Champions Tour on Wednesday in Birmingham, Ala. A stroll around No. 2 elicits all manner of observations of course strategy and the details that give the course its singular character.

He pauses on the second hole to look at the indentation of a long-abandoned bunker that sits a hundred yards in front of the members' tee, to the right edge of the fairway.

"That's beautiful movement," he says. "This ground is a fascinating study. There is always something to find you haven't noticed before."

He looks at the mound in the front of the second green, the same one Bill Coore had talked about two weeks earlier.

"It's like at St. Andrews, the knob on the fourth hole," he says. "It runs the left third of the green. You have to play around it, you have to play to one side or the other. The knob *makes* this hole. All of the play is dictated by this guy. You can bounce it off the knob and it comes back at you. If you hit the backside, it'll propel it off the green. If you hit the sides, it'll bounce Lord knows how far. If you have an opposing wind, you can control it a little better, but then you have two more clubs. It's an amazing green. It's confounded everyone who's ever played here."

He looks at the undulations around the third green—"You can see the old mule working here," he says—and he loves the mounds to the left of the bunkers near the fifth green.

"They keep you in the game. You feel if you miss left, you're in trouble. But if you skip it just inside the mounds, they keep you in the game. You can get a little bounce off them into the green."

The wire grass and hardpan sand contrast with tightly cropped fairways near the second green of No. 2.

He looks at the knob to the right of sixth green.

"God bless, it's beautiful. It controls play on this hole."

He sees the roughs on eight browning out through lack of irrigation and rain.

"Wispy and distressed turf is not a bad thing. That's part of the natural ground you find at Pinehurst."

He brightens walking down the tenth fairway, about a hundred yards from the green, and stepping down into the curious dip that stretches from one side to the other and is there for no apparent reason.

"I love this little dip. I mean, it looks great. But it can be annoy-

ing. You get in it and say, 'Golly, what do I do now?'"

He notes the tightly mown grass around a fairway bunker on the eleventh hole.

"That's good. Before, a ball would be headed into the bunker and just stop. It never had a chance to get there with all the long grass. Then what's the point of the bunker?"

And at any point he might say, "Golly, this is a beautiful hole."

Crenshaw speaks of his deep love of classic golf courses, of the look and feel of the venues created eighty to a hundred years ago that maintain their relevance today—the onslaught of distance notwithstanding. He also notes the challenge of doing restorations of the masters' work versus creating courses from scratch.

"In some ways it's more difficult," he says. "There is more subjectivity involved. You go to a course designed by Donald Ross or Seth Raynor or A.W. Tillinghast and you're trying to climb into their minds. What were they trying to achieve on that particular piece of ground? It's hard. You have to shift gears mentally."

But by reading, by visiting and playing the old courses and talking to other architects, golfers and those with keen understanding and appreciation of shot values, Crenshaw can make an educated guess about the intentions of the old architects. And he knows for certain that having some space to play off the tee was part of Ross's plan for No. 2. He draws parallels to St. Andrews and Augusta—two courses that provide golfers enough paper to work the geometry.

"Bill and I have a great appreciation for Mister Ross's work," he says. "We have read as much as anyone and talked to dozens and dozens of people over the years to try to understand what his principles were and grasp the whole breadth of his work—not just in Pinehurst but everywhere," he says.

"Angles are a huge part of this project. Mister Ross put a premium on *placing* shots in order to set up the next one. But if you only have twenty-five yards to play with, what does it matter? There's never been more of a dichotomy than to have a strategic golf course and neck it down to twenty-five yards. They are polar opposites."

He pauses for effect.

"We disagree with having that restriction on the most beautifully conceived, strategic golf course you can imagine."

Crenshaw and Toby Cobb move to the woods to the right of the twelfth fairway to allow a group to play their tee shots. As they're biding their time, Crenshaw imagines a tee shot rolling through the sand and coming to rest amidst a bed of pine needles. Dealing with a stance and lie of this nature offers some variables unique to No. 2. He takes an imaginary stance.

"You have to find your balance on a shot like this," Ben says. "Can you make a swing and not slip and lose your balance? You can't get very close to the ball. In many instances, you can't ground your club. You sure don't want a penalty from the ball moving on you. Yes, you can make a recovery. But you have to be careful. These are the shots that Pinehurst was known for."

He further elucidates on the idea of the ball hitting and running. Sandy soil makes for a drier, firmer playing surface, and thus more variables.

"You want a ball that runs a bit," he says. "I have always felt that firm and quick conditions lent to the most interesting golf. You hit a ball through the air and then it lands on the ground. If the ball rolls more, you have to plan the shot much more. It's a distant cousin to the British Isles, where you *must* plan your shot along the ground as much as through the air. The British Isles gave us the game. Part of what drew people to this area, namely Mister Ross, was the turf and sand. Pinehurst is all about classic shot values. The game here is wedded to the ground. The curl of the ball and the bounce of the ball are integral parts of the game at Pinehurst."

***

A visit by USGA officials Mike Davis and Jim Hyler to Pinehurst

on the first two days of June 2010 is an important occasion. This will be the first look the USGA brass has gotten at the early chapters of the restoration story, and both are key players in the initiative—Davis because of his creativity in setting up courses for U.S. Opens and Hyler because his platform atop the USGA includes an emphasis on returning golf to an era where water and chemicals are deemphasized out of respect to finances, the environment and the traditions of the game.

Davis grew up in Chambersburg, Pa., won the Pennsylvania Junior Championship as a teen and later played golf at Georgia Southern University. He was working in commercial real estate in Atlanta in 1990 when he talked with fellow Pennsylvania native and USGA executive Mike Butz about joining the USGA staff. Davis learned the craft of setting up courses for national competitions for more than a decade under Tom Meeks, the senior director of rules and competitions, and then succeeded Meeks upon his retirement in 2005.

The U.S. Open during the first five years of Davis's tenure avoided any of the disaster scenarios that occasionally mark the event (think of the eighteenth green at Olympic in 1998 and the seventh green at Shinnecock Hills in 2004) while stimulating players with set-ups diverging from the strict code of suffocating rough that had prevailed for decades. Davis has used a "half-par" philosophy conceived with the idea of inviting golfers to gamble—make a par-four or par-five shorter than normal and give golfers a high risk-reward quotient for being aggressive off the tee. He introduced the idea of "graduated rough" so that drives fifteen yards off-line are penalized more than ones that miss by three yards, and he's a firm believer that bunkers are to be hazardous to players' scores, mandating that sand traps have soft bottoms so that players cannot spin and control the ball as they can on mainstream PGA Tour courses.

Hyler was a lifelong club golfer and a successful banker with North Carolina-based First Citizens when Pinehurst's resurrection under the Dedman regime began with its hosting competitive events in the late 1980s. As First Citizens' CEO, he perceived the PGA Tour Championship in 1991 and '92, the U.S. Senior Open in 1994 and the Women's Open at nearby Pine Needles in 1996 as excellent marketing vehicles for the bank. First Citizens signed on for major sponsorship packages for those events, giving Hyler the chance to meet and hobnob with executives from the resort and the world of golf. One thing led to another and Hyler was appointed in the mid-1990s as chairman of Pinehurst's President's Council, a *Who's Who* group of North Carolina business executives conceived to co-alesce the state's business resources in support of the 1999 Open at Pinehurst. That role introduced Hyler to the USGA's hierarchy, who appreciated his energy, organizational skills, business acumen and love for golf. Hyler was asked to join the USGA Executive Commit-tee in 2004 and then served four years on the Championship Com-mittee. He was introduced as the organization's sixty-first president in early February 2010, the USGA's annual meeting coincidentally held at Pinehurst. He cited Richard Tufts of the Pinehurst founding family and the USGA president in 1956-57 in his president's address.

"The time has come to refocus on the essential mission of this organization, to protecting the ideals which our forefathers like Dick Tufts celebrated, and to work with a renewed emphasis on the game itself," Hyler said. "If we are not careful, high construction costs, soaring maintenance budgets, and declining membership rosters will threaten the survival of many courses and clubs.

"As we have for the U.S. Open, I believe that our definition of playability should include concepts of firm, fast, and yes, even brown, and allow the running game to flourish."

The grass on No. 2 is thick with dew and the early rays of the sun are peeping through the pines to the east on Tuesday morning as Da-vis and Hyler arrive on the first tee to inspect the course with Coore. As they walk down the first fairway, Davis talks of the essential char-acter of a golf course built on sand and how he hopes the restoration of No. 2 will reconnect the course with its roots.

"If you take two golf courses that are exactly the same and one is built on soil and one on sand, the one on sand will always be better," Davis says. "It's going to drain better, the ball is going to bounce bet-ter. That element of waiting to see what happens when a ball lands is a great thing in golf. It's one of the reasons people love links golf, there's that extra element of what's going to happen when the ball lands. That's far more interesting to me than saying, 'I'm 152 yards away and I'm going to hit it 152 yards and it's going to stop.' The turf conditions in sand are better, you can play after a rain, you can play in the winter. Sand will trump soil every time."

Davis and Hyler had been in Pinehurst frequently just two years

earlier, preparing No. 2 for the 2008 U.S. Amateur and then setting up shop for a week in late August to run the championship, won by New Zealand's Danny Lee. During those periods they both wondered what it would be like to wean the course of all the thick rough and replace it with the indigenous hardpan sand.

"Thick Bermuda rough that is three, four inches deep is just chop-out rough," Hyler says. "The whole charm and challenge to No. 2 is the firm, fast greens and the angles into the greens on your approach shots. I think you'll see more shot-making ability by virtue of the slightly wider fairways. They'll bring the strategic value of the greens complexes even more into play."

Does the project fit with the USGA's program of work?

"Absolutely," Hyler says. "I think we'll have a golf course that is firmer, faster and more fun for the average player because they can find their ball and get their club on the ball easier. For the skilled player, the course will offer more challenge because of the options they'll have and the kinds of shots they will have to address. And it's sustainable—it will require less water, less fertilizer, less mowing."

Coore, Davis and Hyler are accompanied by a handful of Pinehurst officials—including owner Bob Dedman Jr. and Chief Operating Officer Don Padgett.

"We have a lot of confidence with Ben and Bill," Dedman says. "They are the very best at rediscovering the naturalness of a golf course. Take the varnish off a masterpiece—that's essentially what we've asked them to do. Technology is a blessing and a curse. It allowed us to grow all this grass. But in Donald Ross's day, they couldn't do this."

The project is still in its very early stages, but there is plenty for Coore to show the visitors from the USGA. Memorial Day weekend is traditionally a slow one at the resort, so the design and construc-tion workers used the opportunity to begin working full-tilt on the first and second holes; acres of sod were stripped on both sides of the fairways, revealing some mounds that had become engulfed by grass, and giving new function to the pine straw settling amidst the hardpan areas.

Seeing the mounds to the right of the first fairway only a day earlier, Dedman remarked to Padgett, "Those mounds look good. It didn't take them long to build them, did it?"

Padgett told his boss those mounds had been there all along; no

HYLER ADDRESSES KEY GOLF ISSUES

Jim Hyler stood in a Carolina Hotel ballroom before hundreds of people making their vocations and avocations in the great game of golf in early February 2010. The retired Raleigh banker had just been introduced as the new president of the United States Golf Association, and Hyler in his president's address touched on a significant initiative facing golf.

"We must re-set the way that we look at golf courses," Hyler said. "As we have for the U.S. Open, I believe that our definition of playability should include concepts of firm, fast, and yes, even brown, and allow the running game to flourish. We need to understand how brown can become the new green."

Firm, fast and brown, less water and fewer chemicals.

As in the opposite of soft, puffy and verdant, over-watered and richly fertilized.

On the very weekend in February 2010 that Hyler addressed the USGA's annual meeting in Pinehurst, plans were being finalized to retain architects Bill Coore and Ben Crenshaw to shepherd a restoration of No. 2, removing some forty acres of grass and more than six hundred sprinkler heads and returning the course to its more natural, rough-hewn look. The result was roundly applauded by the world of golf—competitors, architects, writers, resort guests and club members. The No. 2 project was one of a handful of dominoes that fell over Hyler's two-year incumbency that perfectly illustrated his points.

The 2010 U.S. Open was held at Pebble Beach, with Hyler and USGA official Mike Davis limiting the water applications leading up to the championship, providing a brownish patina to parts of the course. The U.S. Amateurs in 2010 and '11 were held on one hundred percent fescue courses—Chambers Bay in Washington State and Erin Hills in Wisconsin—and viewers watching on television saw quite a contrast to the emerald Augusta National look.

Not everyone is ready for more brown on their golf courses. But more will at least *listen* to a conversation that Hyler initiated in 2010.

"I have been quite frankly thrilled with the reception of those comments," Hyler said as his two-year tenure came to an end in February 2012. "There is a debate and a discussion around sustainable turfgrass management practices and about using less water, and people are *talking* about it.

"Now, has there been any tangible result at your average golf course? It's minimal, I'd say. But this is the sort of thing that takes a drip, drip, drip, drip kind of approach to get people to change their expectations."

Hyler was also encouraged by maintenance practices at Atlanta Athletic Club, the site of the 2011 PGA Championship, where superintendent Ken Mangum reduced his maintenance budget by some twenty percent by eliminating cosmetic practices that golfers did not notice or complain about. The club installed Champion Ultradwarf Bermuda on its greens and Zoysia in its fairways—two strains that allow for optimal playing conditions but less watering.

"Superintendents get it, they totally get it," Hyler says. "They understand the costs involved are exorbitant in today's economy and that we're running out of water. They, more than anyone, understand that things cannot continue as they have for so many years. The people driving the lush look are members, green committees and course owners. The discussions we've had over these two years have been constructive.

"People simply have to wake up and realize what we've known for so many years is just not sustainable."

Jim Hyler at the podium during the 2010 U.S. Open.

one saw them because they'd been hidden by grass.

Davis walks into the waste area near those mounds and tamps the ground with his shoe.

"This is good for Pinehurst, it's good for golf," Davis says. "I think it's great to have a shot in the U.S. Open where a guy is hitting off pine straw."

Also on Davis's agenda is to find any additional yardage available. There won't be much, of course, as nearly all courses a hundred years old have seen their extremities developed to the point there is rarely extra acreage available to lengthen holes. But with the average player in pro golf hitting his driver nearly 290 yards and the longest routinely bombing shots 320 yards or more, Davis will take every inch he can find.

He suggests a new tee for the second hole, pointing to an area tucked in a covey of pine trees to the right of the first green, some thirty yards behind the existing championship tee.

"It would add two, two-and-a-half clubs," Davis says. "It might put a five-iron in their hands instead of an eight-iron. That's a big difference. These guys are like us—they don't hit a four- and five-iron as consistently as they do a short-iron."

Throughout the tour, Coore frequently shows Davis and Hyler the aerial photos from 1943 that have served as a guiding template in the restoration project. Of particular importance to Coore is not only bringing some width back to individual holes but reinstituting some movement to the grass lines. Coore frequently refers to the "bowling alley fairways" that had become prevalent on No. 2. Davis couldn't agree more.

"Today's player bombs it straight," Davis says. "If you put in gentle curves in the fairways, you make him think a little more. It's an aerial game. They pick a center line and bomb it."

Since holes eleven through fourteen were the first to come under the architects' knife in late February, they are the first to provide a reasonable facsimile of what Coore hopes will be a finished product.

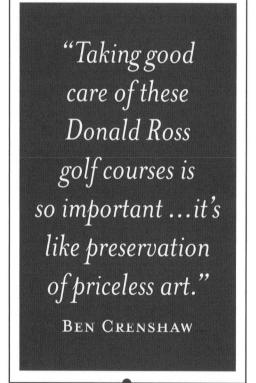

"Taking good care of these Donald Ross golf courses is so important ...it's like preservation of priceless art."

BEN CRENSHAW

Standing on fourteen tee, Davis eyes a panorama that includes a vast wasteland between fourteen and thirteen fairways and a palette of browns, golds and creams.

"What a great look," Davis says, using his hands to mimic the flow of the fairway to and fro. "That's great movement. That's what people remember about Pinehurst No. 2, what made it great. It's what set it apart."

He walks down the fairway and arrives at a spot under trees to the right of the fairway where a pushed or faded drive could land. The spot would have been covered by Bermuda rough in 2005. Today the area has been cleared out, bunkers added and sandy areas reinstated between the traps. He taps his foot on the ground.

"This would be a tough shot," Davis says.

"There's so much give under the ball. They can't pinch it, they can't spin it. Hardpan is a piece of cake for them. In places like this, we can scruff it up a bit, soften it, mess it up a little—just so the ball sinks ever so slightly."

On seventeen, Davis finds a slot in the trees behind the back tee that could accommodate another new tee. The hole played 186 yards in 1951 and 190 yards in 2005.

"Bill, are you opposed to a little more length?" Davis asks. "It's not a four- and a five-iron shot like it used to be. Now it's a seven-iron."

Coore says he has no problem with a new tee for the professionals but quickly admits, "I can't relate to it. A five-iron 215 yards? I'm not opposed to it. I just can't comprehend it."

Davis steps off an area behind the existing championship tee on the par-four finishing hole to add a dozen yards and then wonders along with Coore if anything can be done along the right side of the uphill hole to give players pause for thought before launching another mammoth drive. They look at the elongated and deep bunker that borders the right side.

"It's maybe the best-looking bunker on the course," Coore says.

"But it would be impossible to move it and preserve the look."

Coore amplifies his fondness for the appearance of the bunker—there is nothing smooth or groomed, there are no straight lines and nothing that looks like it was produced by man or lifted from a garden show.

"We've seen pictures from the '36 PGA," Coore says. "The bunkers had a wild look, a gnarly-edge look. This bunker has maintained more of that look than most here. It's important to preserve that look and bring it back."

***

Ben Crenshaw decides at the last minute the third week of June to make a quick trip to Pinehurst. His playing schedule leans toward the West Coast as the summer months evolve, so he's not sure when he'll have a chance to return. He toured No. 2 with Toby Cobb upon his arrival and liked what he saw.

"It's coming along great," Crenshaw says at breakfast at the Track Restaurant the next morning. "We got some good rain yesterday and it tends to quiet it down some, it doesn't look quite so harsh. A lot of things are falling into place."

The conversation over the next hour centers on the big picture aspect of the No. 2 restoration. Can the resort set an example for the rest of the golf world to follow, Crenshaw is asked, in returning a course to a more unkempt look that requires less artificial irrigation and chemical maintenance?

"That's a great question," he says. "The point is this will be a *natural* presentation—it's what was here before there was ever a golf course. Wherever you are in this country, that's what you want. We like that. To us it also makes sense. We know—*we know*—we have to cut down on water usage. We've got to. We have to use it more judiciously. It's not just golf courses and recreational facilities, it's everything we do. Water is scarcer and more expensive and it's only going to get worse.

"We can learn from the Australians. They are amazing. They are some of the best conservationists. They do a beautiful job with their water usage and they have for a long time. Everything has a burnished look—their playgrounds, parks, golf courses. They are the conserva-

tionists of all time. I think it's beautiful. It's remarkable the way they keep their golf courses. The ball hits and runs. It's a great combination between America and the British Isles."

Cobb mentions that he was flagging rough to be removed on the fifth hole a few days earlier when a golfer came up to him.

"Why are you taking out grass?" the man wondered. "Why would you do that?"

"That's the issue, isn't it?" Cobb says. "Lots of people don't understand that. And I can understand them asking."

"It's a reasonable question," Crenshaw adds. "But it's hard to launch into a discussion and give people a little sound bite of an answer. We're trying to replicate what was here before. It was a form of hazard in Pinehurst's history. It's one of the things that helped Pinehurst gain its reputation. It was a region where Donald Ross put his roots down, it was the best land for golf he'd seen in this country. If you have that going for you, why not use it?"

The conversation moves on to the relevance of old courses like No. 2, those built eighty to a hundred years ago that lack the length of modern tracks but make up for it with a sense of history, tradition and a style all their own.

"Taking good care of these Donald Ross golf courses is so important," Crenshaw says. "There will always be a few people who say they're outdated, but the architectural features are so fine, it's like preservation of priceless art. That's what it is. These courses are fun to play. They're a good test but they're fun and enjoyable. This notion that you have to play an extremely hard test is wrong. You reach so many people with classic golf courses and help them have a fun day and a fun game. They're enjoyable and interesting. They are museum pieces."

Instead of going to new courses 7,500 yards long, Crenshaw would love to see the PGA Tour take an event to a course like Wannamoisett, a vintage Ross layout in Rhode Island. The course opened in 1916, was lengthened and tweaked a decade later and, in 1931, hosted the PGA Championship. It's par sixty-nine and stretches to just under 6,700 yards. There is one par-five.

"A course like that brings *everyone* into the picture—long-hitters, shotmakers, guys with great short games," he says. "It would be fun to see what would happen. A modern course with four par-fives is right up today's player's alley. Bill stunned me one day. We were talking about what to do to battle the longer ball. And he said, 'Make the golf course shorter. Do that and you allow more people to have a chance.'"

Another issue of note that has hovered around the No. 2 restoration project has been the idea that the 2014 U.S. Open will be played on a golf course bereft of the very fang that was so promulgated leading into the '05 Open—thick rough surrounding narrow fairways. The advent of longer balls in the late 1990s prompted golf's governing bodies to combat the prodigious length with longer grass.

"One of our first questions for the USGA when we were considering this project was, 'Is wider okay?'" Crenshaw says. "You'll have a different form of hazard than thick Bermuda rough. You'll bring the recovery shot back into the ball game. You hit it into the thick Bermuda and you might be able to get a club on it, but there's not much you can do with it. But there's no recovery. That was a very big question in our minds.

"I remember the Ryder Cup in '99 when the Pro VI was just coming out. I could not believe how far those guys where hitting the ball. Davis Love and Billy Andrade made some comments in the paper that they really liked the new construction ball. It took off. There's no question that was the difference here at Pinehurst from '99 to '05. They felt they had to do something to combat technology. And you had a vastly different golf course in '05 than you had in '99, demonstrably different."

***

Mike Davis from the USGA is returning to Pinehurst the afternoon of August 1 to make another tour of No. 2. Don Padgett is driving around the golf course late in the day before Davis's tour with Bill Coore and Toby Cobb, taking an inventory of what Davis will find. He stops his golf cart near the fourteenth tee and absorbs the view in front of him. This hole and the preceding thirteenth have provided a harbinger of the course to come, as they fell early in the restoration process. The removal of all Bermuda grass between the two fairways provides a good facsimile of the mid-20th century look of No. 2.

"This is what Pinehurst once looked like," Padgett says. "This is the feel right here. It's a cool look. I was out there at 5:30 or so the other afternoon, the late afternoon sun really looked nice. It clicked with me right then—that this is what the entire course will look like. With all of the grass we had before, you never saw any movement to the fairway. Now you do. The pathway goes one way, turns, turns again. You have three or four turns. It looks great."

Meanwhile, Coore and Cobb are on the far side of the course, walking around eight, nine and ten. As dry as the Sandhills area was in the spring, it's been pummeled of late with afternoon thunderstorms, prompting the Bermuda to pop back out in many spots and softening the fairways throughout the course.

Coore is standing on the championship tee of the tenth hole, which sits a hundred yards from the members' tee; between the two tees is a valley covered with rich green grass. Coore envisions more of a gnarly look, the kind he's seen in dozens of photos found in the Tufts Archives.

"We need to make it look sick," Coore says. "It's too healthy."

The softness of the fairways is a frequent topic of conversation. As they reach the tenth fairway, Cobb bends over and picks up a plug of soil. Course maintenance workers have been aerating the fairways over the last two days, and small plugs of fairway matter are scattered about, waiting to be swept away before the next day's tee times. Cobb picks the plug apart with his fingers and points to all the dark soil that crumbles out of the plug.

"That's all organic," he says. "That's a lot of cushion for the ball to land on."

"Organic material is what makes the grass feel soft when you walk on it," Coore adds. "You want the grass on top of the *sand*—not on top of organic."

That will be an ongoing issue for the architects and Pinehurst maintenance staff—finding ways to firm up the fairways over time.

Coore tells of his first trip to Royal Melbourne on the coast of Australia years ago and being smitten with the speed and firmness of those fairways. "They're brown as toast," he told Claude Crockford, the superintendent who reigned over the club's thirty-six holes for four decades.

"You Americans try too hard to grow grass," Crockford responded. "Here, we try to keep it from growing."

"That's a fascinating difference, if you think about it," Coore says.

Ben Crenshaw inspects the areas of hardpan sand that were exposed with the removal of some forty acres of Bermuda rough. The stark transition from fairway to hardpan would be muted with the passage of time and the restriction of water.

"It's a vicious cycle—you fertilize and water and mow, and that leads to more fertilizer, watering and mowing to keep up with what you've already created."

That evening, Coore and Cobb join Davis, Padgett and other Pinehurst golf officials for dinner. Since last visiting Pinehurst in early June, Davis has spent three weeks at Pebble Beach, overseeing the U.S. Open won by Graeme McDowell. A poignant topic of conversation emerges when comparisons are drawn between the restoration project on No. 2 and the touches of brown that were clearly visible on telecasts from Pebble.

Davis tells of receiving at least a thousand pieces of communication—letters, e-mail, phone messages—from viewers aghast that there were actually shades of *brown* on the course.

"They were the most heinous letters and messages," Davis says. "'How could you let that golf course be anything but bright green?!?!?'

It's a subjective thing, and who's to say what's right and what's wrong? There are certainly strong opinions out there that, at least in this country, soft and green are the way to go.

"I always say part of the charm of the game is watching what happens when your ball lands. What's it going to do? Not everyone buys into that concept. You can't take it personally."

Padgett attended the Open and came away convinced any additional length for No. 2 and the 2014 Open was a good thing.

"I stood on the second hole at Pebble, Phil Mickelson hits it 393 yards and has 126 to the hole," Padgett says. "The way some of these guys are hitting it is tough to comprehend. People are hitting it unbelievable distances. I had not seen these guys play since the '05 Open. I was stunned. It will be even more important for us to get it firm and fast so if they do hit it crooked, it's off the beaten path pretty quickly."

As the meal continues, Davis talks about the intricacies and va-

VENERABLE TRADITION

Two of the more well-known caddies at Pinehurst over the years have been Willie McRae (above), who was still on the Pinehurst staff in 2012, sixty-nine years after first looping at the age of ten, and Jimmy Steed (opposite), the long-time caddie of Sam Snead.

C addies have been part and parcel of the Sandhills golf scene from the beginning—much like wire grass, pine straw, two-down presses and nine-teenth hole libations.

John Daniel, better known by his nickname "Barney Google," helped Harvie Ward read the greens of Pinehurst No. 2 and one-putt eighteen times over a thirty-six hole North and South Amateur championship win over Frank Stranahan in 1948. "Ward didn't beat Stranahan today," one spectator was quoted as saying in *Golf World* magazine. "Barney Google did."

Jimmy Steed handed Sam Snead the clubs he used to win three North and South Open titles from 1941-50, finish second three more times and traveled with him to Greens-boro to work most of the eight Greater Greensboro Open championships Snead collected. "Sam had a great many talents, but one of them was *not* selecting clubs," says Bill Campbell, a noted competitor of the era. "Jimmy had the knack of giving Sam the right clubs."

Jerry Boggan dressed like a peacock and trouped through the pine forests chasing Billy Joe Patton's errant shots during Patton's three North and South victories from 1954-63. Boggan delivered newspapers starting at 2 a.m. and then would show up at the golf course to lug Patton's bag, dressed for the weekend in a green suede sweater, green alligator shoes, yellow pants and a yellow and green plaid cap. "I'm ashamed," Patton would say. "My caddie looks better than me."

And then there was Fletcher Gaines, the rotund little elf who carried for Tommy Armour, Gene Sarazen and Porky Oliver in the North and South Open and later for Curtis Strange during the Wake Forest golfer's two North and South Amateur wins in 1975-76. Strange used to ask Gaines to watch him carefully at the top of his backswing and let him know if his hands and the clubhead were "square." Gaines didn't know what Strange meant, but he would answer nonetheless, "Yeah, it looks square to me." Told years later that Fletcher had been shoveling him a load of it way back when, Strange just smiled and said, "Fletcher Gaines, that old son of a bitch."

Daniel, Steed, Boggan, Gaines and other legendary caddies like Hardrock Robinson have graduated to the great caddie yard in the sky, but there remain plenty of fascinating history and an appropriate mix of the new guard in the Pinehurst caddie staff.

"These guys are national gems," Don Padgett Sr., the director of golf at Pinehurst from 1987-2002, said upon the launch of the Pinehurst Caddie Hall of Fame in 2001. "They are walking history books."

And they take the game back to its roots—when Scotsmen walked the links and had time between shots to converse with their playing companions, to give thought to the next shot and to properly inhale the nature. That's even more important on a course like No. 2, which allows golfers to take motorized carts but restricts them to the extremities of each hole.

"You get to the ball too fast when you're riding," says Willie McRae, at 79 the most senior caddie at Pinehurst in 2012. "There's no time to think."

The caddie business has changed throughout golf and in Pinehurst over the last hundred years. Pinehurst used to have more than five hundred caddies on staff in the 1920s and sometimes on busy days the caddie master would dispatch a wagon to the local schoolhouse to get more boys. Resort management has been steadfast in the face of escalating "cart golf" over the last half-century to keep the caddie staff intact. In 1997, Caddie Master Enterprises Inc. took over Pinehurst's caddie operation and has approximately one hundred caddies on staff during the busy spring and fall seasons.

"Our job is to enhance the experience of playing a wonderful, historic golf course," says Eddie McKenzie, a

twenty-two year member of the caddie staff who grew up in Southern Pines and whose experience stretches to the PGA and LPGA Tours. "We help golfers with the subtleties of the greens, with playing the right shots around the greens.

"A good caddie also relaxes the player. The point is, we're out here to play eighteen holes and have fun. This is a hard golf course. It takes its toll. I tell a guy if he's disgusted with the last hole, 'Hey, it's like your first girlfriend. Unless you marry her, she's history. She's done. Forget it and enjoy the rest of the day.'"

Thaddeus McRae caddied for thirty-five years at Pinehurst in the mid-20th century and started his son Willie on the job in 1943 at the age of ten.

"He brought me up here on my tenth birthday," Willie says. "I could make twenty-five cents a loop plus tips—enough for candy for a week."

Willie's been walking the fairways of No. 2 ever since, carrying the bags of golfers such as Donald Ross, Gene Sarazen and Billy Joe Patton, ball players like Yogi Berra and Michael Jordan and politicians including Richard Nixon and Gerald Ford. McRae hesitates to list any of them as "celebrities" given the fact, he says, "everyone's famous to somebody." In 2004 he estimated that he'd walked to Los Angeles and back fifteen times carrying bags around the course. He still works today, though management has made a concession to allow him to drive a golf cart around the course—anywhere except on the putting green. Son Paul is on the golf instruction staff at Pinehurst and grandson Darick is a caddie.

"And I've got a few more miles left," says McRae, who along with Jesse James, Bobby Hill, John Ross and Jeff "Ratman" Ferguson represent the old guard on the caddie staff. "My mama always said you're never old until you die and prove it."

Scott Straight, who visits Pinehurst annually from his home in French Lick, Ind., says he didn't want any help reading greens the first time he played No. 2, despite the fact that a veteran like McRae was carrying his bag. A half dozen holes into the round, Straight's ball looked to break uphill, and McRae said, "You *sure* you don't want me helping you?" Straight succumbed.

"I had a four-foot putt and missed by six inches," he says. "I was thinking, 'My God, I'm not this bad.' Willie did a great job after that hole. I was mystified with some of the reads but everything he said was dead on."

Among the caddie staff in 2012 are two Pinehurst Country Club members who first moved to Pinehurst to retire, but essentially got bored and looked for something to do besides play golf. Tony Smarrelli retired to Pinehurst in 1993 and Tom Harmicar in 2008. They joined the caddie staff and found the work a good way to earn a little extra money, get some exercise, meet interesting people and be around golfers.

"It's a great walk, it's great exercise," says Smarrelli.

"People enjoy caddies. They learn so much more about a course walking and getting a feel for it. On the first hole here, if you hit it left, you're going to walk ninety yards from the cart to your ball. People need help reading these greens.

Southern Pines photographer Tim Sayer captured this image of two caddies on No. 2 that was used on the cover of the March 2012 "Pine Straw" magazine.

There are a lot of double breaks they'd never see. If you miss your line by a couple of inches, you wind up four feet from the hole."

"This job is a lot of fun," adds Harmicar. "There are a lot of good caddies out here. They know what they're doing. There are guys with degrees. But they get caddie fever and wouldn't want to be anywhere else."

The value of having a caddie has risen with the restoration to No. 2 over 2010-11 authored by the architecture team of Bill Coore and Ben Crenshaw. Previously there had been more than a thousand sprinkler heads on the course, many marking yardages to the green, but more than half have been removed and now are found only in the middle of the fairways. It's harder to find a yardage now, but the caddies are required to carry range-finders and thus have an accurate number to the flag at any point on the course. All of the flags on the course are the same color, removing the old red/white/yellow system of marking front-to-back hole locations. And then there is the issue of how to negotiate the areas of hardpan sand, wire grass and gnarly bunkers.

Pinehurst No. 2 now has the look and personality it sported through the mid-1900s and happily is still accented with one of golf's most venerable traditions. To walk these fairways with a caddie in tow is one of golf's purest pleasures.

garies of setting courses up for Opens. One of his tenets is to have consistent green speeds and firmness from hole one through eighteen. Davis treats rough, though, with the opposite mindset. He wrote a memo in 2006 to superintendents of courses on the U.S. Open rota about the evils of thick rough promulgated by triple-row irrigation and the heavy use of fertilizer. He thought the cost to groom untold acres of dense Bermuda grass was unhealthy for clubs and the game itself and stripped it of one of its charms—luck.

"I love inconsistencies in the rough," Davis says. "I love it where you have to look down at your lie and figure out what will happen. One of the worst things that's happened to golf over the last twenty years is triple-row irrigation and having the mindset of consistent rough. Twenty years ago, how many courses had good irrigation in the roughs? Very few. Now with irrigation, over-seeding, eradication of certain grasses and weeds, fertilization—you end up with lush, thick, consistent roughs. You have virtually the same lie every time. In the old days you hit your ball in the rough and had to figure out what you had.

"Part of the charm and challenge of the game of golf is figuring out what kind of lie you have and what kind of shot you can hit from it," he continues. "Bare lie? In the weeds? Sand under your ball? *Figure it out!* That's the joy of the game. It's very much a United States thing. Golfers here don't appreciate that element as much. Once you get out of the United States, they get it. *Figure it out!*"

Coore tells of Harry Colt, the club secretary at Sunningdale Golf Club in England, writing a letter to the membership in the mid-1920s.

"I am very concerned about the condition of the golf course," Colt said. "The fairways are so good that you have a perfect lie every time, and you're taking away from the skill of the game."

Coore elaborates on the point.

"The skill of the best players is tested by figuring out how to play shots out of the cuppy lies and odd lies you can find," he says. "Those situations bring out the best in the best players. Sure, hitting a great shot off a perfect lie is part of the game. Dealing with bad luck and odd bounces is part of it as well."

"Amen to that," Davis says.

***

Bill Coore, Mike Davis and Toby Cobb meet at 6:30 the next morning in the dining room of The Carolina for breakfast before inspecting No. 2. Since much of the conversation at dinner the night before revolved around the recent Open at Pebble Beach, the talk gravitates at breakfast to the 2014 Open at Pinehurst and how the restoration will affect it.

"One of the things that always really bothered me about the U.S. Open was that the set-up tended to become somewhat cookie cutter," Davis says. "Okay, we narrow the fairways, grow the rough, get the greens hard and fast. I think it's really neat when you can take a course and say, 'Okay, what is its architectural personality?' And then you say, 'How can you make it a very stern—yet fun and fair—test for the U.S. Open?' That's what's unique about this project.

"We will still have the challenge of the greens complexes. That's what makes this such a hard test for the world's best players. When the greens are firm and fast, they just repel balls. I do think these changes are going to make it an easier test in terms of driving the ball. That's okay. The trick is to not overdo it and have this become a second-shot and short-game U.S. Open. You have to be able to control the ball off the tee in a U.S. Open."

The greens on No. 2 were rebuilt in 1996 and sprigged with Penn G2 bent grass, at the time one of the leading strains for southern climates. The greens in the 1999 and 2005 Opens hurdled both tests thrown at them that for decades had vexed any idea of holding a mid-June Open on No. 2—they survived in the summer heat (it was in the 90s the entire week of the 2005 Open) while playing with the speed and stiffness the USGA wanted.

"We were blessed both times to have the greens firm and fast," Davis says. "It was never a struggle."

Tee times this morning on No. 2 are running from 7:30 to 10:30, so Coore's plan is to take Davis to the eleventh hole to start their tour. No one will be playing the back nine this early, and by the time they get to the first hole, the last of the groups will have teed off.

One of the things Davis will be most interested in seeing are the new tees that have been built since he visited two months earlier. The second, eighth, tenth, fifteenth, sixteenth, seventeenth and eighteenth holes have some added length; during the winter, new tees will be built on the seventh and eleventh holes.

Davis stands on the existing tee of the par-four eleventh, looks back into the woods where the new tee will be built and nods his head.

"If you can get twenty-five more yards, all of a sudden you're now hitting a five-iron," Davis says. "That's good. If we can find a few mid-iron approaches into these greens, so much the better."

His gaze moves down the fairway, where a bunker has been replaced on the left, two mounds built and the fairway perimeters massaged with gentle curves. Gone are the straight lines that Coore and Crenshaw bemoaned on their first visit in late February.

"This is just a super look here, a great looking drive zone," Davis says. "This has changed dramatically."

They walk up the fairway and into the hardpan area to the right of the landing zone. Davis points to a spot between clumps of wire grass and imagines a ball coming to rest there.

"The player will have to pause a second and ask himself, 'Can I touch that, will it move?'" Davis says. "I love to come in and try to get as many things to have to deal with when the ball is in this stuff. You can be on hardpan, softer sand, pine straw, wire grass, organic."

Coore continues his dialogue with Davis about bunker construction, tweaking and maintenance and how it might affect the set-up for the Open. Coore's memory of the bunkers from the 1960s—supported by the evidence of old photographs—is that there was less of a strict delineation of the bunker edges than exists today and more of a gradual, almost imperceptible, transition from hardpan sand into a bunker. That's particularly true on the side of the bunker closest to where the shot is coming from. The entrance to the bunker is very subtle; the back side has more of a defined edge.

Coore is concerned that such features might create problems during an Open for players wondering if they are in or out of a hazard.

(This came, coincidentally, two weeks before the infamous 2010 PGA Championship at Whistling Straits where Dustin Johnson was penalized two strokes on the seventy-second hole because he grounded his club in a bunker, an area he thought was through-the-green.)

Davis steps into the bunker front-right of eleven green, picks up a rake and shows Coore how they'll be maintained to differentiate between bunker and through-the-green.

"No problem with that at all," Davis says.

He notices in the bottom of the bunker a thin layer of dark material that is neither sand, dirt nor grass. This is organic soil material, which is produced over time as leaves and pieces of wood decompose. These deposits in bunkers will become more common as there is a less defined edge on at least part of the trap. The first impulse of a maintenance worker striving for perfect playing conditions would be to rake or blow the organic material out. Not so, says Davis.

"It takes a little more skill to play off of the organic than it does pure sand," Davis says. "It's just another element to the challenge."

They look at a similar possibility on the hardpan, of a ball coming to rest on a thin layer of the black organic material.

"You can't compress the ball off this stuff," Davis says. "You have to pick it. The ball is just not going to have the same spin. Leave the organic. Leave it just like that instead of having hardpan. It will give the players one more thing to think about—they might be careful about taking a chance and landing on that stuff instead of perfectly manicured hardpan. That's one of the great things about coming to Pinehurst—you get away from the cookie-cutter set-up. You come to Pinehurst and have challenges different from anywhere else."

As they make their way around the course over the next five hours, various elements prompt discussions and ideas.

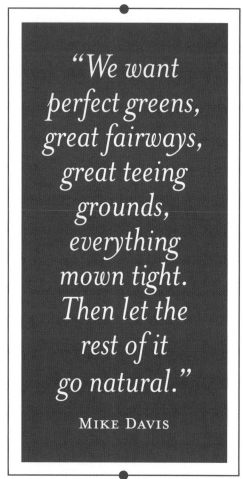

"We want perfect greens, great fairways, great teeing grounds, everything mown tight. Then let the rest of it go natural."

Mike Davis

They stop in the middle of the thirteenth fairway, 150 yards from the green, and Davis paces the width at nearly forty yards.

"That's fine," he tells Coore. "If they're going to lay up to here, give them all the room in the world."

Then he motions to the fairway line to the left, closer toward the green, and asks if Coore can gradually move that boundary toward the center.

"Right now off the tee, they would say, 'I'm going to knock it down there to eighty, ninety, a hundred yards,' and they wouldn't give it a second thought," Davis says. "If we made this turn a little more severe, if we got the fairway down to twenty-six, twenty-seven yards, they would absolutely have to think about it."

They walk up to the fifteenth green and Coore shows Davis the area to the right of the existing putting surface, tucked behind the bunker, where they plan to expand the green when the course closes in the winter.

"This green could use another hole location," Davis says. "It's one of those you change four times, but you really haven't changed it at all."

Davis likes the new tee on sixteen and hopes that a few extra yards will prevent even the longer players from catching the crest and downslope on the fairway. He also approves of the new tee on seventeen.

"I like it," he says. "It's now a solid five-iron."

By late morning, they make their way around to the front nine and find some area of particular interest to the right of the fairway of the short par-four third hole. This is one area of the course that has remained in its natural state throughout the proliferation of grass over the last four decades. Coore suggests this is an area they could show to Kevin Robinson, superintendent of No. 2, and to his staff as a template for how the course should look away from the fairways.

There's cream-colored sand, darker organic material, pine needles, pine cones and wire grass. There's no apparent uniformity or structure.

"We want it kept natural looking, don't over manicure it," Davis tells Robinson. "We want perfect greens, great fairways, great teeing grounds, everything mown tight. Then let the rest of it go natural. The pine needles just blend in.

"You literally can have a thousand different shots."

Coore nods his head, then looks farther up the tree line, his field of vision taking in some mounds around the bunkers to the right of the landing area.

"This is Pinehurst, this is the forties and fifties right here," he says.

They talk about the left side of the fifth fairway, about letting it go wild and scruffing it up so balls will careen easily into the woods between the fourth and fifth fairways. Originally Coore was hoping it would go dormant by turning off the water, but there's still plenty of grass so he and Cobb make plans to bring in some equipment over the next couple of weeks and strip the Bermuda out.

"Ben has talked to old guys on the Senior Tour, and every one of them made the comment that when they walked up to five tee, they said, 'I can't tug this ball. If I just barely tug it, it's going to run all the way down into the trees,'" Coore tells Davis. "That element has been missing. Tug it now and the balls get hung up in the rough."

Don Padgett and Bob Farren, Pinehurst's director of golf course and grounds management, join them for lunch an hour later. One of the points for conversation is the work planned during the winter on the greens. Three of the greens on No. 2 had become polluted with enough *Poa annua* grass by the spring of 2010 that plans were in the works to re-cover them with fresh bent grass when the course closed during the winter. A combination of more *Poa* proliferation and the stress from a record hot summer had escalated the project to seven greens. The plan was to use an improved strain of bent—a combination of Penn A1 and A4—that has been developed since the G2 was installed fourteen years earlier.

Both Davis and Coore wonder if it would be wise to recover all the greens and ensure their consistency.

"It's not a cost issue," Padgett says. "It's a question of finding enough sod. We'll do the work in mid-November, and the greens will be covered all winter. We can make a phone call and find out if they can get enough sod."

They agree on a target of May 2011 to have the course playing as close to Open conditions as possible—firm and fast.

"Generally I think we'll be done a year from now," Coore says.

***

The thirteenth green in all its finely coiffed glory as seen from the fairway in 2005, just before the U.S. Open . . .

Ben Crenshaw spent the third week of September in Cary participating in the SAS Championship on the Champions Tour, drove to Pinehurst Sunday night and is up bright and early Monday morning to meet Toby Cobb for breakfast before walking the golf course. It's been three months since Crenshaw has been to Pinehurst, and he's anxious to see what's happened over the summer. The Track Restaurant is closed on Mondays and Tuesdays, so they opt for the Pinehurst Café, a small diner on a backstreet a few blocks from The Carolina.

Joining them is Kyle Franz, a freelance designer and construction worker from Oregon who was hired in August. Cobb and Franz update Crenshaw on the progress they have made in the last four to six weeks. In addition to Franz, the Coore & Crenshaw team now includes four Guatemalans who specialize in golf course construction; Cobb used them during the building of Dormie Club and likes their skills and work ethic.

"The added manpower has made a world of difference," Cobb says. "Kyle has a great feel for design and the Guatemalans are experienced golf course construction and maintenance guys. They're handy to have around. One of them in particular is really good with irrigation and watering. That's been a major challenge—we've had a dry spell the last month but we've got to get water to these new wire grass plants to get them established. So far, they're holding up well.

"We've probably planted eight hundred a week for four weeks—that's thirty-two hundred or so over a month."

The conversation as they wait for their breakfast orders turns to the role that taut surfaces play in the challenge of the greens and the absolute necessity to continue to firm the course up over the next year.

"Guys are hitting the ball 280 yards and not getting ten yards of roll," Cobb says of players he sees on No. 2. "It's unbelievable. In fact, I've seen a couple hit and bounce backward."

The firmness of American courses—or the lack thereof—has al-

. . . And the same view in the spring of 2011, shortly after the course's reopening, harkening to a look from half a century ago.

ways rankled Crenshaw. He says that golfers who have traveled outside the United States have a much better appreciation for playing on dry ground and a keener understanding of the necessity of planning each shot.

"If you haven't traveled, you can't feel it and sense it," he says. "In the British Isles, in Australia, the ball runs and it runs hard. Green grass isn't as important there. Here you see Scotts Turf commercials all the time—people want perfect green on their lawns and their golf courses. A little brown is more fun. You have to plan the shot more when it runs. On a soft golf course, you have two measurements—the yardage and the wind. On a firm course, you have that plus the bounce and the roll and everything a ball can find while it's rolling. It involves a lot more thought."

An hour later, Crenshaw, Cobb and Franz are walking down the first fairway, hoping to dodge the rain that's predicted for later in the day and indicated by a heavy cloud cover. Crenshaw's first view of the course looking down the first fairway brings a smile to his face.

"There's a lot more color and definition," he says. "It's much more visually stimulating. It's very striking. There are different colors, shades, textures. Visually it's much more appealing."

Crenshaw has not yet seen the new championship tee for the par-four second hole, the one requested by Mike Davis and built over the summer. The hole now stretches to just over five hundred yards, and Ben can only shake his head standing on the new tee.

"Boy. Wow. It's too much for me," he says. "It's almost morbid in length."

His gaze runs down the fairway to the new bunker on the right side, placed within the sandy area. He nods his head.

"It looks good," he says. "We've roughed up the right side, added that bunker. Together they make you say, 'I need to go ten to fifteen yards to the left.' That's fine, but it's another club, a club-and-a-half into the green."

The group advances to the landing area of the third fairway. Crenshaw stands a hundred yards from the green, envisioning the wedge shot into the green and the mental exercise the elite player goes through in picking his club and planning his shot.

"The question here is, how good are you that day?" he says. "What are you feeling right now? What was your warm-up like? It's still early enough in the round. You may be sure, you may not be sure. It's there for the taking if you feel good. But it can trip you up if you try something that you're not good enough on that day to pull off."

Up ahead on the green, Ben sees a small gash in the putting surface, apparently made by a golf club earlier in the morning.

"It looks like somebody threw a club," he says. "What was it Bobby Jones said? 'Some emotions cannot be endured with a golf club in your hands.'"

He chuckles, then bends over and presses the distressed turf back into place.

"I think that's what happened here," he says. "Someone couldn't endure a club in his hands."

Walking to seven tee, Ben notes the sigh of relief golfers feel as they finish two difficult holes—the infamously tough par-four fifth and this long sixth.

"Six to me is every bit as difficult as five," Crenshaw says. "These two you just try to make a par and go quietly, real quietly. You don't want to get nicked and scraped on these two."

The walk continues on this humid morning, Ben offering observations and suggestions along the way.

He looks at the border between the hardpan and fairway on one hole: "That's a pretty straight line. Let's swing it out some, Toby."

He looks at a mound sitting in a sandy area. "Rough it up, scratch it up a little."

He points at a bunker: "Break it up a little, it's too fine."

Bunker re-edging is an ongoing part of the restoration process. Bunkers that are not going to be rebuilt at least will have a trowel or hoe applied to their edges.

"I don't know of a bunker we won't re-edge," Toby says. "Not a lot—just enough to break them up, give them some movement, a little character."

Crenshaw loves the gentle flow of the fairway ground throughout the course. There are little pimples and hollows in curious spots throughout.

"John Low, one of the captains a century ago at the R&A, had a great line: 'Undulation is the soul of the game,'" Ben says.

After lunch, the rain moves in and Crenshaw takes a seat on the veranda outside the golf shop, overlooking the eighteenth green and the Payne Stewart statue. He's joined by Don Padgett, and the conversation turns to the course as it played for the 1999 and 2005 Opens and the one the field will encounter in 2014.

"If the course is at all firm, the greens will hold their own," Crenshaw says. "Forget around the greens—we all know about the problems you have there. But just to negotiate the greens *once you're on them* is another story entirely. The greens keep you at bay. When they get glassy they make you timid.

"This is the hardest set of greens I've ever played in my life. When those greens get hard and fast—wow, watch out."

Padgett notes the greens putted in the eleven to twelve range on the Stimpmeter for the 2005 Open.

"They are hard greens to read," he says. "If you look at Tiger Woods here in '99 and '05, he had all kinds of trouble reading the greens. You look at where he missed and his reaction, and you could tell the ball didn't roll the way he expected it to. He couldn't read the greens and neither could Steve [Williams, Woods' caddie]. These are the hardest inland greens I've ever seen to read. Maybe some mountain courses are a little tougher, but for a course built on a relatively flat piece of land, these are really hard. I still don't know exactly how

Crenshaw and Pinehurst COO Don Padgett, who played the PGA Tour together in the early 1970s, discuss the restoration nuances in the winter of 2011.

to putt these greens and I've been playing them for years."

The image of Payne Stewart draining his fifteen-foot putt on the final hole in 1999, extending his right fist and kicking back his left leg is indelibly forged in the golf world's memory—and preserved for the ages in the statue just a few steps away from where Crenshaw and Padgett sit. But Padgett marvels over the long putt he made on the sixteenth hole.

"*That's* the putt that really won the Open for Payne," Padgett says. "He said afterward, he didn't know which way it was going and neither did his caddie. He said he was going to hit it hard and hit it straight at it. You watch the replay—if it doesn't hit the hole, it's going to run off the green. *Then* what does he do?"

Crenshaw was exempt into the '99 field through his 1995 Masters championship, but the game he brought to Pinehurst that June was a shadow of its former self, due in part to a foot injury that hampered him throughout 1997 and the distractions of his Ryder Cup captaincy that was building to a crescendo three months after the Pinehurst Open. He shot back-to-back 74s and missed the cut by one shot, but that didn't dampen his enthusiasm for seeing the new G2 greens.

"You look at those greens and you scratch your head," Ben said that week. "The movement is magical. You try to grasp it, to put those dimensions in your mind. They're so distinct. It's symphonic."

More than a decade later, his playing resume is essentially complete. Crenshaw is asked when all is said and done, which will be more important—his competitive record or the golf courses he's partnered with Coore in designing?

"Probably the courses—they last longer," he says. "If we've had a hand in doing something good, that's enough. We've been lucky, we've gotten to work in some beautiful spots, with some great raw material. That's more than half the battle, period. God bless, we've had some gorgeous sites for golf courses. That's all you can ask for."

***

Pinehurst is a busy place the first week in November—just as it has been for more than a century. In the old days, the winter season didn't get cranked up until November. In 2010, the resort property is filled with a variety of groups. Bill Coore is back this week and expecting another visit from Mike Davis of the USGA on Friday, and Pinehurst marketing officials have taken advantage of Coore's visit and the fact the restoration project now is eight months along to hold a press conference and give regional media a chance to play the course and interview Coore.

One of the most revealing perspectives of the No. 2 job comes from a video presentation marketing director Tom Pashley has produced. It juxtaposes flyover footage that NBC Sports used in its 1999 telecast of the U.S. Open with footage shot just a week before. On the left side of the screen is an aerial view of the eleventh hole from 1999, on the right a similar view from today. Next are similar aerials of the twelfth hole. Pashley gives Toby Cobb and Kyle Franz a preview of the video late Wednesday afternoon.

"How cool is that?" Pashley asks.

"That's an awesome comparison," Franz says. "It's pretty shocking to compare this course to '99."

"Bill has used the term 'bowling alley fairways' since the beginning of this job," Cobb says. "That's what he means—those old fairways look exactly like a bowling alley from above."

Now the fairways have more the look of those in the aerial photos from 1943 that have helped guide the restoration process. The structure is less rigid and there are fewer straight lines. The fairways meander. There is significantly more sand and less grass.

Cobb and Franz leave the warmth and dryness of the clubhouse to return to the course on a rainy afternoon. They find Coore and arrange to meet on the twelfth hole with Jim Pies, who is in charge of the irrigation system on the five golf courses that play out of the main clubhouse. Coore has some questions about water control issues with the new irrigation system that will be installed over the winter.

The walk from the clubhouse backwards along the thirteenth and twelfth fairways takes only fifteen minutes, but the flow of consciousness from Coore's mind provides an interesting look at the way the architect is constantly processing what he sees and what he *wants* to see in a year or two.

He looks at the hardpan sand to the left of thirteen fairway; so far, the workers have installed several hundred wire grass plants on ground that not long before was covered with Bermuda grass.

"You wouldn't mind seeing that be almost a sea of wire grass at

Toby Cobb (right) was headquartered in Pinehurst full time during the eighteen months of the No. 2 restoration process. Here he and Bill Coore walk the fifth fairway during Coore's visit to Pinehurst in November 2010.

some point," Coore says.

He looks at the line between the tight Bermuda grass of the fairway and the beginning of the hardpan. Coore thinks it's all too neat. He talks to Cobb and Franz about taking a mini-excavator around the course and tweaking the fairway edges.

"Kyle, let's experiment and see what we can do," Coore says. "Let's scruff it up a little. We want it to be roughed up and a little more natural looking. Play with it and see what you can do."

Coore tells Cobb they need to remind the maintenance staff to always be careful where they are spraying fertilizer. He points to the edge of the fairway.

"You don't want a guy driving a tractor, not paying attention and putting water and fertilizer through here," he says. "It will just encourage the Bermuda to keep growing. Keep the water and fertilizer off the edges."

The neatness theme continues as Coore looks at all the pine straw strewn about the hardpan: "It looks like it just happened. It's not manufactured." And it continues as Coore looks at some mounds Franz has built with pine straw haphazardly tossed about: "That's good, Kyle. It doesn't look like a flower bed with mulch. That's the last thing we want out here."

Coore considers the bunkers he sees on No. 2 and reaches into his memory bank for an observation from Robert Hunter, the author of *The Links* and co-architect along with Alister MacKenzie of Cypress Point. "They should have the appearance of being made with carelessness and abandon with which a brook tears down the banks which confine it, or the wind tosses about the sand of the dunes . . . forming depressions or elevations broken into irregular lines."

"That's the thing," Coore says. "We don't have the wind and water here quite like you do along the coast, but the idea is to let Mother Nature take charge."

On twelve tee they find Pies, coincidentally a distant cousin of Coore's—Pies' grandfather and Coore's father were brothers, though Pies himself is a native of Moore County. Pies has been on the Pinehurst maintenance staff for sixteen years and has been irrigation superintendent for ten years. His job at the moment and over the winter when the antiquated irrigation system on No. 2 is replaced is a challenging one—throttling back from having blanket water coverage of

nearly every square foot of the course and its environs to a precision operation that touches very specific areas only.

"What we're moving toward is not the norm at Pinehurst," says Pies. "We trying to get the right head and the right nozzle and the right spring rate to cover certain areas and keep water off other areas."

Coore points to a line of demarcation that typifies the issue on every hole—svelte fairway grass to hardpan sand.

"Jim, we're trying to get the fairway edges where they don't look so perfect," Coore says. "For that to happen, we need the irrigation to stop just short of the sandy area. Can you do that?"

"Absolutely," Pies says.

"Because then they'll start to brown-in."

"You want dry more than green," Pies says.

"Right. These edges are too smooth and pretty."

"We can adjust so the last few drops fall *inside* the line, not beyond it," Pies says. "That's no problem."

It's still raining on Thursday morning as newspaper, radio and television reporters arrive for a midmorning press conference. Crenshaw is sitting in the offices of business manager Scotty Sayers in Austin, Texas, but his image and voice grace the attendees gathered in the St. Andrews Room via Skype.

"I wonder what Leonard Tufts and Donald Ross would say about this technology," Crenshaw says, then adds that it's quite an honor to be asked to take on such a significant project in Pinehurst.

"People make pilgrimages to a couple places in the world," he says. "There are a couple of places they want to visit before their golfing years are over. Those two places are St. Andrews and Pinehurst. First and foremost, there's an atmosphere that pervades that you cannot reproduce anywhere in the world."

Coore addresses the group and explains the restoration project as broken into four phases: the removal of Bermuda grass; the planting of wire grass in its place; the reconstruction of bunkers and the reinstallation of some abandoned ones; and the refinement and growing-in process that will continue indefinitely. He says the job will substantially be complete by the spring of 2011, and he explains the essence of the grass-for-sand trade.

"We can only imagine that Donald Ross when he first arrived here said, 'This is pretty good for golf,'" Coore says. "We believe he looked at these sandy areas and said they are not so penal that every shot hit there is lost or a complete hack-out, but they afford variety and opportunity for recovery. Recovery is such an important aspect for golf throughout its history. We believe, the people at Pinehurst believe, others around the world believe, that as these roughs were lost, some of Pinehurst's character was lost as well.

"It's our belief, and the belief of others in golf, that perhaps it was a bit more interesting in its original form."

Much of the questioning from the reporters centers on the 2014 U.S. Open, and Coore uses the forum to make an important point.

"The perception is this is being done *for* the U.S. Open," Coore says. "That is not correct. The USGA has not dictated this be done. They have certainly supported it. But this work was sought by Bob Dedman and Don Padgett, that they believed this was the right thing to happen for Pinehurst."

Coincidentally in Pinehurst this week is Martin Miller, a photographer and publisher from California who works with retail director Stephen Cryan in producing yardage books, prints, framed artwork and other collateral. He and partner Rob Brown have taken thousands of pictures of the resort's eight golf courses over more than a decade, and, like all photographers, have faced the challenge of shooting a No. 2 course with no mountains, no water hazards and no eye candy to help frame images. Worse, No. 2 had become virtually a smooth carpet of green.

Despite the inclement weather, Miller has been out on the course much of the morning and at lunch is effusive over the changes.

"Shooting this golf course has just gotten a whole lot easier," Miller says. "What I have seen so far is unbelievable, it's spectacular. Thirteen and fourteen really pop. Now, there's a palette to work with. Before, you would stand on the tee or an approach area and all you could see was a green. There was no other visible element."

The sand, in essence, has become a "river" flowing through the eighteen holes.

"The sand is now the ocean," he says. "It's so much more stimulating. People before would say, 'That's a really good golf course, but it's not much to look at.' It's still the same golf course, but there is lot more to see. I'm thrilled by it."

Though Coore is no photographer, he appreciates the challenge of

wielding a camera lens on No. 2.

"You cannot see with a camera the elements that are its strengths," he says. "Its foundation is on detail and subtlety. On most new golf courses, the foundation is on bombastic statements and visual effect. Here there are no rock walls, no fifteen-foot deep bunker, no three and four tiered greens. All those things can work beautifully in the proper situation. Yet the beauty of Pinehurst is, it's avoided all of that."

The press event is the first of two special occasions that day. At 5:30, Pinehurst has invited several dozen community leaders, club officers, top amateur golfers, golf architecture aficionados and others to a reception and presentation from Coore. He tells the group that Pinehurst No. 2 "is at the very foundation of golf architecture in America" and that while no one can accurately discern what Donald Ross would say if he were alive in 2010, he's confident Ross would applaud anything that brought more sand into play.

Coore speaks of all the photographic evidence on the walls of the clubhouse and in the Tufts Archives showing in all its sepia-toned glory what Ross and the Tufts family believed the course should look like. He lists the three prevailing characteristics of No. 2 from its mid-20th century heyday: The native roughs, the width of the holes and the unique green sites. Today only the turtle-backed greens and their accompanying array of undulations, crests and hollows remain.

"Our goal is to go back in history," Coore says.

Mike Davis arrives later in the evening and joins Coore, his staff and assorted Pinehurst officials at dawn's first light on Friday. This is Davis's third trip to Pinehurst since the restoration began. His priorities are to work with Coore on fairway widths in the landing areas, inspect the new tees and monitor the evolution of the native roughs.

"I'm amazed at the contrasts since the last time I was here," Davis says.

"It's starting to happen," Coore agrees.

On the first hole, Davis stands on the right edge of fairway, paces the distance across and asks Coore, "Bill, would you be comfortable coming in two or three yards? In their minds, they start to say, 'Maybe there is some benefit to laying back and having a 140-yard shot in.'"

That theme arises often throughout the tour, Davis finding a few yards here and there in the landing area of the tour pro—280 to 300

SHOCK AND WOW OVER NO. 2

Tom Fazio turned sixty-three in 2008, the year that Bear Stearns and Lehman Brothers went out of business, that the financial world imploded amid a barrage of credit default swaps, government bailouts and tanking home prices. Among the economic pockets hit hardest was the golf business—companies ceased traveling for golf outings, individuals cut back on club memberships and dues, and new courses were quickly dispatched to the back burner. Given his age and the fact that in 2009 Fazio was forced to trim his staff at Fazio Golf Course Designers in half and that by mid-year he did not have one new domestic golf course project on the drawing board, he was content to sit back, enjoy semi-retirement and play golf. He turned the day-to-day operation of his design firm over to his son, Logan.

"He said, 'Dad, go play golf,'" Fazio says. "I do most of my business today on the cell phone."

That freedom brought Fazio to Pinehurst in late September 2010 and to a golf outing at the Country Club of North Carolina. Since Fazio recently had reconstructive knee surgery, he was relegated to riding in a cart and enjoying the evening fellowship. He had also heard of the restoration project on No. 2 and phoned Don Padgett on Sept. 30 and asked if he could drive over and see the course. Padgett invited Fazio, a long-time friend of the resort and club, for lunch and a tour.

"You can say the word *shock* when I first saw the golf course," Fazio says. "The word *wow* is appropriate as well. I also would say that I think it's going to be fabulous. It's such a big deal to do. This is a *big deal*. This is not a little deal. It's a big deal. It takes a lot of guts and good management to do

Tom Fazio on first tee of the opening of Pinehurst No. 8 in 1996.

this. Some people will be shocked at the changes. I think it's pretty much on target. I couldn't be happier, being a Pinehurst fan and having had the opportunity to do quite a few golf courses at Pinehurst myself.

"The look is so unique and so Pinehurst. A couple of generations of golfers never saw the old Pinehurst, they don't understand what it was. Now all of a sudden it's back. This golf course will look strange to some people. There will be a question mark in their minds. But I think they'll come around when they experience it."

Fazio applauds all the pieces of the puzzle—Bob Dedman, Don Padgett, the USGA, and of course the architects themselves.

"You have the perfect storm—a great golf course, all the old traditions, a golf entity that approves it, an owner who knows he's doing the right thing, a guy like Ben Crenshaw who's such an historian of the game, a guy like Bill Coore who knew the old Pinehurst so well. All the pieces fit into place. It's fabulous."

Fazio was a relative newcomer to the golf design business in the mid-1970s when he and his uncle, George, were hired by Pinehurst management to design a new No. 6 course on a rugged site about three miles north of the resort. His career had exploded and he was considered the foremost architect in the 1990s when he was hired to design Pinehurst No. 8 and then a new course on the site of the original Pinehurst No. 4.

"For me, Pinehurst is such a special place for golf," Fazio says. "Put Donald Ross in the equation and it's even more special. It's been an historical destination for over a century. There's a special feeling—a feeling for golf and its tradition and history and longevity."

HOME GAMES IN 2014

From not knowing if a U.S. Open could be financially and logically viable at all to its being one of the most successful ever. That was 1999.

From thinking it would be eight to ten years before another Open would come to Pinehurst to getting one six short years later. That was 2005.

And now to hosting back-to-back Opens for men and women in 2014—something that's never been done before and may never again.

"It's a tremendous honor for the USGA to trust us to do this," says Pinehurst COO Don Padgett II. "It's outside the norm, and Pinehurst is the facility and the people they want to enter into this with. What a show of trust and respect. I think everyone in Pinehurst should be very flattered."

When the world of golf convenes in Pinehurst the third and fourth weeks of June 2014 for first the Men's Open and next the Women's Open, Pinehurst will become the first and only venue to have hosted the U.S. Open, Women's Open, Senior Open, Men's Amateur and Women's Amateur. It will have hosted nine USGA championships following the 2014 double-header.

The USGA announced the novel pairing in June 2009, prompted in part because a venue it planned for the 2014 Women's Open fell through earlier in the year. The 2014 date would follow the last Men's Open on No. 2 by nine years and mark another return to the Sandhills of the Women's Open after last being played at Pine Needles in 2007.

"Somewhere Ernie Banks must be smiling—'Let's play two,'" USGA Executive Director David Fay said in making the announcement.

"I applaud the USGA thinking out of the box on this," Pinehurst owner Robert Dedman Jr. said. "It immediately struck me as a brilliant idea. It shows you how innovative the USGA has become."

Jim Hyler of Raleigh was vice president of the USGA when the deal was made in 2009 and then spent two years in 2010-11 as the association's president.

"I think the '14 championships will be wonderful," Hyler says. "The second week, the crowds won't be as big, the bleachers won't be as full, but I still think having the women at Pinehurst right behind the men will mean a great deal for women's golf."

Reg Jones began working at Pinehurst as an intern for Pinehurst Championship Management in 1994 and his first event was the 1994 Senior Open. Since then, he's helped manage the 1999 Open, worked on the 1996 and 2001 Women's Opens at Pine Needles and had risen to championship director for PCM for the 2005 Open. He joined the USGA in 2006 to direct the U.S. Open on a permanent basis, and the USGA opened a Pinehurst satellite office to its

Far Hills, N.J., headquarters to house Jones and a staff of seven. They work from the second floor of the Pinehurst Department Store building in the center of Pinehurst, and in February 2012, they opened a 2014 operations office in the Members' Clubhouse at Pinehurst.

"There is a strong Pinehurst influence that goes through our organization," Jones says. "And there is a lot of Pinehurst influence in the game of golf. It's a very special place. A lot of it goes back to '99. That was a very special championship, we have a lot of good memories from that week."

The Sandhills area and the state of North Carolina have embraced the two Men's Opens and three Women's Opens that have been played at No. 2 and Pine Needles over the last two decades. Corporate support has been strong, ticket sales have been excellent and the perceived lack of hotel rooms, restaurants and parking venues have proved non-issues. The Men's Open in '99 proved that Pinehurst could successfully host the event both inside and outside the ropes; the dramatic finish with Payne Stewart holing a fifteen-foot putt on the last stroke of the championship is indelibly etched in golf history. Six years later, the Open set the attendance record for the week at some 325,000 spectators, which stood through the 2011 Open at Congressional.

Now the clock is ticking on 2014.

"This will be such an historically relevant championship," Jones says. "That's the driving force behind it. It's something that's never been done before—the opportunity to crown the two best golfers in the world on back-to-back Sundays, on the same golf course, pretty much under the same conditions. The level of discussion and debate and attention these two events will receive will be good for the game."

The footprint for 2014 will remain much the same as the two previous Opens in terms of placing parking, bleachers, merchandise and corporate hospitality—"With a few tweaks here and there," Jones says. The area is fortunate in that it has a deep reservoir of volunteers to handle two weeks' worth of assignments. One of the key questions will be how corporate support shakes out; the banking industry that supported the early Opens was rocked to its core in the Great Recession of 2008, and the state's two largest utilities, Duke Energy and Progress Energy, announced a merger in early 2011.

"Certainly the economy has had an effect on all of us," Jones said in February 2012. "The U.S. Open is not immune. It means the last couple of years we've had to work a little harder to sell tickets and hospitality. Still, the event has been very successful. And at Pinehurst, whether it's tickets or hospitality, it's been one of our more successful events. We expect that again in 2014.

"And it will be a 'home game' for us. That makes it even more special."

Two of the Sandhills' Open champions have been Payne Stewart in 1999, shown lining up a putt with caddie Mike Hicks, and Cristie Kerr in 2007, celebrating her victory at Pine Needles. Both Opens will be contested on No. 2 in 2014.

yards from the tee. He is intent on instilling this thought in the mind of the golfer off the tee: "'Maybe I'm better off *guaranteeing* myself a shot in the fairway from 135, 140 yards out.' I'd like to make them have that thought. Is it worth having a sand wedge versus a nine-iron? Right now on some holes, it's wide enough they won't give it a second thought."

Kevin Robinson, the superintendent on No. 2, points to a footprint in the hardpan sand and tells Davis there will be some areas where footprints will loosen the sand.

"That's okay," Davis says. "If a ball ends up in that, tough luck. I hope some of this is real hardpan, some of it is softer. We really want it to be anything but perfect. The more natural it can be, the more different lies you can find, the better."

Davis further looks at the pine straw, some grass clippings, other assorted matter. He continues to Robinson.

"Kevin, going into the championship, your guys need to know this is fine like it is," Davis says. "Don't clean it up. We want that look. There are so many variables in an area like this. You have to pick the ball perfectly here—a millimeter behind it, the ball comes out dead. If we have a mix of softer sand, hardpan, organic matter scattered about, pine straw, I tell you that will not be easier. Recovery will not be automatic. They might get a green light or a caution light. They might have a clump of organic matter behind their ball. That will make for some interesting shots."

Never far from the mind of anyone involved in the project is the issue of fairway firmness—the thatch underneath the grass makes the fairways softer than anyone would like.

"I don't remember Pinehurst as being a place where the ball would hit in the drive zone and really, really go," Davis says. "I remember the ball hitting and releasing ten to fifteen yards, but I can't remember a time when ball really scooted. There may be sand under there, but what the ball is really hitting is organic matter. That's pretty soft. The firmer you get them, the more you bring the other features into play."

The elements are there for a different kind of U.S. Open in 2014: firm fairways, Pinehurst's signature greens, width to plan shots and angles into hole locations, recoveries from wire grass instead of Bermuda grass. Still, all this planning and scheming by mortals can go only so far. Elements beyond the control of Mike Davis and Bill

Coore will have much to do with how future Opens are played.

"Mother Nature will still have a much, much bigger influence than anything," Davis says. "If we have soft greens because it's been raining, we're going to have a much easier course. These greens are still the defense—*if* they're firm and fast. Same goes for the fairways. If they're running, balls will find trouble and we'll see a lot of recovery shots we've never seen in an Open before. It's going to be so much more interesting. It will be a great dynamic on TV."

After touring the course and having lunch in the Donald Ross Grill, Davis returns to The Carolina and pauses on the West Lawn to give his impressions of the No. 2 restoration to Tom Pashley, the resort's marketing director, who records the conversation on videotape.

"This takes you back to what golf used to be in the golden era of the 1910s, '20s and '30s," Davis says. "Back then, architects were concerned about giving you good teeing ground, good fairways and good greens. The rest of it was the lay of the land, it was whatever was natural for the area and the site.

"It's exciting to see these neat architectural features coming back, the things that made No. 2 what it once was. You owe it to yourself, if you love golf, if you love golf architecture, to see the 'new' old Pinehurst No. 2."

***

For nine months Toby Cobb and the Coore & Crenshaw design and construction workers have had to plan their work around member and resort play on No. 2. They have looked for windows on the tee sheet to schedule tasks that have involved getting close to the playing corridors. They have worked early in the mornings before golfers have shown up and until dusk on the long summer days after golfers have repaired to the nineteenth hole.

Now the golfers are gone, the course having closed in mid-November. Construction work can proceed full bore until early March 2011.

"Toby is finally happy—we've got the golfers off, now he can play in the dirt," Don Padgett says, smiling at Cobb.

Bill Coore and Ben Crenshaw will both be in Pinehurst the week after Thanksgiving, the first time they've been on-site at the same time since late February. A snapshot from Tuesday afternoon at 2:30 illustrates the intensity of the work flow: Crenshaw is standing to the right of the second green, looking into a depression where a bunker once sat and considering the merits of restoring it. There is the sharp buzz from chainsaws removing a tree from the new teeing ground of the seventh hole and the rumble of a bulldozer removing dirt to lower the existing tee. A half dozen workers are putting a protective cover on the first green after it's been laid with new sod, another group is on the eighth green, moving in tandem in a line and scraping thatch from atop the green's sand foundation. Cobb gets a phone call from one of the workers on fifteen green, asking if someone can make a run to the hardware store to get some irrigation pipe fittings. And irrigation chief Jim Pies is in the woods to the left of the sixteenth fairway, waiting for a telephone worker to arrive and tell him exactly where a fiber optic cable runs underneath the ground.

"It's a hundred grand if you tear one of those lines up," Pies says. "You can't guess where they are."

"Now we can ramp things up," Cobb says. "We've been sort of tippy-toeing around, as we should. People paying top dollar to play No. 2 deserve to play without a lot of distractions. But now we can get down to some serious lifting."

The first order of business Nov. 15 was to begin stripping the greens of the Penn G2 bentgrass that had served the course so well for fourteen years but was now showing stress. By early 2010 three greens on No. 2 had developed enough influx of *Poa annua*—a form of bluegrass considered a weed on a golf course—that the putting surfaces were bumpy and inconsistent. Don Padgett and Bob Farren decided by the spring of 2010 that those greens had deteriorated so much they needed to be resurfaced and scheduled that work for the winter. Then by late summer, the record summer heat of 103 days at ninety degrees or higher (more than twice the normal number) had stressed the entire course and four more greens had wilted beyond the acceptable level. Padgett and Farren then decided those would be resurfaced as well. Given that nearly half of the greens were now set to be resurfaced, it only made sense to do the entire course so as to maintain consistency.

Penn G2 was deemed in the mid-1990s as providing the best mix of firmness, playability and resistance to southern heat and humidity and was used in 1996 when the greens on No. 2 were rebuilt to USGA specifications. Since then, the grass seed industry has further evolved and a blend of Penn A1 and A4 has proven even more successful than G2 in southern climates. Farren spent considerable time in the late summer of 2010 shopping sod purveyors and ordering enough to handle Pinehurst's needs in November. Boyd Turf Industries in the Pittsburgh suburbs has some 115,000 square feet growing and ready to ship beginning in mid-November.

Farren and Kevin Robinson, the superintendent on No. 2, knew there would be some degree of thatch—an intermingling of dead stems, leaves and blades—having developed beneath the grass and above the sand that was laid when the greens were rebuilt in 1996. But they weren't sure how much. It turns out, there was quite a bit—as much as two inches on some greens. Rather than lay the new sod on top of the thatch, they quickly made the decision to strip out the layer of thatch, requiring painstaking hand-labor to dig out the organic material across every green surface. That would take roughly an additional week of labor.

"It's better to do it now than sit here in July and say we wish we'd done it," Farren says. "You've got fourteen years of top-dressing and mowing, so you can make a case that the greens have come up an inch and a half to two inches. We're taking them back down to the grade from when we seeded them in '96."

"We only get one chance at this," Padgett adds. "I think we would have been forever sorry if we hadn't done this. They stripped the grass, walked them and they still felt spongy."

One of Coore's priorities over the next several days is to work on the fifteenth and seventeenth greens, the only greens that are being reshaped and re-contoured in any fashion. Both he and Crenshaw on their first tour of the course earlier in the year lamented the lack of any room on the right side of the fifteenth green to stick a pin, and Mike Davis of the USGA had the same opinion of the front of seventeen. The fifteenth is a long par-three and the green is probably as close to a pure "upside down wok" or "turtleback" shape as any on the course. Seventeen is a medium-length one-shot hole, the green sloped from back to front and narrowing at the opening. Coore wants to flatten out the right edge of fifteen and the front portion of seventeen

Bill Coore floats out the new putting surface on the par-three fifteenth hole in December 2010. "I love watching him work his magic," Ben Crenshaw says. "What you're seeing is a perfectionist at work."

and extend both toward bunkers guarding those perimeters.

The interesting thing about the process is that Coore will do the work himself.

"Bill's done every green on every course we've ever done—from Sand Hills to Friar's Head to Dormie and every one in between," Cobb says. "The shapers get it close, then Bill does the finishing work. He loves doing it and he's good at it. He'll stay on the machines for hours and hours and hours. We've turned car and truck lights on greens so he can keep working on short days in the winter."

Coore's favorite tool for "floating out" greens, as the process is called, is a knock-off on a piece of machinery manufactured by Toro called the "Sand Pro." It's about the size of a riding lawnmower, has three wheels and is used to groom bunkers. Some twenty years ago, Coore changed the attachments on the machine to adapt it to working on greens. The machine is big enough to move the dirt but small enough to do precise detailing work. Coore jokes that he missed a sure retirement income by not patenting the apparatus.

"We were the first to do it and now everyone's doing it—but we never registered the idea," he says. "That Sand Pro is not heavy enough to damage a green, so it's great for finishing work. You can do your fine-tuning, your little tweaks when it's just about done."

Coore starts on seventeen on Monday while Cobb and another design associate, Dave Axland, are supervising the extension of the right of fifteen green and the reconstruction of the bunker on that side of the putting surface. Coore works for hours and hours, driving the machine in circles and loops, adding miniscule undulations but stretching and flattening the front finger so that it's not so severe that it cannot hold a pin. At one point Crenshaw and Kyle Franz stop to view Coore's progress tucking and trimming the surface. Crenshaw says he tried getting on a machine in the early days of their partnership but gave it up after seeing Coore's skill.

"I backed right out of that," Ben says with a smile. "I'll just stand to the side and let Bill work his magic. I love watching him do it. What you're seeing is a perfectionist at work."

"You rarely see an architect floating out a green," Franz adds. "It's a great lesson for a young guy in the business—you're never too big to get on a machine and do it the way you want it done."

Two days later, the right side of fifteen has been rebuilt and Coore

moves his machine a few hundred yards and revs it up. It's sunny but cold and windy, and Coore bundles up to spend the afternoon exposed to the elements. A couple of hours later, Crenshaw stops by to check his progress after looking at other parts of the course. He nods encouragement to his partner and notes the added area on the right portion of the green.

"That's the way it ought to look," Crenshaw says. "That's a beautiful piece of work. There was no functionality on the right side of the green. Now there is. On the old pictures, you can see the edge of the green way over to the right. There is a much more inviting look there now. When the pin is over there now, guys will shoot at it. Now you have room to play that shot, that's the lure you want. It's much more inviting. It looks so good."

Crenshaw has seen a lot that he likes on other holes. Cobb shows him a bunker front-right of fourteen green with sandy splotches on the grassy face. That's not sloppy maintenance—it's by design. "It's a cool look," Cobb says. "If we like the way it turns out, we might try it elsewhere."

Crenshaw is amazed at how the sand is much more the star of the visual show from one through eighteen.

"A major theme here is to showcase the sand," Ben says. "The sand is what the place is all about, along with the pine needles. It's amazing how much the sand illuminates the golf course. That monotone green, there was no contrast. What we've done over eight months is like sticking an electrical cord in a wall."

One of the onlookers on Wednesday afternoon is Rich Wainwright, a three-decade veteran of the Pinehurst staff who has worked as a golf professional and now has the title of director of yield management. His job is essentially to manage the use of all of Pinehurst's eight golf courses, breaking the starting times between resort guests and members, ensuring they are not overused and maximizing the cash flow during resort's seasonal ebb and flow. It's been a difficult two years for anyone in the golf business who manages tee times and cash flow, as there has not been enough of either. Pinehurst has held up better than most, given its place in the golf world and the steady ownership of the Dedman family, but Wainwright is excited about what the restoration of No. 2 will mean.

"Essentially what we are doing is rebirthing this golf course,"

Maintenance and construction workers tamp down the new bent grass sod on the eighteenth green in December 2010.

Wainwright says. "I think people who might have played No. 2 years ago are going to have to come back and see it again. I think the demand will be phenomenal. The product is going to be phenomenal. It's just going to be really good."

The return to the golden age of No. 2 from a strategic and appearance standpoint is certainly a marketing hook, and the resurfacing of the greens will help eliminate complaints of late about the quality of the putting surfaces. Like others close to the project, Wainwright is excited about the prospect of a bouncier playing surface from tee to green.

"You get these fairways firm, oh man, how good would that be?" he wonders. "Obviously, the more firm you get the fairways, the more narrow the golf course becomes. It shrinks the fairways."

Padgett joins Crenshaw for a few minutes on the seventh tee. The

dogleg right par-four has so far vexed the architects in deciding how to handle the configuration of bunkers in the right turn of the hole and what to do with the left edge of the fairway. The hole has had as much tinkering as any hole on No. 2, with Richard Tufts doing extensive bunker work prior to the 1962 U.S. Amateur. They also have as reference the 1943 aerial photo and the question is this: Which version, if any, do you use as the template? The new tee will add about fifteen yards, making it next to impossible to try to gamble and clear the bunkers in the corner of the dogleg.

"Ben, I remember you telling me you always thought this golf course gave you options," Padgett says, standing in the middle of the fairway, safely away from the trap on the right, "but this is the only hole on the golf course where you have to aim *right here*."

Crenshaw agrees. "You don't want to try anything here. There is nothing to try, unless you can hit it four hundred yards."

They discuss lopping the last bunker off, giving the long hitter some incentive to try to cut the angle. Ben also considers what might occur *through* the fairway—what trouble a player could find if he drives it through the turn and the fairways are running hard.

"You can spend a lifetime studying what happens *after* the ball hits the ground," Ben says. "There's something new every day at St. Andrews. It's definitely here also. Charlie Price condensed it into one sentence. It was stunning he was so dead on. He said, 'Fine architecture is what to leave out rather than what to put in.' I thought that was so profound."

***

Since leaving Pinehurst in early December 2010, Bill Coore has traveled literally around the world in visiting three Coore & Crenshaw golf courses. He flew to Tasmania off the Australian coast the second week in December for the grand opening of Lost Farm at Barnbougle Dunes. Then he flew to China to inspect the progress at Shanqin Bay, a course on Hainin Island off the southern coast of China. Most recently, Coore was in the Florida heartland working on the routing and hole construction at Streamsong Resort; the Coore & Crenshaw course will be a companion layout to a Tom Doak routing in a resort created on formerly mined phosphate land owned by the Mosaic Company. Coore flies from Tampa the evening of Jan. 19, arrives in Pinehurst and is on No. 2 for a walking tour with Toby Cobb early Thursday morning.

He surveys the greens on the first and second holes, each with a fresh layer of sod knitting in and the bright green of the new grass standing in contrast to the dormant Bermuda and sand everywhere else.

"The greens look good," Coore says. "My first impression is removing that layer of thatch has settled them down a little, calmed them down."

The sun is out and the temperature will creep into the fifties on this day, a welcome respite to what has already been an unseasonably severe winter—following a tough winter in 2009-10 and a brutally hot summer. It's snowed twice and temperature highs have been in the thirties throughout December and early January, creating havoc with the greens resurfacing project.

"You can count in the *hours*, not days, that we've seen fifty degrees or higher the last month," course superintendent Kevin Robinson says.

"We're not asking for a heat wave," Don Padgett adds. "Just normal weather will be fine—days in the fifties, nights in the thirties."

When the decision was made in August to resurface all eighteen greens rather than just the seven with severe *Poa annua* and heat stress, Bob Farren identified a sod farm outside Pittsburgh, Boyd Turf Industries, with an excellent track record of having provided sod for clubs such as Oakmont and for special projects such as the new putting green installed at the White House in 2010. Owner Colin Boyd committed nearly 2.75 acres of sod and planned to begin the deliveries immediately after Thanksgiving. Farren also placed an order for covers to insulate the new greens as needed during subfreezing weather.

The process started smoothly enough, with Boyd's staff cutting layers of sod and rolling them up like carpet, stowing the sod on flat-bed trailers and driving it ten hours to Pinehurst. He sent two of his men to Pinehurst to help with the installation, the process involving unrolling the sod and using a vibrating tamp machine to knit the strips together once they are laid on the green surface. The week after Thanksgiving, however, some snow and cold moved into the northeast, limiting Boyd's ability to harvest the grass. Padgett drew on his years as general manager at Firestone in Akron, Ohio, to locate a Cleveland contractor who could drive three acres of tarps used in laying concrete to Pennsylvania to help keep Boyd's sod from freezing. By the first week in December, greens one through seven as well as eighteen were covered.

Then the bottom fell out when a snowstorm developed throughout the eastern U.S. the first weekend of the month. Western Pennsylvania was covered under heavy snow, forcing Farren to find a back-up sod supplier. The weather was cold but the New Jersey coast had not been hit with snow and ice yet, so East Coast Sod & Seed in Pilesgrove, N.J., was able to supply enough sod for greens eight through sixteen. Those greens were sodded by Christmas. The snow that covered the entire Eastern Seaboard on Christmas night shut down East Coast's ability to harvest and truck enough sod for the final green, so Farren talked to Sandhill Turf, a Moore County company located west of Pinehurst on Hwy. 211. Robinson drove to the nursery the week after Christmas and found enough sod for the seventeenth green.

"At dusk on the last day of the year, we got the last green finished," Farren says.

Though the weather the first two weeks of January was colder than usual, the covers on each of the greens protected them and made a ten-to-twelve-degree difference in their exposure to the cold.

"Those covers are miracle workers," Toby Cobb says. "We used them at Friar's Head, we used them at Dormie on the last few greens that we did in February."

Coore is delighted to learn that since his last visit, Padgett and Farren have made the decision not to overseed No. 2 with ryegrass during the winter, instead opting for a cutting-edge dying process to give the dormant Bermuda turf a little color and visual appeal to visitors coming south for an early wisp of springtime. What's good for the business's bottom line—green grass in the early spring—can be bad for the long-term health of turf.

Applying ryegrass, a strain that grows during the winter when the sun elevates the blade's temperature above freezing, is a cosmetic ruse used on athletic fields and golf courses that detracts from developing the core Bermuda turf once spring arrives. Since the rye grows all year, it has to be mowed, and the clippings left on the ground decompose into thatch—leaving a layer of organic matter that makes the surface softer. Then in the spring, the emerging Bermuda needs more fertilizer to fight through the existing rye, eventually leading to even more thatch. And the planting of the rye introduces more opportunities for winter weed growth such as *Poa annua*.

"It's impossible to overseed and get the firm and fast conditions we want," Padgett says. "We can't get it to play the way we want it to by putting rye grass on the golf course. Overseeding is purely cosmetic. To stay the course, we had to make this decision."

Farren inquired of the USGA's Green Section staff if they knew of any courses using dyes that provided a natural green color, didn't rub off on shoes and balls and were easy to apply and maintain. He was directed to Brunswick Plantation in Calabash, N.C., where the

superintendent had successfully used an organic dye from a company called Geoponics. Farren visited the course in January and liked the results. By mid-February, No. 2 was burnished with a pale swath of green that looked perfectly natural.

"Not overseeding is really good for the turf," Coore says. "The rye grass competes too much with the Bermuda. It's counterproductive to everything we're trying to accomplish."

Beyond the greens, the hot buttons around the course are wire grass and bunkers. Coore & Crenshaw have imported four additional designers/shapers to help Cobb and Kyle Franz, and Pinehurst has assigned one of its maintenance staffers, Alan Green, to spearhead the planting of wire grass. Green and his workers are planting roughly a thousand wire grass plants a week, and Coore spends several hours one afternoon walking the course with Green and talking about the art of planting wire grass.

"The wire grass still has a ways to go," Coore says. "There were areas fifty years ago where you literally had a sea of wire grass. That was a gift of nature. It took generations of reseeding to get that look. It will take a while to come back."

So far, Coore likes what he's seen from Green, a thirty-one year old from Bridge of Allan, Scotland. Green studied turf management at Elmwood College outside St. Andrews and moved to the States nearly a decade ago to serve an internship at Ohio State. He met his future wife, Sara, and they moved to Pinehurst. Green has previously worked on the maintenance staff at course No. 8.

"Golf course maintenance appeals to me," he says. "I'm an avid golfer, I've been working on golf courses since I was sixteen years old. It's incredible to have the opportunity to influence something with the magnitude of course No. 2."

Green, who grew up playing courses all across Scotland, admits he didn't know much about the restoration project when he was working on course No. 8. But when he was given the chance to spearhead the wire grass planting operation in December, he was taken aback.

"My first impression when I walked on site was, it reminds me of home," Green says. "I didn't understand the project at first, but when I saw it I immediately understood what it was all about. It felt a lot more like home. They are going to let nature and the elements dictate the appearance of the golf course. My mother and father are golf nuts, they've played everywhere. I've taken a few snaps and sent them to my dad. He said it looks like the heathlands. It looks like an inland links."

Green isn't the first Scotsman to feel that kinship between home and Pinehurst. One of Donald Ross's favorite stories involved a Scottish pro who had played all his life on links courses. He came to America and was badly off his game on inland courses, then arrived in Pinehurst thinking it was a seaside course.

"As he walked to the first tee, Sandy took a deep sniff and remarked, 'Aye, mon, that's the bonnie breeze right off the sea. That's what I've needed!'" Ross said. "And straightaway he tied the course record his first time out."

Green is walking along the fourth fairway, talking about the look and feel of the heathland courses in Scotland and England. Centuries ago, the glaciers melted and left deposits of sand and silt inland, creating the heathland areas known for their terrific percolating properties. Courses such as Blairgowrie Golf Club in Perth, Scotland, and Ladybank Golf Club, just outside St. Andrews, as well as English pearls such as Sunningdale and Walton Heath have that feel of "inland links."

"The heathlands are the best inland soil for golf—sandy soil and pine trees," he says. "If you pop up Blairgowrie on your computer, you'll think you're looking at Pinehurst."

The American taste for finely coiffed surfaces in every nook and cranny of a golf course migrated to the British Isles as well. As Pinehurst was losing its wire grass, Scotland was losing its heather.

"The heather fell out of favor at the heathland courses," Green says. "They fertilized the dickens out of them and grew grass. Now it's come back around to heather, and it's difficult getting it reestablished. If you have thick layers of organic matter, it's hard to grow heather."

The fairway of the first hole shows a burnished green look in March 2011, just after the reopening. The color actually comes from a dying process that allows the maintenance staff to provide resort guests with some color during cold-weather months without having to overseed the course with ryegrass.

There is a valley running between the ninth tee and green and the championship tee of No. 10 and the fairway. Over the last week, Green has planted a sea of wire grass on the tenth hole and is beginning work on the ninth hole. The placement of the plants on ten is interesting because there are thick patches and others that are bare and sandy—as if positioned by the whims of a roulette wheel or roll of the dice.

"That's a prime example of how to plant wire grass on a blank hillside and not make it look planned," Coore says. "The tendency would be to go all the way across and plant the whole thing with a straight line at the top."

Coore nods his approval of the arrangement—actually, the lack thereof—and since a couple of writers are tagging along, he puts the challenge in a context they can appreciate.

"I don't know anything about writing," Coore says, "but I would venture a guess that planting wire grass is something like writing. How do you look at the same scene and find a different way of describing it? How do you take an area of ground, plant wire grass and make it look different from the last hole? It's so hard to make it look

like it was not thought about."

The redesign of the par-four seventh hole is a different kettle of fish. It will take the best thinking from Coore & Crenshaw to solve what Don Padgett says is "the century-old jigsaw puzzle."

The hole runs 404 yards from the championship tee as used for the 2005 Open, and a new tee erected on the far side of Muster Branch Road will add fifteen yards for the 2014 Open. It was designed by Donald Ross in 1923 by combining the original third and fourth holes into one hole, the dogleg right played today.

Richard Tufts believed the hole was playing too easy by the early 1960s, and prior to the 1962 U.S. Amateur he added bunkers and mounds in the right corner and one trap and mounds on the left side. An illustration in the October 1962 *Golf Digest* shows the fairway in the corner beginning to narrow, a slippery slope that would leave it no more than a dozen yards wide forty years later. When Tom Fazio and Peter Tufts collaborated on a restoration in 1978, they further tweaked the corner by moving bunkers into the gamble zone and even planned the addition of a tree in the corner of the dogleg, though it was never actually planted.

Wire grass has always been a key element of Pinehurst No. 2, whether planted in the 1920s (above) or by Alan Green in 2010 (opposite).

"We're trying to inject a natural sense of life to it," Coore says. "It had such a convoluted look to it. It's apparent over its lifetime it's not been well thought of, you can tell by all the tinkering that's been done to it. We're trying to keep what's good about it, remove what's bad and find something that works from an appearance and strategic standpoint.

"The dogleg had been pushed out so far and the angle was so acute," he continues. "Only the really long hitters could try to carry it. Everyone else had to play out to the left."

Coore's idea to rebuild the hole is to widen the landing area in the corner, giving everyone the opportunity to hit a driver, and rebuild the bunker complex further from the tee to make clearing it a real challenge. The feature bunker will have the highest face of any fairway bunker on the course. Coore spends considerable time with Franz, who will soon climb onto a Mini-Ex and tuck and trim per Coore's instructions.

"We've opened up a whole ton of space over there," Franz says, pointing to where the corner of the dogleg had been deluged with bunkers. "We're trying to open up a little gambling avenue. I'm a nine-handicap and I can't think about trying to cut that corner. Now you have a little room to get closer for your second shot, but you have a price to pay if you miss."

Coore takes his cell phone from his pocket, dials Mike Davis of the USGA and spends ten minutes describing the plan and asking if it works for Davis's U.S. Open preparations. Davis tells Coore that players in the Open never hit driver on seven unless they were trying to clear the entire bunker complex.

"Now they have that option," Coore says, having rung off. "And Mike said he didn't mind if that bunker on the corner was six to seven feet deep."

Coore nods his head and moves on to other tasks as Friday afternoon wears on.

"We've got a chance to get it right," Coore says. "We're off to a good start."

***

The architects, their design associates and the Pinehurst maintenance teams are rounding the far corner and coming into the home stretch in early February. Just one month remains until No. 2 reopens

Bill Coore's reference point to the bunker on the eighteenth hole comes from a photo in a 1927 book authored by George Thomas (opposite). "It's the most beautiful bunker on the golf course," Coore says.

on March 3, 2011, and both Coore & Crenshaw are in Pinehurst the first week of February to inventory the progress and make the final punch list.

Coore has brought with him to show Don Padgett his copy of George Thomas's book, *Golf Architecture in America: Its Strategy and Construction*. Thomas grew up in the eastern United States more than a century ago and, though his expertise was horticulture and landscaping, he took an interest in golf design. Thomas studied first-hand the work of prominent golf designers such as Donald Ross, A.W. Tillinghast, Hugh Wilson and George Crump, in several cases serving as a club committeeman on new projects. After World War I, he moved west and spearheaded the design and construction of Los Angeles Country Club and Bel-Air Country Club.

The book is considered a cornerstone to any serious collection on golf architecture (it's worth up to $500 today), and Coore first saw it in Pete Dye's library back in the early 1970s when Coore occasionally looked after Pete and Alice Dye's home and dog on weekends. Later Coore bought a copy, as did

Ben Crenshaw, and both remembered early in the No. 2 restoration project having seen a terrific old photo of the bunker on the right of the eighteenth fairway at Pinehurst in one of their old books. Coore opens Thomas's book to page 317 and looks at the sepia-toned photograph of the bunker that Coore has pegged "the most beautiful on the golf course" several times during the past year. The picture shows the enormity of the trap—it runs fifty-four yards in length today and twenty paces across—and the jagged edges and the wide furrows made by rake tines. Today a golfer six feet tall cannot see over the highest lip if he's addressing a shot in the bottom of the bunker; the old bunker looks every bit as deep as well.

"It's so rugged and natural looking," Coore says. "It was still highly recognizable even in modern times, but it lacked that old look.

Certainly one of our goals was to restore that look."

Which brings Coore to one of his pet peeves—the hydro-charged ball that flies infinite distances and renders obsolete many of the game's classic courses.

"We've put the cart in front of the horse," he says. "Why are we changing all these golf courses for the sake of the golf ball? Why not just change the ball? Players today bomb it past all these interesting architectural features that have been around forever. You can't just move tees back because you don't always have room. And you can't move the bunkers—certainly not in this case. To try and pick this bunker up on eighteen and move it thirty yards up the fairway would look artificial and contrived."

Coore walks out onto the golf course in the brisk morning air, where he joins Crenshaw and Cobb for a walk around the course. Much of their attention is devoted to the bunkers.

"The golf course is waking up," Coore says. "It's starting to come to life. The bunkers are definitely getting some of that old look, something like those pictures we have from '36 PGA Championship. It's a pretty big move, particularly when you consider that most people think Ross bunkers had sod faces and flat bottoms. It took a little while to get comfortable putting them back. But I think it's working."

Walking along the third fairway, Ben looks at the bunkers ahead of them, the ones to the side of them on the sixth hole, the ones behind them to the west on the second and seventh holes.

"These bunkers, I have flashbacks to Australia and England looking at this stuff," he says. "They look like Royal Melbourne or Kingston Heath. These bunkers look great at a distance. But when you get close, they look even better. I love the little furls and edges."

The bunker work over the last year has involved myriad components. Every bunker has been re-edged to give it a more natural,

Kyle Franz wields his bulldozer in the construction of new bunkers in the corner of the dogleg right seventh hole. "These bunkers, I have flashbacks to Australia and England looking at this stuff," Ben Crenshaw says.

220

weathered appearance. Some have been rebuilt to make the banks sturdier and shave off the build-up of sand being thrown on them over the last fifteen years, since the 1996 renovation leading to the 1999 U.S. Open. Several new ones have been placed in the three hundred yard driving zone at the suggestion of the USGA's Mike Davis, and others have been moved closer to the middle of the fairway. Approximately a dozen bunkers or perimeters have been restored according to the 1943 aerial photography. Nearly every bunker on the course had grass rolling over the top into the face, limiting how well golfers could see them from the tee or approach area.

"We've cut sand up into the faces to make them visible," Toby Cobb says. "On some we've planted wire grass on the top. On some others, we've thrown sand on the turf to scruff them up a little."

The group stands on the fourth tee and looks at the two new bunkers cut into the hillside on the right side of the fairway. Davis believed there was no fear off the tee for elite players in the U.S. Open, particularly on the shortest of the course's two par-fives (eight and sixteen, par-fives on the members' scorecard, are played as par-fours in the Open).

"Those bunkers will influence their thought process," Coore says. "Before, there was nothing to worry about over there."

Up at the green, Coore surveys the newly shaped bunker to the front-right and the small island of turf that Kyle Franz has sculpted amidst the sand. Coore likes the edges of the green; they are craggy and irregular in the golden-age style. The island, though, is a different look for No. 2. The idea is executed well; the question is whether it fits on *this* course.

"You could find some interesting shots in there—particularly this being a short par-five and guys trying to go for it in two," Coore says. "It has a chance to stay. We'll ponder it some more. If this were one of our courses, absolutely, it would stay."

The architects have restored an abandoned bunker about 125 yards in front of the fifth tee on the left side of the fairway and re-edged the two traps in the distance, to the right side of the approach to the green. Crenshaw walks toward the green and motions with his arm at the sweep of the hole from right to left.

"The hole just boomerangs as you approach the green," he says. "Those bunkers are really pretty. There was not much life in those bunkers. All the movements of the course just blended in. The roughs, the bunkers—nothing caught your eye. Golly, this all looks so much better."

Coore stands on the tee of the par-three sixth hole and looks at the new sweep of the bunker to the left; the back side of it has been built up several feet, and there's significantly more sand in the golfer's field of vision as he eyes his tee shot.

"That's it," he says. "That is the old look."

They arrive at the seventh tee, the site of the most extensive bunker work on the course. Coore left two weeks ago with instructions for Franz to continue sculpting six new bunkers on the corner of the dogleg-right hole. The most noticeable new trap has a backside built six feet above ground level; it will certainly affect the thought process of long hitters.

"Ben, you talk about Royal Melbourne," Bill says, nodding in the distance. "That big boy on the right reminds me of number fourteen, the par-five, the bunker that sits on the left. When Kyle first cut it in there, I said, 'That's really high,' but it's nowhere near as high as that big ole monster in Australia."

Crenshaw likes the look and the effect it will have on playing the hole. It's 294 yards to clear the big bunker, 260 to clear the shorter one that sits a little to the left. There is plenty of room to play it safe but still hit the driver—the fairway runs some thirty-five yards across to the left, where a pair of mounds have been sculpted and trimmed with sand and wire grass.

"Before, it was totally void of any options," Crenshaw says.

"Mike Davis put it perfectly," Coore adds. "The really long players hit over the bunker complex without any regard that it's even there. Everyone else has to lay up, and they couldn't hit driver because that corner was necked down so tight. There was nowhere to hit it."

There is not a single round or oval bunker left on the course, no "tiddly-winks bunkers" as Coore terms the uniform traps that ringed the sixteenth green. Some edges are bounded by turf, others melt seamlessly into the sandy roughs. Random wire grass plants have been placed in some bunkers; sand has been thrown on the tops of the turf faces on others.

"The scruffiness takes on a life of its own," Coore says. "You leave it in places, you help it evolve in others. People say, 'Well, this is so easy, you just kill stuff, any fool could do this, you just go out and make a mess.' It's not that simple. There is an art to getting this look. We don't hear it as much today, but fifteen years ago we'd build a course and someone would say, 'When are you going to finish the bunkers?' We'd say, 'What do you mean? They *are* finished.'"

"You see different textures to the edges of bunkers in old photos," Franz adds. "You have a little grass, a little sand, a little wire grass. As we finish off the bunkers, then we'll get to some of the more artistic stuff, that is really fun to do. We're going from well-formed, well-shaped bunkers to a more natural appearance."

On twelve Coore addresses two subtle elements of the new bunker presentation. He nods toward a trap to the left of the fairway filled with sand colored with darker and more golden tints than the dominant bright white color found in most bunkers.

"That's my favorite color of bunker sand," he says. "It has a little color to it. It's not like Florida sand—stark white. The color looks natural, it looks like it belongs. It's got a little bit of a yellowish, cream-color tint to it."

Coore asks Cobb if there will be time to mix some darker sand into every bunker on the course before the reopening.

"It's sand they use for top-dressing," Toby answers. "It's no problem to go all the way through and add it, dirty up the sand a little."

As they near the green, Coore looks at the bunker sitting just below the putting surface on the left side. He runs his foot along the bunker edge closest to the green and describes how there had been a modest upslope of turf surrounding the bunker as well as some Bermuda rough.

"We cut the ridge out," Coore says. "Now the ball can run into the bunker. Before, that little elevation worked like a bumper—it repelled the ball away from the sand. You had build-ups like that all around the golf course. How many balls do you think will roll in there now? A bunch, I'd say."

The architects nod in approval at the work George Waters did on the bunkers on the par-three fifteenth. The right side of the green was extended several yards and the bunker was redesigned. There are two traps there now, one of them built around a knob that stands about six feet tall.

"I'm selfishly proud of number fifteen," Waters says. "It was kind of dreary looking. It was fun to do."

"You should rightly be proud of that," Coore says.

"The knob blends in so well with the green, the broken ground, the patches of wire grass and the sand," Waters says. "Now, you can get some awkward shots. It's a place you *don't* want to be. It adds an element of fear. Many bunkers on golf courses today have become so pure that Tour players don't mind hitting into them. Well, you don't want to hit into *these* bunkers."

Up on eighteen, Franz is working on the cross-bunker about fifteen yards in front of the green. He's built the face up and pushed the sand up higher, particularly in a knob on the right side.

"Now, you can see that bunker, even from the tee," Coore says. "Before, you couldn't see it. In the old pictures, it was cut way up in the right corner like it is now. You could see a mound up there, but you couldn't see the bunker."

Throughout the walk, Coore's step and countenance are the brightest they have been throughout the process.

"Toby and I walked the entire course yesterday," he says. "We found maybe six things—a few odds and ends with bunkers. I thought the crossing bunker on ten needed a little tweaking. We talked to George, and he spent some time later in the day. Boom—it's gorgeous.

"It's looking really good," Coore continues. "We were pretty nervous about this project, to be honest. There will be some who don't understand it. But I like what I see. I'm very pleased."

***

Toby Cobb, Kyle Franz, George Waters and Bryan Caesar gather around a table at Maxie's Pub in the Village of Pinehurst as the noon hour approaches on March 3, 2011. A half a mile away at Pinehurst Country Club, a select group of members and Pinehurst staff are preparing for a 1 p.m. shotgun start and the reopening of Pinehurst No. 2. The work of this quartet of golf course design and construction wizards is essentially completed. Cobb will remain in Pinehurst for three months to tie up any loose ends, Franz will work on the Pinehurst maintenance staff for several months focusing on bunkers and wire grass, and Waters and Caesar will return to their homes on the

The hardpan sand melts into the lower side of the bunkers near the twelfth green. The higher edges are cut with spades to give them a haphazard appearance—the opposite of the smooth, "painted-on" look that many modern bunkers have.

West Coast.

"I feel like an expectant father," says Cobb, who has been at work on the course almost daily the last thirteen months except for occasional trips back home to west Texas to see his family. "I'm ready for the baby to pop on out. I've looked at that golf course so much I'm not sure how objective I am. What have I missed? The four of us have been scouring the golf course the last week. What are we overlooking? What did we need to do that we haven't done?"

"There was never a wasted minute," Franz adds. "I'm content. I'm happy, I'm really stoked. This has been such a rewarding job. It was a huge responsibility. I mean, Donald Ross put his heart and soul into this golf course. It was a challenge. We were on a tight schedule and we had the weather throw us some curves. But it was fun. I'm stoked to see how people like it."

Cobb has already talked to Bill Coore, who called from the other side of the globe, from China where he's working on the firm's new course at Shanqin Bay. Coore joked with Cobb that the Coore & Crenshaw guys in China were saying Cobb had better have done a good job.

"Toby, they're saying that Coore & Crenshaw will never get another job if we botch Pinehurst No. 2," Coore said.

"You know, I wasn't nervous at all during the project," Cobb tells Coore. "But now, I've never been so nervous in my life."

Cobb mentions that Ben Crenshaw has checked in from the Champions Tour, that Coore & Crenshaw business manager Scotty Sayers has e-mailed. He's heard from a couple other Coore & Crenshaw field guys. Everyone wants to know: "Are you ready? Is the golf course ready?"

Cobb sighs. "Hopefully, people will like it."

SUITE LIFE AT THE CAROLINA

"Let me tell you about the very rich. They are different from you and me," wrote F. Scott Fitzgerald in opening a 1926 short story. To which Ernest Hemingway replied, "Yes, they have more money."

More money in the golf travel business can get you a grand piano in the Presidential Suite at the Inn at Spanish Bay, accompanied by breathtaking views of the Pacific Ocean and Del Monte Forest. It gets you an antique telescope and chaise lounge on a balcony overlooking the Atlantic atop the Sanctuary Hotel on Kiawah Island. More money gets you a bar stocked with Finlandia and Glenlivet 12-year-old single malt and a tub with Dead Sea bath salts at The Broadmoor in Colorado Springs. And more money—about $3,000 a night—fetches the upper crust a four-poster bed, silk-covered walls and panoramic views of Scottish meadows at the Gleneagles Hotel's Royal Lochnagar Suite.

Management at Pinehurst recognized in 2007 they had a world-famous golf course and more than a century of tradition ranging from the Ryder Cup to the U.S. Open, but their most opulent offering for CEOs and the very high brow was a suite overlooking the kitchen. So they gutted some prime real estate on the first floor of The Carolina—the back-left area where executive offices had been housed—and converted it to an 1,800 square foot Presidential Suite. The suite opened in the spring of 2008 with a starting rate of $1,200 per person, per night, and that rate had grown to $1,500 by early 2012.

It's a given that you have a comfortable bed (king-size Low Country style with high thread-count linens), lots of technology (four LG flat-screen TVs, one hidden behind a decorative mirror) and soothing décor (the color palette of wheat, russet and loden reflects a New England autumn, and artwork heavy in sepia and duotone images depicts the early days in Pinehurst). But the space is resplendent in the detail work and the little touches throughout the parlor, dining room, bedroom, study and private bath that elevate the experience. To wit:

* A pre-arrival checklist for specifying foam or feather pillows, preferred newspaper delivery, and the time and scent for drawing an evening bath.

* A digital door viewer, allowing occupants to preview their guests on what is essentially a tiny TV screen.

* An assortment of toys, from a chess set with rosewood soldiers and a maple board to a Wii gaming console to a laptop computer nestled in an antique writing desk.

* A shower that douses you not only from above but from the side as well with three bodyspray nozzles mounted at face, chest and waist height, each pulsing fifty-four tiny jets of water onto a body in need of rejuvenation after thirty-six holes of golf.

* A private area on the veranda overlooking the West Lawn with the requisite white rocking chairs, the perfect environment for a late-afternoon libation and scorecard post-mortem.

* Note paper inscribed with the guest's name.

* A sound system that connects to an iPod or that accesses a variety of musical genres—from XM Satellite Radio to a custom-designed channel featuring native Carolinas-based musicians.

* A late-afternoon snack prepared with exquisite detail—mango peeled and scored in a grid pattern, for example, then reversed with the flesh pointing out and arrayed with yogurt, cake, melon, pineapple, nuts and cottage cheese.

* Milk and cookies at bedtime, the beverage delivered in small bottles sealed with chocolate inlaid with the Putter Boy logo, and the cookies displayed on a slate tablet with dehydrated raspberry powder dredged over a stencil.

The Presidential Suite been used primarily by the CEOs of companies holding meetings at the resort and by long-time social guests who are offered the occasional gratis upgrade as a "thank you" for years of repeat business that has continued even in dour economic times. It's also been graced by foreign royalty, a Hall of Fame basketball coach, a governor and a Grammy Award winning singer.

"The suite certainly has the 'wow effect' we were looking for," says Carolina General Manager Scott Brewton. "There has not been anyone not blown away with the size, qual-

The parlor of the Presidential Suite in The Carolina features a mirror above the fireplace that converts into a high-definition TV and a chess set with rosewood soldiers.

ity and finish of the suite. For too long, Pinehurst could not offer a CEO a guest room equal to the best room in the last place he had visited. Now we can."

The Richmond architecture and design firm Glavé & Holmes coordinated the project and brought its experience in historical venues such as Charlottesville, Williamsburg and Old Salem in bridging the desire to link Pinehurst's history with modern comforts. Firm senior associate Gary Inman was intrigued early in the process by his research revealing that Pinehurst founder James W. Tufts and village planner Frederick Law Olmsted were proponents of Transcendentalism—a group of ideas germinating in New England in the 1800s that connect the spiritual being to nature itself and fosters the concept of the "healing landscape."

"Celebrating nature became the master theme for the suite," Inman says.

Architects from that era in the mid-1800s also were fond of weaving text into their buildings and room designs. Irwin found a quotation from the Greek philosopher Epictetus from nearly two millennia ago and displayed the passage in stenciling on the dining room wall: "Bear in mind that you should conduct yourself in life as at a feast."

Indeed, this little corner of Pinehurst nirvana takes the concept of feasting to rich new levels.

It is theory that nature must precede the architect… in the laying out of links. It is futile to attempt the transformation of wholly inadequate acres into an adequate course. Invariably the result is the inauguration of an earthquake. The site of a golf course should be there, not brought there.

PERRY MAXWELL

The view from the fourth tee as (left to right) Bob Dedman Jr., Jim Hyler, Mike Davis and Bill Coore set off down the fairway.

WATCHING ONE OF THE NATIONALLY KNOWN TOURNAMENTS ON NO. 2 COURSE. PINEHURST, N. C.

Golden Age Redux

There is nothing easy about hitting a golf ball hung up in tufts of wire grass, perched three inches above the ground. There is nothing simple about trying to advance a ball resting against a pine cone, pecking about for good contact while not incurring a penalty for moving the ball prematurely, nothing elementary about estimating the "give" under a ball resting in a sandy footprint. And anything less than a full wedge shot with your ball resting on hard-packed sand? Good luck, brother. This golf course reintroduced at Pinehurst on March 3, 2011, is more difficult in some regards, perhaps easier in others. But it has certainly been stripped of its monochrome canvas of green and requires more thought than before.

There are no straight lines on the No. 2 course that reopened in March 2011, as the view from the eighth tee attests.

"This is a whole lot more fun," says John Dempsey, president of Sandhills Community College just northeast of Pinehurst and a member the course rating panel of *GOLF* Magazine. "After all, having fun is what the game is all about. It's sort of like playing golf when you were a kid again. Every shot, you think you can pull off. Of course, you can't. But you *think* you can. It's wonderful."

Dempsey has been in Pinehurst since the late 1980s and has watched the ascension of No. 2, the resort and the community over two decades since the PGA Tour and USGA began visiting regularly with the 1989 U.S. Women's Amateur.

"This course is now a major draw," Dempsey says. "You can count those on one hand. This is a little bit of a different animal than any course around here. I am excited for the resort and the club and the community—and for golf."

There are plenty of interesting features awaiting golfers playing No. 2 on the first day of its reintroduction. First are the visual contrasts. The sandy roughs and bunkers yield a cacophony of creams, golds, browns and every hue in between. There is no long grass—*anywhere*—and the dormant Bermuda has been given a subtle tint of green dye, a concession to the early season visitors from the North. As the weather warms up later in March, the dye will wash out and the Bermuda will pop through.

Still visible down the middle of the fairways are the paths of the old center-line irrigation pipes, first laid by architect Donald Ross and superintendent Frank Maples in 1933. Those pipes have been removed in favor of a new

Pick your poison: Before on No. 2, errant balls had to be slashed out of thick rough. Now the golfer has to precisely clip his ball off sand that could be fluffy, firm or a multiple of variables in between, like this expanse to the left of the eighteenth fairway.

state-of-the-art irrigation system that utilizes main lines along the sides of fairways. Strips of sod have been laid where the ground was dug up, and they run in serpentine fashion this way and that, a road-map of sorts of how Ross envisioned the movement of the fairways. From this clue alone if from no other, Ross was saying there were no straight lines to be found on Pinehurst No. 2.

The fairways are wide—fifty-one yards across on the fifth fairway at one point, forty-seven on the eighth, and most are in the thirty-five yard range. But they neck down in some places where bunkers or mounds encroach from the perimeters—twenty-two yards on the first hole, nineteen on the third, twenty-three on eight, twenty-one on twelve, twenty-eight on thirteen. Again, no uniformity at all.

The greens are smooth and have knitted-in remarkably well given the snow and ice and cold of December and early January.

"God's grace," resort President and COO Don Padgett says humbly, thinking back to the travails of two months ago.

"What's neat to see is all the little subtleties are still in the greens," Director of Golf Chad Campbell says. "Like on fifteen, when you're putting across the green from the left side, that putt used to hold the line even though it looked like it wanted to move six inches to the right. But it doesn't, that's still there. Those little things are still there, those places where the ball goes opposite what you think it should do."

The first group off the tee the next morning, Friday the fourth, is made up of Toby Cobb, Kyle Franz, George Waters and Brian Caesar—four Coore & Crenshaw employees who labored around the clock the last two months to ensure the course was ready to reopen on schedule. After months of wielding heavy machinery, shovels and rakes, they now have a go with their golf clubs.

"It's just sweet," Waters says. "It's everything you hoped for. The greens are still the thing you remember the most. You miss so many greens and you think, 'I'd better not go long, I'd better not do this or that …' It just makes it hard to hit good shots with that stuff creeping into your head all the time. And it makes you respect the guys who play so well here, the guys who win championships here.

"There is just nothing like this with the greens and the roughs and the wire grass and now the bunkers. I can't think of anything similar in this country. That's a cool thing."

"I had the time of my life," Franz adds. "The corridors are so much better. It's amazing how well it works. I'm not a great player, a nine handicap, but at least I'm a pretty accurate driver. The width encourages you to hit to spots, to nudge it over to the grass line to get the best view of the pin. You have just enough rope to hang yourself. There are double bogeys waiting to happen if you play the angles and miss and you're stuck in the wire grass."

Behind them is a group that includes David Eger, who at fifty-eight years of age has one of the most complete competitive and administrative perspectives as anyone on the history of No. 2. Born in Maryland and raised in Charlotte, Eger played No. 2 as a teenager in the 1960s, as a collegian in the 1970s and later as a young member of the PGA Tour. He returned as an amateur, winning the North and South in 1991 and again in 2000. And he traveled to Pinehurst as a tournament official, setting up No. 2 for the 1991 Tour Championship as a member of the PGA Tour staff and the 1994 U.S. Senior Open as a USGA official. Eger has seen the course and played it Tufts-era, Diamondhead-era and Dedman-era; with Bermuda greens and bent greens; in April, August, October and December.

"Unfortunately, over the years as the grass grew in with rough and what not, the angles for approach shots significantly changed," Eger says. "You basically had to drive the ball where they wanted you to. The angles that the architect originally built into the holes were taken away."

Now, the honor of the course has been rescued.

"I think the work Ben and Bill did here is just fabulous," Eger says, standing beside eighteen green in the late afternoon sun. "They've restored it, renovated it back to a place it was long ago. Unless you're seventy or eighty years old, you've never seen Pinehurst like this with the roughs down both sides of the fairways. You can see how Donald Ross designed it, how it played in the old days. It's a whole different concept but one people will latch onto quickly. If you miss a fairway,

you're not gouging it out of thick rough. You're hitting off of sand, and for many people, that's not an easy shot.

"The distinction between grass and the sand is wonderful. It's the way golf courses from the golden age looked. Pinehurst had that distinctive look of the scrub rough areas and wire grass. Putting it back took a lot of courage, but ultimately it was the right thing to do."

***

By mid-May of 2011, the course has been open to the world for ten weeks. Some still cannot fathom why anyone would remove grass from a golf course. Some are so attuned to the luxuriant and ornate presentation of modern courses that the bumpy and stark appearance outside the fairways is quite the shock. And to some golfers, as unpleasant as thick rough can be, the ability to get their club *under* the ball makes the rough preferable to the exacting challenge of picking a ball cleanly off a tight lie—no matter that they can only pound it out twenty yards from the grassy thickets.

Yet the majority of golfers embrace the new iteration of Pinehurst No. 2.

Pinehurst marketing director Tom Pashley spoke with a handful of resort players in March and collected some opinion snippets for a video posted on YouTube.

"The course is wonderful," says Max Shaull. "Look at it. It's rugged, it's natural, it's beautiful."

"I've played the golf course the way it was before, and you walk to the first tee and you have that same feeling, no matter how many times you play it," says Glenn Davis. "I teed off on No. 2 today, and I felt it again."

"I like how there are no straight lines, it's really rustic, kind of old school," says Brent Gasper.

"You feel like you're walking on hallowed ground around here, in a time machine almost," adds David Gasper. "It's very pure."

Some seventy-five golf writers and assorted other media representatives visited for a press outing the Monday after the Masters or on their own at other times during the spring. *Golfweek's* architecture specialist Brad Klein toured the course and saluted the result in an early April missive:

"Donald Ross' most famous design from a century ago has been utterly transformed through a restoration by Bill Coore and Ben Crenshaw that is as radical and path-breaking as any in the history of golf-course architecture," Klein wrote. "The result is stunning. Pinehurst No. 2 is strategically more compelling than ever—and a whole lot more fun, too. Golf here used to be about the greens and surrounds. Now it's about every shot."

Two golfers who played the course shortly after its reopening knew it from the last decade of the Tufts era in the 1960s and, as rating panelists with the two major golf publications in the country, had a broad scope of architectural knowledge to form their opinions.

Bill Phipps of Akron, Ohio, attended golf camp at Pinehurst as a sixteen-year-old in 1966. The kids stayed in The Holly Inn as The Carolina was closed, and Phipps remembers a fire breaking out in the Village and resort owner Richard Tufts responding as a member of the Volunteer Fire Department to help douse the flames. Years later, Phipps was the marker for the Payne Stewart/Phil Mickelson twosome in the final round of the 1999 U.S. Open. He is green committee chairman at three clubs and a course rater for *Golf Digest* magazine, thus his bona fides are sound for putting Pinehurst and the new No. 2 in proper context.

"It was beyond my expectations," Phipps says. "It's pure golf. It's an easy walk. There is plenty of room to play, and it was firm and fast. But you have problems if you hit it off-line or are trying to hit those greens from the wrong side. I never get tired of those greens. I even liked seeing a few brown spots in the fairways. That's fine. It's like links golf in Ireland and Scotland. I wish we didn't use so much water here in the States. Just because grass is brown, doesn't mean it's dead.

"This project will reconnect Pinehurst with its traditions and its past," he continues. "That's important. In this era of target golf and souped-up equipment and a generation raised on Tiger Woods, I'm not sure today's generation *gets* Pinehurst. They get Phoenix and Pebble Beach. I don't know that they get Pinehurst."

Bob McCoy of Springfield, N.J., is a rating panelist for *GOLF* Magazine and gained a measure of acclaim in the spring and summer of 1997 when he played the magazine's top one hundred courses in the world in as many days. That trip brought him to Pinehurst just after No. 2 had reopened following greens, tees and bunker rebuilding in advance of the 1999 U.S. Open. McCoy figures he's played No. 2 a couple dozen times over four decades. He saw photos of Coore & Crenshaw's work before visiting in mid-April and thought the course bore some resemblance to Pine Valley, where he's a member.

"Then I got there and was absolutely thrilled," McCoys says. "I've always liked No. 2, but I thought you had to be somewhat of a golf aficionado, an architectural aficionado, to appreciate what you were looking at and what you were playing. Some of my friends would visit Pinehurst and say, 'I think No. 8 is better.' I would say, 'What are you talking about?' No. 2 can be an acquired taste. When I played in '97, it was really getting green and bland. It looked and played conventionally. I could understand why people would not be taken with it."

McCoy likes the rugged look of the course and how it echoes the appearance and feel of a seaside links course—minus the ocean. He boosted the course in his personal ballot for *GOLF's* 2011 edition of "Top 100 Courses in the World." But with the voting closing in early June and results announced in September, he doubts enough panelists will have seen the restored course to noticeably impact its standing (the course was ranked No. 19 in the 2009 list and moved up to No. 15 in 2011).

"It was a bold decision and a home run," McCoy says. "One thing I really like is that it has reintroduced the concept of luck. Once you're off the short stuff, you're into a game of luck. And that's good. Luck is part of golf, though you wouldn't know it listening to today's pros. They want to dial in the yardage from a perfect lie. But at Pinehurst now, you can roll up on the side of a mound and have an awkward shot, you can get into the wire grass and not have a chance. It's like playing links golf. Luck is supposed to be part of the equation."

All of these visits are a prelude to the most important event of the spring—the convening of the President's Council for the 2014 U.S. Open and the return of Bill Coore and the USGA's Mike Davis and Jim Hyler on May 15-16. The President's Council is a group of North Carolina business executives organized by Pinehurst officials prior to the 1999 and 2005 Opens to help build corporate awareness and support for the event throughout business circles statewide. Hyler was president of the group in 1999 while leading First Citizens Bank. The council assembled for 2014 includes Johnny Harris of Charlotte and

Bobby Long of Greensboro, two leaders in establishing PGA Tour events in their respective cities, as well as scions from banking, utilities, department stores and other pockets of the statewide economy.

Scheduled are a reception and dinner at The Carolina on Monday night and a round of golf on No. 2 Tuesday morning, with the featured foursome of Pinehurst owner Bob Dedman, Coore, Davis and Hyler. They are scheduled to meet at the Pinehurst clubhouse Monday afternoon for a photo session, Tom Pashley orchestrating the idea to replicate some vintage photos of former owners Leonard and Richard Tufts and architect Donald Ross.

Hyler is the first to arrive and stands beside the eighteenth green of No. 2. The president of the USGA will soon be off to Washington to help administer the 2011 Open at Congressional Country Club, but for the moment his focus is on the 2014 venue.

"I had fairly high expectations, and they exceeded those," Hyler says. "A few fairways are really generous, so we might narrow them a little by cutting grass out and extending the sand. We're not going to grow any rough. I think the players will like it, and I think you'll see some good scoring."

Beyond the issue of the U.S. Open, Hyler likes how the No. 2 restoration fits into the big-picture scheme of golf in the 2010s. Money will be tight for the foreseeable future and water will be precious, all the more reason to cultivate golf grounds with reasonable maintenance demands.

A game of luck: How your ball snuggles up to the thousands of wire grass plants throughout the course is an important quotient to playing Pinehurst No. 2.

"The sustainability statement is off the charts," Hyler says. "To say we reduced water usage by fifty percent, that's quite a statement. To let the rough areas go dormant and distressed, to take out forty acres of turf and go to a single-row irrigation system—that's quite a statement. What's happening here is the future of golf."

Hyler's gaze moves to the statues to the side of the green, to the likenesses of Robert Dedman Sr., Richard Tufts and Donald Ross—each a leader and visionary in his own right. Hyler considers the Blackberry held in his hand, the device he uses to reach literally anyone in the world he desires in a matter of seconds, and compares it to the communications tools available in the mid-1950s, when Tufts was USGA president. Tufts spoke into a dictation machine that he hated and wrote letters by longhand that his secretary transcribed. Long distance phone calls were expensive and cumbersome.

"I was thinking about Mister Tufts this morning and his two years as president of the USGA, the things he got done and the communications challenges they had," Hyler says. "Think of the areas he's touched: the Green Section, course set-up, handicapping, the Rules of Golf. His fingerprints are all over everything we do. What he accomplished in a short period of time is nothing short of amazing."

Hyler's attention moves to Dedman, who bought the resort and club out of distress from the banks in 1984.

"And where would this place be if not for Robert Dedman?" Hyler wonders. "He might have been the one man in golf at the time who could pull it off. He literally saved the place."

Later that evening at dinner, Coore gives the group an overview of the restoration project and tells of the forty acres of Bermuda grass stripped from the course and the 650 irrigation heads removed.

"The photos and the old mainline irrigation pipes took the guess work out," Coore says. "We could base what we did on fact, not on supposition or opinion. We were tip-toeing around and a little reluctant at first. We got bolder once we had those pieces of the puzzle. We had evidence."

CUTTING EDGE ACADEMY

What goes around does indeed come around. Pinehurst officials in 2010 gave the raspberry to the modern look on their esteemed No. 2 course, taking it back half a century to its roots of short grass, wide corridors and disheveled perimeters.

Meanwhile in the Pinehurst Golf Academy, instructors are spending more time teaching the game in the manner of early 1900s golf pros—the on-course playing lesson.

"Our students have asked for and we've responded by spending more time teaching on the golf course," says Eric Alpenfels, head of the Pinehurst Golf Academy and one of *GOLF* Magazine's Top 100 Teachers in America.

"Across the board, top teachers are saying we need to do more on-course instruction," Alpenfels says. "We kind of got sidetracked with this 'perfect swing' idea. People were not performing better on the golf course. What good is it to hit it flush on the range if you go to the first tee and top it?"

Early 1900s architects like Donald Ross and Alister MacKenzie never considered setting ground aside for practice in laying a course out because the instruction mode of the day was to take a beginning golfer out on the course. As the game became more popular and courses became busier, instructors looked for nearby parcels of open ground for beginners to hit multiple shots unimpeded by other golfers.

Ross built the first dedicated practice facility in the United States at Pinehurst in 1913 when he rerouted the No. 1 course and carved out the huge open space that remains today. Since then, Pinehurst has been at the epicenter of golf instruction and research.

Lionel Callaway, creator of the Callaway Handicapping System, was a mid-1900s pro at Pinehurst. The early 1980s teaching staff included Hank Haney, Jack Lumpkin, Mike LaBauve and Mike Abbott—all instructors to PGA Tour players. Haney met Mark O'Meara at Pinehurst in 1983 and began a long and productive teacher-pupil relationship. Haney returned to Pinehurst for the 2005 U.S. Open as Tigers Woods' instructor, a union that lasted from 2004-10.

"I owe a lot to this place," Haney said that week. "The three years I spent in Pinehurst were probably the most instrumental of my career. This is where it all started."

In recent years Alpenfels and a veteran staff that includes Paul McRae, Kelly Mitchum and Geoff Lynch have operated the resort's golf schools successfully and profitably in the face of a major economic downturn in 2008-09 and overall softening of golf school participation nationwide. One of the niches of the Pinehurst Golf Academy has been its interest in research and compiling test results on what drills and methods work best in golf instruction. Much of those results have been published in *GOLF* Magazine and other publications and prepared in tandem with the PGA of America.

"Pinehurst should be leading the way in finding new ways and better ways to teach the game," Alpenfels says. "We've been a leader for more than a century in every element of the game."

Research in 2011 confirmed the growing sense that golfers benefit from focusing on external cues in learning the swing versus internal cues. Alpenfels cites the example of a golfer's swing fault of an out-to-in swing path (or "coming over the top") and how an idea *external* to their minds and bodies can produce a better fix than one found *within* their minds.

"We have seen significantly better results placing two clubs on the ground, one along the target line and one pointed to the right of the target," he says. "We have the golfer envision swinging to the right along the line of the second club.

"That works better than an 'internal cue,' which in this case would be telling the golfer, 'Keep your right elbow close to the body on the downside as your right shoulder drops.'"

Other research projects have determined, for example, that a golfer can benefit from practicing lag putting by looking at the hole while making the stroke instead of at the ball; that the best drill for curing a slice is one called the "toe-in" drill; and that a full turn in the backswing can best be learned with a

Eric Alpenfels surveys the firing line at the Pinehurst Golf Academy; getting golfers to take good shots in this practice environment to the first tee of the golf course is priority No. 1 for one of the nation's leading golf schools.

golfer practicing in bright sunlight and using his shadow on the ground to improve the depth of his shoulder turn.

The results of such research benefit not only golfers and instructors in general but, more specifically, students attending the various Golf Academy sessions throughout the year. Sessions are held from March through October from Sunday to Thursday and Thursday to Sunday in the Golf Academy headquarters at the east end of the Maniac Hill practice range. The state-of-the-art facility was built in 2005-06 and designed to allow practice of a myriad of situational shots like one encounters on the golf course.

"Taking the game from the practice tee to the course is a focal point today," Alpenfels says. "We're teaching golfers to mimic what they find on the course on the practice tee. Don't hit fifty six-irons in a row. Hit a driver to a specific point, then hit a six-iron approach, then maybe hit a fifteen-yard pitch shot. Do your pre-shot routine each shot.

"Golf is performance based. What did you shoot? We're trying to take you from the lesson tee to lower scores on the golf course. That's the important thing."

Davis then addresses the group and first recognizes Dedman Jr. and the relationship the USGA enjoyed with first Dedman Sr., who died in 2002, and now his son.

"The Dedmans are the 'anti-Wall Street,'" Davis says. "They don't think about the next quarter. They think long-term. You cannot put a value on that. We simply don't have another relationship like the one we have with Pinehurst. They genuinely care about the game of golf, preserving and protecting the game."

Davis compliments Coore for the work he and partner Ben Crenshaw did in reclaiming No. 2's mid-20th century personality and notes the risk that Dedman, Coore, Crenshaw and the USGA itself were taking in pulling the trigger.

"This was a scary proposition for the owners, for the (USGA) president, certainly for the architects," Davis says. "You have a Mona Lisa here, and you're going to fiddle with it. A lot of things could go badly."

Davis tells of getting to know the late P.J. Boatwright, the executive director of rules and competitions for the USGA, in 1990 when Davis joined the staff. Davis knew of Boatwright's history in Pinehurst—Boatwright lived in the village for four years in the 1950s while running the Carolinas Golf Association—and his familiarity with No. 2.

"I knew a little something about No. 2," Davis says. "I had been here as an amateur, I had played in the North and South Amateur. P.J. and I had dinner one night and we talked about courses that had not had a U.S. Open but could or should. No. 2 came up and I said, 'Why not?'

"Well, P.J., in that deep southern drawl of his, said, 'You can't get the conditions right.'"

Boatwright meant that he was not particularly happy with the state of the course's greens, which had been rebuilt in 1987 and planted with bentgrass. The quality of sod used at the time was suspect and Boatwright didn't believe the greens could play with the quickness and tautness the USGA demands of its U.S. Open greens.

"Well, he was correct—*at that time*," Davis says. "Fast forward a few years and now you have the hybrid bents that don't use as much water. You *can* get them firmer and faster in hot weather. You know what? Now we can have a U.S. Open here."

The next morning, Coore arrives on the first tee with more than a little angst that the neglected state of his golf game might be a distraction and even a little embarrassing in the midst of three others who play the game on a more regular basis. He's hardly touched a club since the official opening of his course in Tasmania in early December. But Coore makes a nice par on the second hole after his drive lands high in a wire grass plant next to a left-side bunker, requiring an almost "baseball swing" back to safety. The convivial atmosphere of the group—"This is like your regular foursome at the club," Coore says—and the fact there's no punishing rough anywhere helps Coore settle into a nice comfort level.

"If we were playing the 2005 Open set-up, this would be a miserable round of golf—at least for me," Coore says. "But you don't have a feeling of hopelessness. If you hit it off-line, you have a chance. Off the fairway, it's an adventure. But you can find your ball and, in most cases, get the club on it. Three-inch rough? No way."

Davis parses the new course first with a wide lens. What he hoped for two years ago when he met with Dedman and Don Padgett at Bethpage has turned out better than he'd imagined.

"Standing on the tee, visually it's night and day," Davis says. "You really understand what you're supposed to do, and that will become even more pronounced as the roughs mature. And then when you miss a fairway, the kind of shots you have are so interesting. There are just a multitude of things out there. It's wonderful."

He likens the scope of the project to what Oakmont did in the decade leading up to the 2007 Open—it took out more than 3,500 trees that robbed the course of its early 1900s links persona and competed with the turf for sunlight and nutrients.

"When Oakmont cut down all those trees, it was a huge change for the better and had an impact around the country and the world," Davis says. "The message: Don't over-tree a golf course. What has happened here is such an incredible statement for the game of golf: Take it back to a more natural state, work with the land, use half the water. It's a great thing for golf and the environment. And oh, by the way, it makes the golf course so much more visually stimulating and brings so many more shots into the game. Now you have to look down and see what kind of options you have left."

With each step around the course and each shot, Davis is also

A television crew sets up to get Ben Crenshaw on camera during a media appearance at Pinehurst in April 2011.

dissecting the course for its presentation three years hence—the 2014 U.S. Open. He visited three times in 2010 to walk the course with Coore and suggest fairway widths in the professionals' landing zones, but there remain some areas that are too friendly for the top drawer player. Case in point—the left of seven on the opposite side from the ornery cluster of new bunkers.

"They've created some wonderful architectural features on the right," Davis says. "But we need to narrow it on the left. It's so wide, those features on the right will never come into play, never. There's too much room down the left."

Davis marvels at the novel idea of playing a U.S. Open with no rough, but he's committed to the new presentation of two cuts of grass—one for greens, a second for everything else. That's why the maintenance of the sandy roughs will be an integral element to the 2014 set-up.

"It will be a work in progress with the grounds staff," Davis says. "We don't want perfect conditions in the hardpan areas. Loose sand with footprints is fine. Pine needles and pine cones are fine. Leave them there. Will it be easier? Maybe. But it will be a much more interesting golf course in 2014. It will really allow the players to showcase their shotmaking skills."

As he tours the course, Coore is perhaps most pleased that he and Crenshaw, prodded by Padgett and emboldened with each successful step of the process, grew comfortable enough to remove huge swaths of grass and rebuild dramatic bunkers. The four-hole stretch of six through nine, in particular, serves up a cacophony of dramatic edges, humps and scratchy surfaces in another time zone from the look from five years ago.

"There was a danger the result would be 'neither-nor'—no longer a parkland course but one still not restored to what it looked like sixty years ago," Coore says. "I admit, we were careful, a little gun shy, in the early stages."

Coore remembers watching a historical video about the course and resort in his hotel room one night and being struck by a reference to the "restoration of the sandy roughs" prior to the 1999 U.S. Open. That would have been part of the 1996 project that included total rebuilding of the greens complexes and the reconstruction of all the bunkers. At the time, the sandy roughs were prevalent only to the right of three, eight, eleven and twelve.

"'Middle ground' was not what we wanted," Coore says. "I think that's what they had prior to '99. And then nearly all the roughs were gone by '05 after they'd installed all the sprinkler heads."

Coore, Crenshaw and design associate Toby Cobb began the project working on holes eleven and twelve in February 2010, then continued on thirteen and fourteen by completely stripping every blade of grass between the parallel fairways. That rugged look helped set the template for the rest of the project.

"The good news," Coore says after the round, "is there is absolutely nothing major wrong with this golf course. We'll make some minor refinements to accommodate the world's greatest players in our National Open. But for day-to-day play, I couldn't be happier. It's turned out better than anyone could have imagined."

***

Pebble Beach has its dramatic seaside setting; Augusta National has its nursery and historical echoes and back-nine casino; Pine Valley confounds golfers with acres of sand, brush, bramble and pines; Merion and Winged Foot and Shinnecock glow in their Old World Eastern patina.

And Pinehurst No. 2 has its greens and its short grass. The former have been part and parcel of its character since Donald Ross converted the sand-clay greens to grass in 1935. The latter has only made a recent return after four decades of grassy creep.

"They are simply the best greens complexes any architect has ever built, transforming an elegant but unremarkable property into a supremely interesting test of golf," architect Tom Doak wrote in the 2005 U.S. Open Championship magazine. "The undulations around every green are different, and you have to be intimate with them to understand how (or how not) to attack various hole locations."

The story of the greens on No. 2 begins in the early 1930s when Donald Ross felt a special motivation to take his existing course—one with sand-clay greens and one that did not yet include the current fourth and fifth holes—and retool it into a venue that would further clamp down its status as one of the nation's finest tests.

Though golf champion Bobby Jones of Atlanta did not participate regularly in the North and South Open or Amateur, he termed Ross "an old and very highly esteemed friend of mine" and visited Pinehurst at various times throughout the 1920s and early 1930s. Jones admired Ross's work at Augusta Country Club and Forest Hills Golf Club in Augusta and told Ross of his vision to build a golf course in or near Atlanta upon his retirement from competitive golf. According to journalist and historian Charles Price, Ross believed he had a deal to design the course at whatever time Jones located at a site and established a business plan; that, of course, would turn out to be a club in Augusta, 145 miles to the east of Atlanta.

Jones's mind changed, though, in 1929 when he traveled to California's Monterey Peninsula for the U.S. Amateur at Pebble Beach. Jones inexplicably lost in the first round to nineteen-year-old Johnny Goodman and was left with a week of free time until his return back to the East. Jones visited a newly christened course nearby named Cypress Point and was introduced to the architect, Dr. Alister MacKenzie, a British physician who left the practice of medicine to design golf courses. Jones and MacKenzie spent considerable time together that week playing Cypress Point and talking golf architecture.

"Ross was a notorious individualist," Price explained in *A Golf Story*, his 1986 book about Jones and the Masters Tournament, "and Jones wanted a course with *his* designs incorporated into it, not a course entirely of somebody else's. Now, here he was three thousand miles from home, with nothing but time on his hands, and in the company of one of the world's most highly regarded architects. MacKenize and Jones talked, and they talked a lot. The more they talked, the more impressed Jones became with MacKenzie's theories. While neither was aware of it, the Augusta National Golf Club—and, hence, the Masters Tournament—was being born."

In another piece in *GOLF* magazine, Price expanded on the affront Ross took to the Jones-MacKenzie partnership.

"Ross was a proud, reserved, standoffish man, almost egotistically so," Price said. "He was miffed. He considered himself … to be America's foremost architect."

This motivation to not allow a neophyte Augusta National (the club opened in early 1934) to steal Pinehurst's thunder worked in tandem with two more variables to make the mid-1930s the ideal time to initiate significant changes to No. 2. One, the Great Depression had crippled the golf design and construction businesses, so Ross had few other commitments. And two, agronomic advances presented Ross with viable options for planting the greens in a grass that would survive the winter "high season." Ross and superintendent Frank Maples maintained a nursery in which they experimented with various grass strains and maintenance practices, and by the summer of 1934, Ross had cultivated a strain of Bermuda grass that he believed was hearty enough. He built three trial greens on No. 2 for the 1934-35 season. They were well-received and held up during the resort's heavy play from November through March, so he abandoned all the original greens for the new grass greens for the fall of 1935.

Just as Old Tom Morris, one of Ross's mentors from his formative days in Scotland, made frequent use of the plateau green complex, so too did Ross in his design work at Pinehurst. He scooped out greenside bunkers and dredged the pocks and swales around what would be the putting surfaces, using the displaced sand to build up the green. His experience as a greenkeeper provided him with an awareness of drainage issues, and the crowned greens that sloped off around the sides discarded water quickly. Once the water coursed into the hollows a few feet away, the sandy loam allowed their quick drainage. The result was an excellent venue for creating a fascinating short-game test.

> ## "Only in a sandy soil will the drainage problem permit construction of the rolling contours and hollows natural to the Scottish seaside courses where golf was born."
>
> DONALD ROSS

"Only in a sandy soil will the drainage problem permit construction of the rolling contours and hollows natural to the Scotch seaside courses where golf was born," Ross said prior to the 1936 PGA Championship on No. 2. "This contouring around a green makes possible an infinite variety in the requirements for short shots that no other form of hazard can call for. I am sure that as you watch play, you will be interested to see how many times competitors whose second shots have wandered a bit will be disturbed by these innocent appearing slopes."

Peter Tufts, great-grandson of the Pinehurst founder, and Ellis Maples, son of the superintendent, both remembered as children watching Ross build greens. The Scotsman would begin by standing in the center of the area designated for the green surface.

"A mule, guided by a laborer, would walk around the circumference, pulling a drag pan," Tufts said. "Ross would watch them walk, and he might say, 'Okay, now cut and scoop, now drop.' Sometimes he worked from plans in his hand, sometimes not. After the drag pan, he'd shape with rakes, hoes and shovels. And he took his time. Architecture was in the details, he thought. It came naturally to him."

Maples, who became a golf professional and then an architect himself, explained why there exists no printed documentation of the greens on No. 2.

"They didn't have a single blueprint," Maples said. "They did it all from their head."

The post-1936 identity for Pinehurst No. 2 had been established: wide fairways cut through the native sandy roughs and greens in many instances elevated and surrounded by undulating chipping areas.

"The greens were small and convex," remembers Bill Campbell, a regular in the North and South Amateur from the 1940s onward, "in many cases so that the ball tended to bounce and run off the greens. So the problem was how to get up and down if you missed a

The infamous tiny target greens of No. 2 are represented on the par-three fifteenth, shown at left in 2003 and at right in 2011. The right side of the green was extended, and all the bunkers were rebuilt in 2010-11.

green. The greens were not meant to be pitched to in all cases. The old Pinehurst way was to play a run-up shot because you couldn't stop it otherwise."

Herbert Warren Wind, the renowned author and historian, was good friends with Richard Tufts and a regular visitor to Pinehurst.

"The hallmark of a Ross course is a sparingly bunkered green perched on the crown of a slope, but the qualities that made his courses so popular were the variety of the holes, the exceptional number of interesting shots they set up for the fairly good and the accomplished player, the leeway they gave the average player, and their extraordinary pleasing aspect," Wind wrote in *The New Yorker* in his account of the 1962 U.S. Amateur held at Pinehurst.

David Eger grew up in Charlotte and played junior golf competitively. His early exposure to No. 2 was in the mid to late 1960s, when he visited Pinehurst for the Donald Ross Junior as well as other state

and regional competitions.

"I remember as a kid thinking I'd never seen anything like it and probably haven't seen much like it since," says Eger. "It was built on this pure sand base, and the greens were the identity of the course. The greens all sat up and had plateaus where you had to invent shots around the greens. It was very challenging if you missed the greens."

The greens Campbell, Wind and Eger remembered from the Tufts era were the original Bermuda base, overseeded in the winter with rye. As agronomists improved the ability of smoother bent surfaces to withstand southern summer heat, Pinehurst converted its greens in 1996 to Penn G2. The slick putting surfaces combined with closely cropped slopes and hollows around the greens vexed the world's finest golfers in the 1999 and 2005 U.S. Opens. Brad Kocher, Pinehurst's head of course and grounds maintenance from 1984 until his retirement in 2008, said the greens "might be the smallest targets in golf."

The greens are modest in size to begin with, averaging five thousand square feet each. Kocher estimated that if the greens were putting at 11 to 11.5 on the Stimpmeter as they do for an Open, the effective area to hit and hold on the greens is in the 1,500-square-foot range.

"The pros are frustrated by the really, really, *really* small targets," Kocher said prior to the 2005 Open. "They don't see targets like this anywhere else. When they miss, they're faced with the lowest-percentage shot they face anywhere. A pro would rather miss the green in a bunker than hit one of the little recovery shots they have from the dips around the greens."

The greens were a challenge both years unlike anything Open competitors were accustomed to.

"What's amazing is that from off the green, you have one shot if the ball comes to rest at any given point," Ben Crenshaw said in 1999. "If it moves just three feet you've got a totally different shot. The ground is continually moving. As a result you never have the same shot twice. That's why it stays so fresh.

"There's nothing like it. There's nothing like it at all."

A dozen years later, Crenshaw surveys the gently pitched ground surrounding one of No. 2's greens. His opinion hasn't changed.

"This golf course has the most fascinating set of decisions you'll ever see," he says. "You can always put the club on the ball. The question is, where do you land it and where does it bounce and where does it roll? You get confused. You have three or four different options, it plants that indecision in your mind. It's hard to commit to a shot."

Tiger Woods missed the first and second greens of the final round in 2005. *With putts.*

Retief Goosen's shot to the second green rolled off the far side. *On a chip shot.*

Vijay Singh hit—and *held*, an important word on No. 2—the

green of the long and difficult par-four eighth hole with his second shot. *And his third rolled off the back of the green.*

"There should be a special stat for golf at Pinehurst No. 2—'GV' for 'greens visited,'" quipped David Fay, executive director of the USGA.

"It's not the hardest course I've ever played, but it may be the hardest to get the ball close to the hole on the green," Tom Watson said.

Payne Stewart reflected on having to hit a two-iron on the fifth hole in 1999. "You look at the size of the green, and then you look at the *real* size of the green, and they're two different things," he said. "You've got a rectangle that's maybe twelve by twenty-five feet, and it's the only place you can keep the ball on the green."

"It's the most draining course I've played in a long time," Lee Westwood added.

"People sometimes ask what's the hardest course I've ever played," said two-time Open champion Lee Janzen. "Now I know."

Those greens combined with the chipping areas, the flow of the holes and the strategic nuances are what led Tom Weiskopf to venture in a 1995 conversation that Pinehurst No. 2 is a better year-round test than Augusta National.

"Augusta National is good one week a year," Weiskopf said. "Augusta does not compare to this golf course. Augusta is only such one week a year. Augusta only shows its teeth and demands when the greens are so fast and with those unbelievably difficult pin positions.

"I've played Augusta two or three weeks before [the Masters] and it's a piece of cake—*a piece of cake.* Pinehurst No. 2 is never a piece of cake."

The template for U.S. Open set-ups since the 1950s called for long, stringy rough to border fairways and greens. A seven-iron approach that missed a green five feet to the right at Olympic Club in the 1998 Open required one shot and one shot alone—a lob wedge hit hard enough to dislodge the ball from its lie. Pinehurst presented the golfers with choices as they contemplated recovery shots. The

putter was the predominant choice in 1999; the USGA allowed for a slightly longer cut of grass in 2005, enabling players to more easily get a wedge under the ball and broaden the universe of pitches and chips.

"You have so many options that you can actually get confused," Woods said in 1999. One of his options was a putter with four degrees of loft and a three-wood with fifteen degrees. In the opening round, Woods used a three-wood for chipping and successfully managed one up-and-down; on the weekend a similar try rolled over the green and resulted in a double bogey.

"When you have to hit a putt that hard and try to judge the pace, you take it back further than you normally do and you're not used to the motion," Woods said. "You don't get a chance to do that very often, unless you play on links courses in Europe. But a three-wood motion, you can hit it easier and it gets up the hill easier.

"Every hole here, over the green is not good. If you hit the ball in the rough, play short. If it comes out hot, great. If not, I'm chipping straight up the hill or putting or bumping-and-running or whatever it is."

Some observers looked at the greens and said they were too domed on their horizons, that they were not the greens left by Ross upon his death in April 1948. Golf architect Pete Dye, who played No. 2 frequently during World War II while stationed at Fort Bragg in nearby Fayetteville, says the application of top-dressing over the years raised the surfaces beyond their profiles from the mid-20th century.

Certainly the vision of the plateau green is accurate. They are evident in many of the greens at Dornoch, where Ross grew up, and some at St. Andrews, where he worked for a year under Old Tom Morris. Morris tweaked the design of the Old Course and was wholly responsible for the New Course, and plateau greens are key parts of those designs. Ross spoke of the importance of the chipping areas around the greens, and the sand he excavated to create them had to go *somewhere*. Trucking it off was not as simple in 1935 as it is today.

"I think everyone realizes some of the crowning of these greens

The turtleback greens and hollows around them are reflected well in this elevated view of the first green.

PINEHURST'S PIED PIPER

T op executives throughout Club Corporation of America knew company founder Robert Dedman to be a cool, level-headed and strong-minded leader and negotiator atop the far-flung company that owned and operated country clubs across the United States.

But in 1984 as Dedman considered the addition of the distressed Pinehurst resort to his portfolio, one of them noticed a difference.

"Robert took himself out of the front line of the negotiations because it was the only thing we ever looked at buying that he knew he was emotionally involved with," says Don Padgett II, at the time general manager of another CCA property, Firestone in Akron, Ohio, and today the chief operating officer at Pinehurst. "He was emotionally involved in it, and he knew if he was the guy out front, he'd pay too much. I saw that and said, 'Wow, this is a different deal.'"

Robert Dedman poses beside The Putter Boy statue during his 1984-2002 stewardship of Pinehurst.

For eighteen years, from his purchase of the resort in 1984 to his death in August 2002, Dedman was a frequent visitor to Pinehurst from his home in Dallas as his company grew into ClubCorp International, which at the time of his death owned and operated more than two hundred country, city and athletic clubs and resorts worldwide.

"Robert was very dynamic, he was a leader, a pied piper," says Beth Kocher, a club executive for Dedman at Inverrary Country Club in Florida and later at Pinehurst. "He had a way of making people really go above and beyond to deliver for him. He made them achieve far more than they believed they could. He was extremely inspirational in his speeches. I never left the room after one of his speeches not feeling re-energized."

Dedman enjoyed a lifelong passion for poetry, and verses from masters such as Emerson, Kipling, Longfellow and Browning provided guidance, structure and inspiration throughout his life. "Poetry became the umbilical cord for my positive mental attitude and nurtured my heartfelt inspiration to do good for others," Dedman said in his 1999 autobiography, *King of Clubs*.

Dedman often quoted a favorite stanza from Elizabeth Barrett Browning and told associates, "That's what separated me from picking cotton the rest of my life and doing what I've done." From Kipling's poem *If*, Dedman found inspiration for managing his time and guarding against waste and the "unforgiving minute" mentioned in the verse. He worked out the math and noted there were 168 hours in a week. "I figured, if I set aside fifty-six to sleep, I still have 112 waking hours. If I invested eighty hours in gainful endeavors, I would still have thirty-two hours left to do with whatever my heart desires," Dedman said.

Dedman led and taught with poetry and also with stories, jokes and witticisms. He always had a saying appropriate for an occasion or point-of-emphasis.

"We're in the repeat business."

"We're in the business of selling fun."

"Members vote with their feet."

"There are two rules of membership. No. 1, the member is always right. No. 2, if you think the member is wrong, refer to No. 1."

"This hotel is just a country club with rooms."

"A deal is only good if it's a win-win."

"The less I do, the better we are."

"Everyone is either a goal-scorer or a goal-keeper. Decide which one you are."

"They don't put luggage racks on hearses." (Dedman was noted for his philanthropy, having donated more than $100 million over the years to higher education, much of it to Southern Methodist University in Dallas).

"Trash begets more trash." (Pieces of trash were like magnets—Dedman would find them and gather them up. His golf cart after eighteen holes invariably was full of drink cans and empty cigarette packs.)

Dedman loved the game of golf. "He was passionate about it," says his son, Bob Jr. "He'd have played every day if he could."

Dedman was a five-handicap golfer when he started ClubCorp in the 1950s and also made time to play several sets of tennis a week. "It's still impossible for me to pick the sport I like the best," he said. He liked the physical exertion of tennis, the release of tension through the pounding of the ball and competitive nature of playing an opponent one-on-one. Golf was more of a mental challenge and a total immersion in nature—the grass, the trees, the birds, the landscape.

"Golf is truly a metaphor for life," Dedman said. "The game involves keeping score, hoping to win, and learning to lose. In any given round, you get some good shots and bad ones."

When Dedman learned in the early 1980s that Pinehurst was for sale, he was naturally interested, though getting into the resort business strayed somewhat from the confines of the country club business.

"Robert loved golf, but I don't think that he or any of us realized when we first bought Pinehurst its true historical significance to golf in the United States," says Jim Hinckley, a top CCA executive at the time. "Over the years, Robert would run into people like Pete and Alice Dye, or Jack Nicklaus or Arnold Palmer, who would tell him about their experiences at Pinehurst. Everyone loved Pinehurst.

"It was one of the few situations we took over where *everyone* wanted to see it succeed."

has come from years of top-dressing," Don Padgett said in June 2010. "Are the greens sitting up higher than where they were years ago? Yes. Does anyone know exactly when and how they got there? No, not really. But regardless of how they got that way, at the end of the day, they are an incredible set of greens and unlike anything in this country."

On that point, there is no argument.

"It was nobody's grand plan," *Golf Digest's* Ron Whitten wrote in 2005. "They just slowly mushroomed, a quarter of an inch at a time, into what are now the best set of greens in golf."

"So Ross's original greens were probably not as severe as the greens that pros will play this June," Tom Doak offered in 2005. "But then again, Ross probably didn't contemplate 325-yard drives, either."

***

And then there is the matter of long grass. Or in the case of No. 2's Golden Age Redux, the lack thereof.

Charles Price lived in Pinehurst in the 1940s while working for *The Pinehurst Outlook* and playing competitive golf. He played No. 2 dozens of times and knew how to juxtapose that to the modern look he found in returning to Pinehurst to live in the 1980s and up to his death in 1994.

"There was no Bermuda rough here," Price said in 1990. "Every blade of grass on the golf course was cut. Everything else was sand. All this Bermuda grass today is doing is hurting some poor lady who comes out here playing with her husband. You might as well cut the whole thing as fairway. The rough here should not be anything but wasteland sand, which is all it ever was in the beginning."

Bobby Jones said the thing about playing with average golfers he disliked the most was "looking for their damned ball." Architect Alister MacKenzie said that among the essential features of an ideal golf course was a "complete absence of the annoyance and irritation caused by the necessity of searching for lost balls." Further, he said, "Narrow fairways bordered by long grass make bad golfers. They do so by destroying the harmony and continuity of the game, and in causing a stilted and cramped style by destroying all freedom of play."

Author Curt Sampson spent the week of the 1999 British Open at Carnoustie Golf Links researching his book *Royal and Ancient—Blood, Sweat and Fear at the British Open.* That championship is best remembered for Jean Van de Velde's final-hole meltdown and beyond that for the awful scores promulgated by a golf course marked by heinously long grass and narrow fairways. Was the course set-up, Sampson posed, fair?

"No, Alister MacKenzie and Donald Ross would have said," Sampson offered. "Both of the 20th century's greatest golf architects abhorred high rough, even for major championships. They put trouble near their greens, not off their tees."

That's an important prong in the philosophy Ross used at Pinehurst, and it survived for at least two decades following his 1948 death. Bill Coore played No. 2 often as a teenager and collegian in the 1960s and remembers that the wide berth off the tee was an enduring personality trait of the course.

"Pinehurst No. 2 used to be about wide fairways, not narrow fairways," Coore says. "They were wide for a reason."

Coore extends both arms in front of him and holds his hands about a foot apart.

"It was not like hitting between this and this," he says, looking at his hands.

Now he moves them much farther apart, illustrating the concept of a wide fairway.

"The concept behind No. 2 originally was that you can hit the ball here, here, or here," he says, nodding toward different points between his hands. "Depending on the wind and conditions and where the pins

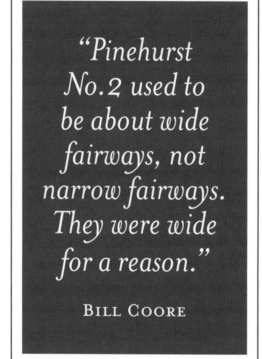

> "Pinehurst No. 2 used to be about wide fairways, not narrow fairways. They were wide for a reason."
>
> BILL COORE

are, you had to plan every shot. The width allows the golfer to make the decision instead of the golf course dictating one way to play it."

Visit the website for Tom Doak's firm, Renaissance Golf Design, and you'll see a queue of wide-angle photographs melting across the top of the page from courses Doak has designed: St. Andrews Beach in Australia, Sebonack on Long Island, Old MacDonald on the Oregon coast, Ballyneal in the hills of Colorado. One thread is the utter lack of long grass—unless it's well off the fairways and is indigenous to the native ground.

"Of all the courses I have seen around the world, only a few have taken advantage of the possibilities of short grass—probably because it requires a good budget to manicure extra acres of fairways," Doak says. "But consider the list: the Old Course at St. Andrews, Augusta National, Pinehurst No. 2, Royal Dornoch, Muirfield, and Ballybunion at the front. With so many new courses lusting after this sort of status, you'd think a few would try to implement this technique."

Doak caddied at St. Andrews for a year after graduation from Cornell University and got his real education, he says, "on exciting courses which had cost nothing to build and which were affordable for all to play. Ever since, I've felt a responsibility to build courses which reflect the ideals of the game as the Scots still play it."

And the Scots are certainly not playing a lot of the sixty and sixty-four-degree lob wedges so popular in the United States. They can run their ball along the taut surfaces of the British Isles, they play their shots under the brisk winds and they use their imaginations to picture a ball in flight, striking ground and then running along the surface to an eventual stop. American courses with stringy rough surrounding a soft green allow for essentially one shot—a fierce swipe with a heavy club with lots of loft.

"On a course like Pinehurst, you have more options, but at the same time, that makes a lot of people uncomfortable," Doak says. "You don't know which shot to play and don't really commit one way or the other and you mess it up. So many people are just not comfortable putting from off a green or chipping the ball. They reach for the lob wedge automatically. We've done two courses at Bandon Dunes, and there's nothing but short grass there. The caddies try to keep the wedge in the bag. But people keep trying that thirty-yard wedge off a tight lie and a firm fairway. They hit it halfway up the bank and the ball comes right back to them."

The width, the sand, the wire grass and the persnickety green settings were among the elements that struck Ran Morrissett when he first saw and played No. 2 in the early 1980s. Morrissett grew up in a golfing family in Richmond, Va., and remembers a trip in 1981 that included golf at Harbour Town on Hilton Head Island and No. 2 in Pinehurst.

"Driving home, we were saying, 'Gosh, Harbour Town is really neat. It's got marshes and these plank boards and cool green shapes.' But for some reason, we all liked No. 2 better," Morrissett says. "We debated with some vigor the plusses and minuses of both. From that point on, I have always had an interest in golf architecture."

That trip planted a seed for what would become a cyberspace forum for talking design: *GolfClubAtlas.com.* Morrissett and his brother, John, created the website in 1999 to feature classic golf course reviews, interviews with architects and a discussion board. Today he maintains the site with help from partner Ben Cowan-Dewar, and the site has no commercial contributions or subscription fees. It exists merely with voluntary contributions from readers that Morrissett asks be no higher than the par of the contributor's favorite golf course.

Log on today and you might find British golf architect Donald Steel talking in a feature interview of his love of Rye Golf Club on England's southeast coast, a discussion of the best sources for antique persimmon wood heads and reviews of classic courses worldwide—from Lahinch in Ireland to Yeaman's Hall in South Carolina to Mid Ocean Club in Bermuda.

Morrissett works in equipment finance and can live most anywhere. Years ago he chose Southern Pines because it's an excellent place to raise a family and is ideally suited for a golfer. He loves three-hour rounds on late afternoons at Southern Pines Golf Club, another Donald Ross design. He has some roots in the area as well. His great-grandfather was a lawyer in Carthage and did some work for Pinehurst founder James Tufts; Morrissett has old letters from Tufts written on Pinehurst letterhead. His Sandhills vantage point has allowed Morrissett to watch the evolution of No. 2 over the last two decades.

"In the last five years, I might have played No. 2 once," Morrissett says one afternoon in October 2010. "You could have been anywhere in the southeast United States where there is Bermuda grass and pine trees. The course no longer reflected that it was in the Sandhills of North Carolina. The golden age fairways typically were forty-two to forty-seven yards wide. The last time I was on No. 2, I paced off the first fairway at twenty-four yards and at one point on the seventh fairway—I think the crook of the dogleg—it might have been twelve yards wide.

"That's not how Donald Ross defended par. He defended it at the greens. But what happened was some guy plays it for the first time and you ask, 'What did you think of thirteen?' and he says, 'Well, which hole was that?' The holes were no longer distinctive."

Morrissett invokes the name of one of golf's grandest impresarios, Seve Ballesteros. The Spaniard thrived in a short grass environment and had the imagination to turn wild drives amidst the pine trees of Augusta National or the links turf of Great Britain into highlight reel recoveries. Ballesteros' five major championships were collected in those environments; in the U.S. Open, the bastion of narrow fairways and thick rough, his best effort was a tie for third in 1987.

"Short grass scares the ace player, so much more than a hack," Morrissett says. "That's a great combination. I mean, you can play No. 2 every day of the year and never lose a golf ball, which is a wonderful thing. MacKenzie wrote all that stuff about how bad it was to hack through wet grass and look for your golf ball and it defeated the whole purpose of being outdoors and enjoying nature. Can you imagine Seve Ballesteros at his absolute peak playing Pinehurst No. 2 after this restoration? I would love to have seen that. He would hit some wild shots off the tee but would have had a chance to make recovery shots. Nobody made recovery shots like Seve in his prime."

Sadly, Ballesteros succumbed to brain cancer in May 2011, but golfers of all rank and file can now stoke his memory by finding an errant drive in the sandy wasteland and manufacturing a recovery. The short grass throughout No. 2 now means the ground game is part of the quotient. Stark are the contrasts between the verdant and well-fed grass of American golf courses and the sparse and lean grasses of British golf.

"The guy who has been to the U.K. appreciates that golf at its base, and the enduring aspect of the game, is the ball on the ground," Morrissett says. "For the last six, eight, ten years, Pinehurst did not deliver an on-the-ground game. And it didn't deliver on fun and playing angles and it became too one-dimensional. So it's great that it's returning. It's long overdue, it's the way it should be."

What goes around, comes around, in other words. Golf on television brought us the concept of heroic finishing holes. The Masters gave us perfect maintenance. Developers stretched golf courses out to squeeze in more homesites. Marketing chiefs lusted after golf course images with flowers and waterfalls.

"In an era where people have tried to build eighteen signature holes, Pinehurst in its own quiet, dignified way set the standard for presenting one great hole after another without beating you over the head," Morrissett says. "Golf has gotten itself in quite a mess over the last fifteen years with overbuilt features and high maintenance issues, and Pinehurst has always been there as a shining example of what's good about the game. Yes, it got tarnished a little over the years. But it's so important that it's back in its full glory, that it show people that golf isn't about water hazards and gimmicks and tricked-up features that sit well for the camera."

***

Lanny Wadkins is grinding on another shot on the eleventh hole at Pinehurst No. 2 on this afternoon in late June of 2011, just as he did so many times back in the 1960s as an elite amateur golfer. Wadkins grew up in Richmond, played collegiately at Wake Forest and learned the course playing the Donald Ross Junior Invitational, the North and South Amateur and assorted other times he and the Demon Deacon golf team visited throughout the year.

"Okay, time for a birdie, we need to get moving," Wadkins says.

Only it's not Wadkins himself with a golf club in hand. Out in the fairway is eighteen-year-old Tucker Wadkins, the younger of Lanny's two sons who is opposing Mike Miller in the first round of the 2011 North and South Amateur. The elder Wadkins and his wife, Penny, are visiting from their home in Dallas and are following from the pine forest to the right of the par-four hole.

"Watching is brutal," Wadkins says of following the golf careers of Tucker and older son Travis. "They wear me out. I probably wear *them* out."

These two mounds to the right of the first fairway have been there for many years, but no one really noticed them because they were covered with thick Bermuda rough.

"A lot of us thought this was the best golf course in the country. It was a wonderful environment for golf."

LANNY WADKINS

Wadkins, sixty-one, plays little golf these days as a result of years of back injuries, surgery and extended recovery. But his credentials from decades ago are stellar: 1970 U.S. Amateur champion, 1972 PGA Tour Rookie of the Year, 1977 PGA Championship winner, twenty-one career professional victories, twenty matches won over eight Ryder Cup appearances. Pinehurst was a bedrock of his formative golf years.

"A lot of us thought this was the best golf course in the country," Wadkins says, meandering through the pine trees. "It was pure golf, it was a wonderful environment for golf. I just loved it. I always said it was my favorite golf course. Then over the years, I'd say it was my favorite—the way it *was*.

"Eleven was the hole I always loved the most. I loved the sandy pine straw. The wire grass look down the right was spectacular. I loved

the front-right pin. It was my favorite pin on this hole. I'd hit a seven-iron to that pin with a little wind. Otherwise, it was a six-iron."

"Didn't Hogan say this was his favorite hole?" Penny wonders.

"Hogan said his two favorite par-fours were the eleventh here and the sixth at Seminole," Lanny answers.

Wadkins played No. 2 in June 2008 with Don Padgett and told Padgett the scanty fairways and burdensome rough had robbed the course of its texture and character. He hardly recognized what he had known decades earlier.

"Eleven, twelve and thirteen are the ones I remember when I saw them three years ago," Wadkins says. "They were just screwed up. You were walking single-file down the fairways. There was one bunker thirty yards deep in the rough. That's silly. What purpose does that serve? It was ridiculous. I didn't like it."

Wadkins' opinion was among a handful of dominoes that fell in Padgett's mind and led to the eventual decision on the part of Padgett and resort owner Bob Dedman Jr. to dig up the framing of the course and start over, to take the bones back to what Donald Ross left more than half a century ago.

"I love what Ben and Bill have done," Wadkins says. "It's my favorite again. The thing I like is that they have really taken it *all the way* back, even more than I remembered. It really looks good. They're getting it right."

He nods toward the fairway.

"The fairway would kind of serpentine along," he says, using his hands to illustrate. "It went this way and that way. Now it's got that old look again. It's just spectacular. It couldn't be better.

"You've got people in Coore & Crenshaw who respect and believe in the history of a place like this. They're not going to shove their ideas down your throat. They're going to try to put back what was here. I admire everyone involved for taking the leap and doing this. As Bob Dedman said, it was going to be the best thing they ever did or the worst."

The Wadkinses continue to follow Travis around the course, his game unfortunately not sharp enough to overcome Miller, who wins 3-and-1. Lanny watches as the golfers examine their recovery shots from around the greens and remembers the challenge of chipping to the Bermuda greens of the 1960s.

"I always thought this was one of the best chipping courses I'd ever played," he says. "Chipping, hitting a bump-and-run into the humps, it was really spectacular when it was firm with those old Bermuda greens."

The twelfth and fourteenth greens are in close proximity to one another, and as Wadkins circles behind the back of twelve he notes the creases and crinkles in the ground behind the green and looks over toward fourteen, where there's a dramatic plunge off the rear of the putting surface.

"Behind the greens you see some of the great character they have," he says. "Lots of times you missed that because you never came back here. This is such a great match play course. So many things happen. Pinehurst would have made for an unbelievable Ryder Cup. I'd love to have played a Ryder Cup here."

As Lanny and Penny follow their son around the course, Bob Farren is watching many things from his maintenance cart in the shadows—the health of the new greens and wire grass plants in the summer heat, the miscellaneous plant growth in the sandy roughs, the nuances of golf balls bouncing in an environment so different from that of two years earlier. Farren, Pinehurst's director of golf course and grounds management, has been at the club for nearly three decades and rose to his present position in 2008 upon the retirement of Brad Kocher, who was one of Robert Dedman Sr.'s first appointees in 1984.

Kocher and Director of Golf Don Padgett Sr., hired in 1987, took their marching orders from Dedman to take the considerable financial resources he provided and get all of Pinehurst's courses in outstanding condition following their deterioration under Diamondhead and the banks in the early 1980s.

"It was hard to believe the conditions I saw," Kocher remembers of his arrival. "They were very poor. Obviously money for maintenance had been a problem with the banks. They were mowing the greens with riding mowers at the time because it was the cheapest way to do it. The problem is that the riding mowers wear out the turfgrass on the sloped perimeters of the greens. Pinehurst No. 2 is meant to be mowed with walking green mowers."

Padgett Sr., a former president of the PGA of America, understood No. 2 from a big-picture perspective when he arrived in 1987 and began working with President and CEO Pat Corso in developing Pinehurst's relationship with the USGA, the PGA Tour and the PGA of America. Padgett understood that when people asked about "Pinehurst," what they were really asking about was a golf course—Pinehurst No. 2, the resort's crown jewel. From Padgett's first day on the job, he stressed to fellow management and employees alike that, as goes No. 2, so goes Pinehurst itself—the resort, the private country club and the village itself.

"He was good about reminding people that fact … whether it's sales, food and beverage, whoever," Kocher said in 2004. "No. 2 is why people come here. His was a steady, consistent voice. This is a *golf* resort. If you think anything differently, you lose your perspective and profitability."

The desire on the part of Kocher, Farren and their staffs to keep

A golf architect must approach each bit of country with an absolute open mind,

with no preconceived ideas of what he is going to lay out; the holes have to be found, and the land in its natural state used to its best advantage. Nature can always beat the handiwork of man and to achieve the best and most satisfactory results in laying out a golf course, you must humor nature.

WILLIE PARK JR.

Bill Coore has one foot in the bunker, one foot out on the second hole as he tries a recovery after a wayward tee shot.

the entire Pinehurst campus—hotel and club grounds as well as golf courses—in immaculate condition and on a level equal to or above their club and resort competitors subliminally led the No. 2 course to lose that roughhewn look that was part of its early DNA.

Farren remembers one talk he gave in San Diego to fellow superintendents and highlighted some of Pinehurst's lofty maintenance practices.

"I said at Pinehurst, one of our standards was catching pine cones on the first bounce," Farren says. "I said it off the cuff, but it made an impression on people."

He smiles.

"Now Bill and Ben tell us, 'Don't pick them up any more.'"

Therein lies the rub.

The marketplace, much of it, anyway, likes smooth and green. How much can you surrender in the interest of historical and natural integrity?

"Brad and I and everyone else were responding to what the market wanted and our bosses were demanding," Farren says. "We succeeded in doing what we intended to do. Now I have the satisfaction being part of it of going back the other way."

Farren remembers the lead-up in the spring of 1996 to Pine Needles hosting the U.S. Women's Open. The event was scheduled for late May, and course officials at the Donald Ross course in nearby Southern Pines used liberal amounts of water and fertilizer coming out of winter to ensure a thick covering of Bermuda rough and a rich green look for television.

"We saw the writing on the wall that spring," he says. "They had to overseed that year to have good rough. People liked that green look, particularly those coming from up north. We said, 'If they're going to be pretty and green, we're going to have to be also.'"

Now it's a new set of challenges built around the demolition of nearly forty acres of grass and its replacement with the native sand, pine cones and needles, wire grass and whatever else Mother Nature stirs into the pot.

"It's such a change of culture from day-to-day habits of how to take care of things," Farren says. "You will literally be able to play this golf course every month of the year and see different conditions in the sandy roughs. They will change all the time."

Mike Davis from the USGA was intrigued in mid-May by a plant that produced purple and yellow flowers known as a Johnny Jump-Up.

"This will look really cool," Davis said.

Farren told him not to count on that particular plant still being there a month later.

"We could have a whole new set of flowering plants here in June," Farren told him.

Dr. Tom Rufty, a professor in the Department of Crop Science at N.C. State University, visited Pinehurst earlier in June to help identify and catalogue the various species of plants that are appearing in the native roughs. Farren and his staff will catalogue the plants over the course of a year and determine which ones to eradicate and which to keep. One plant that has sprouted in abundance as hot weather has arrived is the portulaca, which sports a bright purple flower in the mornings before closing up under the midday sun. There are a few cactus plants as well.

"We also have a learning curve in the course's ability to withstand thunderstorms and heavy rain events," Farren says. "It's much different from when we just had heavy turf. We had a storm in early June with 3.7 inches of rain in just over an hour. We had an incredible mess. Some of the sand moves and washes out. If it's part of a design feature, we'll build it back. If it's sand that's going to move every time we get a heavy storm, we'll just let it go where it's going to go."

***

Wynn Solle tees his ball up at 5:59 p.m. on a crystalline fall afternoon on Pinehurst No. 2 and eyes his 162-yard shot on the seventeenth hole. The sunshine filters through the pine trees to the right, casting a mellow glow across the cathedral of grass and sand and pine needles. Perhaps this was Van Gogh's vantage point when he mused, "There is no carpet imaginable as splendid as that deep brownish-red in the glow of an autumn evening sun."

Solle addresses his shot, waggles, eyes the flag, waggles again, then pulls the trigger. Just as he does, the carillon in the Village Chapel a quarter of a mile away sounds off with its medieval and majestic notes heralding the six o'clock hour. Nonplussed, Solle completes his

backswing, makes crisp contact and watches the ball fly through the air and land fifteen feet left of the flag.

Playing companion Les Fleisher smiles.

"Even through the church bells, he can stay focused," Fleisher says. Solle waves off the praise.

"You get used to it," says Solle, a member of Pinehurst Country Club since 1988. "Your mind is kind of trained to say, 'I haven't heard them in a while, maybe it's about time …'"

Sweater weather, a century-old golf course, the church bells wafting through the breeze, autumn's palette cloaking the moments in a warm glow, good friends walking and lugging their bags—purity by definition.

"This harkens back to when I was a kid, when I first learned the game," Solle says. "Everyone showed up on the putting green, formed groups, put their ball in the rack, slung the bag on their shoulders, and away you go.

"When we're out here in the summer, the beauty is that you don't see a soul. You have the whole front nine to yourself late in the afternoon. You're out here with the shadows and the golf course and guys like you who enjoy walking."

Fleisher nods in agreement. He and Solle are among a group of some forty Pinehurst Country Club members who regularly take advantage of the club's walking policy—golf on foot allowed at any time on courses 1, 3 and 5 and during specified times on Nos. 2, 4 and 6. They have a special "Walking Club" tag on their bags, a certain badge of honor that binds them to one of golf's most ancient traditions.

"We're the fanatics," says Fleisher. "We may be the last of a dying breed. We enjoy playing the game in its simplest form. The sad thing is that most guys have lost the ability or interest to walk. It's not a walking game anymore. One guy the other day said, 'Why would I walk if I can ride?' Well, I don't have an answer for that."

The answer, of course, is that walking is what Harry Vardon and Ben Hogan and Donald Ross did on these very acres. On foot you feel all of the curls and furrows of the ground. Your legs and back and lungs are taxed; this is a *sport*, after all. You converse with all three playing companions, not just your cart mate. On foot you hear only nature—never a motor. On foot you have time to contemplate the next shot, to take in the angles and consider the architecture. Over

eighteen months visiting Pinehurst to shepherd the restoration of No. 2, Bill Coore never once set foot in a golf cart.

Fleisher considers the pealing of the carillon just after six o'clock and mentions being aghast at having played a few holes one time with a teenager who was actually wearing ear buds attached to a *gadget du jour* while walking the hallowed fairways of No. 2.

"Today there is so much stimulation for kids—video games, computers, a hundred and fifty channels on TV," he says. "The bells are just the right touch—stimulation of the finest kind."

Holy, Holy, Holy …

"It's almost mystical late in the day," Fleisher says. "It's hard to describe."

The experiences mount up as the fall of 2011 unfolds, the Coore & Crenshaw iteration of No. 2 exposed for the first time to the special circumstances of autumn. It's a busy time at the club and resort as it always is when cooler weather arrives—new challenges for the maintenance crew, inspections by USGA staff, tweaks by the architects, evaluations by golf course ratings panelists.

The routing of No. 2 is the same as it's been for decades, the rumpled ground the same, the devilish greens still persnickety as ever. But everything *looks* different—to the naked eye and through the camera lens as well.

"Gosh, it looks so much better," says Thomas Toohey Brown, a Pinehurst club member and commercial photographer. "No. 2 used

Aerial photos of the seventh hole from 2005 (above) and 2011 contrast the old and new No. 2—straight lines and green grass before, haphazard dimensions and earth tones now.

THE GOLDEN AGE OF PINEHURST

to be very difficult to photograph, there wasn't much to it. There was no elevation and it was all green. There's a lot more here now."

Brown visited the course at 10:30 one night in April and used the full moon to capture a unique glow to the course. He set his camera on a tripod and used a fifty-second exposure in the still of the night.

"It turned out pretty neat," Brown says. "The contrasts stood out in the moonlight. Before the restoration, what would have been the point?"

Those who evaluate and rate courses for the various magazines find it a refreshing change as well.

"It's brilliant, absolutely brilliant," says Jim Simmons, a member of the *Golfweek* rating panel who visited in early October. "The shape of the holes is outstanding. You have to be very precise. You have to hit to the right slots or the right corners and not go two yards over. It's like Augusta in that respect. There you can hit it as wide as you want, but the precision demanded on your approach shots and short shots makes all the difference in the world."

Simmons remembers visiting Pinehurst some years ago when the course was getting green and lush.

"I remember eleven and twelve being a boring, nondescript corner of the golf course," he says. "Today, it's radically different. Six was a carpet of grass and a turtle hump out there with no depth perception at all. Now, it's a golf hole."

Merchants in the village who spend considerable hours talking golf with customers and townsfolk detect an uptick in sentiment—despite some early skepticism spawned from the understandable mindset of, *They're removing grass from a golf course?!?!?*

"I knew I would like it because it fits my eye," says Tom Stewart, a former PGA professional and owner of Old Sport & Gallery. "It's brilliant. I did have some concern about how the average bloke would perceive it. But to a person—high handicap, scratch, in between—I don't know anyone who hasn't enjoyed it. It's still up in the air how the professionals will play it in the Open. I think they'll get to eight or ten under-par. No one can play from thick Bermuda to those greens. But they can spin the daylights out of it off hardpan. Advantage to the pros, but that's okay. Who cares?"

Former USGA Executive Director David Fay visits in early November and loves the look. He says that his former boss at the USGA,

the late P.J. Boatwright Jr., would certainly approve of the restored character of No. 2. Boatwright was a connoisseur of No. 2 during the mid-20th century but was not a fan at all of the 1970-80s modernization mode.

"If P.J were alive, he'd be nodding his head in approval," Fay says. "Kudos to Bob Dedman and Don Padgett for making it happen. I'd like to believe their fathers would be very proud of the decision-making by their sons."

Dedman received in his Dallas office every scrap of opinion about the No. 2 restoration—from magazine pages, from e-mail or traditional letters, from resort and member comment cards. Thinking after a while that Pinehurst staff was screening the messages, he told Lori Kish, Don Padgett's administrative assistant, "Send me everything—even the bad staff."

"We are," Lori answered. "You're getting everything."

Perhaps no group has felt the pulse of the No. 2 restoration project over eighteen month more than the caddies, a staff that numbers approximately one hundred in high season and provides a key service to golfers. With carts restricted to the far extremities of the holes on No. 2, walking with a caddie is the preferred method of play.

"There was a lot of frustration during the early stages," says Tom Harmicar, a caddie since 2008. "You had to handle golfers with kid gloves. It was really difficult."

"During the renovation, we caught a lot of heat," adds Eric Stang, who's looped on No. 2 since 2006. "People didn't really understand what was happening."

Since the reopening in early March 2011, the caddies have heard nothing but accolades about the new experience on No. 2.

"Not one person has had anything bad to say," Stang says.

"Nobody says they liked it better the old way," adds Marshall Maynor, a caddie for nine years. "They definitely added more character to the golf course. It's not so much wide open. You have to actually think about your tee shot more than before. You can still hit it out of the hardpan and score, but you have to be a decent player to connect with it cleanly." Stang points to Donald Ross's quote from 1936 about the playing characteristics of No. 2 that is chiseled into a stone monument by the first tee.

"He believed in making you play every club in your bag, and now

KIDS AT PLAY

For one week every August, traditional and staid Pinehurst is flipped on its ear. Seven-year-olds are putting golf balls and running down the halls of the venerable Carolina Hotel. Nod at someone and say, "Morning," and there's no telling what accent will come back at you. A lunch buffet is set up at the resort clubhouse with pigs-in-a-blanket as one offering, and the kitchen staff knows an onslaught is coming every morning for the French toast on the breakfast buffet.

The venerable golf writer Dick Taylor once mused that if you listen hard enough at night in Pinehurst, "you can hear the arteries hardening." Perhaps, but for one week a year now the collective age of the Sandhills golf community drops precipitously. Instead of Tommy Armour and Babe Zaharias cracking balls on the practice range during the old North and South Open and Women's Amateur, today you have teeny tots with perfect grips and on-plane swings. Captain Kangaroo could serve as starter.

"Honey, they've shrunk the PGA Tour," is how John Bryan, an administrator with U.S. Kids Golf, likes to catalog the annual conclave of more than a thousand young golfers on nine courses throughout the Sandhills. "Their attire, their mannerisms, their fundamentals—they look like tour players in miniature."

Lifelong Pinehurst resident Marty McKenzie has seen everything from the 1951 Ryder Cup to the 2005 U.S. Open on Pinehurst No. 2 and the attendant Hall of Fame golfers that events of that ilk import to the community.

"But I have *never* seen anything like these kids," he says. "These are the highest quality of youth on the planet participating in the greatest sport on the planet, and it all takes place in our beloved Pinehurst."

On the afternoon before the first round of the 2010 U.S. Kids Golf World Championship, the clubhouse is teeming with activity as the last of 1,234 contestants from three dozen countries registers. Every inch on the practice tee is taken. The putting green is a swarm of kids and parents. The retail shop is slammed with traffic. Out behind the eighteenth green, one family after another stops in front of the Payne Stewart statue, with parents snapping photos of their kids assuming the requisite "Payne Pose."

"Coming to Pinehurst is awesome," says Russ Jones, who's brought eleven-year-old daughter Aubree from their home in Memphis to compete for the fourth straight year. "Our year revolves around this trip. It's the culmination of the year."

Jones is standing behind his daughter as she rips beautiful drives down the practice range. Next to her is Cade Jones, six years old and proudly sporting a black golf shirt with the Putter Boy mark. One assumes the size is quadruple small.

"Cade's been playing a lot of T-ball, but I want him to play more golf next year," Jones says as the tyke launches a clean strike with a miniature five-iron fifty yards downrange and then wheels around with a smile to make sure Pop saw the shot. "I hope next year, both kids will play here."

A couple of stations down the line are the Smiths from Rockville, Ill.—dad Marcus and son Marcus James. Young Marcus is nattily attired in navy shorts with a white belt, white shirt, white visor and white shoes. His wardrobe is set for the week, but his dad can't understand the boy's plans to wear long pants in ninety-degree-plus heat.

"They wear pants on the pro tour," Smith says. "I guess that's it."

This avalanche of adolescent golf revelry comes compliments of an Atlanta engineer-cum-entrepreneur named Dan Van Horn. The father of three noticed in the mid-1990s that Little League baseball players had lighter bats but young golfers had nothing but crude sawed-off golf clubs, so he launched a company to manufacture quality junior golf clubs—with proper swing weights and shaft flexes. One thing led to another and in 2000 he staged a tournament for kids aged six to twelve at Jekyll Island, Ga., in part to promote his clubs but also to foster the idea of golf as the consummate family activity. He had the vision to name it a "world championship," and some 250 players and their families attended.

Van Horn tweaked his version of junior competition by grouping players into narrow age brackets, allowing eight-year-olds to compete only against other eight-year-olds, for example, to set hole yardages according to age and to allow parents to caddie

Parents and kids on the golf course (opposite), like this pair as they examine the roll of a putt in the 2010 U.S. Kids Golf World Championship; a birdie putt (above) yields a fist pump and celebratory roar from a teen-age competitor.

for their children. And lest the urge to become an overbearing parent afflict someone during the course of play, a strict code of conduct for parents was instituted. One violation and they're given a "yellow card," disallowed from caddying and forced to pass an online behavioral course before regaining their caddie privileges.

Van Horn says the launching of Tiger Woods onto the golf landscape in 1996 and the attendant views of his appearance as a two-year-old on *The Mike Douglas Show* with a picture-book swing certainly were serendipitous for his new venture. Money, fame and golf were suddenly the holy trinity and lured many to the game. But as 2010 proved with Woods and his infamy of infidelity, the core values of fun and family prevail in the end.

"Some of the parents here really think their kid is the next Tiger Woods," Van Horn says. "But to most people, that doesn't matter. They're here because their kids are having fun, and it's a sport the family can enjoy together."

"As a parent to have your child play in international competition at age twelve and you participate as a caddie, that's big," adds Bryan, formerly director of the Georgia section of the PGA of America. "How does it get any better than that? You can go to the Little League World Series, but you're in the bleachers. You're not out there with your kid."

The 2010 U.S. Kids World Championship took 550 volunteers, twenty-one rules officials, forty-seven U.S. Kids Golf staff members and an estimated 4,000 parents and family members to organize and usher the kids around the resort and community. The event was being held in Pinehurst for the sixth straight year after two years in Jekyll Island and three in Williamsburg.

"Where else for a world championship in golf would you want be, other than Pinehurst?" Bryan asks.

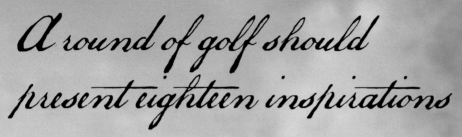

A round of golf should present eighteen inspirations

—not necessarily thrills, for spectacular holes may be sadly overdone. Every hole may be constructed to provide charm without being obtrusive with it.

A.W. Tillinghast

The view of the thirteenth green from the wide expanse of hardpan, bunkers and wire grass between the thirteenth and fourteenth fairways.

you're going to play every one," Stang says. "You can't just wail away with the driver without thinking, not anymore. The pros can't rip the driver. You're going to have to hit some long irons and fairway woods off tees."

Among the caddie staff are two Pinehurst Country Club members—Smarrelli and Harmicar. Both retired to Pinehurst—Smarrelli in 1993 and Harmicar in 2008—but both got tired of playing golf every day. They joined the caddie staff and found the work a good way to earn a little extra money, get some exercise, meet interesting people and be around golfers. Both say the No. 2 experience has been significantly elevated—from their perspectives as members and as caddies.

"Before, it looked like a driving range," Smarrelli says. "It was all grass, you hit between the trees. Now you see the angles, you play the angles, it's more of a thinking-man's course. Every hole is beautiful. The resort guests love the look. It's frustrating for some playing off the hardpan. That's a tough shot for them."

"It reminded me of a bowling alley, there was grass everywhere," Harmicar adds. "It's such a better golf course now. Ninety-nine percent of the guys I caddie for now say they'll be back. The good golfers really enjoy the subtleties and the high-handicappers can play it."

Ben Crenshaw was in Cary for the SAS Championship on the Champions Tour the third week in September and drove to Pinehurst one afternoon to ride around the course with Padgett. He called Coore with a glowing report.

"Bill, you're really going to like what you see," Crenshaw said. "The areas between the bunkers are looking terrific. The colors are marvelous. The golf course looks more natural, more rustic. It's amazing what nature will do, given a little time."

Coore sees for himself ten days later when he arrives the first Monday in October for four days. The week begins with a luncheon address to a group of business and sports executives from around the state; they have been invited to play the course and get an early overview of plans for the 2014 U.S. Men's and Women's Opens. Coore tells them of being approached two years earlier by Dedman and Padgett with the idea for the restoration.

"Are you *sure* you want to do this?" Coore says of his response. "This is not an ordinary golf course. Do you really want to do this? They were steadfast. They had had enough conversations with people

who knew it and could say this is *not* the golf course it once was. It had lost its visual character. It looked like it could have been anywhere in the United States."

Coore reviewed the key statistics of the venture: a thousand sprinkler heads reduced to four-fifty; forty acres of turf removed; some eighty thousand wire grass plants established; forty percent less water used in maintenance.

"This was a huge risk for Pinehurst," Coore says. "Ben and I were out on a limb, too. But it was worth doing. I hated that so much of what I knew forty years ago was no longer here. This golf course was so instrumental in my understanding what good golf architecture can be and should be."

The next day, Coore walks the course with an entourage that includes brothers Mike and Chris McCartin, the former a member of Tom Doak's construction crew and the latter a former Wake Forest University golfer and aspiring tour pro. Mike is a 2003 Duke University graduate who served an internship under Doak in 2005 and returned to school to earn his masters degree in landscape architecture at the University of Georgia. He has been working for Doak ever since and recently has been assigned to Doak's new course at Streamsong Resort in Florida; Coore & Crenshaw are doing a separate course there as part of a thirty-six hole complex east of Tampa and south of Orlando.

Coore provides the background to the No. 2 restoration as they make their way around and is paying close attention to the condition of the sandy roughs. He stands on the edge of the second fairway, looking at the color and health of the grass as it melts into the sandy hardpan. He would like to see a little scruffier grass at the edges but recognizes that a wet August and September have made for an ideal Bermuda grass growing environment. The summer was difficult for managing weed growth outside the fairways; as soon as the maintenance staff caught up with clipping and spraying the undesired infestations, another deluge of heavy rain would nudge Mother Nature into a new round of growth. Don Padgett occasionally pitched in to pull some weeds and one day wound up in the emergency room for treatment of fire ant bites up both of his arms.

"I didn't have gloves on and grabbed the wrong thing," he says. "It was a perfect storm for growing weeds. It was so wet. We'd get a bunch of stuff under control and have a gulley washer come and undo everything. It was hot and every three or four days you'd get another storm dump on us."

What Coore does like, though, is that the Pinehurst maintenance staff has done a good job keeping the perimeters of the fairway from extending any farther out than where they were in March when the course reopened.

"It hasn't browned in," Coore says. "But the good news is, it hasn't *greened out.* That's most important."

Farther down the fairway, Coore surveys the cornucopia of material in any given swath of ground outside the fairways.

"It looks like the old pictures," he says. "It's just perfect. There is different stuff happening everywhere you look.

"There's some fluffy sand, some hardpan, some pine straw, some organic. You can't compress a ball off organic. You don't know where it will go. Some spectator in the U.S. Open will be standing there and say, 'It's teed up for him.' But he might hit it thirty yards over the green."

Mike and Chris nod in agreement.

"Sand is so unforgiving," Mike says. "You look at it and think, 'I can pull this off, I'm going to blast this baby.' This makes you want to play aggressive. It lures you into thinking you can do things you might not pull off. Nine times out of ten, it doesn't work out."

McCartin stands on the tee of the par-three ninth hole, eyes the green and the array of rugged bunkers surrounding it.

"This just makes me want to hit a ball," he says. "I want to hit over all that stuff. You cannot walk around here without itching to play golf."

They examine the ebbs and flows of the ground and Coore explains the idea behind going to two grass heights—one for greens and one for everything else.

"There are so many interesting features to the land here," Coore

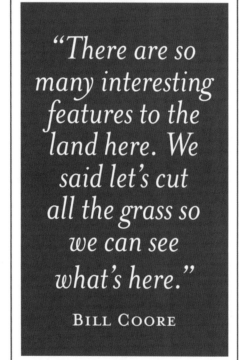

"There are so many interesting features to the land here. We said let's cut all the grass so we can see what's here."

BILL COORE

says. "We said let's cut all the grass down so we can see what's here. Now the challenge is to get the turf top-dressed and aerified. It'll probably be another two years before they get as firm as we'd like them."

When the tour is complete, the McCartins thank Coore for his time.

"It's fantastic, and I had high expectations," Mike says. "It's what Pinehurst should be."

"It's tough because you're so close to it, but you try to remove yourself and be as objective as possible," Coore says. "But you have to say, 'It's pretty damn good.' You look out there say, 'Okay, this will work.' You just shake your head thinking about that sea of green you used to see."

There is a sweet element to the result, a bitter one as well given that the business of golf and golf design remain gripped in the economic morass that commenced nearly four years earlier with the collapse of Lehman Brothers and continued with the unraveling of the housing industry. Coore & Crenshaw are finishing their course at Streamsong Resort in Florida, but beyond that they have no new design projects in the hopper. The irony is not lost on Coore that had the "Golden Age" flavor of Pinehurst No. 2 remained intact over the last half century, the game of golf might not be so expensive to play and the business of golf so difficult to maintain.

"The cymbals just kept getting louder and louder and louder, the cost more and more and more over the years," Coore says. "The golf business would have been better suited to withstand the downturn if it had not been for the cost of building individual courses spiraling upwards and upwards and upwards, the idea of building one course that is better than the one down the street or the one just ranked in some list."

Coore is in Pinehurst this week not only to inspect No. 2 but also to spend time on a parcel of 925 acres the resort owns five miles south of the Village and consider its suitability for another golf course—Pinehurst No. 9. The land is situated to the east and northeast of Hwy. 5 as it runs toward its intersection with U.S. Hwy. 1 near Aberdeen; it includes 275 acres bought from golf architect Robert Trent Jones in 2000 as well as additional acreage purchased in February 2011 that includes the abandoned holes of what once was the Pit Golf Links.

Golf architect Dan Maples, grandson of Pinehurst golf course superintendent Frank Maples, surveyed the land in the early 1980s and thought it ideal for a new course of dramatic edges, stark fall-offs and gonzo forced-carries. He named the course for its heritage as a sand quarry; parts of the land were mined as far back as the late 1890s, much of the sand finding its way in the 1950s into concrete and asphalt used in building the Blue Ridge Parkway. More than thirty feet deep of sand across two hundred acres had been dug out, leaving a pocked landscape of pine trees growing through sandy mounds and all manner of dramatic sweeps and swales. It had become a haven for area dirt biking enthusiasts.

Maples pooled his resources with a group of investors and in 1985 opened the Pit, which did well in the Sandhills golf market for twenty years as a daily-fee course. But the opening of architect Mike Strantz's Tobacco Road thirty miles to the north in 1998 took the quirky and extreme niche of golf courses to a higher level and robbed the Pit of some of its usual customers, and the recession of 2008 tipped it over the edge into financial distress. Maples and his group lost the property in bankruptcy proceedings in late 2010 and the golf course was closed that December.

The Pit site is adjacent to land that Pinehurst planned originally for No. 9 more than a decade ago. Jones bought the land in the 1970s when he found it while building the Country Club of North Carolina Cardinal Course on adjoining acreage. He sold it to Pinehurst and son Rees Jones was contracted to design the new course. Plans were announced in 2000; the course would sit amidst a village concept including an inn, a clubhouse, townhouses and a retail center. The original projection included a cost of more than $100 million and a timeline with the course opening as early as the spring of 2002; trees were cleared on the property before course construction commenced. The resort was flush in the glow of the success of the 1999 U.S. Open and the 1990s economic and golf booms, which saw Pinehurst open

the Tom Fazio designed No. 8 course in 1996 and No. 4 in 1999. Plans were made for a No. 10 course within the same project; Jack Nicklaus was going to be the designer.

That vision went *poof*, however, in the wake of the 9/11 terrorist attacks and the recession of 2001-02. The site sat idle for a decade until Dedman decided to buy the Pit land and have a significant expanse of property available for development at the proper time—whenever that might be.

Coore and Toby Cobb walked the land earlier in the year after the Dedman purchase and were intrigued by the possibilities. Now Coore has returned to put pencil to map and hand Dedman and Padgett more concrete ideas on what could be done with the site. Early on Wednesday morning, Coore, Dedman, Padgett and Bob Farren meet at the abandoned Pit clubhouse, mount golf maintenance vehicles and set off on a tour of the property.

There is one large lake within the envelope of the Pit course that had been a focal point of play on the back nine. Coore says it wouldn't be a significant part of the new course, that it might kiss up to a couple of holes but would be more of a visual in the distance; the lake would provide a nice backdrop for the clubhouse and building lots. In fact, Coore eschews any thought of using the original Pit course and proceeds to the eastern extremity of the site. There he finds acres and acres of land not touched in probably half a century. There are moguls and mounds and mature pine trees popping through them.

"You could fake that look, but it wouldn't look the same for thirty or forty years," Coore says, surveying the elements of the landscape around him. "A dune like that with a tree growing through it? That just doesn't happen. If you can figure out a way to utilize that, you've got a fascinating feature for a golf course."

They trek through the woods and traverse several overgrown fairways that were once on the back nine of the Pit.

"This is an interesting piece of ground," Coore continues. "The golf course in my mind would incorporate some of the quarry. It would have some more gentle, rolling ground, a little more like the traditional Pinehurst look. Other parts would have a glimpse of the lake. Overall, it's a spectacular place. I don't get the sense there are a lot of wetlands. Two things are expensive: wetlands and rocks. It's hard to get around them without spending some money. But I don't see either as being a problem."

That Coore & Crenshaw will design the new course is not at issue. Dedman has to decide if the economic environment in 2011-12 is conducive to taking such a bold step. *Wall Street Journal* golf columnist John Paul Newport noted in November 2011 that there were only four courses on track to open in the United States in 2012 and one in Canada. Pinehurst's inventory of eight courses is sufficient at the moment to handle the demand from members and resort guests. The idea is to be ready for whatever time the demand ramps up. There is also the concept that a new course by two of golf's most popular architects would attract demand—particularly when positioned within a resort menu that includes their restoration of No. 2. That the eyes of the golf world will be on Pinehurst throughout 2014 leading up to the Open double-header is not lost on resort management.

"Bill, how long would it take to build it?" Padgett wonders.

"You're not dealing with rock, you're not dealing with wetlands," Coore says. "Probably fourteen months. You can work here all year around. You'd have to hit the planting window right.

"I would hope people who appreciate No. 2 would appreciate this course. But it would be a totally different experience. It would be more rugged looking than No. 2, have more rugged features. I would think we would have really big fairways—give people room to play around these rugged parts. At first glance, maybe it would look harder, but you'd invariably shoot better scores because those greens are so difficult on No. 2."

Dedman peppers Padgett, Farren and Coore with a variety of questions, wondering where the clubhouse would be, how large it would be, how much parking would be required, would they use bent grass or one of the new heat-tolerant Bermuda strains for the greens? They mentally parse the calendar: If Coore could furnish a routing and budget by November, construction could start perhaps in the winter of 2012, the course could be grassed a year later and grow in toward an opening in the fall of 2013 or spring of 2014.

Coore observes the vistas around him and then nods toward the crude routing sketched on the topo map.

"It gets me excited when I come out and look at this stuff," he says. "I'm not particularly thrilled with what we have on the plan, but I think it's here. It makes you want to go stumbling through

Sand splashed on the tops of the bunker faces and wire grass plants randomly scattered within the traps are indicative of how Mother Nature might have arranged the landscape over decades.

the woods."

They agree to continue the due diligence on No. 9, and Coore walks the ground some more when he returns to Pinehurst in early November. But the priority of this visit is to meet with Mike Davis of the USGA and discuss immediate and long-range tweakings to the No. 2 restoration that apply only to the 156 competitors in the 2014 U.S. Open. Crenshaw has come in for the conversations as well. Davis has not been back to Pinehurst since mid-May—it's been a busy summer in his new role as executive director of the USGA after taking over for David Fay in the spring—and he's interested to see how the course has evolved in five months.

"It's fabulous, it's maturing, it doesn't look brand new," says Davis as he and Coore walk down the first fairway early one November morning.

"I am really happy with it," Coore says. "If you had shown me photos of what I see now and said, 'Bill, this is what it will look like in the fall of 2012,' I would have said, 'Great, I'll take it.' We're essentially a year ahead of where I thought we might be. It looks great."

Particularly keen to his eye are patches like those to the left of the fairway near the second green.

"If you took a photograph right here, how much better could this be?" Coore enthuses. "You've got pine straw where nature wants it to be, wire grass right up to the bunkers and in some cases *in* the bunkers. You've got patches of odd stuff. It's all pretty neat. And yet everyone can play it."

Though Davis agrees the course is outstanding and remains one hundred percent committed to the idea of a playing a U.S. Open without a blade of long Bermuda grass, there are some fairways he believes are too generous in the landing area for the pros. He wants to suggest places where the competitor in the Open might need to take more care in planning and executing tee shots.

"To put my cards on the table," Davis says, "here is my concern. In 1999 and 2005, we had firm greens and a very narrow course. My only trepidation is, as wide as it is now, if we have soft greens because it rains, I could see without exaggeration sixteen-under winning it. I think people would say, 'They've taken some of the championship part out of the No. 2 course.' Historically, accuracy has always been a part—probably too *big* a part—of the test of the U.S. Open. We need

to get a little more of that back."

A case in point is the first hole. Davis points to a strip of dew he made earlier with the tire of a golf cart about six to eight yards to the left of the existing fairway border on the right side. He asks Coore if they can pinch in the fairway line at the three hundred yard area.

"We want to say, 'Okay, you can't possibly miss this fairway if you lay back to one-fifty, we're going to give you that eight-iron shot,'" Davis says. "But if they go a little further, there's some risk. The fairway is thirty yards wide at the 128 sprinkler. If a guy is going to try to get to wedge or nine-iron range, he's got to hit a good tee shot.

"In general around the course, we just want to say that accuracy is going to be a bigger part of the equation. I am hypersensitive to not harm what you've done here. I love it. But I'm also sensitive to not let this thing backfire. Pinehurst as a resort doesn't want to see the championship course have only a modest challenge to players off the tee."

Another issue for consideration throughout the course is the concept of breaking up the areas of hardpan sand. Davis says a clean lie on firm hardpan is "a green light" for elite players.

"I would like to see a few areas here and there with softer sand," he tells Kevin Robinson, the superintendent of No. 2. "But it's not something we need to worry about right now. We probably won't address it seriously until the spring of 2014. Maybe we rake it out, maybe we throw a little more sand into the natural areas—just something to trim back a little on all the hardpan."

Davis looks at the firm sand a hundred yards short of the third green, to the right of the fairway.

"You've got a green light here. But if it's soft, you are saying, 'Awwww, man,' and you're looking at maybe a six."

Several significant tweaks are planned, and Toby Cobb has returned from his Texas home to knock them out over the next several weeks. To provide more peril off the tees, Coore & Crenshaw have agreed to narrow the fairway on the seventh hole and sculpt a fall-off area to the left covered by sand, wire grass and random moguls; to build some mounds to the left of the eighth and sixteenth fairways; and to build two new tees on the fourth and fifth holes.

Four and five have been a nexus of conversation from the beginning of the project. Neither Coore nor Davis like the tee built on the par-five fourth prior to the 1999 Open. The tee stretches the hole to

The dogwoods are blooming in the spring of 2012 between the third tee and sixth green of No. 2; note how the tightly-mown turf of the tee and green melds directly into the pine straw without a hint of long rough anywhere.

565 yards, but the new angle straightens the hole and robs it of its original right-to-left shape. They discussed at the beginning of the restoration the idea of building a new tee along the original sight line of the hole, but to do so would mean losing a prime grandstand area between the third green and sixth tee. Davis has since discussed the issue with Reg Jones, the USGA official who handles all outside-the-ropes issues of the Open. Jones says he can relocate the grandstand, giving Davis the green light to lengthen four while maintaining the original angle. Davis walks to an area between three green and six tee.

"This will essentially be a players-only area," he says. "We can put the new tee for four right here. This looks so much better from here. The angle is wonderful. We'll get about twenty-five, thirty more yards. Right now four is essentially a long par-four to arguably one of the easiest greens on the course. I would like to put a little more club in their hands."

There is also room behind the existing fifth tee to add a few more yards to a hole that played 472 yards for the 2005 Open. Despite the hole's historical significance as the most difficult hole on the course and one of the hardest in Open history—the collected fields in 1999 and 2005 averaged 4.47 shots—modern equipment and players' strength have them hitting short irons on a hole Donald Ross envisioned requiring a fairway wood or two-iron. With a new tee sculpted from a slope running up toward to location of the now-demolished World Golf Hall of Fame, the hole can stretch to 507 yards.

"The last go around, we saw so many guys hitting eights and nines," Davis says. "This new tee will put them on a down-slope and a side-slope. That's one of the scariest shots in golf."

Davis also revisits his idea to play the fourth hole as a par-four and the fifth as a par-five for the men's Open. He and Coore both have agreed at various points the last eighteen months that the idea has merit. For one reason, five was conceived by Donald Ross as a par-five; it was played as a five for the 1936 PGA Championship (the eighth hole was originally a par-four and the pars of the holes were flopped prior to the 1951 Ryder Cup Matches). And for another, the green of the fourth is relatively sanguine while the fifth green is one of the most severe and heavily bunkered.

"Four just feels like a long par-four to me and five feels like a short par-five," Davis says. "It makes sense architecturally to switch pars.

But you're losing a little of that mystique of the past."

"Five has been known as one of the toughest par-fours in the U.S. Open," Coore says. "You would lose that little historical connection.

"On the other hand, five was originally a par-five. So you have that history there as well.

"I can see both sides of it."

Ten minutes later, Davis stands in the fifth fairway, eyeing the green from the canted fairway.

"Even if we play this as a five and you lay up and you've got eighty yards left, that's still a brutal shot as tough as this green is," he says.

A few minutes later, he's inspecting the caustic perimeters of the putting surface. He points to some areas where he might place a flag if the hole is played as a par-five.

"As a five, you can push the hole locations," he says. "It'll be the shortest five they play all year long. We won't feel guilty. I would put the holes more in the center as a four than a five."

The issue is tabled for further consideration. A betting man, though, would process the fact that Davis has floated the idea of switching the pars on nearly every visit to Pinehurst over the last eighteen months with the assurance there are no logistical concerns with a new tee on four. And he would lay his wager that in 2014 the fourth hole will be a par-four and the fifth a par-five.

(That bet would have paid off. When Davis returned in April 2012, he flagged a new tee for the fifth hole and made a final decision to play it as a par-five at 575 yards.)

"But the bottom line is, *together* these holes are a par-nine," Davis says. "Maybe we could put 4.5 on the card for both of them."

The par-four seventh hole has seen some of the most dramatic changes of the restoration project, the entire right side of the fairway being re-sculpted with a series of bunkers, mounds and gnarly hardpan. A pair of mounds was shaped to the left of the fairway, but Davis doesn't think they're penal enough to give the left side equal peril with the right. Coore suggests letting the left drop like a shelf to a lower area of sandy rough and wire grass.

"The right side is so dynamic," Davis says. "But we need something on the left. I'd like to see it narrowed down some—if you want play from 180, fine, we'll give you all the fairway you want. But you're going to have to hit a more exacting shot if you're going to chase it up

The approach shot on the long and arduous fifth hole presents many problems. But prior to the 1951 Ryder Cup, the fifth hole was actually a par-five, and the eighth hole was a par-four.

THE GOLDEN AGE OF PINEHURST

WEBB AROUND PINEHURST

A s the final strokes of the 2012 U.S. Open were being waged on a foggy and creaky old hill in San Francisco in June, eyeballs in Pinehurst were glued to television sets, excited phone calls were exchanged, hurried text messages were whizzing about. If Webb Simpson is not officially a son of Pinehurst, he's definitely a kissin' cousin.

When Simpson made par on the seventy-second hole at the Olympic Club with a delicate chip from the cabbage and a nervy four-foot putt, Country Club of North Carolina director of golf Jeff Dotson remembered a similar up-and-down Simpson made to win the Southern Amateur five years earlier. He short-sided himself on the par-five eighteenth of CCNC's Dogwood Course, lobbed the ball from a gnarly lie and rolled in a six-footer to win one of amateur golf's most prestigious titles by a slender stroke.

Such precision around the greens is happenstance with Simpson. Sam and Debbie Simpson have been members of CCNC since the late 1980s, and Dotson remembers frequent weekends and summer days on the family's visits from their Raleigh home as young Webb spent hour after hour around the short-game practice area at the club.

"He spent as much time practicing as he did playing," Dotson says. "Even at that age, he had a sense of how important the short game was—that it would bail you out when your ball-striking was off and allow you to take advantage of your good ball-striking days."

Pinehurst Country Club member Ron Crow, a leader of the club's volunteer forces for its annual amateur tournaments and special events like U.S. Opens and Amateurs, remembered the late Fred Webb, the octogenarian maternal grandfather of Webb Simpson who visited Pinehurst each summer from 2005-07 to watch Webb in the North and South Amateur. Crow and his tournament volunteers arranged for a chauffeured cart to take Mr. Webb around the course to watch his grandson.

"He was such a pleasure to see every July," Crow says. "He could not have been more excited to watch his grandson play. He was so proud of Webb. He's since passed away, and I couldn't help but think when Webb won the U.S. Open how much pleasure his grandfather would have gotten. When Webb turned pro and shot a good score, I'd get a phone call from Mr. Webb—'Did you see Webb shot 3-under?'"

Don Padgett, Pinehurst's chief operating officer, had spent the week at Olympic on official business; his club was a scant two years out from its 2014 Open return engagement. Padgett returned home late Friday and watched the Open on television on Sunday and thought Simpson had positioned himself perfectly: at no point did Simpson actually strike a shot while in sole possession of the lead.

"He was on no one's radar," said Padgett, a tour pro from the early 1970s. "They didn't show him on TV until the tenth hole Sunday and then the last three holes. He posted a score and let everyone come back to him. I was so happy for him. What a great young man. He's so humble. Of all the talented young guys out there today, he's probably got the world in as good a perspective as you can have it."

Simpson was born in 1985 and started playing golf at age eight by following his dad to the range to hit balls. He loved it from the beginning and grew up playing at Carolina Country Club in Raleigh and CCNC, the family bunking at their townhouse near The Holly Inn in the village on their retreats to the Sandhills.

"CCNC is probably my favorite place in the whole world," Simpson says. "I've always loved the courses. The back nine of the Dogwood is probably the prettiest nine holes in the state. The finishing holes there along the lake are really special. The whole atmosphere is just hard to beat.

"I've been in love with Pinehurst my whole life," he says. "I love getting down there, knocking around the village and enjoying the atmosphere of the place. I've always loved going to Pinehurst. A lot of times in middle school and high school, my dad and I would go away for the weekend or just the day, or I'd go play golf with my friends. I have a lot of great memories in Pinehurst."

Webb Simpson (kneeling center at right) was ten years old when he won his age division in the 1995 Mid Pines Junior. Seventeen years later, he used his razor-sharp short game to save par on the seventy-second hole of the U.S. Open to win the championship.

Simpson was ten years old when he won his age group in the Mid Pines Junior Invitational; also collecting trophies in that 1995 competition were future PGA Tour players D.J. Trahan and James Driscoll. He was fourteen when he served as a standard-bearer in the 1999 Open at Pinehurst. He walked the first and second rounds with Tom Watson and Aussie Stephen Allan.

"It was awesome, it was cool to be inside the ropes, walking the course, seeing these great players up close," Simpson says. "I remember how smart they were and how they made decisions that, at a young age, I would never have considered. I was blown away by how well they drove the ball also."

Simpson turned pro after his senior year at Wake Forest in 2008, just missing the chance to play in the U.S. Amateur on No. 2.

"Will I point toward 2014?" he said in 2008. "Absolutely.

I tried to qualify for the '05 Open but missed. To play the Open in '14 would be awesome. I'll still come to Pinehurst as often as I can, depending on my schedule. But I'll definitely always have that Open in the back of my mind."

Simpson was true to his word four years later, escaping to the Sandhills the week before the U.S. Open with a group of buddies to play golf on two of his favorite area courses—CCNC and Mid Pines.

"I love going down to Pinehurst and that was my pre-U.S. Open warm-up," he said. "I worked hard early in the week but once I got to Pinehurst, it was all fun and games. We had tons of laughs and we grilled out every night. For me to get with my buddies and get my mind away from golf and the U.S. Open was the best thing I could do. I showed up at the Open more refreshed and rested than most people. We were joking about how that's got to be a yearly thing now."

there closer to the green."

The entourage walks up eight fairway, where Crenshaw notes the hairline spine that runs into the green, tending to pitch approaches one direction or the other depending on which side the ball lands. Features like that beg the course to play with taut and rigid fairways.

"If you've been to Dornoch, you can understand why Donald Ross was trying to make the ground game so much a part of playing this golf course," Crenshaw says. "At Dornoch, you can really see the natural movement in the ground around the greens. This spine is a perfect example. But in order for it to really work well, the ground needs to be firm.

"Firm fairways will help with some of the widths Mike is worried about," Crenshaw says. "If the fairways get really firm and all of a sudden they run more, then those widths aren't as much an issue."

Coore makes an occasional housekeeping observation to superintendent Kevin Robinson. Maybe a bunker edge is a little too smooth on one hole, perhaps the pine straw looks too much like a nursery on another. But on the whole, he's pleased with the work done by Robinson, his two assistant superintendents, John Jeffreys and Alan Owen, and the rest of the maintenance crew. Bob Farren suggested in the spring and Padgett approved the addition of one worker to concentrate on the non-grass areas of the course—the bunkers and sandy roughs. That position was filled by Tom Lineberger, a native of Pinehurst and May 2011 graduate of the turf science program at N.C. State University.

"I've said from the beginning that getting the maintenance staff to buy into the process would be a huge thing," Coore says. "They have to commit to do the work. The guys have got to believe in what we're doing. It's a culture change."

The club is saving on the use of water and chemicals to groom all the acres of Bermuda grass that are now sand and wire grass. It's simpler to mow the course at two heights only—one for greens and one for everything else. But there is more meticulous hand labor in other regards. Labor has risen, Farren estimates, from about six thousand man hours a year to closer to eight thousand.

"The mowing we're doing now is more intense," says Robinson, who moved from course No. 7 to replace Paul Jett as superintendent on No. 2 in April 2010. "You don't just have a guy on a tractor mow-ing rough and then blowing it out. Rough that is 2.5 inches high is mowed once a week. Fairway at half an inch is mowed five times. We used to not patch divots in the rough. Now a lot of that is played as fairway so we're patching those areas."

Jeffreys, a five-year veteran of the No. 2 staff, walks along behind Coore, Crenshaw and Davis and looks at the myriad of elements of the native roughs.

"Anyone can come out here on a rough mower and mow rough," he says. "But it takes someone with talent and a keen eye to spray these areas. It takes more skilled labor. Some weeds are acceptable to a certain growth level. When they get past that, you have to spray them out. Without a doubt, it's more interesting to play the golf course now, and it's certainly more interesting to maintain it. There are so many more variables. Golfers in the spring can see a totally different golf course than in the fall."

Before the Coore & Crenshaw restoration, the natural areas of hardpan sand were restricted to parts of holes three, eight, eleven and twelve. Those areas were blown with a back-pack blower to rid them of pine needles and other debris, and pine cones were removed by hand. It's a challenge to wean the staff of the habit of making everything look neat.

"Now we leave the debris that accumulates," Jeffreys says. "Some guys at the beginning wanted to keep cleaning it out. You have to say, 'Stop, don't do that.' We've grown accustomed to the change. It took a while. You'd turn around and see a guy blowing and raking because he thought that's what looked good, looked clean. But they read the articles, they heard Coore & Crenshaw talk about certain things, about why they were doing this or doing that. We have a pretty smart crew. They're golf smart. They picked it up pretty fast."

Lineberger worked part-time on the Pinehurst staff on weekends, summers and holidays during college and remembers a comment from the spring by Kyle Franz, a shaper on the Coore & Crenshaw staff.

"The rugged look is not what you learn working on other golf courses," Lineberger says. "Kyle said, 'Forget everything you've learned.' I love the new look. They've brought the golf course back to life."

Among those enjoying and appreciating that renewed life are Les

Fleisher and Wynn Solle on their late afternoon excursions. There's plenty to talk about as they stride briskly down each fairway, their goal to putt out on eighteen with just enough daylight left.

They talk about shots they've seen from the professionals during previous U.S. Open competitions:

"Final round of '05, I was standing with a buddy just to the right of the second fairway," says Fleisher, a native of Wilmington and brother of PGA Tour veteran Bruce Fleisher. "We were just a couple of feet from Retief Goosen. He'd missed the fairway, and we could hear him and his caddie talking. The pin was back-right, they were talking about a six or a seven. The caddie told him to take the seven and hit to the middle of the green, make a four and go on to the next hole. Goosen was arguing for the six. I turned to my buddy and said, 'He could lose it right now if he doesn't make the right choice.'

"He hit the six *over* the green, chipped back long, made six and we went and watched someone else." (Goosen went on to shoot an 81 and fall from first to a tie for eleventh).

Solle remembers watching players on the sixth hole, the seventh and the seventeenth at various tournaments, everyone aiming for the pin tucked to one side or another.

"They don't play the percentages," he says, shaking his head. "They would be well served to get a local caddie who knows how this course plays. One day on seven in the '99 Open, the pin is back right. Everyone fires at the pin all day. They end up either long or in the bunker. Nick Price finally comes through, aims for the middle of the green, hits a nice little cut, ends up right beside the flag. Only one guy all day plays a cut into the green. Amazing."

They talk about what attracted them to Pinehurst in the first place:

"No. 2 is now more like what I remember when I first came here in the seventies," says Solle, a building contractor and a native of Pennsylvania who moved to Pinehurst in 1988. "It was unlike anything I had ever seen before. This was a ground game golf course. You had to bounce the ball and see where it would land. That was so much fun."

Fleisher grew up in Wilmington, and he and brothers Bruce and Jerry learned golf playing at Pine Valley Country Club. He spent most of his working life in Washington, D.C., in commercial real estate; then he and his wife retired to Maine. But the winters were too

brutal, and despite having numerous friends in Florida, they didn't like the heat and clutter. Pinehurst was the perfect compromise, and in 2004 they found a home just a short stroll from the ninth green of No. 2.

"I can play nine holes and walk in," Fleisher says. "It's perfect."

And they dissect the little nuances of the course. Solle nods toward a bunker on the left of the tenth fairway and notes the tufts of wire grass popping up through the sand.

"A guy the other day says, 'Why did they put wire grass in a bunker?'" Solle says. "I tell him to go look at that photo of Ben Hogan winning at Merion in 1950. Look at the bunkers on the left side as he's hitting his one-iron. You'll see wire grass *in the bunkers*.

"One of the most famous photographs in golf history and there is wire grass in the bunkers! Hey, that's part of golf."

But mostly they talk about the quaint experience of playing golf with like-minded players. Fleisher remembers meeting fellow Walking Club member John Dempsey on the first tee several years ago.

"We'd never met but we had an instant connection walking this golf course," Fleisher says. "It was getting dark and there was no way we could finish. By the sixteenth tee, it was pitch black, the moon was rising over the clubhouse. He said, 'This is just like when I was kid. I've got to go in, call my wife and have her come pick me up.' I said yes, 'It was the same with my mom.' That was absolutely fascinating."

That was the same John Dempsey who five months earlier at the President's Council meeting had talked of feeling "like a kid again" playing a course that was a hundred and four years old. Not a bad theme to crop up more than once.

***

It's a bright but brisk winter day in early 2012 when Bill Coore returns to Pinehurst with Toby Cobb to handle a laundry list of tasks around the resort. Coore first wants to inspect the work Cobb did on No. 2 in November—the new tees on four and five, the hardpan and wire grass on the left of seven, undulations and hillocks scattered about, fairways pinched in on several holes.

Coore is also still looking for the best eighteen holes he can find on the site of the abandoned Pit Golf Links, the course that will one

Walking Club members have access to Pinehurst's courses at certain times on certain days, and this foursome has made it to the delicate ninth, a one-shot hole with peril to every side.

day be Pinehurst No. 9. He makes three trips to the site over four days and works well into the night in his room in The Carolina drawing on a topographical map of the site.

"It's like any puzzle—you try to figure out the best way to put it together," he says. "There are some fascinating features on that site you want to work into the golf course—some old mounds with trees growing through them, some of the old sand pits. You want to have some neat stuff on it and showcase these parts, but still not let it become goofy. You could take a bulldozer and make the land fit the golf course, but you'd lose that personality of that piece of ground."

Coore and Cobb will also peck about in a triangle of woods in the middle of the ninth, tenth and eleventh holes on Pinehurst No. 1. From this area Coore will design and Cobb and Dave Axland will construct a new par-three that will follow the eighth hole on No. 1 and become the new ninth, allowing the club to discard the current par-three eighteenth. That area will then be upgraded along with the existing practice green and bunker on the south side of the clubhouse into an elaborate short-game facility—with at least three greens and a putting course fashioned in the manner of the Himalayas course at St. Andrews. Part of the idea is to replicate the greens complexes on No. 2. The project will be implemented at some point after the 2014 Opens.

But the focus this afternoon is No. 2, which on a forty-degree day is mostly vacant except for several hardy souls. The Bermuda fairways have gone dormant for the winter and display a slight greenish tint from the dye applied in limited quantities to appeal to guests from northern climes.

"It looks really good," Coore says. "Get the turf a little tighter and firmer and we could hold the U.S. Open tomorrow."

Coore looks at the fourteenth green and the undulations surrounding the putting surface. He stands to the left of the green, envisioning a recovery shot that could be played with a putter, eight-iron, pitching wedge or sand wedge, depending on the hole location and a player's personal preference.

"This is a great hole," he says. "We need to mimic some of this on the new practice area. Look at this swale—that would be a great feature to implement around a practice green, give people a chance to practice this shot. That area to the left of two, the hump on two green, we need to mimic that kind of stuff."

Throughout the afternoon, eighteen times Coore walks to the tee of a hole, gazes down the fairway, processes all the elements of the landscape and then fixates on the green in the distance.

"To me, this is more visually striking now than it was all those years ago, thirty or forty years ago," Coore says. "Maybe someone would say, 'Well, there's a little too much eye candy.' That's possible. But if you get rid of forty acres of turf, you have to put *something* back. We'll keep an eye on the wire grass. We certainly don't want it to look like it did when Diamondhead put in all that love grass and you had areas where there was nothing but a sea of love grass. That got out of hand."

It has been 582 days since Coore and Ben Crenshaw first walked the course in February 2010 to begin the process of wringing Pinehurst No. 2 through a time capsule—delivering the course from its svelte sheen of green to a multilayered prism of earth tones.

Since then, Coore has visited the resort fifteen times and walked the course probably fifty times. He's made no notes, no noise and staged no arguments. He has directed the removal of forty football fields worth of grass and the installation of nearly six digits worth of wire grass plants. He has quietly communicated his visions and instructions to his staff with hand gestures and verbal illustrations drawn from some six decades of life on golf courses—building, designing, playing and studying. Sometimes he'll take a rake or a hoe and chip at the ground himself.

At long last, Coore embraces the result of a job that he and Crenshaw hesitated to accept in the first place because the idea was, well, so audacious. *You're digging up grass on a golf course?*

Coore is walking down the ninth hole when his phone rings, his wife Sue calling from their home in Scottsdale.

"How does it look?" she asks.

Coore is navigating his way through all the sand and wire grass plants, toward the green perched on a hillock surrounded with gnarly and nasty bunkers, pine straw strewn all about in a manner that old Charles Price and Ben Hogan might have found half a century ago.

"If we never did anything right in all of these years," Bill Coore tells his wife, "we got this one right." ❦

THE AURA OF NO. 2

"There's nothing like it, nothing like it in the world."

Ben Crenshaw has seen thousands of golf courses around the globe in four-plus decades of competition and design work with partner Bill Coore. Since first seeing Pinehurst No. 2 in November 1973, he's revered its unique qualities.

What makes Pinehurst No. 2 special? Let us count the ways.

* Wide fairways. Donald Ross and superintendent Frank Maples installed the first irrigation system on No. 2 in 1933. The pipe was laid down the middle of each fairway and water was thrown roughly seventy feet on either side. That ground was maintained as fairway, everything else was the natural hardpan sand that had defined the region for generations. That breathing room off the tee allowed golfers the opportunity to aim tee shots to one side or the other in order to have the best angle to approach the green and the hole location that day.

* No rough. The 2014 U.S. Open will be the first since the 1950s, when the USGA established its template for Open course set-ups, that the national championship has been played with no long grass bordering the playing avenues. No. 2 is now maintained with two lengths of grass—the greens at one very tight measure and the fairways and everything else only slightly longer. Instead of hacking out of thick Bermuda rough, golfers now have to play a myriad of shots off hardpan, amid pine needles and cones, and off a variety of textures, firm in some places, soft in others.

* Unkempt bunkers. Modern bunker maintenance calls for smooth lines on the edges, uniform grass blankets on the faces and neatly coiffed bunker bases. "They're so perfect, they look like they've been painted on the course," Coore says. No more. The edges of the bunkers are rough and haphazard. There are tufts of wire grass on the faces and in some of the bunkers themselves. Some of the borders blend seamlessly into the surrounding hardpan sand. The odd wisp of pine straw or organic material in the sand

is fine, all the more to resemble Ross's native Scotland and the condition he left the course when he died in 1948.

* Firm and fast. This element will take the most time to evolve as the course maintenance staff works to remove the thatch that has built up over years in the fairways and tends to make them play soft. Toward that end, Pinehurst has begun using an organic dying process each winter to give the course some of the green color that visitors from the Northeast covet—without having to overseed the course with bright green ryegrass. Overseeding breeds more thatch—it's the antithesis of grooming a taut playing surface.

* Inverted saucer greens. The greens on No. 2 are surrounded by a medley of swales and hollows covered by closely cropped grass. Golfers can recover by putting, chipping or pitching. Mid- to high-handicappers are advised to keep the wedge in their bag. It's tough to get the club under the ball on the tight lies around the greens. The smart money plays to the front-center of the greens on No. 2, no matter where the flag is located. A shot landing on the perimeters of the dome-shaped greens is sure to slide off the putting surface, so the percentage play is to aim to the center and putt toward the corners.

* A myriad of colors of visual stimulation. The appearance of No. 2 had evolved over the latter stages of the 20th century into monochrome green with neat circles of white bunkers. Now it's anything but. The emerald fairways give way to the natural colors of the bunkers (filled with a darker hue of sand) and the sandy roughs. "What I see is the attractiveness of a different palette of color," Coore says. "Before, you had just one shade of green everywhere. Now you have everything from all shades of green and brown to all the stuff in between. That, in and of itself, is an attractive picture."

* The hazards it does *not* have, i.e., water. There is only one water hazard on No. 2, the pond fronting the tee of the sixteenth hole, and it's only in play for the high-handicap player prone to topping his tee ball. The pond was never conceived as a strategic part of the course; in the early days, it was merely a low-lying area that drained poorly and looked unsightly. Donald Ross and superintendent Frank

Walking No. 2 with a caddie is one of most venerable traditions in golf today; (inset) the Sunday flag on the eighteenth hole features the commemorative "Payne Pose" celebrating his 1999 U.S. Open win.

Maples filled it with water so it would look better.

* The hazards it *does* have, i.e., pine straw and hardpan sand, two features indigenous to Sandhills golf. The key to recoveries off both surfaces is to make sure you hit the ball first. Play the ball back in your stance with your hands slightly forward at address. And be careful in the pine straw; it's easy to dislodge your ball and incur a penalty stroke.

* Caddies. A round on No. 2 is infinitely more pleasurable in the company of one of the club's caddies. Carts are restricted to sand paths that are set well back from the fairways; it's difficult to get the feel for the course by walking at right angles to the line of play all day.

*And it's pure Donald Ross. As architect Tom Doak notes, No. 2 is "the only Ross course that you can be sure got one hundred percent of Donald's attention. It's a course he had the luxury of evolving on the ground over a period of more than thirty years."

THE QUINTESSENTIAL AMATEURS

The inaugural North and South Amateur began on April 1, 1901, on Pinehurst No. 1, a course playing to a length of 5,176 yards. Contestants walked to the golf course from The Holly Inn or the brand-new Carolina or took a horse-drawn carriage. They wore long-sleeve shirts, neckties and flannel plus-fours—no wonder their swings were wristy and compact. Their clubs had hickory shafts and their irons were still about a year away from being improved with grooves on the faces (the better to impart backspin). Golfers played the fancy new rubber balls just created by the B.F. Goodrich Company, and they were *hot*—the winner of the long-drive contest cracked his 180 yards. They positioned their tee shots on little clumps of moistened sand and, after putting on sand/clay green surfaces, smoothed them for the group behind with a rug attached to a broom handle. No expert player was without the ability to "hop a stymie"—that is, loft a putt over a ball resting between your ball and the cup.

George C. Dutton was the champion, defeating A.J. Wellington by a score that wasn't published in *The Pinehurst Outlook* and seems to have been lost to the ages. The Women's North and South was added in 1903.

The original title of "United North and South Championship" was the invention of Henry Haynie of Boston, chairman of the first tournament committee. Later the word "United" was dropped, for one reason because concerns of a stronger bond between North and South in the aftermath of the Civil War had diminished over time.

Since then, the mission has been simple, according to

Richard Tufts of the Pinehurst founding family: "To provide an annual gathering of those who love the game, rather than a spectacle."

Tufts was USGA president from 1956-57, the developer of the long-standing U.S. Open course set-up procedure and a staunch supporter of amateur golf. He authored the *Creed of the Amateur*, in which he noted that amateurism must be the "backbone of any sport, golf or otherwise."

"[The amateur] accepts cheerfully all adverse breaks, is considerate of his opponent, plays the game fairly and squarely in accordance with its rules, maintains self-control, and strives to do his best, not in order to win, but rather as a test of his own skill and ability," Tufts said.

Tufts chafed at what he perceived as a growing attitude of smugness and greed on the part of professionals in the early 1950s—ergo his decision to cancel the long-standing North and South Open in 1951. At the time, the tournament was considered a "major" on the professional circuit and listed among its champions Byron Nelson, Sam Snead and Ben Hogan. Tufts substituted in its place the North and South Seniors for men and women.

As Tufts wrote in his 1962 book, *The Scottish Invasion:* "Golf came to America as a great amateur sport, rich with tradition and enjoying the highest possible standard of ethics and good sportsmanship in its play. The idea has been to accept the game at Pinehurst in this form and to maintain and preserve these standards in order that amateur golfers might find at Pinehurst those things which James Tufts sought to provide."

Today the North and South Amateur, North and South Junior, North and South Senior and the Donald Ross Memorial

Junior are key components of the Pinehurst golf calendar. The men's North and South is the longest consecutive running championship in the country—though not the oldest. The U.S. Amateur started in 1895 but was interrupted for two years because of World War I and four years because of World War II.

"Think about the history of this resort," Don Padgett Sr., director of golf at Pinehurst from 1987-2002, said in 1999. "Thirty-six years after the Civil War, cousins and brothers and families with people on both sides met in Pinehurst to play in the North and South. That's pretty strong.

"These tournaments are extremely important to Pinehurst. This place has been a bastion of amateur golf for a century."

Win a North and South event at Pinehurst and you're in exalted company. The Heritage Hall area of the Pinehurst clubhouse is lined with boards listing the champions of all of its North and South events. It's heady territory, for sure.

For the men there are Francis Ouimet, George Dunlap, Harvie Ward, Bill Campbell, Billy Joe Patton, Jack Nicklaus, Curtis Strange, Corey Pavin and Davis Love III.

For the women there are Glenna Collett Vare, Maureen Orcutt, Estelle Lawson Page, Peggy Kirk Bell, Louise Suggs, Babe Zaharias, Carol Semple Thompson, Donna Andrews, Kelly Robbins and Beth Bauer.

For the senior men there are Tom Robbins, Curtis Person, Bill Hyndman, Harry Welch and Dale Morey. And for the senior ladies there are Carolyn Cudone, Ceil MacLaurin, Betty Probasco and Barbara Young.

Juniors who have won the Donald Ross Memorial include Leonard Thompson and Chip Beck; Woody Austin and Hunter Mahan have won the North and South Junior Boys, and Donna Andrews and Morgan Pressel have captured the Junior Girls.

"It's pretty neat to have your name up there with all the others," says David Eger, a Charlotte native who won the 1991 and 2000 North and South Amateurs and now is a regular on the PGA Champions Tour. "Jack Nicklaus is up there, Bill Campbell won a few times. There are some great names up there, wonderful players dating back a century."

Dick Chapman grew up aiming at coffee tins buried in the backyard of his family's winter home in Pinehurst. He credits learning golf on the small sand greens of Pinehurst with helping him develop the uncanny short game he used

Jack and Jackie Nicklaus grin from ear to ear (opposite) over the latter's win in the 1985 North and South Amateur; among their predecessors in collecting Putter Boy trophies were Dick Chapman (inset), the 1958 champion, and Harvie Ward (above), the winner in 1948 and runner-up a year later.

in winning the U.S. Amateur in 1933.

Chapman was defeated 4-and-3 by Dunlap in the 1934 North and South final. In the next twenty-four years, Chapman would win the U.S., British, French and Canadian Amateur titles—but it would not be until 1958 that he would return to the North and South final, popping Herb Durham of Dallas 11-and-10 in the championship match.

"Winning this is a greater pleasure than I enjoyed when I won the other titles because this one was the hardest to win," Chapman said.

The North and South was originally played in the spring but in recent years has been played in early July, with the Women's North and South following later in the month. Pinehurst officials have adjusted the format from time to time, seeking to keep the tradition of match play intact while working around scheduling nuances of other tournaments as well as the resort and country club. A new competitive format was planned for 2012 to help take agronomic pressure off the greens of No. 2 leading into the 2014 U.S. Men's and Women's Opens.

The new format called for a 132-player field to play three rounds of stroke play on Pinehurst No. 8, the field being cut to the low sixty and ties through thirty-six holes and then to sixteen through fifty-four holes. Those sixteen would then advance to four rounds of match play on No. 2.

"We can't have the North and South going and have a 103-degree day and 150 players out there," says Pinehurst COO Don Padgett II. "We can't shoot craps and lose those greens. We think going to No. 8 for three days and having a smaller match-play field play gives us the best chance to maintain the great tradition of the North and South while not taxing No. 2 too severely in the middle of summer."

Curtis Strange won back-to-back North and South Amateurs in 1975 and '76 while attending Wake Forest University.

Holiday Back Home *by Bill Fields*

When I returned home to the Sandhills for a vacation in the summer of 2011, I had in mind playing a little golf, enjoying time with family and friends and getting rested up for a busy upcoming slate of coverage for *Golf World*. Upon getting in town, though, and realizing that the North and South Amateur was happening on the recently restored No. 2 course, my week off turned into—happily—a busman's holiday.

Not only was I eager to see and document the extensive and excellent work Bill Coore and Ben Crenshaw had completed on returning Donald Ross's gem to what it had been, I had a rooting interest in one of the North and South participants. Jack Fields is the son of my old friend Mike Fields, with whom I had many fun days on Pinehurst area courses growing up in the 1970s (even though he often beat me!). The allure of No. 2 and Jack was a strong two-fer.

After tweeting some photographs from the opening day of match play (many people hadn't yet seen the restored No. 2 and were excited to have a look), I decided to photograph the tournament more seriously the rest of the week. I did so digitally but in black and

David Erdy found himself in a natural, old-school area right of the sixteenth fairway (left), but he and his caddie gauged the situation with modern tools: laser rangefinders. At right, Jack Fields hits his second shot on the thirteenth hole.

white, with shorter lenses than I would have preferred in the 1980s and 1990s while on assignment at dozens of major championships.

Since No. 2 had been taken back to a look it had roughly in the middle of 20th century, I wanted my photography to also have a retro feel. To that end I thought about all the images captured by John Hemmer, who was the resort's official photographer for nearly fifty years starting in 1925. Most of Hemmer's golf pictures offered a good feel for Pinehurst's distinct landscape, and by shooting wider and including more than just a golfer in the frame, I was trying to do the same thing.

I made some interesting photographs of a course that had been reborn, including some of Jack Fields en route to winning the championship, the first native son to claim the North and South. It turned out to be a busier week than I had anticipated but also a most enjoyable one.

The gallery gathers short of the tenth green as David Erdy (opposite) plays a shot in his final match against Jack Fields; left-hander Brad Benjamin (below) plays his approach on the par-4 fourteenth hole.

BEYOND GOLF

They ache and sweat and fuss over the details at the 1895 Grille, the Four-Diamond restaurant tucked in the center of The Holly Inn in Pinehurst.

The experience begins with an *amuse-bouche*, a tiny morsel to stimulate the palette that one night might feature a bite of trout or the next a dollop of tartare. There is a warm basket of bread—perhaps sweet potato biscuits with pecans and slices of an onion loaf. The shrimp cocktail appetizer is accompanied by a glass of yellow-tomato gazpacho and crackers dusted with a zesty spice mix. The filet of beef is rubbed with sea salt and truffle oil and nestled alongside a ramekin of macaroni, fontina cheese and morsels of lobster, the ingredients morphing into a den of comfort-food nirvana.

The wait staff in the 1895 Grill is pleasant and attentive—"They have an innate smile on their face and come across as happy individuals; that's a prerequisite," says Ed Peckels, Pinehurst's director of food and beverage. And the waiters and waitresses are adroit and precise in lifting a gooseneck sauceboat laden with molten white Godiva chocolate liqueur high above the table, tipping it ever so carefully and letting the liquid cascade down into a pillow of chocolate soufflé. There are veterans on the staff who team up to "double-pour"—the liqueur flowing from one sauceboat to a second and then into the soufflé.

"I've heard talk of a three-tier pour and even a four-tier pour in the works," Peckels says with a twinkle in his eyes. "One guest was so overcome he leaned his head back, opened his mouth and asked if they'd pour the chocolate directly into his mouth."

And you're sent on your stuffed and sated and merry way with a bit of sweet homemade bark, with white and dark chocolate melded together—no pre-packaged mints wrapped in foil at the 1895 Grille.

"Savor the moment," says Thierry Debailleul, the executive chef over Pinehurst's broad dining catalogue. "Dinner at the 1895 will take a little longer. Every morsel is an experience. There is always something happening on your plate."

"We get a lot of special occasions—birthdays, anniversaries, graduations," adds Peckels. "Creative food, creative service. Our guests remember their night at the 1895."

Beyond the fanciful dining experience at the 1895 Grille, Pinehurst offers a dozen venues for fueling the caloric fires—from the lavish breakfast buffet in the Carolina Dining Room to a relaxed evening repast in the Ryder Cup Lounge, which was tripled in size in a 2010 renovation. The Holly also features the Tavern, a casual dining experience created around a century-old, hand-carved Scottish bar. You can enjoy a bison burger in the Tavern, perhaps bison short ribs in the 1895 if you hit the dates just right. The beef for hamburgers is ground and formed daily at the Tavern, and there are always homemade potato chips fresh out of the fryer delivered to your table in newspaper wrap.

"Something for everyone somewhere at the resort," says Debailleul, who came to Pinehurst in 2008 after twenty years of international culinary experience. "There is a rich history here. The restaurants are a lot more intimate, and you have the ability every day to do something a little different. There are so many different options—fine dining, casual, banquets all present opportunities to be creative."

Creative food and attentive service are the hallmarks of the dining experience in the 1895 Grille—so named because that's the year The Holly Inn (above) opened as Pinehurst's first lodging facility.

The grandeur of the dining adventure at the 1895 Grille sets an appropriate tone for the Pinehurst experience beyond the resort's 144 holes of golf. There is so much more to this multifaceted playground—from a turn-of-the-century inn (turn of the *last* century, that is) to an opulent spa to a playground of pools and boats and racquets.

The Spa at Pinehurst opened in the spring of 2002 and affords guests a "sanctuary within a sanctuary." The front façade of the white building is reminiscent of the conservatory that once stood near the original Carolina Hotel. It opens into a spacious reception area, and beyond are 31,000 square feet of escape from sensory overload. Inside you hear only the flutes, harps and cellos of background

A serene, tranquil and spiritually nourishing environment—The Spa at Pinehurst.

music. You feel only the strong hands of a masseuse rubbing out lower back or neck stress. You taste only the strawberries and bananas of the smoothies served poolside.

"The spa is a serene, tranquil, spiritually nourishing environment," says Kim Parker, the spa director.

In the decade since its opening, the Spa has become less about luxury and pampering as it is health and well-being. Men are more interested than ever in taking care of their skin and their feet. Corporate visitors to the resort are treating their employees to massages that decrease stress levels and increase productivity. Yoga and pilates classes are popular.

The Spa serves a special niche among golfers as well with programs geared to stretching and strengthening tired and aching back and shoulder muscles post-golf. Michael Campbell called the Spa after the third round of the 2005 U.S. Open, complaining of soreness and tightness, and the staff treated and massaged him for nearly three hours that Saturday night before he won the Open the next day.

The Spa's menu of services reflects a resort-wide

expansion of attention to families, teenagers and children. Mothers and daughters can enjoy a morning retreat into the Spa with a facial, manicure and pedicure; pedicures for kids feature a "peaches and berries" foot bath.

The West Lawn at The Carolina features an Olympic-size pool, cabana and children's play area. Guests can fish at Lake Pinehurst or go kayaking, canoeing and paddle-boating. The tennis club features twenty-four courts and is listed among the Top 50 U.S. Tennis Resorts by *Tennis* magazine. The two hundred acres of Lake Pinehurst offer sailing, canoeing, paddle-boating, kayaking, fishing and swimming.

The genteel set adorned in all-white remains a fixture on the lawns at the clubhouse, one group wielding its mallets in croquet, the other rolling balls toward the jack across the lawn in the ancient sport of bowls. Games of that ilk are actually older at Pinehurst than golf; founder James Tufts was pictured in grandson Richard's book, *The Scottish Invasion*, playing roque, a game similar to croquet that actually replaced croquet on the docket for the 1904 Olympic Games.

Upon the 1895 founding of Pinehurst, Tufts entertained no thought of golf—he simply wanted relaxation and recreation. That began with the Holly.

The Holly Inn opened on New Year's Eve of 1895 and, at three dollars a night, promised the finest amenities—including electric lights, steam heat, telephones and "an abundance of choice food, daintily served by girls from the North." Amusements included a room for billiards, whist and dominoes.

The five-story facility was originally designed to resemble the inns along Cape Cod in Tufts' native Massachusetts. It

The fireplace in the lobby of The Holly Inn sets an inviting tone for Pinehurst's oldest lodging establishment.

was situated at the head of the Village Green, the oval parcel of land in the Village of Pinehurst that today is the site of the Given Memorial Library and the Village Chapel. It had forty-five rooms in the beginning and did so much business that Tufts doubled its size two years later. It still flourished, leading Tufts to decide to build The Carolina Hotel on a grander scale.

The Holly fell destitute during the 1970s but was revitalized in the mid-1980s as part of a hotel/condominium project. Officials at Pinehurst expanded their operation in 1990 with the purchase of the Manor Inn and decided in 1997 to take another step with the Holly; the inn closed in late-1997 and was restored and renovated into a luxurious facility, reopening in the spring of 1999.

The inn has eighty-five guest rooms, including eight suites (two of them bi-level). The furnishings and appointments are a blend of the old (full-length cheval mirrors, rocking chairs, porcelain pedestal sinks, beds with padded headboards) and the new (two phones in each room, work tables, Internet access, in-room safes and plenty of shelf space in the bathroom).

The heart of pine floors in the lobby and the fireplace and stage in the octagonal Music Room are original fixtures from nearly twelve decades ago. The floors creak and the hallways on the upper floors tilt just a hair after more than a century of settling. The wooden doors are dense and heavy; framed antique postcards showing the inn as it looked in 1905 hang from the picture molding in each room. The sheets are high-count cotton and the pillows substantial yet fluffy with feathers, all the better to drop into a deep sleep after a day on the go and a meal at the 1895 Grille.

PINEHURST No. 2

THE GOLDEN AGE OF PINEHURST

APPENDIX

No. 2 Hole By Hole

Course Overviews

Pinehurst Chronology

Tournament Results

Index

Photo Credits

Par 4 391 Yards

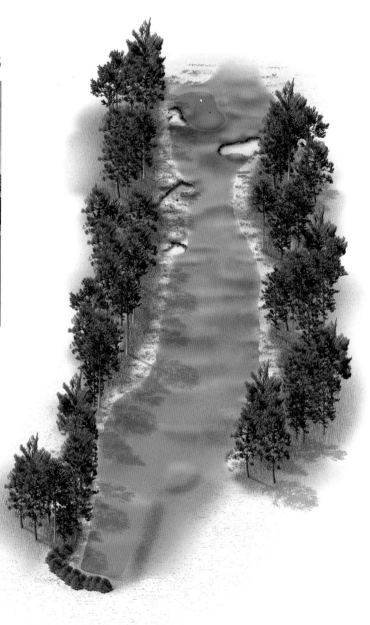

The first hole on Pinehurst No. 2 is not difficult—a medium-length par-four with a wide fairway. But the green complex throws down the gauntlet from the beginning—these are quite possibly the most distinctive set of greens in American golf, and they will test your skill, touch, nerves and creativity for eighteen holes. The approach shot is easier if played from the right side of the fairway, and the green is angled invitingly and appears to be a generous target from that side. Misjudge your distance or pull or push your iron shot just a hair, and the ball will bounce on the slopes at the perimeter of the green and leak into the bunker front-left or the chipping area to the right. The bunker front-right of the green is actually about twenty yards short of the putting surface, fooling many golfers into doubting the yardage and under-clubbing.

Yardages listed are from the Blue Tees / 6,912 yards, Par 72; new championship tees 7,485 yards, Par 70.

Par 4 438 Yards

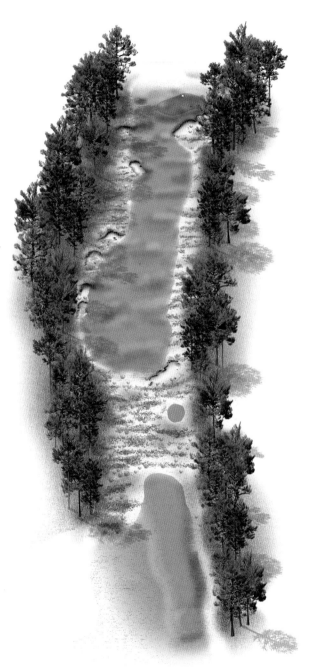

Architect Donald Ross begins his mosaic of shot-shaping demands on the second hole. A well-struck draw off the tee will position the golfer on the left side of the fairway, offering a more inviting angle into the green—the exact opposite of the first hole. Of course, there's more trouble on the left side of the fairway, where a cluster of bunkers await the shot hooked or pulled too much, and the approach shot is longer from the left. The right side of the fairway is trouble, particularly to a back-right flag, as there is a hump in the green and a bunker to negotiate. Most players can hit a short-iron into the first green, but now they see how difficult it is to hit a mid-iron or long-iron onto the table-top putting surfaces. "One of the great par-fours in golf," says Jack Nicklaus. "It's a sucker play when the pin is on the right. You just want to hit to the middle of the green and move on."

3 Par 4 350 Yards

R oss presents one of the finest short par-fours in golf with the third hole. After a medium par-four followed by a long par-four, the golfer now has the opportunity to fire at the flag with a pitching wedge, if he has smartly positioned his tee shot. The cross-bunker that protrudes from the right of the fairway, some 240 yards from the blue tees, gives the player pause; there is a sliver of fairway to the left of the hazard, but a tee shot struck too far will find the bunker and leave one of the hardest shots in golf—the hundred-yard bunker shot. The green is well-bunkered in front and slopes sharply from back to front. There's not a flat putt on it unless you're lucky enough to be below the hole aimed straight up the fall-line. Any approach hit too boldly can roll off the back of the green and not stop until it's nestled beside the fifth green or fourth tee.

Par 5 507 Yards

The view from the tee of the fourth hole is one of the most visually striking on the golf course as this hole has the most topographical movement—cascading down from the tee and climbing upward to the green, the fairway canted from left-to-right the first three hundred yards. Both championship and regular tees were moved in the 2010-11 restoration back to their original angles on the left side of the hole, preserving the original right-to-left dogleg. The tee shot needs to avoid a large bunker on the left side of the fairway, and new bunkers added to the right of the fairway raise a caution flag to long hitters. The second shot for the average golfer must be carefully aimed to avoid the bunkers on each side of the fairway, the left one about seventy yards out and the right one a hundred yards from the green. Miss those and you'll have a good lie and a wedge shot into what is probably the most benign green on the course. For long-hitters the hole is a gambler's delight.

5 Par 4 436 Yards

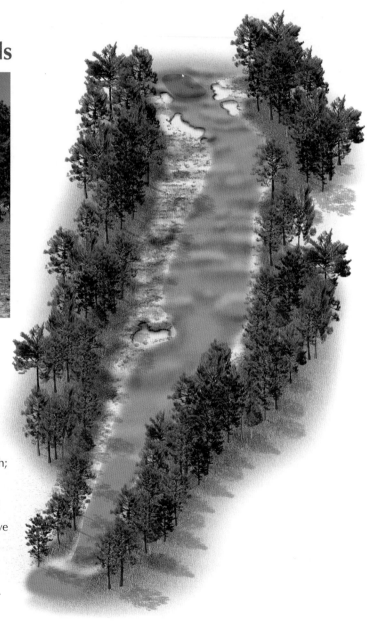

All you need to know about the brutal fifth hole is that only twenty-seven percent of all second shots in the 1999 U.S. Open landed on the putting surface. "You're dealing with hitting a five-iron into a thirty-foot circle," Phil Mickelson noted. Add up the problems: The hole plays just under 440 yards; the fairway slopes from right to left, making for a testy sidehill lie on the approach; the green is elevated, severely crowned and guarded front-left by a yawning bunker. The golfer faces an interesting decision off the tee of the dogleg-left hole. The safest route is to play out to the right and have an open angle into the green. But the hole plays significantly longer from that side. Or you can aim down the left side and cut off some distance, but you'll have to carry the greenside bunker into the green. Left of the green is jail; missing right is relatively safe.

6

Par 3 204 Yards

The long and difficult sixth hole combined with the treacherous fifth might well be the toughest back-to-back holes on the course. Golfers trudge up from the fifth green, likely having been dealt a bogey or worse, and now are faced with pulling a long iron or fairway wood from the bag and drilling it toward a well-guarded green. And generally you're hitting into the prevailing wind. Ross left the opening of the green unfettered to allow run-up shots, but as golf courses in general and No. 2 have gotten softer over the years, a swale in front of the green essentially mandates a full carry to the putting surface. Golfers erring to the left or right with their tee shots will find bunkers on either side of the putting surface. The bunker on the left side was significantly rebuilt in 2010-11 to match photos from the early 1900s.

Par 4 402 Yards

The dogleg right seventh underwent the most significant changes of any hole during the 2010-11 restoration. The previous version offered two options: the longest hitters could bomb their tee shots over the bunker complex in the right corner of the turn; everyone else had to lay up short of the fairway neck between those bunkers on the right and thick rough on the left—the fairway measuring only a dozen yards across at its narrowest point. Now there are more bunkers in the right corner—seven compared to five—and they are deeper, and one has a menacingly high back wall. But they are set farther to the right, giving players more room to hit a standard driver shot but not have to carry the bunkers. The hole now offers options for every level of player. The fairway falls off on the left side to a wasteland of hardpan sand and wire grass.

Par 5 469 Yards

P layed as a par-five for resort and member play, the eighth offers the rare opportunity on No. 2 for a birdie or less. Played as a par-four in professional competition, it's a difficult hole—extracting an average of 4.5 shots from the field in the 1999 U.S. Open and 4.3 shots in 2005. A good tee shot will get some fuel from the slope of the fairway and leave a second shot from two hundred yards or so out. Anything missing the green left or long, however, is purgatory. From the left side, John Daly twice missed hitting the green with his putter in 1999. Hole locations in the back portion of the green are sucker plays—get too aggressive and the ball will finish down a steep slope behind the putting surface. An up-and-down from there is next to impossible.

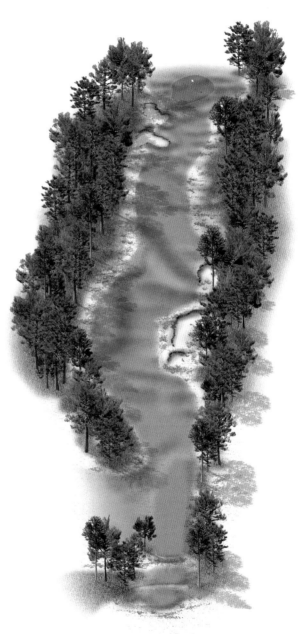

Par 3 174 Yards

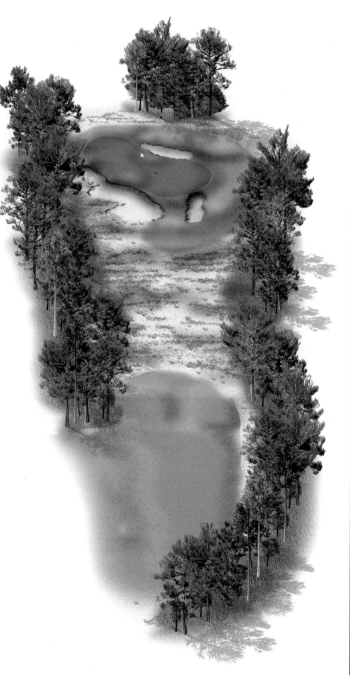

This par-three is the shortest hole on No. 2 but it offers one of the best hole locations on the entire golf course—the front-left corner just beyond the expansive, gnarly bunker on that side. It might require only a seven-iron, but the distance has to be perfect. If your tee shot is short, you'll be playing from the bunker. If it's long, the ball can roll down a severe slope behind the green into hardpan and then underbrush. A tee shot to a right-side flag must have enough juice as well; there's a sharp fall-off in front of the green that will funnel poorly judged or under-struck shots back down the hill toward the tee. The par-threes on No. 2 have excellent diversity and each runs in a different direction, giving the player a taste of every wind variable on a given day. This one provides an interesting contrast from the brutish sixth.

10 Par 5 580 Yards

Tiger Woods was hole-high in two shots on this mammoth par-five in the 1999 Open, just going to show you there are almost no defenses against modern technology and length. For mere mortals, however, this is an interesting and solid hole. Position off the tee is important as the right side of the fairway offers the best angle for the second shot. The player who can draw the ball can play his second shot down the right side of the fairway—away from a bunker on the left—and let it curve back toward the green as it settles toward land. That left-side bunker is about a hundred yards from the green; avoid it at all costs because a full wedge from a deep bunker is not an easy shot. There's plenty of movement in the fairway from a hundred yards in, adding a twist to your approach to the green.

Par 4 439 Yards

The eleventh hole perhaps more than any other provides a template for the 2010-11 restoration by Bill Coore and Ben Crenshaw. The hole bends slightly from left-to-right and in its original form was a prime example of Ross working the angles. The fairway appeared wide from the tee, but the good player would note the hole location from the tee and attempt to place his drive on the side of the fairway opposite the side of the hole. If the pin was on the right side of the green, it was easier to fire an iron shot from the left side of the fairway. If the pin was on the left, the green was more open from the right portion of the short grass. Much of that strategy was lost as the fairways narrowed to fewer than twenty-five yards across throughout the 1990s and early 2000s. Now there is room to play and to work the angles as Ross intended. The green appears to slope markedly from left to right, but in truth the two bunkers on the left side get much more play because the green can reflect shots landing on the left portion into the bunkers.

Par 4 418 Yards

A new tee added thirty-two yards to this hole for the 1999 U.S. Open and the hole required an average of 4.39 shots, but the twelfth doesn't play as severely during normal conditions. The fairway resembles the tenth in that there's plenty of movement to the ground; the trough running across from 125 yards away from the green can provide a funky lie. This hole unfolds like the second in that the left side of the fairway affords the best angle into the green. The right side is fraught with two bunkers and more hardpan sand and wire grass. The front portion of the green has plenty of movement. The left third portion will funnel many shots landing there into a chipping area to the left of the putting surface. The right two-thirds will reflect approaches to the right, some of them all the way into the bunker front-right.

Par 4 375 Yards

Donald Ross often designed golf courses and holes backwards—that is, he found the best and most natural looking sites for greens and then built the holes and connected the dots from there. At Pinehurst, he found a ridge at 625 to 630 feet above sea level with ground to one side some fifteen to twenty feet below it and deemed it an ideal spot for a green—ergo the putting surface to the par-four thirteenth. This is a relatively short hole, but the starkly elevated green has given golfers fits since the early days. Hole locations tucked to the left or right extremes of the green are particularly challenging as they sit behind a set of foreboding bunkers; only thirty-seven percent of the field hit the green in the third round of the 2005 U.S Open because the hole was only five paces from the right edge and nine from the front.

Par 4 375 Yards

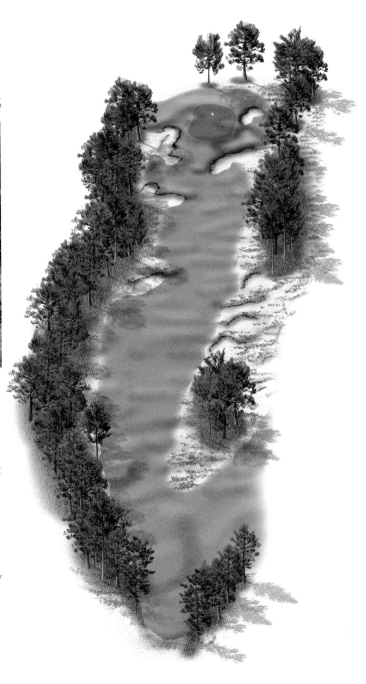

Plenty of length and a narrow green make this one of the most difficult par-fours on the course. The right side of the fairway shares with the thirteenth a vast expanse of bunkers, hardpan sand and wire grass that was restored in 2010-11, and the left side is clipped by a bunker that protrudes into the fairway. Golfers are often fooled by the placement of the bunker to the front-right of the green; it looks to be snuggled up to the putting surface but is actually twenty yards short. Over the green is one place you don't want to be; the slopes are severe to the rear, and the ball can take off and run forty yards into the trees bordering the tenth fairway. The easier recovery shot is to the left of the green; miss to that side and you can still putt the ball. Miss to the right side, however, and your fate is a series of deep hollows.

Par 3 183 Yards

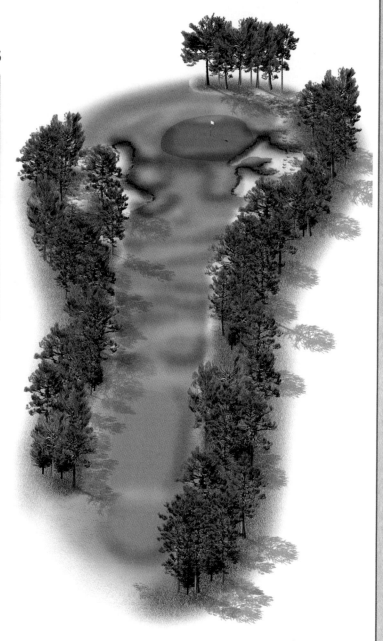

Long iron to a tiny green—it doesn't get much more difficult than that. The fifteenth green embodies the "tortoise-backed" shape perhaps better than any other green on No. 2. The high point is slightly to the front half of the green, and the putting surface gradually slopes off in every direction. It doesn't matter which area of the perimeter your tee shot lands; the ball will trickle down into one of the dips and hollows bordering the green. A ball that hits dead center or beyond is likely to be thrown by the tilt of the green off the back edge. The 2010-11 restoration included the extension of the right side of the green to provide an additional hole location. No. 15 is similar to the par-three sixth in that the green-front is open, but a swale running across tends to trap many shots running along the ground.

16

Par 5 511 Yards

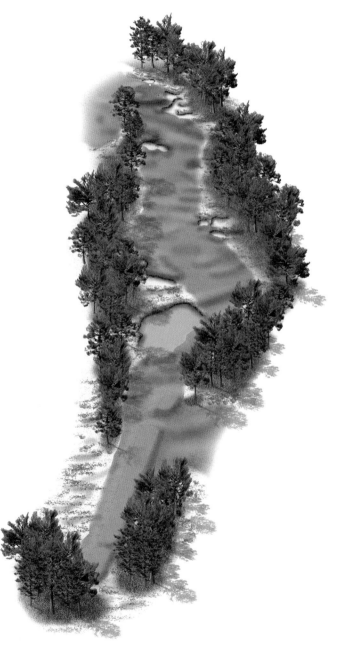

This hole features No. 2's lone water hazard, which is there more by default than as a strategic feature of the design. There was a depression in the area in front of the tee that simply would not drain very well, and it looked unsightly. So Ross filled it in with water to make it look less scraggly. But the pond has nothing to do with playing the hole. The second shot demands as much skill and strategy as any juncture on the course. With a good drive, many players can reach the green in two, but it has to be a perfect shot because the green sits on a rise and deflects run-up shots. If you miss your shot and find one of the bunkers around the green, the recovery shot could be far more difficult than having played safe and being left with a wedge from eighty or ninety yards. The sixteenth played as a par-four from 489 yards during the 1999 and 2005 U.S. Opens, and a few additional yards have been added for 2014.

Par 3 186 Yards

The final par-three on the course runs through a funnel of pine trees, and late in the afternoon the shadows and sunlight from the right make for a memorable setting. Then you have to figure out how to play the hole. A five-to-seven iron will do the trick for most golfers. The prevailing wind is from the right after you have played the sixth into the wind, the ninth with the wind, and the fifteenth with it coming from left-to-right. Any shot aimed center to left-of-center can get a boost from the wind and wind up in the bunker to the left. One of the course's most severe bunkers stretches across the front of the green. Underclub and land in the bunker and you'll have a difficult recovery shot with the putting surface above your head. Coore & Crenshaw extended and flattened the front portion of the green in 2010-11 to add a hole location to an area that had been too severe for a pin.

Par 4 415 Yards

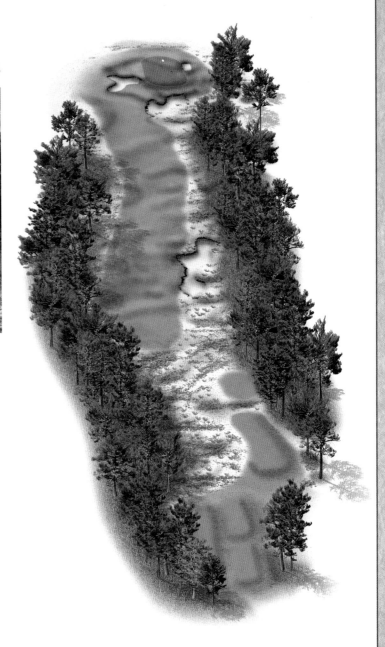

The eighteenth is one of the finest and most difficult finishing holes in golf. It's consistent with the design of No. 2 in that angles are very important, but it's unique in the framework of the course in that it is the only hole that plays uphill from tee to landing area and then to the green—and it runs into the prevailing wind. The fairway looks plenty wide from the tee but the margin is much smaller in reality; by far the better position is the right side of the fairway. To get there, however, you have to challenge a long, deep bunker that runs along the fairway. There's plenty of wire grass in that bunker, making it play even more difficult. It's a harder approach shot from the left side because you have to play across one bunker to a green angled against you from a slightly sidehill lie.

This 210-yard par-three on course No. 1 is one of the most difficult one-shot holes at Pinehurst. It was the eleventh until the 2012 addition of a new ninth hole bumped this hole up to the twelfth. A hole in this location with the water hazard has been a part of the Pinehurst golf scene since 1900.

PINEHURST COUNTRY CLUB

Course No. 1

NO.	PAR	YDS.	HCP.				
1	4	386	3				
2	4	397	1				
3	4	349	9				
4	5	462	17				
5	3	170	11				
6	4	370	5				
7	3	165	15				
8	4	359	13				
9	3	148	7				
OUT	35	2,806					
10	4	367	2				
11	4	405	10				
12	3	220	6				
13	4	407	12				
14	4	332	8				
15	4	349	4				
16	4	387	16				
17	4	327	18				
18	4	423	14				
IN	35	3,217		IN			
				OUT			
				GROSS			
TOTAL	70	6,023		H'D'P			
				NET			
Date							

LENGTH OF THIS CARD IS STYMIE MEASURE

No.1

THE GOLDEN AGE OF PINEHURST

The No. 1 course goes back to the beginnings of the game in the late-1800s at Pinehurst. The course has at least two holes and one water hazard directly linked to opening of No. 1 in 1899—the pond fronting the tee of the par-three hole known for years as the eleventh and the stream in front of the hole known as the twelfth tee are shown on course maps from 1900.

"No. 1 is like a history lesson," says Don Sweeting, Pinehurst's EVP for golf and club operations. "It's a classic design; it takes you back to the very beginning with Donald Ross. You see how he designed a course as a young man. All of the features are right in front of the golfer. You can see the hole and know exactly how to play it."

The course that exists today is routed in the same general vicinity as the original eighteen-hole layout. Early holes on course No. 1 were abandoned by Ross to area now made up of the first and eighteenth holes of No. 2, and the original first, second and eighteenth of No. 1 were deleted in 1913 to allow for construction of "Maniac Hill," the resort's practice range.

Ross rebuilt the course in 1939 and completely changed seven holes. "No. 1 is proving about as popular as No. 3 this year," Richard Tufts said. "Some people claim it makes the best course now."

Two significant changes were in the planning and execution stages for the spring and summer of 2012.

First, the par-three eighteenth hole was abandoned to allow for expansion of the short-game practice area to the south side of the clubhouse. A new par-three was designed by Bill Coore and inserted in a kite-shaped patch of woods between the eighth through eleventh holes. Golfers now play the par-four eighth hole and then play a hole measuring approximately 145 yards from the blue tees as the new ninth. The old ninth becomes the tenth and so on through the back nine. The course now concludes on the old par-five seventeenth—the new eighteenth.

Coore, who along with partner Ben Crenshaw coordinated the restoration of No. 2 from 2010-11, designed the new hole on follow-up visits to Pinehurst in the winter and spring of 2012.

"Bill designed the new hole as he does all of his work—meticulously and with a lot of thought," says Sweeting. "He walked the course twice to get the feel and character of the course and designed a hole that would fit naturally."

And second, the Penn G2 bentgrass that had been on the greens since 1998 was replaced with MiniVerde ultra dwarf Bermuda, representing Pinehurst's initial foray into the world of the next generation of putting surfaces. Bermuda was a dominant strain for southern greens for decades until the development in the 1990s of bent grasses that could remain healthy and provide fast and smooth putting surfaces in the summer. Now the story has come full circle, and many superintendents have found excellent results with the new Bermudas. If the conversion is as successful as hoped, the resort could make similar changes to its other courses over time.

"Our summers have changed a great deal over the last twenty years," says Bob Farren, Pinehurst's director of grounds and golf course management. "We have more full-time residents and members who play golf twelve months a year. The hotel has more golfers in the summer than ever. The new Bermudas handle that demand very well."

The greens conversion and new hole construction were planned between mid-July and mid-September 2012.

The course measures just under 6,100 yards and doesn't require a lot of power. But it does test every other component of your game—accuracy off the tee, course management and the ability to create recovery shots around the small greens. No. 1 is now maintained similar to course 2—no overseeding to promote firm and fast fairways and little or no rough.

The tiny first green of course No. 3 lays down the gauntlet: This is the most target-oriented course at Pinehurst. The greens average less than five thousand square feet each and most are elevated—with slopes from gentle to severe falling off around the putting surfaces.

PINEHURST COUNTRY CLUB

Course No. 3

NO.	PAR	YDS.	HCP.		
1	4	288	17		
2	4	350	9		
3	4	336	7		
4	4	388	1		
5	4	391	3		
6	4	351	5		
7	3	148	11		
8	4	291	15		
9	3	148	13		
OUT	34	2,691			
10	4	376	2		
11	4	327	8		
12	4	342	4		
13	5	494	16		
14	3	196	6		
15	5	434	18		
16	3	187	12		
17	4	317	14		
18	4	314	10		
IN	36	2,987		IN	
				OUT	
				GROSS	
TOTAL	70	5,678		H'D'P	
				NET	
Date					

LENGTH OF THIS CARD IS STYMIE MEASURE

No.3

THE GOLDEN AGE OF PINEHURST

Jay Harris has been a member at Pinehurst Country Club since 1996 and played in the North and South Amateur often in the 1960s. At the height of his game as a scratch golfer, he loved nothing better than to tee it up from the tips on No. 2 against top-flight competition.

But he has a suggestion.

"Trying taking your woods out of the bag one day and go play No. 3," he says. "Try it. You've got a challenge on your hands. Hitting those knobby little greens is not easy."

Fellow member Les Fleisher agrees. He's seen any number of long-knocking limberbacks struggle on a course that measures under 6,000 yards and has postage-stamp size greens.

"Length is not an issue, but No. 3 is a shot-maker's course," says Fleisher. "You need to be able to work the ball. If you can't work it, you can get frustrated out there. It's the most target-oriented course of any at Pinehurst. There are some blind shots, and the greens are tiny targets and they're quite undulating. If you hit it off-line, No. 3 can play games with your mind. The course appeals to older players—not just because it's shorter, but they can invent shots and play the finesse shots the course demands."

Ben Crenshaw played courses 1 and 3 in the 1970s when the PGA Tour came to Pinehurst and both layouts made an impression.

"Courses 1 and 3 are wonderful golf courses," Crenshaw says. "They have some marvelous holes, little holes only 320 to 380 yards. I just don't think people understand how good those holes are. They're filled with interest. They're shorter, but there's plenty of character to them."

No. 3 is the shortest of the eight courses at Pinehurst, measuring just 5,682 yards from the back tees. So it's not overrun with visiting golfers with mid-to-low handicaps. It is, however, full day after day with folks getting along in life who hit their drives two hundred yards or less. There are nine par-fours playing three-fifty or less, allowing the short hitters to hit some mid-irons into greens.

The greens complexes are the most similar to those on No. 2 as any other Pinehurst course. The greens measure about 4,500 square feet each, somewhat smaller than those on No. 2, and most are elevated, with slopes from gentle to severe falling off around the putting surfaces.

The course is an excellent complement to the more difficult courses. You can play eighteen holes in three hours or less, and it puts a premium on approach-shot accuracy more than any course at Pinehurst. It's a stiff challenge from a hundred yards in.

"No. 3 is about four hundred yards shorter than No. 1, but it's actually a more difficult scoring course because of the difficulty of the greens," says Don Sweeting, Pinehurst's EVP for golf and club operations. "The greens are more like those on No. 2 than any other course we have."

No. 3 opened in 1910, and *The Pinehurst Outlook* was quick to hail this new work of Donald Ross. The course is "almost as popular as the No. 2 course, and in another year or so will, without question, be the finest course at Pinehurst. The general topography of the ground is decidedly of a more rolling character than the other two courses, and Donald Ross has shown excellent judgment in laying out the holes," the newspaper said.

Many of the holes exist as they did originally, though some with different numbers. Some holes were lost to course No. 5 upon its opening in 1961. The first hole is on the site of the old tennis courts and the current second hole used to be the first on No. 3—only it ran in the opposite direction. Water comes into play on only one hole. There's a pond on the 145-yard seventh that sits between the green and tee, requiring a full carry to safety. That hole was the fourteenth on No. 3 in the early days.

Another tie to the past between courses 1, 2 and 3 is that none are overseeded in the winter—the better to promote taut playing surfaces—and rough is limited on 1 and 3 and completely banished from No. 2.

British-style pot bunkers dot the landscape of the par-four fifteenth on No. 4. Tom Fazio and associate Tom Marzolf drew on the bunker style of Donald Ross's native Dornoch for the bunkers, most of them with ground shaped around the hazard to swallow an errant shot.

PINEHURST COUNTRY CLUB
Course No. 4

NO.	PAR	YDS.	HCP.			
1	4	402	7			
2	5	495	15			
3	4	428	3			
4	3	197	11			
5	4	450	1			
6	3	182	17			
7	4	445	5			
8	4	406	9			
9	5	522	13			
OUT	36	3,527				
10	4	400	10			
11	4	451	6			
12	3	210	18			
13	5	510	8			
14	3	229	12			
15	4	381	4			
16	4	405	14			
17	5	548	16			
18	4	456	2			
IN	36	3,590		IN		
				OUT		
				GROSS		
TOTAL	72	7,117		H'D'P		
				NET		
Date						

LENGTH OF THIS CARD IS STYMIE MEASURE

No.4

THE GOLDEN AGE OF PINEHURST

The timeline of Pinehurst No. 4 over nearly seventy years underscores the reasons why Pinehurst management arrived at a bold decision in the late-1990s.

1919 – Original Donald Ross layout opens.
1936 – Difficult economic times force closing of nine holes.
1939 – Remaining nine holes closed.
1950 – Nine new holes open, designed by Richard Tufts.
1953 – New eighteen-hole routing completed.
1973 – Course lengthened and renovated by Robert Trent Jones in preparation for World Open on PGA Tour.
1983 – Rees Jones rebuilds greens to accommodate longer shots instituted by his father a decade earlier.

The result was a soup kettle of Ross, Tufts and the Jones family.

"It had become a hybrid of designers and ideas with no thread to tie it all together," Pat Corso, Pinehurst's president and CEO from 1987 to 2004, said in 1998.

"Right now, No. 4 is just a golf course," Tom Fazio added. "It's not a Donald Ross, it's not a Trent Jones, it's nobody's. It just evolved. The opportunity is here to start over and create an outstanding golf course."

Fazio Golf Course Designers were retained a year ahead of the 1999 U.S. Open to take the land occupied by No. 4 and turn it into a blank canvas. Start over from scratch. And time the project so that part of the property could be used for the corporate entertainment village for the 1999 Open with the holes completed immediately after the event.

"We were told to start the golf course and stop it at the same location, but that's the only constraint," says Tom Marzolf, a design associate of Fazio's. "We came out and walked the site and said, 'What if there were no holes here? What could you do? What is the best golf experience to be found out there?' It's a great site, there are no limitations on money, it's at Pinehurst, in the sand, and we've got time to do it and do it right. What's missing? The only thing it won't have is some cliffs and the Pacific Ocean."

Fazio, Marzolf and their associates began brainstorming when first awarded the job about touches the new course could have. They wanted to embrace Pinehurst's history. They wanted to underline Fazio's long-time involvement with the resort, from building No. 6 in the 1970s to No. 8 in the mid-1990s. And they wanted to acknowledge that right next door was one of the finest courses in the world.

The result, the designer proclaimed, was "Tom Fazio's Tribute to Pinehurst."

"It's been a challenge and a thrill to design golf courses within a driver and a couple of three-woods of No. 2 in recent years," Fazio said when construction began. "Now we're doing one just a sand wedge away. It's a major responsibility and a major challenge."

The course features some of the tortoise-backed greens in the tradition of No. 2, dozens of British-style pot bunkers and fifteen acres of exposed sandy areas. A three-and-a-half-acre lake and an adjunct half-acre pond are fixtures in the interior of the new course and add considerable visual impact.

The course opened in 1999 and has been consistently ranked among the top fifteen in the state of North Carolina. Having it as a companion course to No. 2 for stroke-play qualifying was one reason Pinehurst was awarded the 2008 U.S. Amateur.

"If someone calls me and wants to get on at Pinehurst, No. 4 is the toughest," says Don Padgett II, president and COO at Pinehurst. "The members love the golf course. It's the prettiest course we have playing out of the main clubhouse. It's popular with resort guests. And if you play it from the white or green tees, it's not as severe as No. 2."

PINEHURST COUNTRY CLUB
Course No. 5

NO.	PAR	YDS.	HCP.			
1	4	391	9			
2	4	412	3			
3	5	484	13			
4	4	393	11			
5	4	428	7			
6	3	168	17			
7	4	407	5			
8	4	374	15			
9	4	434	1			
OUT	36	3,491				
10	4	381	6			
11	4	369	4			
12	4	386	12			
13	3	185	16			
14	5	523	14			
15	3	188	10			
16	4	437	2			
17	5	504	18			
18	4	384	8			
IN	36	3,357		IN		
				OUT		
				GROSS		
TOTAL	72	6,848		H'D'P		
				NET		
Date						

LENGTH OF THIS CARD IS STYMIE MEASURE

The par-three fifteenth on No. 5 is known as the "Cathedral Hole," so named for the majestic pines that encircle the greens, resembling organ pipes in a church. This hole was originally the sixth hole on No. 3 before architect Ellis Maples retooled that course and built a new No. 5 in 1961.

No.5

THE GOLDEN AGE OF PINEHURST

mong the assorted memorabilia Dan Maples proudly displays in his Pinehurst office is a 1950 poster announcing a golf exhibition at Raleigh Country Club with tour pros Sam Snead and Lloyd Mangrum facing club pros Ellis Maples and Orville White. This was when Ellis, the son of former Pinehurst green keeper and course construction chief Frank Maples, was plying his trade as an amalgam of pro, builder, superintendent and designer before focusing full-time on golf architecture.

"Daddy was a super player, a super teacher," Dan says. "He once shot a 62 at Raleigh Country Club. He shot a 68 on No. 2 in 1930 back when it played long, when you were hitting woods and long-irons into greens. That's why his golf courses were so good. He brought such a great all-around foundation in the game to his work."

Pinehurst No. 5 is often overshadowed by the names of Donald Ross and Tom Fazio, the architects of four of the five courses emanating from the main clubhouse. But Ellis Maples' design appeals to a variety of golfers—it doesn't carry the surcharge of courses 2 and 4 and, at more than 6,800 yards from the gold tees, appeals to the lower-handicap player more than 1 and 3.

"No. 5 has flown under the radar, probably because Donald Ross's name isn't on it," says Les Fleisher, a Pinehurst Country Club member. "That's a shame. It doesn't get the respect it deserves. The scores in North and South Seniors and any of the men's golf association events are always higher on No. 5. There are some strong holes out there. It's a good challenge, there are a lot of risk-reward holes."

No. 5 opened in 1961 when Richard Tufts hired Maples to expand the club's inventory of golf on the west side of Hwy. 5. Course No. 3 had been there since 1910.

With the land available for the new course, it was impractical to restrict a course to making a ring around the perimeter of the existing No. 3 course. So Maples took the southernmost holes on No. 3, built new holes and made that course No. 5. He took the northern side of No. 3 and added it to new holes and that became No. 3. The "Cathedral Hole," for example—so named because the tall pines framing the greens resemble an organ's pipes—was the sixth on No. 3 and became the fifteenth on No. 5.

The resulting course had plenty of length, five water hazards and some tight out-of-bounds markers as well—thanks to the rows of condominiums built in the Diamondhead era of the 1970s. It was renovated in 1998 to replace the old Penncross bent greens with Penn G2. A new set of tees was built for ladies, seniors and beginners, measuring 5,248 yards.

One other noticeable change was the repositioning of the green on the par-four eleventh hole closer to the water hazard fronting the green. Previously the hole was 395 yards from the men's tees and required a long and difficult approach over a pond to an elevated green. The hole now plays 334 yards from the men's tees.

Some greens were redesigned to better accept approach shots, and several bunkers that had been largely out of play were repositioned. The green of the par-five seventeenth hole was moved approximately thirty yards to the left to allow it to get better sunlight. Many cart paths were relocated for convenience, safety and aesthetics.

"Ellis emulated the work of Donald Ross, and No. 5 has a nice classic feel to it," says Don Sweeting, Pinehurst's EVP for golf and club operations. "Like Ross, he used the land so well. It's challenging but fair, there are no gimmicks. Seniors enjoy it because it's around 6,200 yards from the men's tees, but it appeals to the better player because you can stretch it out to more than 6,800 yards. There's something for everyone at No. 5."

NO.	PAR	YDS.	HCP.									
1	4	441	1									
2	5	537	5									
3	3	198	17									
4	4	402	7									
5	4	415	9									
6	5	515	15									
7	3	213	13									
8	4	385	11									
9	4	441	3									
OUT	36	3,547										
10	4	437	2									
11	4	417	6									
12	4	413	8									
13	3	212	16									
14	4	391	10									
15	5	499	14									
16	3	225	18									
17	4	415	12									
18	4	436	4									
IN	36	3,443										
TOTAL	72	6,990										

PINEHURST COUNTRY CLUB

Course No. 6

IN
OUT
GROSS
H'D'P
NET

Date

LENGTH OF THIS CARD IS STYMIE MEASURE

The rugged No. 6 course opened in 1979 and was the first built away from the core Pinehurst campus. The tenth was originally a par-five but was rebuilt in 2004 and shortened into a par-four, the green being moved forward and requiring an uphill approach with a long iron or fairway wood.

No.6

THE GOLDEN AGE OF PINEHURST

om Marzolf visited Pinehurst as a junior golfer from Ohio frequently in the 1970s and watched with interest as the resort added its first new course away from the central resort campus in the late-1970s. That's when George and Tom Fazio built No. 6 on a rugged and hilly site about three miles northeast of the Village of Pinehurst.

The job was important for the Fazios—George, a former tour pro now designing golf courses, and Tom, his nephew who began building George's designs as a teenager. They were trying to get established as a firm in the throes of the 1970s recession, and to get a job from Pinehurst was a significant boost to the future of a firm that soon would be run by Tom.

"We were a struggling business trying to get known and get recognition," Fazio says. "No. 6 coming along when it did was a dream come true. It was the biggest piece of cheese we'd ever thought about. It had amazing potential."

The Fazios were actually given a routing that had been done by a local land planner; they took that plan and designed a golf course within the corridors allowed. The result that opened in 1979 was something totally different for Pinehurst—dramatic topographical movements and holes weaving around and over four lakes.

By the early 1980s, Marzolf was studying landscape architecture at Virginia Tech with plans to become a golf course architect. For his fifth-year thesis in 1983, he acquired the original land plan from the Fazios and designed a new course—a stadium-course concept in the mold of the Tournament Players Clubs that were the trend of the day.

"That thesis helped me get my foot in the door," Marzolf says. "Tom hired me out of college in 1983, and I've been with him ever since."

So it was with considerable interest that Pinehurst officials asked Fazio Golf Course Designers in 2004 to engineer a major facelift of No. 6—with Marzolf coming full circle to lead the project. All of the greens were rebuilt and resurfaced, bunkers were moved to accommodate modern equipment, fairway grades were altered, some new tees were constructed. The tenth hole was converted from a par-five to a par-four to alleviate an unfair landing area between two lakes tightly pinched together.

The golf course is part of a residential community that has grown into maturity over nearly three decades. Residents at No. 6 enjoy having a course in their backyard and are fiercely loyal to their course. The facility has a driving range and putting green, and a short-game practice area was built in 1998.

"No. 6 was twenty-five years old, so it was time for some work," says Marzolf. "It was a function of modernizing the golf course and correcting a few problems that were the result of the original land plan and a limited construction budget. We are really proud of the finished product.

"Needless to say, that golf course is close to my heart. It helped me get my start in the business."

No. 6 set the tone for the evolution of golf beyond the central core of the club and resort. Courses 7 and 8 followed over the next two decades on land similarly diverse from the gentler slopes near the Village.

"When we came in to do No. 6, I was amazed at the contrast in the land compared with No. 2," Fazio says. "It was a very dramatic site with lots of elevation change. You didn't have the subtleties and the soft flow of No. 2. I welcomed the change. No. 2 is so special I didn't want to do a course and have anyone compare it to No. 2.

"I think it's important in a club like Pinehurst that you vary the golf courses, have different styles so people have options and don't get bored."

NO.	PAR	YDS.	HCP.						
1	5	520	5						
2	4	462	1						
3	4	406	13						
4	4	418	11						
5	3	205	17						
6	4	479	3						
7	4	394	9						
8	5	543	7						
9	3	191	15						
OUT	36	3,618							
10	4	399	6						
11	4	421	10						
12	5	525	4						
13	3	207	16						
14	4	408	8						
15	4	435	14						
16	3	197	18						
17	4	406	2						
18	5	600	12						
IN	36	3,598		IN					
				OUT					
				GROSS					
TOTAL	72	7,216		H'D'P					
				NET					
Date									

PINEHURST COUNTRY CLUB
Course No. 7

LENGTH OF THIS CARD IS STYMIE MEASURE

The par-three sixteenth hole on No. 7 features "Rees's Fingers," a series of elongated strips of sand that were shaped within a vast expanse that runs from tee to green. Golfers must also traverse a number of wetland features that were protected during the mid-1980s design and construction.

No.7

THE GOLDEN AGE OF PINEHURST

**R**ees Jones was in the preliminary stage of designing Pinehurst No. 7 in the mid-1980s when he found three ancient relics of Donald Ross's old work. Amid the pine trees near the old PGA/World Golf Hall of Fame building, where the tee of the par-four fourth hole would be, was one large bunker and two smaller ones that had been part of an old, long-abandoned employees' course.

"It was pretty exciting to find a little piece of history like that," Jones says. "I said, 'Clear this by hand, don't bring any machinery around this bunker.'"

Jones left the bunkers right where they were. The large bunker is just to the right of the championship tee, and there's a pine tree growing through one side of it. Down the fairway, about a hundred yards, are the two smaller bunkers. None have anything to do with playing the current hole, but they survive as testaments to the storied heritage of Ross and the ancient golf holes he built the first half of the 20th century.

Nearly three decades after its opening, No. 7 retains its connections to the history of Pinehurst, offering the finest playing surfaces available and the best ideas of Jones, one of the giants in modern golf course architecture. The course opened in April 1986 and was renovated in 2002 with new putting surfaces, new greens complexes, a revamped bunker configuration and some new tees.

Just as No. 2 evolved over the years and decades under Ross's scrutiny and the evolution of agronomic and golf equipment technology, so too does a course like No. 7.

"I was pretty excited back in the eighties to be asked to do a golf course in Pinehurst," Jones said upon the course's reopening in 2002. "I designed it in one day at my kitchen table. I didn't go to bed until 3 a.m. I think I made everyone pretty happy. To get a plum job like that and have it so well received was a turning point for me.

"We cut the cloth properly the first time around," he continued. "Now we've just gone back and given it the finest putting surfaces available today and improved the contours."

No. 7 is situated on a rugged piece of land about a three-mile automobile drive from the main clubhouse. But it's actually adjacent to No. 2. From the ninth green of No. 2, you can see across the street to the fifteenth tee of No. 7. It has as much mountain feel as any of Pinehurst's courses and includes two dramatic par-threes that require a carry over a natural berm (the thirteenth) and a series of sandy fingers that stretch from tee to green (the sixteenth). There's a lot of hitting down from the tee and then hitting up to greens.

This course and No. 8 have more wetlands than any of the Pinehurst courses, partly because of their natural occurrence on the land and because environmental laws were more restrictive than ever when these courses were built. Jones on No. 7 and Tom Fazio on No. 8 couldn't touch many of the wetlands they encountered. One of the interesting uses of the wetlands on No. 7 occurs on the seventh hole, a short par-four known as "Devil's Gut." The approach shot must carry a broad expanse of marsh.

"I think it's one heck of a golf course," Jones says. "It's a spectacular piece of ground. The golf course fits very naturally, hitting from elevated tees, down into the valleys and back up."

Today Pinehurst No. 7 has matured into one of the most respected golf courses at Pinehurst. The private "club-within-a-club" has some three hundred members, many of them residents within the 393-acre site officially named Fairwoods-On-Seven. The community sold out in 1996 and now only resales are available. No. 7 has its own clubhouse, complete with the Pinehurst trademark copper-covered cupola.

PINEHURST COUNTRY CLUB

Course No. 8

NO.	PAR	YDS.	HCP.		
1	4	361	15		
2	5	559	9		
3	4	386	11		
4	4	464	5		
5	3	149	17		
6	5	604	1		
7	4	370	13		
8	3	238	7		
9	4	441	3		
OUT	36	3,572			
10	4	441	6		
11	5	579	4		
12	4	358	18		
13	3	209	12		
14	4	402	8		
15	3	184	16		
16	4	400	10		
17	5	500	14		
18	4	447	2		
IN	36	3,520		IN	
				OUT	
				GROSS	
TOTAL	72	7,092		H'D'P	
				NET	
Date					

LENGTH OF THIS CARD IS STYMIE MEASURE

The par-three eighth hole on No. 8 requires a full carry over wetlands and is indicative of the variety offered on Tom Fazio's 1996 design—marshes, thick vegetation, stretches of native hardpan sand and wire grass, uphill and downhill shots. "Every hole is different," Fazio says.

No.8

THE GOLDEN AGE OF PINEHURST

Pinehurst No. 8 was conceived in 1994 when Pinehurst's popularity was escalating in the aftermath of two PGA Tour Championships, the 1993 landing of the U.S. Open for 1999, and the hosting of the 1994 U.S. Senior Open. The resort needed more golf as it approached the anniversary of its first century in business.

Its eighth golf course would be called The Centennial Course.

"No. 8 is the crowning glory for us," Pat Corso, the resort president and CEO at the time, said upon the course's opening in 1996. "We considered the various things we could do to celebrate our centennial. We thought of the Jubilee Course at St. Andrews and said, 'Why not build a golf course?' We needed another golf course."

Pinehurst retained the services of Tom Fazio for the job, and Fazio knew he had the makings of a special course the first day he set eyes on the property.

"One thing about golf courses in this region is that there can be a sense of sameness to them because of the land," Fazio says. "The positive here is that there's a lot of variety. I'd like to say it was planned that way. But it's just the way the land fits. It's one of the major plusses of the site.

"The challenge is to have each hole have an individual and unique style and feel. I think we've accomplished that."

As he's speaking one morning in October 1995, Fazio is standing on the seventh fairway of the No. 8 course. Barely a third of the way into a preview tour of the course with Pinehurst officials, Fazio is already running out of adjectives to describe the variety of terrain and features integrated into the course.

Uphill, downhill, sidehill—the topography runs the gamut.

Shots demanding a cut, others a draw; shots that can be bumped into a green, others that must fly to the flag—there's no stereotype anywhere.

Marshes to cross and skirt, thick vegetation lining some fairways, stretches of native hardpan sand and wire grass bordering others—the collection points for wayward shots come in every size and shape through these eighteen holes.

"There's a variety of changes in yardages, visuals, ups-and-downs," Fazio says. "The par-threes are varied. You've got a flat par-five in the second hole and then the sixth is uphill with a strong slope from right to left. There are strong par-fours, easier par-fours.

"The wonderful thing is, you come to every hole and say, 'This is different.'"

The golf marketplace certainly agreed with Fazio. In *Golf Digest's* 2011-12 listing of America's 100 Greatest Public Courses, it was ranked No. 68.

No. 8 is restricted to resort guests alone. With a separate clubhouse located three miles from the main clubhouse, it has a secluded and special feeling all its own. Service is ratcheted up a notch—from the greeters at the bag stand to the locker room attendants.

This unique marriage of nature and challenging golf provides Pinehurst with another important source of pride. The Centennial Course has been named an Audubon Signature Cooperative Sanctuary and is among an elite group of golf courses which serve as models for sound land management practices and natural resource conservation. The essence of the Audubon International program provides for using natural resources, without depleting them, in ways that will support human activity.

"This is what a golf club ought to look like," noted Don Padgett Sr., the Pinehurst director of golf from 1987 to 2002. "This site was left as pristine as possible. The clubhouse facility is perfect—full service but not overdone. It's pure golf. It's not sold as anything else."

Some dates of interest in the evolution of Pinehurst.

1895 James Walker Tufts of Boston begins purchase of a half dozen contiguous tracts of land in "Pine Barrens" area of North Carolina; Holly Inn opens on Dec. 31.

1896 Magnolia Inn opens.

1898 Nine holes of No. 1 Course open; course of 2,561 yards designed by Dr. D. LeRoy Culver of Southern Pines.

1898 First clubhouse.

1899 18 holes of No. 1, length 5,176; construction begins on Carolina Hotel.

1900 Harry Vardon plays four exhibition rounds in Pinehurst. Donald Ross is hired as golf professional.

1901 Nine holes of No. 2, length 1,275 yards. Clubhouse enlarged. Carolina Hotel opens with 250 guest rooms.

1902 James Tufts dies of heart attack in his apartment in Carolina Hotel; only son Leonard inherits Pinehurst.

1903 Nine holes of No. 2 lengthened, 2,750 yards. Clubhouse enlarged.

1907 18 holes of No. 2 completed, length 5,860 yards; Donald Ross designer. Nine holes of No. 3 added, length 2,900 yards.

1910 18 holes of No. 3 open; Donald Ross designer.

1912 Six holes of No. 4 open for practice.

1912 Sculptress Lucy Richards uses "Golf Lad" caricature as model for bronze statuette to be used on sundial outside the Pinehurst Country Club clubhouse. The "Sundial Boy" later becomes the world-famous "Putter Boy."

1913 Five new holes of No. 1 added by Donald Ross. "Maniac Hill" practice range opens. New shop. Pine Crest Inn opens.

1914 Nine holes of No. 4 open.

1917 Ross rebuilds sand/clay greens on No. 2 from square, flat surfaces to allow curvature to the edges and some undulation.

1918 Walter Hagen wins first of three North and South Open titles with 293 total in the first year the event lasted 72 holes.

1919 Eighteen holes of No. 4 completed; Donald Ross designer.

1921 Mid Pines golf course, designed by Donald Ross, opens in November. Inn opens in January, 1922.

1923 Present third and sixth holes of No. 2 replace old third and fourth. Manor Inn opens.

1928 Pine Needles golf course, designed by Donald Ross, and hotel open in January.

1928 Nine holes of No. 5 open (present fourth and fifth of No. 2 were first and ninth holes of No. 5).

1930 Management of Pinehurst passed from Leonard Tufts to his sons— Richard, Albert and James.

1934 Experimental grass greens on first three holes of No. 2.

1935 Grass greens on all of No. 2. Course No. 5 abandoned. Present fourth and fifth holes of No. 2 replace old ninth and 10th.

1936 Grass greens on No. 3. Nine holes of No. 4 abandoned. Denny Shute wins PGA Championship on No. 2 with a 3-and-2 final victory over Jimmy Thomson.

1937 Grass greens on No. 1.

1938 Remaining nine holes of No. 4 abandoned.

1940 Present fifth, sixth and 11th holes of No. 1 replace old 10th and 11th. Ben Hogan wins North and South Open for first professional golf win.

1941 Sam Snead uses an eagle on the par-five 10th hole to help win the first of three North and South Open titles.

1948 Donald Ross Memorial Junior inaugurated following April passing of architect.

1950 Nine holes of No. 4 reopen.

1951 No. 2 lengthened from 6,952 yards to 7,007 for Ryder Cup Matches. North and South Open discontinued following victory by Tommy Bolt and replaced with Men's North and South Senior Amateur.

1953 Second nine holes of No. 4 reopen.

1958 Women's North and South Senior inaugurated.

1959 Jack Nicklaus wins the North and South Amateur, edging Gene Andrews 1-up.

1961 No. 5 course opens; Ellis Maples designer. Son of ex-greens superintendent Frank Maples creates new course on west side of Hwy. 5 by building 18 new holes and parceling holes from No. 3 into two new courses.

1962 No. 2 lengthed to 7,058 yards for U.S. Men's Amateur. Labron Harris Jr. defeats Downing Gray Jr. 1-up for championship.

1970 Pinehurst sold by Tufts family to Diamondhead Corp. (Dec. 31).

1972 Greens on No. 2 changed from Bermuda to bent.

1973 Professional golf returns to Pinehurst for World Open, a 144-hole tournament won by Miller Barber by three strokes over Ben Crenshaw. No. 4 redesigned by Robert Trent Jones to be used with No. 2 for World Open.

1974 World Golf Hall of Fame opens. World Open reduced to 72 holes; Johnny Miller wins tournament in playoff with Jack Nicklaus, Frank Beard and Bob Murphy.

1977 World Open renamed Colgate/Hall of Fame Classic. Hale Irwin shoots 20-under-par 264 to win tournament.

1979 Greens on No. 2 converted from bent to Bermuda. No. 6 course opens; Tom and George Fazio designers.

1980 Colgate drops sponsorship of PGA Tour event; it continues for three years as the Hall of Fame Classic.

1982 Hall of Fame Classic, beset by no title sponsor, no TV and dates opposite college football, discontinued, to be replaced the following year by the Hall of Fame Senior. Greens, tees and bunkers on No. 4 revised by Rees Jones.

1984 Pinehurst acquired in July by ClubCorp of Dallas, Texas, Robert Dedman founder and chairman.

1985 PGA of America purchases World Hall of Fame; name officially changes to PGA/World Golf Hall of Fame.

1986 No. 7 course opens; Rees Jones designer. Patrick A. Corso named chief executive officer of Pinehurst Inc., a position he would hold until February, 2004.

1987 Clubhouse for No. 7 opens. Donald E. Padgett Sr., former president of the PGA of America, named director of golf, a position he would hold until his semi-retirement in the fall of 2002.

1987 Greens on No. 2 converted from Bermuda to bent and rebuilt to USGA specifications.

1988 Pinehurst hosts PGA Club Professional Championship in first official outreach effort in tournament golf under new ownership.

1989 Pinehurst hosts first USGA event in effort to bring championship golf back to Pinehurst when U.S. Women's Amateur contested on No. 2; Vicki Goetze champion.

1990 Pinehurst Conference and Exhibition Center opens in March. Facility costs $5 million and includes 9,600-square-foot Grand Ballroom and 14,000-square-foot Exhibit Hall. Pinehurst Inc. purchases the Manor Inn.

1991 Greens rebuilt, some fairways recontoured on No. 6. "Maniac Hill" practice range rebuilt, resort clubhouse remodeled. PGA Tour returns to Pinehurst for the Tour Championship; Craig Stadler beats Ross Cochran in playoff.

1992 Paul Azinger collects three-shot victory in Tour Championship.

1993 Pinehurst No. 2 awarded U.S. Open for 1999 in June announcement at Open at Baltusrol.

1993 PGA/World Golf Hall of Fame closes for eventual move into new World Golf Village in Florida.

1994 Simon Hobday wins 1994 U.S. Senior Open.

1996 The Centennial Course, Pinehurst No. 8, opens in March, designed by Tom Fazio. In June Pinehurst is named a National Historic Landmark by the U.S. Department of the Interior.

1997 Pinehurst No. 2 reopens after nine-months of renovations, highlighted by greens being rebuilt and planted with Penn G-2 bentgrass. Collars around greens changed from common Bermuda to 419 Bermuda. New tees built for fifth, sixth, ninth and 12th holes.

1997 The Centennial Course, Pinehurst No. 8, hosts its first national championship with the PGA Club Professional Championship.

Event will return to No. 8 again in July, 1998.

1998 Course No. 1 reopens in February after a renovation that includes converting the greens to Penn G-2 bent, reconfiguring bunkers and lengthening several holes. Course measures 6,128 yards following previous count of 5,780 yards.

1998 Course No. 5 reopens in December. Renovation includes converting greens to Penn G-2, repositioning two greens and several bunkers and building new women's tees. New short course of 5,247 yards available.

1999 Holly Inn, purchased in 1997 by Pinehurst Inc., reopens after $14 million renovation.

1999 Course No. 4 closed for complete redesign by Tom Fazio; reopens in December. New Learning Center facility at the top of "Maniac Hill" practice range opens and is named for long-time director of golf Donald E. Padgett.

1999 Payne Stewart makes 15-foot putt on 72nd hole for par, winning U.S. Open over Phil Mickelson by one stroke.

2000 Pinehurst awarded 2005 U.S. Open.

2002 Course No. 7 closes in June and reopens in December following extensive renovation by architect Rees Jones. Green complexes resculpted and putting surfaces planted with Penn G-2 bentgrass. In addition, several tees relocated and bunker configuration totally revamped.

2002 The Spa at Pinehurst opens in April. The $12 million facility includes 31,000 square feet, 28 treatment rooms, lap pool, steam, sauna, whirlpool and exercise room.

2003 Pinehurst awarded 2008 U.S. Amateur. Courses No. 2 and 4 to be used. Course No. 3 renovation completed; greens converted to Penn G-2, marking eighth and final course to have its greens built to USGA specifications with G-2.

2004 Minor renovations to No. 2 initiated looking toward 2005 U.S. Open. Holes four, 11, 12 and 14 to be lengthened, course to measure in excess of 7,300 yards.

2005 New Zealand's Michael Campbell shoots a final-round 69 to edge Tiger Woods by two shots to win the U.S. Open.

2006 Four years following the death of his father, Robert Dedman Jr. sells the family's ClubCorp assets but retains ownership of Pinehurst Resort & Country Club.

2008 Danny Lee beats Drew Kittleson 5-and-4 to win the U.S. Amateur.

2009 USGA announces the 2014 U.S. Open will be held at Pinehurst and that the U.S. Women's Open will be held the following week.

2010 Architects Bill Coore and Ben Crenshaw hired to supervise restoration of No. 2. Work begins in February, course closes from November-March 2011. Greens resodded with A-1/A-4 bent.

1999 U.S. Open

Player	R1	R2	R3	R4	Total	Money
Payne Stewart	68	69	72	70	279	$625,000
Phil Mickelson	67	70	73	70	280	370,000
Vijay Singh	69	70	73	69	281	196,792
Tiger Woods	68	71	72	70	281	196,792
Steve Stricker	70	73	69	73	285	130,655
Tim Herron	69	72	70	75	286	116,935
Hal Sutton	69	70	76	72	287	96,260
Jeff Maggert	71	69	74	73	287	96,260
David Duval	67	70	75	75	287	96,260
Darren Clarke	73	70	74	71	288	78,863
Billy Mayfair	67	72	74	75	288	78,863
Paul Azinger	72	72	75	70	289	67,347
Davis Love III	70	73	74	72	289	67,347
Paul Goydos	67	74	74	74	289	67,347
Colin Montgomerie	72	72	74	72	290	58,215
Justin Leonard	69	75	73	73	290	58,215
Dudley Hart	73	73	76	69	291	46,756
Jim Furyk	69	73	77	72	291	46,756
Jay Haas	74	72	73	72	291	46,756
Jesper Parnevik	71	71	76	73	291	46,756
Scott Verplank	72	73	72	74	291	46,756
John Huston	71	69	75	76	291	46,756
Brian Watts	69	73	77	73	292	33,505
Nick Price	71	74	74	73	292	33,505
Tom Scherrer	72	72	74	74	292	33,505
D.A. Weibring	69	74	74	75	292	33,505
Miguel A. Jimenez	73	70	72	77	292	33,505
David Berganio Jr.	68	77	76	72	293	26,186
Tom Lehman	73	74	73	73	293	26,186
Geoffrey Sisk	71	72	76	75	294	23,805
Bob Estes	70	71	77	76	294	23,805
Stewart Cink	72	74	78	71	295	22,449
Sven Struver	70	76	75	74	295	22,449
Gabriel Hjertstedt	75	72	79	70	296	19,084
Corey Pavin	74	71	78	73	296	19,084
Brad Fabel	69	75	78	74	296	19,084
Craig Parry	69	73	79	75	296	19,084
Steve Pate	70	75	75	76	296	19,084
Carlos Franco	69	77	73	77	296	19,084
Esteban Toledo	70	72	76	78	296	19,084
Rocco Mediate	69	72	76	79	296	19,084
Stephen Allan	71	74	77	75	297	15,068
Len Mattiace	72	75	75	75	297	15,068
Chris Perry	72	74	75	76	297	15,068
Gary Hallberg	74	72	75	76	297	15,068
Lee Janzen	74	73	76	75	298	12,060
David Lebeck	74	70	78	76	298	12,060
Robert Allenby	74	72	76	76	298	12,060
Jim Carter	73	70	78	77	298	12,060
Brandel Chamblee	73	74	74	77	298	12,060
Steve Elkington	71	72	79	77	299	10,305
Chris Tidland	71	75	75	78	299	10,305
Greg Kraft	70	73	82	75	300	9,562
Jason Tyska	72	74	75	79	300	9,562
Spike McRoy	70	74	76	80	300	9,562
Phillip Price	71	73	75	81	300	9,562
Jerry Kelly	73	74	79	75	301	8,840
Tom Watson	75	70	77	79	301	8,840
Kaname Yokoo	68	74	78	81	301	8,840
Tom Kite	74	72	80	76	302	8,460
John Cook	74	73	77	78	302	8,460
Bob Tway	69	77	79	78	303	8,178
Chris Smith	69	77	77	80	303	8,178
Larry Mize	69	75	84	76	304	7,966
a-Hank Kuehne	72	75	81	78	306	---
Bob Burns	71	76	84	77	308	7,755
Ted Tryba	72	75	82	79	308	7,755
John Daly	68	77	81	83	309	7,543

a-Amateur

Player	R1	R2	Total
Andrew Magee	73	75	148
Thomas Bjorn	70	78	148
Stephen Leaney	76	72	148
Chris Zambri	73	75	148
Ben Crenshaw	74	74	148
Scott Hoch	71	77	148
Mathias Gronberg	70	78	148
Nick Faldo	74	74	148
Ernie Els	72	76	148
Bobby Wadkins	75	73	148
Steve Flesch	75	73	148
Jim McGovern	71	77	148
Michael Muehr	74	74	148
Richard Zokol	73	76	149
Lee Westwood	73	76	149
Stuart Appleby	73	76	149
Glen Day	70	79	149
Fred Funk	71	78	149
Peter Baker	75	74	149
Scott Gump	74	75	149
Dennis Zinkon	71	78	149
Jeff Sluman	74	75	149
Sam Torrance	75	74	149
Mike Weir	73	76	149
Omar Uresti	72	77	149
Steve Lowery	74	75	149
Keith Clearwater	73	76	149
Mark O'Meara	71	79	150
Mark Brooks	74	76	150
Olin Browne	73	77	150
Bob Heintz	73	77	150
Mark Slawter	72	78	150
Notah Begay III	74	76	150
Robin Freeman	73	77	150
Fred Couples	73	77	150
Shaun Micheel	73	77	150
Bob Gilder	74	77	151
Gary March	72	79	151
Jay Williamson	73	78	151
Greg Norman	73	78	151
Barry Cheesman	72	79	151
Joey Sindelar	73	78	151
Erik Ciotti	72	79	151
Garrett Willis	77	74	151
Greg Gregory	73	78	151
Jeff Street	76	75	151
Bob Friend	74	77	151
Fuzzy Zoeller	74	77	151
Bradley Hughes	71	80	151
a-Bryce Molder	73	78	151
Per-Ulrik Johansson	75	77	152
Kirk Triplett	71	81	152
Patrik Sjoland	75	77	152
Alberto Ochoa	77	75	152
Curtis Strange	78	74	152
Keith Kulzer	75	77	152
Grant Masson	74	79	153
Jeff Freeman	72	81	153
Chris Riley	74	79	153
a-Andrew Barnes	74	79	153
Jack Nicklaus	78	75	153
Joe Durant	74	79	153
Mark Calcavecchia	79	74	153
Doug Barron	77	77	154
Jumbo Ozaki	80	74	154
Steve Jones	72	82	154
Craig Bowden	75	80	155
Bill Glasson	77	78	155
Jeb Stuart	77	78	155
a-Tom McKnight	72	83	155
a-Matt Kuchar	76	79	155
E.J. Pfister	79	77	156
Ronald Philo Jr.	77	79	156
David Toms	74	82	156
Chad Campbell	74	82	156
Jeff Gallagher	77	80	157
Retief Goosen	75	82	157
Tim Loustalot	79	78	157
Mike Stone	77	80	157
John DiMarco	79	79	158
Scott Fawcett	79	79	158
Jim White	76	83	159
Mark Mielke	78	81	159
Robert Russell	77	82	159
a-Matt Call	81	79	160
Ryan Welborn	82	78	160
Hale Irwin	76		WD
Jose Maria Olazabal	75		WD

2005 U.S. Open

Player	R1	R2	R3	R4	Total	Earnings
Michael Campbell	71	69	71	69	280	$ 1,170,000
Tiger Woods	70	71	72	69	282	700,000
Sergio Garcia	71	69	75	70	285	320,039
Tim Clark	76	69	70	70	285	320,039
Mark Hensby	71	68	72	74	285	320,039
Davis Love III	77	70	70	69	286	187,813
Rocco Mediate	67	74	74	71	286	187,813
Vijay Singh	70	70	74	72	286	187,813
Nick Price	72	71	72	72	287	150,834
Arron Oberholser	76	67	71	73	287	150,834
Bob Estes	70	73	75	70	288	123,857
Corey Pavin	73	72	70	73	288	123,857
Peter Hedblom	77	66	70	75	288	123,857
Retief Goosen	68	70	69	81	288	123,857
Stewart Cink	73	74	73	69	289	88,120
Fred Couples	71	74	74	70	289	88,120
Ernie Els	71	76	72	70	289	88,120
Ryuji Imada	77	68	73	71	289	88,120
John Cook	71	76	70	72	289	88,120
Peter Jacobsen	72	73	69	75	289	88,120
K.J. Choi	69	70	74	76	289	88,120
David Toms	70	72	70	77	289	88,120
Fred Funk	73	71	76	70	290	59,633
Justin Leonard	76	71	70	73	290	59,633
Paul Claxton	72	72	72	74	290	59,633
Kenny Perry	75	70	71	74	290	59,633
Olin Browne	67	71	72	80	290	59,633
a-Matt Every	75	73	73	70	291	44,486
Geoff Ogilvy	72	74	71	74	291	44,486
Jim Furyk	71	70	75	75	291	44,486
Adam Scott	70	71	74	76	291	44,486
Steve Allan	72	69	73	77	291	44,486
Steve Elkington	74	69	79	70	292	35,759
Brandt Jobe	68	73	79	72	292	35,759
Phil Mickelson	69	77	72	74	292	35,759
Bernhard Langer	74	73	71	74	292	35,759
Angel Cabrera	71	73	73	75	292	35,759
Ted Purdy	73	71	73	75	292	35,759
Shigeki Maruyama	71	74	72	75	292	35,759
Tim Herron	74	73	70	75	292	35,759
Lee Westwood	68	72	73	79	292	35,759
Mike Weir	75	72	75	71	293	26,223
Tom Pernice	74	73	73	73	293	26,223
Chad Campbell	77	71	72	73	293	26,223
Peter Lonard	71	74	74	74	293	26,223
Rob Rashell	74	72	73	74	293	26,223
Colin Montgomerie	72	75	72	74	293	26,223
Paul McGinley	76	72	71	74	293	26,223
J.L. Lewis	75	73	76	70	294	20,275
Nick O'Hern	72	71	78	73	294	20,275
Jason Gore	71	67	72	84	294	20,275
Richard Green	72	72	78	73	295	17,667
Soren Kjeldsen	74	71	77	73	295	17,667
Thomas Levet	75	73	73	74	295	17,667
Thomas Bjorn	71	74	75	75	295	17,667
Nick Dougherty	72	74	74	75	295	17,667
Frank Lickliter II	75	73	78	70	296	15,223
a-Ryan Moore	73	75	73	75	296	15,223
J.J. Henry	73	73	76	74	296	15,223
Lee Janzen	74	74	74	74	296	15,223
Tommy Armour III	70	72	79	75	296	15,223
Jonathan Lomas	72	74	75	75	296	15,223
Ian Poulter	77	69	74	76	296	15,223
Steve Jones	69	74	74	79	296	15,223
Keiichiro Fukabori	74	67	75	80	296	15,223
Luke Donald	69	73	74	80	296	15,223
Michael Allen	73	72	77	75	297	13,553
Steve Flesch	72	71	78	76	297	13,553
John Mallinger	74	72	73	78	297	13,553
Bill Glasson	74	73	71	79	297	13,553
Stephen Ames	71	75	76	76	298	12,551
Rory Sabbatini	72	74	76	76	298	12,551
D.J. Brigman	74	73	75	76	298	12,551
J.P. Hayes	77	71	74	76	298	12,551
John Daly	74	72	77	76	299	11.674
Omar Uresti	75	73	75	76	299	11.674
Charles Howell	77	68	73	81	299	11.674
Bob Tway	71	75	79	75	300	11,048
Jeff Maggert	72	75	75	78	300	11,048
Chris Nallen	76	72	78	75	301	10,547
Graeme McDowell	74	74	72	81	301	10,547
Craig Barlow	76	71	76	80	303	10,171
Jerry Kelly	76	71	78	80	305	9,921

Player	R1	R2	Total
Peter Hanson	76	73	149
Shingo Katayama	74	75	149
Robert Allenby	72	77	149
Carlos Franco	74	75	149
Tom Lehman	77	72	149
Robert Karlsson	75	74	149
Zach Johnson	74	75	149
Toro Taniguchi	70	79	149
Euan Walters	76	73	149
Jerry Smith	78	71	149
Derek Brown	75	74	149
John Rollins	75	74	149
Matt Kuchar	75	74	149
Todd Hamilton	75	74	149
Eric Meichtry	75	74	149
Spencer Levin	73	77	150
a-Trip Kuehne	75	75	150
Jose-Filpe Lima	75	75	150
John Merrick	77	73	150
Scott Verplank	76	74	150
Lee Rinker	76	74	150
Troy Kelly	83	67	150
Padraig Harrington	77	74	151
Stephen Gallacher	79	72	151
Ian Leggatt	75	76	151
Eric Axley	81	70	151
Nick Gilliam	76	75	151
David Oh	74	77	151
James Driscoll	76	75	151
Shaun Michael	78	74	152
Stuart Appleby	81	71	152
David Duval	76	76	152
Craig Parry	77	75	152
Jay Haas	82	70	152
Steve Lowery	78	74	152
Steven Conran	77	75	152
Patrick Damron	79	73	152
Kyle Willmann	75	77	152
Miguel Angel Jimenez	79	74	153
Carl Petterson	77	76	153
Bart Bryant	79	74	153
Casey Whittenberg	75	78	153
Clint Jensen	77	76	153
Yong Eun Yang	74	79	153
a-Luke List	82	71	153
Chris DiMarco	71	82	153
Scott Parel	76	77	153
Josh McCumber	73	80	153
Joe Ogilvie	78	75	154
Rich Beem	78	76	154
Brandt Snedeker	79	75	154
Scott McCarron	76	78	154
a-David Denham	77	77	154
Robert Gamez	77	78	155
Scott Gibson	77	78	155
Nick Jones	80	75	155
Len Mattiace	76	79	155
a-Michael Putnam	76	79	155
Franklin Langham	74	81	155
Ben Curtis	76	80	156
Aaron Barber	74	82	156
David Hearn	77	79	156
Simon Dyson	79	78	157
Michael Rulz	79	79	158
a-Lee Williams	79	79	158
Jim Benepe	82	76	158
Rod Pampling	80	79	159
a-Pierre-Henri Soero	83	77	160
Sal Spallone	79	81	160
Wil Collins	82	79	161
Conrad Ray	80	84	164
David Howell	74		WD
Paul Casey	85		WD

Men's North and South Open

Year	Champion	Scores	Runner-up
1902	Alex Ross	75	Donald Ross
1903	Donald Ross	73-74—147	Jack Jolly
1904	Alex Ross	81-71—152*	Jack Hobens
1905	Donald Ross	72-74—146	Alex Ross
1906	Donald Ross	72-74—146	Alex Ross
1907	Alex Ross	73-79—152*	Donald Ross
1908	Alex Ross	72-71—143	Bernard Nichols
1909	Fred McLeod	77-71—148	Gil Nichols
1910	Alex Ross	73-68—141	Gil Nichols
1911	Gil Nichols	68-73—141	Donald Ross
1912	Tom McNamara	75-69—144	Charles "Chick" Evans **
1913	Tom McNamara	74-72—146	Mike Brady
1914	Gil Nichols	73-72—145	J.J. McDermott
1915	Alex Ross	71-75—146	Francis Ouimet **
1916	Jim Barnes	71-73—144	Clarence Hackney
1917	M.J. Brady	67-74—141	Fred McLeod
1918	Walter Hagen	76-72-73-72—293	Emmet French
1919	Jim Barnes	76-75-72-75—298	Mike Brady
1920	Fred McLeod	73-73-72-75—293	Clarence Hackney
			Walter Hagen
1921	Jock Hutchison	144-147—291	Fred McLeod
			George Fotheringham
1922	Pat O'Hara	73-75-72—220	Clarence Hackney
1923	Walter Hagen	70-68-76-75—289	Cyril Walker
1924	Walter Hagen	68-68-74-73—283	Cyril Walker
1925	Macdonald Smith	68-70-70-73—281	Walter Hagen
1926	Bobby Cruickshank	74-71-74-74—293	Arthur Yates **
			Tom Harmon Jr.
			Macdonald Smith
1927	Bobby Cruickshank	68-75-73-69—285	Walter Hagen
1928	Billy Burke	73-69-74-75—291	Tommy Armour
1929	Horton Smith	74-71-67-76—287	Tommy Armour
			Roland Hancock
1930	Paul Runyan	72-77-72-70—291	Frank Walsh
1931	Wiffy Cox	69-74-74-71—288	Joe Turnesa
1932	Johnny Golden	74-69-72-71—286*	Craig Wood
1933	Joe Kirkwood	68-67-70-72—277	Harry Cooper
1934	Henry Picard	69-68-74-72—283	Horton Smith
			Harry Cooper
			George T. Dunlap Jr. **
1935	Paul Runyan	65-71-72-68—276	Felix Serafin
1936	Henry Picard	71-72-73-72—288*	Ray Mangrum
1937	Horton Smith	67-73-77-69—286	Paul Runyan
1938	Vic Ghezzi	68-73-68-70—279	Paul Runyan
1939	Byron Nelson	71-68-70-71—280	Horton Smith
1940	Ben Hogan	66-67-74-70—277	Sam Snead
1941	Sam Snead	69-66-73-69—277	Clayton Heafner
1942	Ben Hogan	67-68-67-69—271	Sam Snead
1943	Bobby Cruickshank	71-72-74-75—292	Joe Kirkwood
1944	Bob Hamilton	73-72-76-71—286	Bobby Cruickshank
1945	Cary Middlecoff	70-69-69-72—280	Denny Shute
1946	Ben Hogan	71-71-70-70—282	Sam Snead
1947	Jim Turnesa	71-66-74-73—284	George Schoux
1948	Toney Penna	72-73-70-70—285	Sam Snead
			Julius Boros **
1949	Sam Snead	68-70-70-66—274	Johnny Bulla
1950	Sam Snead	68-71-66-70—275	Johnny Palmer
1951	Tommy Bolt	71-72-71-69—283	John Barnum

* Won playoff
** Amateur

1994 U.S. Senior Open

Simon Hobday, $145,000	67-67-66-75—274	Gibby Gilbert, $9,070	73-73-68-73—287
Jim Albus, $63,419	66-69-66-74—275	Jimmy Powell, $7,288	70-76-73-69—288
Graham Marsh, $63419	68-68-69-70—275	Dale Douglass, $7,288	72-68-74-74—288
Tom Weiskopf, $30,608	72-66-72-67—277	Jack Kiefer, $6,589	69-75-71-74—289
Tom Wargo, $30,608	69-70-69-70—277	Larry Ziegler, $5,738	71-76-75-68—290
Dave Stockton, $30,608	74-67-68-68—277	a-Johnny Stevens	75-71-74-70—290
Bob Murphy, $21,651	71-70-71-67—279	Larry Mowry, $5,738	72-73-72-73—290
Jay Sigel, $21,651	73-66-70-70—279	Tommy Aycock, $5,738	74-70-73-73—290
Jack Nicklaus, $21,651	69-68-70-72—279	Chi Chi Rodriquez, $5,050	70-76-76-69—291
Isao Aoki, $18,313	69-71-73-67—280	Bill Hall, $5,050	70-76-73-72—291
Lee Trevino, $17,169	69-71-72-69—281	Terry Dill, $5,050	70-74-72-75—291
Ray Floyd, $16,044	69-68-74-71—282	Ben Smith, $5,050	71-73-72-75—291
Dave Eichelberger, $14,280	74-72-69-69—284	Bobby Nichols, $4,292	76-73-75-68—292
Gary Player, $14,280	72-67-73-72—284	Larry Laoretti, $4,292	75-73-76-68—292
Rocky Thompson, $14,280	70-74-69-71—284	Bob Irving, $4,292	76-72-74-70—292
Mike Hill, $12,760	72-68-70-75—285	Charles Coody, $4,292	74-73-73-72—292
Dewitt Weaver, $11,429	74-73-70-69—286	Marion Heck, $4,292	76-70-73-73—292
Jim Ferree, $11,429	71-75-69-71—286	Bill McDonough, $4,292	76-72-71-73—292
Kermit Zarley, $11,429	74-68-71-73—286	Bob E. Smith, $3,690	75-73-74-71—293
Bob Dickson, $9,070	76-73-69-69—287	Jim Dent, $3,690	75-74-70-75—293
Mike Joyce, $9,070	74-73-69-71—287	a-Vinny Giles	71-70-75-77—293
Calvin Peete, $9,070	73-70-72-72—287	Tommy Aaron, $3,164	72-76-72-74—294
Jim Colbert, $9,070	72-74-69-72—287	Bruce Lehnhard, $3,164	75-72-72-75—294

Steve Bull, $3,164	70-72-76-76—294
Jim Stefanich, $3,164	76-72-69-77—294
Tom Shaw, $3,164	69-72-74-69—294
Ray Vanyo, $2,562	72-77-74-72—295
J.C. Snead, $2,562	71-75-75-74—295
Bill Krickham, $2,562	74-75-72-74—295
Bill Lytle, $2,318	72-69-80-75—296
Jack Rule Jr., $2,318	71-73-77-75—296
Jim Collart, $2,230	76-71-79-71—297
a-Robert Housen	76-72-74-75—297
Miller Barber, $2,139	74-75-76-73—298
Dick Howell, $2,139	73-76-75-74—298
Arnold Palmer, $2,139	74-74-73-77—298
Dean Sheetz, $2,051	73-74-76-76—299
Wayne Carey, $2,051	69-73-78-80—299
a-John Reichert	74-74-78-74—300
Mike McGinnis, $2,022	75-73-78-74—300
Gary Wiren, $2,000	75-72-76-79—302
Robert Pfister, $1,978	72-76-79-78—305
Buddy Overholser, $1,945	76-73-79-78—306
Labron Harris, $1,945	72-77-82-75—306

World Open
Colgate-Hall of Fame Classic
Hall of Fame Classic

Year	Champion/Runner-up	Score
1973	Miller Barber (144 holes)	68-74-73-74
		67-73-72-69—570
	Ben Crenshaw	
1974	Johnny Miller *	73-63-73-72—281
	Jack Nicklaus, Frank Beard, Bob Murphy	
1975	Jack Nicklaus *	70-71-70-69—280
	Billy Casper	
1976	Raymond Floyd *	69-67-67-71—274
	Jerry McGee	
1977	Hale Irwin	65-62-69-68—264
	Leonard Thompson	
1978	Tom Watson	72-67-67-71—277
	Hale Irwin, Tom Kite, Howard Twitty	
1979	Tom Watson *	70-68-65-69—272
	Johnny Miller	
1980	Phil Hancock	71-67-67-70—275
	Scott Simpson	
1981	Morris Hatalsky	65-71-68-71—275
	Jerry Pate, D.A. Weibring	
1982	Jay Haas *	70-70-70-66—276
	John Adams	
	* Won Playoff	

1991 Tour Championship

Craig Stadler, $360,000*	68-68-72-71—279
Ross Cochran, $216,000	68-69-71-71—279
John Daly, $138,000	68-76-68-70—282
Bruce Lietzke, $96,000	71-69-72-71—283
Chip Beck, $71,000	72-70-72-71—285
Jim Gallagher Jr. $71,000	71-74-69-71—285
Nolan Henke, $71,000	69-70-74-72—285
Nick Price, $71,000	70-67-75-73—285
Steve Elkington, $60,000	69-75-71-71—286
Ian Baker-Finch, $54,000	68-76-71-72—287
Corey Pavin, $54,000	74-69-72-72—287
Jeff Sluman, $54,000	74-71-69-73—287
Jay Don Blake, $46,467	69-72-74-73—288
Ted Shultz, $46,467	70-71-75-72—288
Billy Andrade, $46,467	73-74-68-73—288
Mark O'Meara, $41,067	72-72-72-73—289
D.A. Weibring, $41,067	71-73-74-71—289
Fred Couples, $41,067	72-73-66-78—289
Davis Love III, $38,800	72-72-75-71—290
Andrew Magee, $38,800	74-72-70-74—290
Scott Hoch, $37,200	69-75-76-71—291
Payne Stewart, $37,200	69-76-75-71—291
Lanny Wadkins, $36,000	74-73-72-73—292
Paul Azinger, $34,800	69-68-78-78—293
Mark Brooks, $34,800	78-72-71-72—293
Rocco Mediate, $33,400	73-74-72-75—294
Steve Pate, $33,400	75-74-71-74—294
John Cook, $32,600	73-71-75-77—296
Tom Purtzer, $32,400	73-72-75-77—297
Mike Hulbert, $32,000	75-75-73-79—302
* Won Playoff	

1992 Tour Championship

Paul Azinger, $360,000	70-66-69-71—276
Lee Janzen, $177,000	70-69-72-68—279
Corey Pavin, $177,000	74-68-69-68—279
Keith Clearwater, $96,000	68-75-72-66—282
Fred Couples, $76,000	73-78-66-66—283
Raymond Floyd, $76,000	72-71-72-69—283
Greg Norman, $59,000	70-70-73-71—284
Duffy Waldorf, $59,000	70-73-70-71—284
Brad Faxon, $59,000	70-71-72-71—284
David Frost, $59,000	69-68-74-73—284
Jay Haas, $59,000	73-66-72-73—284
Dan Forsman, $59,000	71-67-72-74—284
Jeff Sluman, $43,114	73-73-74-65—285
John Cook, $43,114	74-70-73-68—285
Nick Price, $43,114	74-70-72-69—285
Tom Kite, $43,114	73-68-74-70—285
Tom Lehman, $43,114	70-70-73-72—285
Craig Stadler, $43,114	69-71-72-73—285
John Huston, $43,114	70-68-70-77—285
Chip Beck, $38,000	71-70-75-70—286
Bruce Lietzke, $38,000	72-72-72-70—286
Billy Ray Brown, $36,000	72-71-73-72—286
Steve Elkington, $36,000	71-73-71-73—286
David Edwards, $36,000	71-71-72-74—286
Davis Love III, $34,000	68-76-75-72—291
Jim Gallagher Jr., $34,000	73-74-73-71—291
David Peoples, $33,000	75-72-73-73—293
Mark Brooks, $33,000	73-73-72-75—293
Mark O'Meara, $32,400	72-75-76-71—294
Steve Pate, $32,400	71-76-76-72—295

CHAMPIONS OF MAJOR EVENTS IN PINEHURST AREA

1936 PGA Championship: Denny Shute.
1951 Ryder Cup Matches: United States 9.5, Great Britain and Ireland 2.5.
1962 U.S. Men's Amateur: Labron Harris Jr.
1965 Southern Amateur: Billy Joe Patton.
1966 Western Amateur: Jim Weichers.
1971 PGA Club Professional Championship: Sam Snead.
1972 PGA Club Professional Championship: Don Massengale.
1973 PGA Club Professional Championship: Rives McBee.
1974 PGA Club Professional Championship: Roger Watson.
1977 Southern Amateur: Vinny Giles.
1980 U.S. Amateur (Country Club of North Carolina): Hal Sutton.
1980 World Amateur Team Championship: United States won men's and women's competitions.
1982 NCAA Championship: Houston team champion, Billy Ray Brown individual champion.
1983 PGA Senior Hall of Fame Classic: Rod Funseth.
1987 Independent Insurance Agents Junior Golf Classic: Brian Craig.
1988 PGA Club Professional Championship: Robert Boyd.
1989 U.S. Girls Junior Championship (Pine Needles): Brandie Burton.
1989 U.S. Women's Amateur: Vicki Goetze.
1991 PGA Tour Tour Championship: Craig Stadler.

1991 U.S. Senior Women's Amateur (Pine Needles):Phyllis Preuss.
1992 PGA Tour Tour Championship: Paul Azinger.
1992 Independent Insurance Agents Junior Golf Classic (No. 7): Tiger Woods.
1993 Maxfli PGA Junior Championship (No. 4): Pat Perez, boys champion, Erika Hayashida girls champion.
1994 U.S. Senior Open: Simon Hobday.
1995 LPGA Pinewild Women's Championship: Rosie Jones.
1996 U.S. Women's Open (Pine Needles): Annika Sorenstam.
1997 PGA Club Professional Championship (No. 8): Bruce Zabriski.
1998 PGA Club Professional Championship (No. 8): Mike Burke Jr.
1999 U.S. Open Championship (No. 2): Payne Stewart.
2000 U.S. Women's Amateur Public Links (Legacy Golf Links): Catherine Cartwright.
2001 U.S. Women's Open (Pine Needles): Karrie Webb.
2002 U.S. Senior Women's Championship (Mid Pines): Carol Semple Thompson.
2005 U.S. Open Championship: Michael Campbell.
2007 U.S. Women's Open (Pine Needles): Cristie Kerr.
2008 U.S. Men's Amateur (No. 2): Danny Lee.
2010 U.S. Girls Junior (CCNC): Doris Chen.

Low Competitive Scores On No. 2

Year	Name	Score
1973	Gibby Gilbert	62
1973	Tom Watson	62
1977	Hale Irwin	62
1974	Johnny Miller	63
1977	J.C. Snead	63
1978	Hale Irwin	63
1979	Dana Quigley	63
1979	Johnny Miller	63
1973	Ben Crenshaw	64
1977	Leonard Thompson	64
1980	Scott Simpson	64
1980	Fuzzy Zoeller	64
2003	Casey Wittenberg	64
2006	Phillip Mollica	64

Men's North and South Amateur

Year	Champion/Runner-up	Score
1901	George C. Dutton	
	A.J. Wellington	
1902	Charles B. Cory	3-and-1
	E.A. Thomson	
1903	T. Sterling Beckwith	1-up
	John M. Ward	
1904	Walter J. Travis	8-and-7
	Charles B. Cory	
1905	Dr. L. Lee Harban	1-up
	Fred Herreshoff	
1906	Warren K. Wood	2-up
	C.L. Becker	
1907	Allan Lard	12-and-11
	Nathaniel F. Moore	
1908	Allan Lard	5-and-4
	John E. Porter	
1909	James D. Standish Jr.	3-and-2
	C.L. Becker	
1910	Walter J. Travis	5-and-4
	W.R. Tuckerman	
1911	Charles Evans Jr.	6-and-4
	Robert Hunter	
1912	Walter J. Travis	6-and-5
	Henry J. Topping	
1913	Henry J. Topping	1-up, 37
	Hamilton K. Kerr	
1914	Reginald S. Worthington	6-and-5
	Paul E. Gardner	
1915	Fillmore K. Robeson	4-and-2
	Henry J. Topping	
1916	Philip V.G. Carter	5-and-3
	Frank W. Dyer	
1917	Norman H. Maxwell	2-and-1
	William C. Fownes Jr.	
1918	Irving S. Robeson	1-up
	Robert A. Stranahan	
1919	Edward C. Beall	4-and-3
	Frank C. Newton	
1920	Francis D. Ouimet	5-and-4
	Samuel J. Graham	
1921	B.P. Merriman	9-and-8
	Gardiner W. White	
1922	Henry J. Topping	3-and-2
	Fillmore K. Robeson	
1923	Frank C. Newton	6-and-5
	Charles T. Lansing	
1924	Fred W. Knight	1-up
	B.P. Merriman	
1925	Arthur W. Yates	10-and-8
	William C. Fownes Jr.	
1926	Page Hufty	2-and-1
	L.E. Sherrill	
1927	George Voight	4-and-2
	Eugene V. Homans	
1928	George Voight	1-up
	John W. Dawson	
1929	George Voight	9-and-8
	William C. Fownes Jr.	
1930	Eugene V. Homans	3-and-1
	C. Ross Somerville	

Year	Champion/Runner-up	Score
1931	George T. Dunlap Jr.	6-and-5
	Samuel M. Parks Jr.	
1932	M. Pierpont Warner	5-and-3
	John B. Ryerson	
1933	George T. Dunlap Jr.	6-and-5
	Jack Toomer	
1934	George T. Dunlap Jr.	4-and-3
	Richard D. Chapman	
1935	George T. Dunlap Jr.	1-up 38
	Johnny Johnson	
1936	George T. Dunlap Jr.	8-and-7
	A.C. Giles	
1937	Robert W. Dunkelberger	5-and-3
	James T. Hunter	
1938	Frank Strafaci	5-and-4
	George T. Dunlap Jr.	
1939	Frank Strafaci	1-up
	Robert W. Dunkelberger	
1940	George T. Dunlap Jr.	7-and-6
	John B. Ryerson	
1941	S.M. Alexander Jr.	3-and-2
	Frank Strafaci	
1942	George T. Dunlap Jr.	10-and-9
	Powell Crichton	
1943	Harry C. Offutt Jr.	2-and-1
	Ronnie Williams	
1944	Mal Galletta	8-and-6
	George McAllister	
1945	Ed Furgol	6-and-5
	Frank R. Stranahan	
1946	Frank R. Stranahan	6-and-5
	H.S. Covington	
1947	Charles B. Dudley	6-and-5
	Felice Torza	
1948	E. Harvie Ward Jr.	1-up
	Frank R. Stranahan	
1949	Frank R. Stranahan	2-and-1
	E. Harvie Ward Jr.	
1950	William C. Campbell	1-up 37
	Wynsol K. Spencer	
1951	Hobart Manley Jr.	1-up
	Billy Joe Patton	
1952	Frank R. Stranahan	8-and-7
	Frank Strafaci	
1953	William C. Campbell	2-and-1
	Mal Galletta	
1954	Billy Joe Patton	1-up 37
	Alex Welsh	
1955	Donald M. Bisplinghoff	5-and-4
	William C. Campbell	
1956	Hillman Robbins Jr.	1-up
	William Hyndman III	
1957	William C. Campbell	3-and-2
	Hillman Robbins Jr.	
1958	Richard D. Chapman	11-and-10
	Herbert Durham	
1959	Jack Nicklaus	1-up
	Gene Andrews	
1960	Charles B. Smith	5-and-3
	Peter Green	

Year	Champion/Runner-up	Score
1961	William Hyndman III	4-and-3
	Richard D. Chapman	
1962	Billy Joe Patton	7-and-6
	Hobart L. Manley Jr.	
1963	Billy Joe Patton	7-and-6
	Bob Allen	
1964	Dale Morey	3-and-2
	Billy Joe Patton	
1965	Tom Draper	1-up
	Don Allen	
1966	Ward Wettlaufer	4-and-2
	Marion Heck	
1967	William C. Campbell	10-and-9
	William Hyndman III	
1968	Jack Lewis	7-and-6
	William Hyndman III	
1969	Joe Inman	2-and-1
	Lanny Wadkins	
1970	Gary Cowan	5-and-4
	Dale Morey	
1971	Eddie Pearce	5-and-4
	Vinny Giles	
1972	Danny Edwards	3-and-1
	Eddie Pearce	
1973	Mike Ford	1-up, 38
	Bill Harvey	
1974	George Burns III	4-and-2
	Danny Yates	
1975	Curtis Strange	2-up
	George Burns III	
1976	Curtis Strange	6-and-5
	Fred Ridley	
1977	Gary Hallberg	5-and-3
	Mike Donald	
1978	Gary Hallberg	5-and-4
	Hal Sutton	
1979	John McGough	1-up
	Scott Hoch	
1980	Hal Sutton	12-and-10
	Kevin Walsh	
1981	Corey Pavin	11-and-10
	Steve Jones	
1982	Keith Clearwater	2-up
	Jay Sigel	
1983	Bryan Sullivan	8-and-7
	Mike Taylor	
1984	Davis Love III	4-and-3
	John Inman	
1985	Jack Nicklaus II	2-and-1
	Tom McKnight	
1986	Billy Andrade	3-and-2
	Kurt Beck	
1987	Robert Goettlicher	3-and-2
	Billy Andrade	
1988	Uly Grisette	2-up
	Henry Cagigal	
1989	Lee Porter	4-and-3
	Eoghan O'Connell	
1990	Tom Scherrer	1-up
	Tee Davies	

Year	Champion/Runner-up	Score
1991	David Eger	2-and-1
	Tee Burton	
1992	Duane Bock	2-up
	Darrett Brinker	
1993	Kelly Mitchum	3-and-2
	Ron Whittaker	
1994	Mark Slawter	6-and-4
	Kevin Kemp	
1995	Paul Simson	3-and-1
	Jimmy Flippen	
1996	Paul Simson	1-up
	Scott Newton	
1997	Jake Kransteuber	1-up
	Paul Simson	
1998	Tim Jackson *	211
	Chuck Trickle, Danny Green	
1999	James Driscoll	9-and-7
	John Pitt	
2000	David Eger	2-and-1
	Jedd McLuen	
2001	Michael Sims	1-up
	Bryce Molder	
2002	Eric Jorgensen	4-and-3
	Nathan Smith	
2003	Chris Stroud	2-and-1
	Jeff Overton	
2004	Martin Ureta	3-and-2
	Ryan Posey	
2005	Sean Moore	1-up
	Ryan Posey	
2006	Brady Schnell	5-and-4
	Robert Gates	
2007	Phillip Mollica	8-and-6
	Raymond Sheedy IV	
2008	Matt Savage	1-up
	Jamie Lovemark	
2009	David Chung	4-and-3
	Wes Bryan	
2010	Donald Constable	4-and-3
	Kelly Kraft	
2011	Jack Fields	5-and-4
	David Erdy	
2012	Peter Williamson	4-and-3
	Thomas Bradshaw	

* 1998 North and South played 54 holes at stroke play due to scheduling conflicts.

Women's North and South Amateur

Year	Champion	Year	Champion
1903	Myra D. Paterson	1958	Mrs. Philip M. Cudone
1904	Myra D. Paterson	1959	Ann Casey Johnstone
1905	Houghton Dutton	1960	Barbara McIntire
1906	Myra D. Paterson	1961	Barbara McIntire
1907	Molly B. Adams	1962	Clifford Ann Creed
1908	Julia R. Mix	1963	Nancy Roth
1909	Mary Fownes	1964	Phyllis Preuss
1910	Mrs. C.H. Vanderbeck	1965	Barbara McIntire
1911	Louise Elkins	1966	Nancy Roth Syms
1912	Mrs. J. Raymond Price	1967	Phyllis Preuss
1913	Lillian B. Hyde	1968	Alice Dye
1914	Florence L. Harvey	1969	Barbara McIntire
1915	Mrs. Roland H. Barlow	1970	Hollis Stacy
1916	Mrs. Roland H. Barlow	1971	Barbara McIntire
1917	Elaine Rosenthall	1972	Mrs. Michael Booth
1918	Dorothy Campbell Hurd	1973	Beth Barry
1919	Mrs. Roland H Barlow	1974	Mrs. J. Douglas Streit
1920	Dorothy Campbell Hurd	1975	Cynthia Hill
1921	Dorothy Campbell Hurd	1976	Carol Semple
1922	Glenna Collett	1977	Marcia Dolan
1923	Glenna Collett	1978	Cathy Sherk
1924	Glenna Collett	1979	Julie Gumlia
1925	Mrs. Melville Jones	1980	Charlotte Montgomery
1926	Louise Fordyce	1981	Patti Rizzo
1927	Glenna Collett	1982	Ann Sander
1928	Opal S. Hill	1983	Ann Sander
1929	Glenna Collett	1984	Susan Pager
1930	Glenna Collett	1985	Lee Ann Hammack
1931	Maureen Orcutt	1986	Leslie Shannon
1932	Maureen Orcutt	1987	Carol Semple Thompson
1933	Maureen Orcutt	1988	Donna Andrews
1934	Charlotte Clutting	1989	Page Marsh
1935	Estelle Lawson	1990	Brandie Burton
1936	Deborah Verry	1991	Kelly Robbins
1937	Estelle Lawson Page	1992	Stephanie Sparks
1938	Jane Cothran	1993	Emilee Klein
1939	Estelle Lawson Page	1994	Stephanie Neill
1940	Estelle Lawson Page	1995	Laura Philo
1941	Estelle Lawson Page	1996	Kristen Samp
1942	Louise Suggs	1997	Kerry Postillion
1943	Dorothy Kirby	1998	Beth Bauer
1944	Estelle Lawson Page	1999	Beth Bauer
1945	Estelle Lawson Page	2000	Candy Hannemann
1946	Louise Suggs	2001	Meredith Duncan
1947	"Babe" Didrikson Zaharias	2002	May Wood
1948	Louise Suggs	2003	Brittany Lang
1949	Peggy Kirk	2004	Morgan Pressel
1950	Pat O'Sullivan	2005	Ya-Ni Tseng
1951	Pat O'Sullivan	2006	Jenny Suh
1952	Barbara Romack	2007	Alison Walshel
1953	Pat O'Sullivan	2008	Christine Smith
1954	Joyce Ziske	2009	Amelia Lewis
1955	Wiffi Smith	2010	Cydney Clanton
1956	Marlene Stewart	2011	Danielle Kang
1957	Barbara McIntire	2012	Austin Ernst

Men's North and South Senior

Year	Champion	Year	Champion
1952	Judd L. Brumley	1982	Brown McDonald
1953	O.V. Russell	1983	Edward Ervasti
1954	Spencer S. Overton	1984	Howard Derrick
1955	B.F. Kraffert Jr.	1985	Fred Zinn
1956	Tom Robbins	1986	Joseph Faison
1957	J. Wood Platt	1987	Gael Coakley
1958	J. Wolcott Brown	1988	Moot Thomas
1959	Walter F. Pease	1989	Denis Biron
1960	Tom Robbins	1990	Chuck Smith
1961	Robert R. Bell	1991	Carey Schulten
1962	Col. William Lanman	1992	Chuck Smith
1963	James H. McAlvin	1993	Jim Keim
1964	James H. McAlvin	1994	Bill Cox
1965	David Goldman	1995	Deane Hundley
1966	Curtis Person	1996	Bill Cox
1967	Robert E. Cochran	1997	Chip Stewart
1968	Curtis Person	1998	Robert Kulp
1969	Curtis Person	1999	Mike Rice
1970	Robert E. Cochran	2000	Robert Kulp
1971	David Goldman	2001	John Crooks
1972	William Hyndman III	2002	William Boles Jr.
1973	Raymond Palmer	2003	Robert Kulp
1974	David Goldman	2004	Berger Warner
1975	Harry Welch	2005	David Brookreson
1976	Paul Severin	2006	Paul Simson
1977	George Pottle	2007	Paul Simson
1978	Edward Ervasti	2008	Rob Hess
1979	Dale Morey	2009	Paul Simson
1980	Dale Morey	2010	Chip Luts
1981	Richard Remsen	2011	Paul Simson

Women's North and South Senior

Year	Champion	Year	Champion
1958	Mrs. Harrison F. Flippin	1985	Barbara Young
1959	Mrs. Charles E. Bartholomew	1986	Ceil H. MacLaurin
1960	Maureen Orcutt	1987	Barbara Young
1961	Maureen Orcutt	1988	Barbara Young
1962	Maureen Orcutt	1989	Betty Probasco
1963	Ada McKenzie	1990	Betty Probasco
1964	Mrs. John S. Haskell	1991	Barbara Young
1965	Mrs. Reinert M. Torgerson	1992	Ceil H. MacLaurin
1966	Mrs. John Pennington	1993	No championship
1967	Mrs. Frederick C. Paffard	1994	Ceil H. MacLaurin
1968	Mrs. Douglass C. Coupe	1995	Barbara Vandeweghe
1969	Mrs. Philip J. Cudone	1996	Barbara Vandeweghe
1970	Mrs. Philip J. Cudone	1997	Sharon Gonsalves
1971	Mrs. Harton S. Semple	1998	Sheila Hopkins
1972	Mrs. Philip J. Cudone	1999	Nancy Smith
1973	Mrs. Philip J. Cudone	2000	Patty Moore
1974	Mrs. Philip J. Cudone	2001	Nancy Smith
1975	Mrs. Philip J. Cudone	2002	Nancy Smith
1976	Ceil H. MacLaurin	2003	Nancy Fitzgerald
1977	Ceil H. MacLaurin	2004	Nancy Smith
1978	Mrs. I. Wayne Rutter	2005	Patty Moore
1979	Ceil H. MacLaurin	2006	Carolyn Creekmore
1980	Ceil H. MacLaurin	2007	Patty Moore
1981	Betty Probasco	2008	Carole S. Thompson
1982	Jan Calin	2009	Sherry Herman
1983	Barbara Young	2010	Brenda Pictor
1984	Barbara Young	2011	Lisa Schlesinger

Donald Ross Memorial
Junior Championship

1948	Charles B. Smith		1980	Seishi Tanaka
1949	Ken Worthington		1981	Chris Kite
1950	Billy Ford		1982	Art Roberson
1951	Joe Correll		1983	Danny Hockaday
1952	Bobby Sisk		1984	Matt Peterson
1953	George Warren		1985	Kem Rodgers
1954	Ed Justa		1986	Doug Stone
1955	Burnham Uhler		1987	Robert Sevier Jr.
1956	Ed Justa		1988	Jason Widener
1957	George Smith Jr.		1989	Trey Jervis
1958	Buddy Baker		1990	Brent Patrick
1959	Bobby Littler		1991	Paul Carpenter
1960	Don Hedrick		1992	Edward Kurpeil III
1961	David Bennett		1993	Thomas Parker IV
1962	Russell Glover		1994	Ryan Felty
1963	Leonard Thompson		1995	Whitten Meares
1964	Leonard Thompson		1996	Chad Webb
1965	Mike Cheek		1997	Matt Kruze
1966	Davis Williams		1998	Jonathan Hill
1967	Johnny Gregory		1999	Sutton Barbrey
1968	Randy Hoft		2000	David Vallina
1969	David Eger		2001	Luke List
1970	David Thore		2002	Brendon Todd
1971	David Thore		2003	Drew Weaver
1972	Chip Beck		2004	Canceled, bad weather
1973	Chip Beck		2005	Henry Zaytoun
1974	Chris Tucker		2006	Ryan Sullivan
1975	Charles Schaffernoth		2007	Austin Cody
1976	Eric Moehling		2008	Keith Mitchell
1977	Mike West		2009	Davis Womble
1978	Gray Linzel		2010	Canceled, bad weather
1979	Chris Kite		2011	Joshua Martin

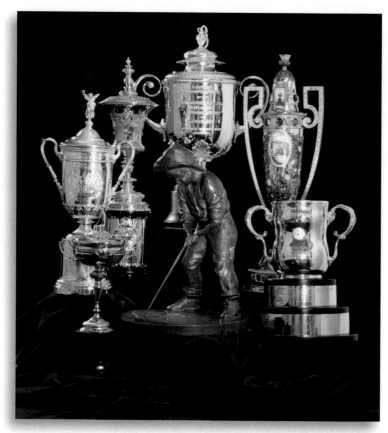

The Putter Boy surrounded by trophies (clockwise from front left) of the six major championships Pinehurst has hosted: Ryder Cup Matches 1951; U.S. Open 1999 and 2005; U.S. Amateur 1962 and 2008; PGA Championship 1936; U.S. Women's Amateur 1989; and the U.S. Senior Open 1994. Pinehurst is the only public-access facility in the nation that has been the site of as many major golf events, and in 2014 it adds the U.S. Women's Open to the list.

North and South Junior Boys

1979	Mark Bucek		1991	Robert Dean		2002	Jared Texter
1980	Bruce Soulsby		1992	Gary Shankland		2003	Nathan Stamey
1981	Woody Austin		1993	Robert Floyd		2004	Drew Weaver
1982	Mike Taylor		1994	Don Hill		2005	Aaron Eckstein
1983	Greg Parker		1995	Sal Spallone		2006	Lee Bedford
1984	Russell Mason		1996	Taylor Walsh		2007	Michael Cromie
1985	Kem Rodgers		1997	Taylor Walsh		2008	Justin Clemment
1986	Francis Holroyd		1998	John Carter III		2009	Grayson Murray
1987	Brian Craig		1999	Hunter Mahan		2010	Jake Nutter
1988	Frederick Chew III		2000	John Fizer		2011	Chad Cox
1989	Jack Patterson		2001	Rodney Thomas		2012	Kendrick Vinar Jr.
1990	Robert Dean						

North and South Junior Girls

1979	Cathy Ayers		1991	Kim Marshall		2002	Chris Brady
1980	Debbie Thomas		1992	Rachel Poston		2003	Ann Laney
1981	Kristal Parker		1993	Heather Graff		2004	Corrine Carr
1982	Robin Gamester		1994	Marcy Newton		2005	Courtney Harter
1983	Vanessa Castellucci		1995	Marcy Newton		2006	Hunter Ross
1984	Donna Andrews		1996	Beth Bauer		2007	Courtney McKim
1985	Karen Jefferson		1997	Ashley Durham		2008	Brittany Altomare
1986	Shirley Trier		1998	Ashley Leonard		2009	Allison Emrey
1987	Susan Slaughter		1999	Lindsay Knowlton		2010	Sarah Bae
1988	Tonya Blosser		2000	Jackie Beers		2011	Kari Bellville
1989	Barbara Paul		2001	May Wood		2012	Catherine Ashworth
1990	Meredith Tucker						

PINEHURST'S AMATEUR IDEAL

Pinehurst has long prided itself on its place in amateur golf. Indeed, Richard Tufts of the founding family spoke often of the value of a wonderful game played in winsome surroundings with the proper mindset: "Amateur golf can be a most valuable antidote to the high pressure, artificial life we lead today," Tufts noted in 1969. "But only if the game's ancient traditions and standards are maintained and golf is enjoyed for itself in friendly competition amid such natural surroundings as we find on the old links courses of Scotland. Golf should be a medium for relaxation and not commercialization."

No. 2 has been venue for two U.S. Amateur championships (1962 and 2008), and the Country Club of North Carolina was the site for the 1980 event (with No. 2 used as one of the stroke-play qualifying courses). Labron Harris Jr. (top right) edged Downing Gray Jr. 1-up in 1962; Hal Sutton (sporting a Putter Boy-logo shirt) cruised 9-and-8 past Bob Lewis in 1980; and Danny Lee, shown above left accepting his championship trophy, downed Drew Kittleson 5-and-4 in 2008.

Index

Acknowledgments

Among those I owe a significant debt of gratitude in the planning and creation of this book are the following:

To the Pinehurst LLC administration for having the confidence to entrust their story to me, most significantly Don Padgett, the president and chief operating officer, and Stephen Cryan, the director of retail operations from 1995-2012. They and others have become good friends over the years and are among the reasons that the "Off for Pinehurst" poster as displayed on page sixty is also prominently framed on my office wall.

To Bill Coore and Ben Crenshaw, both consummate gentlemen and golf purists, for welcoming me into their circle to tell a most remarkable story. Their thoughts on golf design and maintenance should be required reading for everyone in golf.

To Toby Cobb, whose yeoman's work from dawn to dusk turned Coore & Crenshaw's thoughts into reality, for the fascinating insights he provided into the design and construction realm. Dittos to Kyle Franz and the rest of the Coore & Crenshaw team.

To Tom Pashley, Kerry Andrews and Patricia Felder of the Pinehurst marketing and public relations staff and Jeff Anderson in desktop publishing for helping bird-dog photographs.

To Don Sweeting, Chad Campbell and Eric Alpenfels of the golf staff; to Bob Farren and Kevin Robinson of the golf maintenance staff; to Scott Brewton, Matt Chriscoe, Ed Peckels and Thierry Debailleul of the hotel and food and beverage staffs for opening the window into the workings of a distinguished resort.

To John Gessner, the lead photographer in the book, for his tireless efforts and keen eye in documenting the work of Coore & Crenshaw and assembling a myriad of images of the resort and village.

To Audrey Moriarty, Melissa Bielby and the staff at the Tufts Archives for their help locating many of the vintage photographs included in these pages.

To David Woronoff, Jim Dodson and Andie Rose of the excellent *Pine Straw* magazine, the repository of my monthly "Golftown Journal" pieces, some of which formed the basis for sidebars in this book.

To Art Chansky for his editing expertise and to Paul Betz for his keen proofreading eye.

To Marty McKenzie, the genial repository of more Pinehurst color and trivia than any other human alive. Marty has been on speed-dial for a quarter of a century in case I needed to know what happened on a random date in 1967 or where a particular body was buried.

And to the lovely and talented Sue Pace, whose design skills turned more than 100,000 words and hundreds of images into a cohesive, tasteful and classy visual presentation. Technology is an amazing thing today; this book was written on a Dell laptop, emailed across the hallway and assembled into a handsome package on an Apple desktop. With little to no marital strife along the way.

LP

Photography

A majority of the archival photographs and those from competitions of various golf tournaments over the years at Pinehurst came from the files of Pinehurst LLC, the Tufts Archives and the author's personal files. A majority of the Tufts Archives images were taken by John Hemmer, the long-time staff photographer at Pinehurst.

Other designations are as follows:

John Gessner: Coore & Crenshaw page 25 and 147; Village Chapel 65; Bagpiper Ian Staten 80; Pine Crest Inn (2) 86-87; Tom Stewart 97; Mike Davis, Jim Hyler, Robert Dedman Jr., Bill Coore 134 and 226-27; Dedman and Coore 149; Ben Crenshaw putting 154; Tufts Archives 161; Crenshaw 162, 191 and 237; Carolina Hotel, Village (4) 170-73; golf course 184, 215, 233, 255, 265, 267, 277; Crenshaw and Don Padgett II 200; Lanny Wadkins 250; Bill Coore 252; Jim Hyler 274-75; Holly Inn and 1895 Grill 285, 287; No. 2 flag 288; "Thistle Dhu" putting green, back end sheet.

Martin Miller and **Rob Brown**: Dust Jacket cover; ninth and eighteenth holes No. 2 front matter; Payne Stewart and Michael Campbell panoramas Gatefold; seventeenth green pages 174-75; sixth green 177; eighteenth hole 218; seventh hole 220; eighth hole 229; eighteenth hole 230; fifteenth hole 241; sixteenth hole 264-65; No. 2 hole by hole 290-307.

Larry Lambrecht: Sixth green No. 2, front end sheet; opposite Contents; thirteenth hole page18; twelfth green 179; first fairway 249; eighth hole 336.

Mark Henninger: Pinehurst Clubhouse pages 12-13.

Old Sport & Gallery: Early 1900s golf match pages 10-11; Bobby Jones exhibition 45; Richard Chorley painting 97.

Corbis Images: Billy Joe Patton page 16, Ben Hogan and Jack Nicklaus Gatefold.

Getty Images: Malcom McLean page 110; Ben Crenshaw (3) 151; Sand Hills Golf Club 164; Robert Dedman Sr. 244.

Willie Skinner and **Royal Dornoch Golf Club**: Postcard page 70; Tom Watson group 74; John Sutherland 83.

Royal Golf Hotel: pages 78 and 79.

Kevin Murray: Royal Dornoch Golf Club pages 72-73, 84 and 92-93.

Gladys Ravenscroft Collection donated to the Tufts Archives by Anthony Nottingham: Donald Ross foursome page 90.

Hugh Morton/UNC Wilson Library: Ben Crenshaw 1973 World Open page 109; World Golf Hall of Fame Induction 114; Crenshaw 152.

Thomas Toohey Brown: Bill Coore and Mike Davis page 163; Coore and Toby Cobb 202; Coore 210; eighteenth green resodding 212; Alan Green 216; Kyle Franz 220.

Elizabeth Shapiro: Donald Ross page 24.

American Society of Golf Course Architects: Tom Marzolf page 101.

Pine Needles Lodge & Golf Club: Hickory golfers page 116; Cristie Kerr 2007 U.S. Women's Open 207.

USGA: P.J. Boatwright page 120; Jim Hyler 187, Webb Simpson 271.

Janine Driscoll: Aaron Stewart (2) page 143.

Coore & Crenshaw: Bill Coore and Ben Crenshaw page 164.

Mark Brown: Chechessee Creek page 165.

Craig Disher: Aerial No. 2 pages 182-83.

Dunlop White and **Jaeger Kovich**: Before/After of thirteenth hole pages 198-99.

Tim Sayer: Caddies on No. 2 page 194.

Tom Pashley: First green pages 242-43.

Norma Pittman Stilwell: U.S. Kids Golf (2) pages 258-59.

Chip Henderson: Fifth hole page 269; ninth hole 272.

About the Author

The Golden Age of Pinehurst is Lee Pace's fourth book documenting the story of Pinehurst. The initial one was the 1991 edition of *Pinehurst Stories—A Celebration Great Golf and Good Times*; the second edition, published in 1999, was a substantial revision. *The Spirit of Pinehurst* followed in 2004.

He has written books with former Pinehurst Director of Golf Don Padgett Sr. and LPGA founding member Peggy Kirk Bell. He has also authored the story of Pine Needles and Mid Pines in the 1995 book, *Sandhills Classics*. Pace wrote and coordinated the production of the Carolinas Golf Association's centennial book in 2008.

He has written about the Sandhills golf scene for twenty-five years for a variety of magazines, including *GOLF*, *Links*, *Golfweek*, *Private Clubs*, *Delta Sky Magazine* and *US Airways Magazine*. Today he writes a monthly golf column for *Pine Straw* magazine.

Pace's passions beyond golf and Pinehurst extend to the University of North Carolina, where he graduated in 1979 with a degree in journalism. He lives today in Chapel Hill and covers the football program through his *Extra Points* online feature and is now in his ninth year as sideline reporter for the Tar Heel Sports Network.

PRACTICE FIELD

No. 3

No. 4

No. 1

No. 10

No. 9

No. 5

No. 14

No. 7

CLUB AREA

No. 6

No. 18

No. 12

No. 11

No. 16

No. 17

Pinehurst

PINEHURST 1895

Course No. 9

Aberdeen, North Carolina   May 2012

1 Inch = 100 Feet

An Early Look at Pinehurst No. 9

Bill Coore presented this routing to Pinehurst management in late May 2012 after close study for more than six months of a 925-acre parcel of land south of the Village of Pinehurst. No timetable had been established as of that time for the construction of what would one day be Pinehurst No. 9.

The site is located just off Hwy. 5 near Aberdeen on land that was once used for the Pit Golf Links, a 1985 Dan Maples design that went out of business in 2010. Nothing of the original Pit course will remain, though the new course will use corridors from the back nine for the first

and ninth holes of the new course, and parts of holes five, six, seventeen and eighteen will be located on ground once occupied by the front nine of the Pit. The third and fourth holes will be positioned on a unique patch of ground marked by mounds, moguls and mature pine trees popping through the undulations.

"It's a spectacular piece of ground," Coore says. "I think we can build something really interesting and really dramatic out here. We have a quarry and a lake. We have some very rugged ground and some gentle, rolling ground more like the traditional Pinehurst look."

THE GOLDEN AGE OF PINEHURST